OUR STORIES

Our Stories

AN INTRODUCTION TO SOUTH ASIAN AMERICA

PUBLISHED BY

South Asian American Digital Archive

Cover Images

Top row (left to right):
A South Asian American activist and member of the Desis Rising Up and Moving (DRUM) organization, name unknown, at a protest. DRUM "builds the power of South Asian and Indo-Caribbean low wage immigrant workers, youth, and families in New York City to win economic and educational justice, and civil and immigrant rights." In SAADA, courtesy of DRUM.

Semona Rodriguz Sidhu, Bisham Singh Sidhu, and their son. The Sidhus were one of the many Punjabi Mexican families living in the American West in the early and mid-twentieth century. Their photo was featured in the "Beyond Bollywood: Indian Americans Shape the Nation" museum exhibit at the Smithsonian Asian Pacific American Center. In SAADA, courtesy of Alicia Phillips.

Middle row (center):
Radhika Balakrishnan with her father, mother, cousin, and two brothers on a family road trip from Chicago to Orlando in July 1972. In SAADA's Road Trips Project, courtesy of Radhika Balakrishnan.

Bottom row (left to right):
A 1970 passport photo of Sarmistha Bhattacharjya. Bhattacharjya immigrated from Kolkata, India, to Boston, Massachusetts, on March 1, 1970, at the age of twenty-two. She recalled landing in Boston's Logan Airport "excited to see the airport covered with snow. My first impression was that it looked like a fairy tale. . . . I felt a sense of freedom, though there was both fear and joy in the back of my mind." In SAADA's First Days Project, courtesy of Nilanjana Bhattacharjya.

Front row, left to right: Mahesh Chandra and Vaishno Das Bagai (not pictured: Ramesh Chandra). Back row, left to right: Unknown, potentially Ishwar Chandra and Krishna Chandra. Vaishno Das Bagai immigrated to San Francisco, California, with his wife, Kala Bagai, and their three children in 1915, becoming one of the early South Asian families to immigrate together to the United States. Mahesh, Ramesh, Ishwar, and Krishna Chandra were brothers who also immigrated from India, lived in San Francisco, and became close family friends with the Bagais. In SAADA, courtesy of Rani Bagai.

ISBN: 978-1-7371759-7-1 (Hardcover)
ISBN: 978-1-7371759-3-3 (Ebook)

Library of Congress Control Number: 2021940223

South Asian American Digital Archive
1900 Market Street, Floor 8
Philadelphia, PA 19103
saada.org

In loving memory of Aparna Sharma.

ABOUT SAADA

The South Asian American Digital Archive (SAADA) is a 501(c)(3) not-for-profit organization based in Philadelphia, PA.

Mission

SAADA creates a more inclusive society by giving voice to South Asian Americans through documenting, preserving, and sharing stories that represent their unique and diverse experiences.

Vision

We envision American and world histories that fully acknowledge the importance of immigrants and ethnic communities in the past, strengthen such communities in the present, and inspire discussion about their role in the future.

Values

We believe South Asian American history is an integral part of American and world histories.

We believe in a broad conception of South Asian America, centered on those in the U.S. who trace their heritage to Bangladesh, Bhutan, India, Maldives, Nepal, Pakistan, Sri Lanka, and the many South Asian diaspora communities across the globe.

We believe that diversity is a strength. We strive to build archival collections that reflect the vast diversity of South Asian Americans on the basis of national, religious, regional, caste, socioeconomic, gender, sexual orientation, and cultural identity.

We believe that immigrants are central to the story of America's past, present, and future.

We believe that individuals make history, that ordinary people make extraordinary contributions to society, and that everyday stories matter.

We believe that history is not a spectator sport.

We believe communities can use history as a tool for empowerment.

We believe in the possibility of technology to encourage participation in archival collecting.

We believe that strong archives are vital to community well-being and that archives should be dynamic spaces for dialogue and debate.

saada.org

CONTENTS

Chapter 6
Faith & Religion

Chapter 7
Civic Engagement

Chapter 8
Arts & Popular Culture

LIST OF INSETS

CHAPTER 1

EARLY SOUTH ASIAN AMERICAN HISTORY (PRE-1923)

CHAPTER 2
FORGING LIVES IN UNCERTAIN TIMES (1923–1965)

CHAPTER 3
IMMIGRATION AFTER THE CIVIL RIGHTS MOVEMENT (1965–)

CHAPTER 4
POST-9/11

CHAPTER 5
IDENTITY & EQUALITY

CHAPTER 5

IDENTITY & EQUALITY (CONTINUED)

CHAPTER 6

FAITH & RELIGION

Chapter 7
Civic Engagement

Chapter 8
Arts & Popular Culture

CHAPTER 8
ARTS & POPULAR CULTURE (CONTINUED)

CHAPTER 9
WORK, LABOR, AND ENTREPRENEURSHIP

CHAPTER 10
FAMILY

FOREWORD

Our Stories: An Introduction to South Asian America began in 2015 as a Kickstarter campaign led by the South Asian American Digital Archive (SAADA). Four hundred and seven donors raised more than $38,000 to bring SAADA's archived stories to life in a book intended for a younger and broader audience. The original goal of the project was ambitious: to create a "first-of-its-kind" print book and digital edition that would be available to libraries, schools, and families.

What you hold in your hands represents the fruits of an even more ambitious undertaking: the recruitment of sixty-four scholars, activists, authors, and members of the South Asian American community who crafted well-researched and deeply personal contributions; the curation of primary sources from the SAADA archive and other repositories; the identification (and sometimes creation) of additional resources; and the cultivation of networks around the country that illuminate the extraordinary variety of experiences captured under the label "South Asian American." There is no singular South Asian American experience, but in depth and breadth, this book is indeed one of a kind.

This book also represents the loving labor of hundreds of people over five years. Above all, Samip Mallick, SAADA's cofounder and executive director, has remained the staunchest advocate of *Our Stories*. He has thoughtfully expanded the project with dedication to SAADA's core values: that diversity is our strength, that ordinary individuals make history, that history can be a source of empowerment, and that we all have a role to play in fostering dynamic dialogue and community well-being. He has presided over SAADA's growth from a small community of dedicated archivists to an essential archive that houses the largest digital collection of South Asian American historical resources. He has encouraged SAADA to grow as a community-building organization that cultivates artists and their art, teachers and their work, scholars and their research, community members and their voices, activists and their advocacy, young people and their growth. That we are able to share the stories in this volume is largely due to his dedication to the important work that SAADA undertakes every day.

As someone who has been involved with SAADA for almost a decade, I am often asked why it means so much to me. SAADA makes available invaluable items for research that I incorporate into my teaching as a historian, and it provides a site for my own and my students' oral history work in South Asian American communities. Through this work, I have learned more about the communities that make up South Asian America—their histories, their challenges, the privileges they hold, and the ways they are marginalized. But SAADA's greatest value for me personally has been what it has taught me about myself.

I am a third-culture kid. I was born in Saudi Arabia to a Pakistani American father and a white American mother. I didn't have a clear sense of home or of where I belonged; we visited Pakistan frequently and the U.S.A. annually, but both were foreign to me. Growing up, I couldn't be a Saudi citizen, and I didn't know much about what it meant to be an American one. Attending college in the American South, I studied Hindi and Urdu, but people looked askance at me at South Asian student association meetings, so I left. Studying abroad in England, my friends asked me to order for them at the "Paki" restaurant, but nothing on the menu looked like the food we had at home. (The menu listed Madras Curry; at home we just had chicken curry: would they taste the same?) Studying abroad in India, my Hindi was accented, and sometimes speaking "Indian English" was the best way to be understood, especially outside of cosmopolitan urban areas. On a Fulbright in Pakistan, I lived with my Dadi (my paternal grandmother) and my Urdu improved, but I still required a translator to speak to people from rural Punjab. Going back and forth was natural to me, but it didn't help anchor my experience.

It was not until I became involved with SAADA and the communities that surround it that I began to develop a sense of being South Asian American. My reflections as a mixed-heritage person who has studied and lived in South Asia sit in conversation with the work of other scholars through the pages of *Tides*, SAADA's online magazine. The wealth of stories there, as here, illuminate great diversity and the range of experiences South Asian Americans have navigated as immigrants and citizens. SAADA's inclusive approach ensures that all of these stories are *Our Stories*.

In this book, the story of my father's experience as a foreign exchange student in 1959–60, which seemed so singular to me, finds company among the stories of other students from South Asia who arrived throughout the twentieth century. My parents' interreligious, interracial marriage in Norman, Oklahoma, appears less rare when I watch *Lavaan*, Zain Alam's film that sets silent footage of the marriage of Sharanjit Singh Dhillonn and Dorothy Dhillonn to music. As a parent, I want my child to experience the cultural multiplicity I grew up with, and to feel at home with it—to be as comfortable eating daal chawal as tacos or hamburgers or peanut butter dosa—and the stories SAADA shares show that this is possible.

SAADA has helped me connect with individuals and communities, both intimate and distant, who recognize or share parts of my family's story. It has helped me grow into my identity as a South Asian American woman, teacher, and leader, as I hope that *Our Stories* will help you grow into yours.

Amber Abbas
President, SAADA Board of Directors, 2019–21
Associate Professor of History, Saint Joseph's University, Philadelphia, PA

PREFACE

My parents immigrated to the United States from India in the late 1960s, part of the first wave of immigration from South Asia made possible by the 1965 Immigration Act. Growing up in Michigan in the 1980s and '90s, I knew nothing of the rich and diverse histories of South Asian Americans before me. To understand myself and my story, I believed, I would have to spend time in South Asia. And that is what I did, traveling to India and Sri Lanka for education and work. But, as many people of the South Asian diaspora have felt before me, I found myself completely at home neither here nor there. It was not until college that I began to learn about the histories of South Asians in the United States. When I first learned about Congressman Dalip Singh Saund and the Ghadar Party and Dr. Anandibai Joshee, I began to see American history completely differently. I also saw myself differently. I felt rooted in the American story in ways that I never had before.

With SAADA, I have always hoped to share that personally transformative feeling I had with others in our community. SAADA cofounder Dr. Michelle Caswell's research later gave a name to that transformative feeling: "representational belonging." As one respondent in Dr. Caswell's research put it, to see yourself reflected in the archive is to "suddenly discover yourself existing."

Over the last thirteen years, SAADA has documented, preserved, and shared stories from our community, making them freely available to the public through our work. We have built the largest publicly accessible collection of archival materials related to South Asian Americans, including rare photographs, newspaper clippings, correspondence, oral history interviews, and other ephemera dating from the late 1800s up to the present day. We have also worked creatively in partnership with artists, scholars, filmmakers, activists, and journalists to reimagine these stories and materials and connect them with our community and the broader public. SAADA's "Revolution Remix" walking tour, for example, shares stories of South Asians in Philadelphia all the way back to the 1780s and reframes some of the most historic places in the American republic to include our community's voices. In 2019, we partnered with five South Asian American musicians to create a soundtrack to the walking tour, bringing these historical stories to life in an entirely new way.

But all along, I have kept thinking about why it took so long for me to learn about these histories in the first place. These are American stories, not just South Asian American stories, and yet they are rarely, if ever, taught in classrooms or found in textbooks. As I had experienced years before, most young South Asian Americans, even today, never get the opportunity to see themselves reflected in the legacies of individuals who helped shape the American story. Our stories are vibrant and powerful, but they have been hidden from view.

Today, there are nearly 5.4 million individuals in the U.S. (or more than one in every hundred Americans) who trace their heritage to South Asia. If you imagined that all of the South Asians in the country lived in one state, it would be the twenty-third most populous state in the country, larger than the state of South Carolina and almost as big as Minnesota. To ignore the history of South Asian Americans in our classrooms is, to my mind, like removing the state of South Carolina (or any one of the twenty-eight smaller states) from our curriculums—there would undoubtedly be a national outcry. But for communities like ours that have been excluded from and marginalized in the American story, it is only when we begin to advocate for our own stories that we ever have a chance of being included.

When we launched the Kickstarter campaign for *Our Stories* in 2015, SAADA was a relatively new organization. The tremendous outpouring of support for this project, with 407 backers supporting the book before a single page was written, is testament to our community's widespread recognition of the need to provide the next generation of South Asian Americans with the education and resources we did not have. We hope that finding *Our Stories* on the bookshelf in their school or library will help ensure that young South Asian Americans will never question where their story fits into the American story.

It has taken a lot of time and effort to bring this book together. I am deeply grateful to the hundreds of individuals who have contributed to this project, without whom this book would not exist today.

We had initially hoped to publish *Our Stories* in 2016, and many of the stories in the book were written and submitted to us at that time. Although a number of years have passed since then, and certain recent events are not included, *Our Stories* continues to serve as a snapshot of our community and its history and an archival document of its own.

The sixty-four authors who contributed to this volume did so because they believed in its mission to make South Asian American stories available to younger readers. And because of their generosity, all of the profits from book sales will go directly to supporting SAADA further. Information about each of these contributors can be found in the Author Bios section, and I encourage you to learn more about their work as you continue your exploration of South Asian America. I also want to especially thank the editors of each chapter for all of the time and labor they put into inviting contributors and providing feedback: Dr. Seema Sohi, Dr. Kritika Agarwal, Dr. Fariha Khan, Dr. Rajini Srikanth, Dr. Radha Modi, Dr. Khyati Y. Joshi, Dr. Bandana Purkayastha, Dr. Monisha Das Gupta, Dr. Nilanjana Bhattacharjya, Dr. Shilpa Davé, Dr. Pawan Dhingra, Dr. Amy Bhatt, and Dr. Amber Abbas. Twenty-two community members also donated their time to providing feedback on an early manuscript. Their input improved this project immeasurably and I am thankful to each of them for their part in this project.

The hundreds of insets, image captions, and other ancillary materials in this book were primarily authored by two individuals, Imran Siddiquee and Nivetha Karthikeyan. Their commitment to this project and thoughtfulness about ensuring that a wide range of voices were included has been so important to fulfilling its vision. It is also because of Nivetha's heroic efforts that this project was finally able to cross the finish line.

The editor for *Our Stories* is Heidi Hill, the design was created by Brian Cook, and layout was done by Varisa Tantiwasadakran. I am so grateful to them for their unwavering commitment to seeing this project through, from start to completion.

Our Stories is a product of all of the love and labor that has gone into SAADA over the past thirteen years. I want to thank SAADA's cofounder, Dr. Michelle Caswell, for our years of collaboration and friendship, and all of SAADA's board members for believing in and supporting this project. I especially want to thank our past and current board presidents, Dr. Pawan Dhingra, Dr. Seema Sohi, and Dr. Amber Abbas (who are also all contributors to the book) for their leadership and vision in helping to make SAADA what it is today.

From the bottom of my heart, I would like to thank my partner, Kinnari, who makes it all possible, and our daughter, Sejal, who lights up our lives, and makes it all worthwhile.

This book would not exist without the generosity of our 407 backers on Kickstarter, who are listed in the Acknowledgments section. And because of their support, as soon as *Our Stories* is published, it will be donated to hundreds of schools and libraries. I also want to thank Saint Joseph's University for providing a grant to support the book's publication and distribution. It is our goal to have *Our Stories* on the bookshelves of schools and libraries across the country. We invite you to join us in that effort by visiting saada.org/ourstories.

S.M.

INTRODUCTION

As a person of South Asian heritage reading this book, you have perhaps wondered how your story fits into the American story. While South Asian American stories are rarely taught in classrooms, found in textbooks, or reflected in popular media, it is not because they do not exist. As you will soon read, our stories have existed for centuries. You are part of a community that has helped build, shape, question, challenge, and make this country what it is today. Our stories have been etched into the very landscape and character of the nation.

Throughout this book, you will be introduced to scores of individuals who have pushed back against the circumstances they encountered to fight for justice and make a place for our community in the American story—like Kartar Dhillon, known to many simply as Kar. As a young girl born in California's Simi Valley in 1915, Kar grew up during a period of intense xenophobia directed at South Asian Americans. Yet, despite the limitations placed on her, Kar went on to organize farmworkers, support the Black Panthers, and engage in India's struggle for independence.

You will also read about the ways that South Asian Americans have carved out space for our communities in the geography of cities across the country—our restaurants, stores, cultural venues, religious centers, and more. You will encounter the Little Guyana neighborhood of Queens, New York, where Indo-Caribbean "twice migrants" have settled, and Banglatown in Hamtramck, Michigan, where Bangladeshi immigrants make up half the members of the city council.

Elected officials of South Asian heritage now include representation at all levels of politics, from local school board members all the way to the vice president of the United States. These individuals are part of a long history of political and civic engagement by members of our community: from the Ghadar Party, founded in 1913, whose members rebelled against British rule in India and racial discrimination here in the U.S., to Dalip Singh Saund, who in 1956 became the first South Asian American (and Asian American) elected to U.S. Congress.

South Asian Americans have also helped shape American culture through our creativity. You will be introduced to South Asian American novelists, performers, musicians, architects, comic book artists, and others who have interacted with broader American cultural movements while navigating the expectations placed upon them—like Dhan Gopal Mukerji, who won the prestigious Newbery Medal in 1928 for his children's book *Gay-Neck: The Story of a Pigeon*, and whose other writings raised American consciousness about India's anti-colonial movement, casteism, and India's inequities related to those in the United States.

Since our earliest days in the country, South Asians have forged solidarities with other marginalized communities. You will read about Jaswant Krishnayya and Ahmed Meer, two MIT students who spent their summer vacation working with activists during the sit-ins of the Civil Rights movement, a series of protests against whites-only lunch counters, restaurants, movie theaters, pools, and beaches; and the correspondence between the Dalit anti-caste leader and architect of India's constitution Dr. B. R. Ambedkar and Pan-Africanist and civil rights leader Dr. W. E. B. Du Bois reflecting on the commonalities of their struggles. You will also read about the ways in which groups in our community continue to be marginalized by others in our own community, such as the decades-long fight by LGBTQ+ community members to march in the India Day Parade in New York City.

And you will read about the many ways in which South Asian Americans have found love and formed families—like Mala and Vega, queer South Asian Americans who share reflections on their experiences growing up, coming out, building a relationship together, and discovering communities of support and care.

The stories in this book are stories of our roots in this country. South Asian Americans have made homes, nurtured families, and formed communities in this country for centuries. The legacies they have built are yours to claim, if you choose. As you read this book, we hope you will feel grounded and inspired by their stories.

Before you begin your exploration of *Our Stories*, we would like to draw your attention to a few notes that will help you navigate and understand what you read in the pages ahead.

First, you will notice various geopolitical terms—such as "India," "South Asia," and others—referenced throughout the book to mean different things at different times to different people. Many of these terms have had their meanings defined and redefined throughout the nineteenth and twentieth centuries, as forces of colonialism and postcolonial movements have shifted borders and shaped national identities. As Dr. Shweta Majumdar Adur summarizes in chapter 3:

> The modern-day countries of India, Pakistan, and Bangladesh were all a single colony of the British government until their independence in 1947. After independence, the subcontinent was partitioned into two nations, India and Pakistan; the latter consisted of two noncontiguous territories under one state's rule, West and East Pakistan. In 1971, East Pakistan declared a war of liberation and, with India's support, seceded from Pakistan. The newly independent nation is what we now know as Bangladesh.

The modern-day countries of Bhutan, Maldives, Nepal, and Sri Lanka similarly have their own complex histories. While Bhutan and Nepal were not colonized by European states in the twentieth century, both Sri Lanka and Maldives were classified as part of the British Empire (with British-controlled Sri Lanka referred to as Ceylon) until they achieved their independence in 1948 and 1965, respectively.

These changes mean that an individual from the 1920s may refer to a South Asian migrant as "Indian" or "Ceylonese" even though, today, we may refer to that same migrant as "Pakistani," "Bangladeshi," or "Sri Lankan."

More likely, however, as you will read in chapter 1, they would have been referred to as a "Hindu" or a "Hindoo," a racialized term (not related to religion) adopted by the U.S. government to describe all people of South Asian origin. This term quickly came to carry a strongly derogatory connotation and was frequently used to "other" South Asian immigrants, collapsing a community with a diverse range of religious, linguistic, cultural, and geographic origins into a single, non-American entity.

A few decades later, according to anthropologist Aminah Mohammad-Arif, "the word 'South Asia' officially emerged as a category to divide the Asian continent, in the wake of the establishment of area studies in the United States." In other words, "South Asia" was being used as an academic term to represent a specific area of study—"South Asian studies"—similar to disciplines like "Middle Eastern studies." Beginning in the 1940s, the term "South Asia" was also used by policy-making in-stitutions such as the U.S. State Department, the United Nations, and the World Bank. So, like the term "Hindoo" decades before, "South Asian" was also a term created to describe us, but not chosen by us.

But the term "South Asia" and its derivatives "South Asian America" and "South Asian American" have evolved beyond their early academic and bureaucratic ori-gins to hold deep and complex meanings for the individuals who identify with them today. As V. V. Ganeshananthan writes in chapter 5:

> As an activist in the larger South Asian community, I have sought out spaces that have chosen to label themselves South Asian, and not In-dian. The latter would, no doubt, be expedient in a variety of ways—India and Sri Lanka are both easier for people to recognize. But South Asia is a concept that lies beyond nation or ethnicity; it's a collective idea rooted in cross-border solidarities. To elect South Asia bespeaks a generosity of vision and a desire to be inclusive. It's an invention and a reclamation of space. So when the South Asian American Digital Archive asked me to write about Sri Lankan American identity, and I thought about why I was willing, I returned to the idea of South Asia. It's true—it might be something that doesn't exist, something made after the fact to try to contain an odd mishmash of pasts. But perhaps that is not a mistake, but a victory. Perhaps this is what the South Asian diaspora has in common, regardless of national or ethnic origin—our relentless ability to rename and invent ways to belong to each other.

It is important to know that the specific geographic borders of "South Asia" are also not universally agreed upon. In general, this book defines South Asia as including Bangladesh, Bhutan, India, Maldives, Nepal, Pakistan, and Sri Lanka. Some also include Afghanistan and Burma in their definitions of South Asia. South Asian Americans are those in the U.S. who trace their heritage to these countries as well as to the many South Asian diasporic communities across the globe, such as those in Trinidad, Guyana, Uganda, Fiji, and the United Kingdom. As you read this book, remember to note the specific historical, political, and even personal contexts in which such geopolitical terms are being used in order to understand their intended meaning—and note the ways that the terms we use, even just to describe ourselves, constitute meaningful and inherently political acts.

In SAADA's work, we subscribe to an inclusive view of South Asian American identity, one that recognizes our shared histories and, more importantly, our shared futures. "South Asian American" may not be a term that you use regularly to describe yourself, or it may be a term that you deploy only in certain circumstances. Or perhaps, as Dr. Amber Abbas has written in the foreword to *Our Stories*, you have felt out of place in South Asian American spaces and wondered about how you fit in. We hope you will find stories in this book that will resonate with your experiences and help you see your personal story in the context of our community's story. Each of us, in our own way, is contributing to the larger South Asian American story.

This brings us to our second note. In any community, no matter how narrowly defined, there are dynamics of power that result in some voices being amplified and others being silenced. The stories of community members who are working-class, undocumented, LGBTQ+, Dalit, Indo-Caribbean, and from other groups that have been historically marginalized continue to be excluded from dominant narratives about what it means to be South Asian American. For example, many are surprised to learn that there are more than half a million undocumented South Asians living in the United States today. This represents nearly ten percent of the South Asian American population, and yet, stories of undocumented South Asian Americans are often not heard due to the uniquely vulnerable status of these members of our community. Sharing your story publicly if you are undocumented can lead to being stigmatized or even under threat of arrest and deportation.

In *Our Stories*, we center the perspectives of a wide range of members of our community in an attempt to reflect the true richness and diversity of South Asian American experiences. We have also not shied away from a range of difficult topics that are a reality in our lives. Some of the stories in this book include historical or personal accounts of identity-based violence, sexual assault, and self-harm. These stories are crucial to understanding the lived experiences of what it means to be South Asian American. It is also important to remember that for every account that is included in the chapters that follow, there are countless others that have not. We hope that this book serves as a starting point for your exploration of South Asian America, but that you do not end here.

In addition to the stories within each chapter, the book also contains hundreds of insets and images that provide additional context and information. Many of these insets and images include archival sources that are housed in SAADA's digital collections, the largest publicly accessible archive of South Asian American history, containing rare photographs, letters, newspaper clippings, oral history interviews, videos, born-digital materials, and other ephemera. You will read first-person accounts from SAADA's participatory storytelling initiatives, such as our First Days Project (sharing stories from immigrants and refugees about their arrival in the U.S.) and Road Trips Project (sharing stories of travel across the country to reframe an American tradition). You will also read excerpts from *Tides*, SAADA's online magazine, which seeks to connect the past to our understanding of the present, and from oral history interviews conducted by SAADA's Archival Creators Fellows, sharing the experiences of community members who have historically been marginalized and excluded from the archival record. We encourage you to engage with these projects and others at saada.org. *Our Stories* is also accompanied by a website that provides links to the archival sources in this book and other relevant materials. We hope you will visit the companion website at saada.org/ourstories to continue your exploration.

Samip Mallick
Executive Director, SAADA

Nivetha Karthikeyan
Special Projects Coordinator, SAADA

A NOTE FROM SAADA

Our Stories: An Introduction to South Asian America is accompanied by a website, where you can find more information about the stories, insets, and images in this book.

This companion website links the content in the book to relevant resources and more ways to continue exploring the richness and diversity of South Asian American experiences.

You can visit the companion for each chapter by scanning the QR code you find on its title page, or by visiting the website for *Our Stories* and navigating from there.

Get started now by visiting saada.org/ourstories or by scanning the QR code below:

CHAPTER 1

Early South Asian American History

PRE-1923

Men sitting on a wooden sidewalk. San Francisco, 1910. Courtesy of the University of California, Berkeley.

INTRODUCTION

Seema Sohi

South Asian Americans are one of the fastest growing immigrant groups in the United States, yet their long and complex histories in the country are little known. As the stories in this chapter demonstrate, South Asians traveled to the United States as lascars, or sailors, as far back as the 1700s; as merchants, tourists, and religious and political leaders in the late-nineteenth century; and as laborers, agricultural entrepreneurs, students, and intellectuals in the early decades of the twentieth century.

Rajender Kaur's story about Sick Keesar reveals the earliest traces of a South Asian presence in the ports of the East Coast during the late 1700s. In "Jumping Ship," Vivek Bald highlights the subsequent arrival of Muslim seamen on British steamships in the early twentieth century, many of whom jumped ship and settled in the urban spaces of New York, Baltimore, and Detroit. As Bald has chronicled elsewhere, Bengali Muslim peddlers had previously journeyed to the United States to sell "Oriental" goods, including silk, shawls, rugs, jewelry, and embroidered cotton, to American consumers who desired the "exotic" goods of India and the "Orient." These peddlers arrived at a time in which "Oriental" goods from India were highly desirable and a sign of fashion and social standing even as the actual people from the subcontinent were vilified, attacked, and excluded. The men who sold these goods moved among the resorts, amusement parks, and beach board-walks of New York, New Jersey, and southern cities like New Orleans. Though most of them returned to the subcontinent, some stayed and integrated into work-ing-class neighborhoods of color, including Tremé, West Baltimore, and Harlem, by marrying local women, having children, and developing African American, Puerto Rican, and West Indian extended families.

While most of these early arrivers were men, there were also a few women, in-cluding Anandibai Joshee, who, as Anupama Arora's story tells us, was the first South Asian woman to earn a medical degree in the United States, in 1886. Kartar Dhillon, whose autobiographical story is excerpted in this chapter, grew up amid South Asian revolutionaries fighting for Indian independence from Great Britain. She would go on to become a political activist in California until her death, in 2008, at the age of ninety-four.

By the early twentieth century, South Asians also began migrating in greater numbers to the West Coast of North America, where they found employment in the lumber mills of British Columbia, Washington, and Oregon and the orchards, ag-ricultural fields, and vineyards of California. In 1907, the number of South Asians who had entered Canada was 2,623, and 1,072 had entered the United States. At the same time, a smaller group of Bengali and Punjabi intellectuals fleeing imprison-ment and political repression in India for their anti-British political organizing came to the urban centers of Vancouver, Seattle, San Francisco, and New York.

Like other Asian immigrants who had come before them, South Asians were targeted by organized labor and elected officials, who pushed for their exclusion by insisting that they were economic competitors willing to work for lower wages. At times these exclusionary demands erupted into acts of racial violence. The Bellingham Riot, in September 1907, marked the first large-scale outbreak of violence against South Asians in North America. As Paul Englesberg's story in this chapter illustrates, the riot culminated in the expulsion of South Asian workers from the town of Bellingham, Washington. Only a few days later, the largest race riot in Canada's history tore through Vancouver, British Columbia. These interconnected events on both sides of the U.S.–Canadian border were followed, only eight months later, by Canada's passage of the Continuous Journey Law, which declared it unlawful for any immigrant to enter Canada who did not arrive by continuous journey from their country of birth or citizenship.

The Continuous Journey Law effectively prohibited the entry of South Asians into Canada. The number of South Asians who entered Canada through official channels in 1907 was 2,623; in 1908, this number dropped to 6, and in 1909, only 10 Indians were allowed entry to Canada. The passage of the 1908 law in Canada also affected the number of Indians entering the United States. In 1908, the number of South Asians who entered the United States was 1,710, more than in any previous year. However, U.S. immigration authorities seemed to have been alarmed by the increase, and in 1909, only 377 South Asians gained entry. Immigration officials began denying admission to more than fifty percent of arriving South Asian migrants by using what was known as the "public charge" clause, disallowing those who they said would likely become dependent on the government for subsistence. Officials argued that public prejudice against South Asians on the Pacific Coast had grown to such a fervor that it was unlikely they would be able to secure employment and thus were "likely to become public charges." The "public charge" clause worked to exclude thousands of South Asians in the coming years. When pushed by South Asians on the West Coast to prove that they were in fact becoming public charges, immigration and labor authorities were unable to provide even a single name.

Although the total number of South Asians to gain entry to the United States never exceeded 1,800 in any given year between 1906 and 1917—making the total number who entered the United States through official channels under 8,000—to immigration officials, even this number was too large. Years of anti-immigrant sentiment against South Asians would culminate in the passage of the Immigration Act of 1917 (also known as the Barred Zone Act), which in effect excluded South Asians from entering the country for decades.

South Asians were never passive in the face of these calls for exclusion or acts of racial violence. Many joined the ranks of the Ghadar Party, a revolutionary party that, as my story chronicles, rebelled against both British rule in India and racial discrimination and exclusion in North America. The Ghadar Party mobilized and inspired thousands of South Asians in North America, and in doing so prompted the U.S., Canadian, and British governments to begin spying on South Asians from California to New York and exchanging their surveillance reports with one another in order to quell the growing anti-colonial movement. One highly dramatized act of defiance occurred in the summer of 1914, when 376 South Asians aboard the *Komagata Maru* sailed into Vancouver harbor to protest the injustices of the Continuous Journey Law. The *Komagata Maru* became the platform upon which South Asians demanded the right of entry into Canada as British subjects. In this defiant act, South Asians dramatized anti-colonial struggle by linking the fate of the passengers on board the ship to the broader movement for self-rule in India.

Taken together, the stories in this chapter illuminate the multifaceted pasts of South Asian Americans. The complexity and richness of South Asian migration and settlement in the United States are central to the formation of the early republic, the economic growth and capitalist development of the American West, and the larger histories of tourism and struggles for immigrant equality throughout U.S. history. As the multilayered stories in this chapter demonstrate, South Asian migration, labor, and political activism have shaped the nation in ways that we are only beginning to uncover.

Seema Sohi (she/her/hers) is an associate professor of ethnic studies at the University of Colorado Boulder.

SICK KEESAR'S PETITION TO BENJAMIN FRANKLIN

Rajender Kaur

It was August 9, 1785, and the *Pallas* had just returned to Baltimore harbor from Canton (now Guangzhou, China) under the stewardship of Captain John O'Donnell, an adventurous Irishman who had made his fortunes in India. *The Maryland Journal and Baltimore Advertiser* of August 12, 1785, detailed with excitement the *Pallas*'s valuable cargo of "teas, china, silks and satins" and noted the "not unpleasing sight" of its motley crew of Chinese, Malays, Japanese, Moors, and a few Europeans, "all employed together as brethren." Among this motley crew was a Bengali lascar, Sick Keesar, the first lieutenant of the *Pallas*.

There is little known about Keesar other than the fact that he filed a petition of "redress and grievance" against O'Donnell, charging the captain with reneging on his promise to secure a return passage home to India for this crew of thirty-five men. The petition, dated November 3, 1785, was addressed to Benjamin Franklin,

President of the Supreme Executive Council of Pennsylvania, and was filed in Philadelphia. Keesar and his men had originally traveled to the city hoping to secure a return voyage on one of the many ships set to sail to India from there, including the *Canton*, captained by Thomas Truxtun. But the passage fees of forty guineas per person that Truxtun demanded were too onerous, and Keesar pleaded for Franklin to intervene on his behalf and those of his fellow sailors, who had sold all their belongings to survive. There is no record of Keesar and his men having succeeded in sailing back home, although it is thought that they may have returned with Captain O'Donnell on the *Chesapeake*, the first American merchantman to sail to India, in 1786.

This little-known saga of a Bengali lascar demonstrates the presence of South

"Lascars" shown in the Philadelphia Inquirer (December 25, 1903).

Asian sailors, servants, and indentured workers in early America. As trade between the fledgling new nation and India flourished between 1784 and the late 1840s, South Asian men would become a familiar sight in port cities like Salem, Newburyport, Baltimore, Boston, Philadelphia, and New York along the Eastern Seaboard. These men were a significant presence in the United States by the 1850s and an important part of the cultural imaginary, as evidenced by characters like Fedallah in Herman Melville's *Moby Dick* (1851) and the lascars described by Melville in *Redburn: His First Voyage* (1849).

The story of Keesar and his men illustrates the global circuit of maritime labor in the late eighteenth and the nineteenth centuries. It also highlights the vibrant presence of South Asia in the form of goods, people, and ideas within early

---

LASCAR

From the sixteenth to the middle of the twentieth century, men from South Asia, Southeast Asia, the Arab world, and other areas of Asia east of Africa were employed on European ships as sailors or militiamen. These men were often known as lascars.

The name is a translation of the Hindi word *lashkar* (meaning "army"), which itself derives from *al-askar*, an Arabic word for a "guard" or "soldier." The Portuguese military would later adapt this term to *lascarin*, which meant Asian militiamen or seamen, specifically those from the area east of the Cape of Good Hope (mostly Indian, Malay, Chinese, and Japanese crewmen).

The British of the East India Company initially described Indian lascars as "Black Portuguese" or "Topazes" but later adopted the Portuguese "lascar." These men served on British ships under "lascar agreements." The agreements allowed ship owners more control than with ordinary contracts, since the sailors could be transferred from one ship to another and retained in service for up to three consecutive years. The name "lascar" was also used to refer to Indian servants, who were typically engaged by British military officers.

HISTORIES OF INDENTURE

Following the formal abolition of slavery in the British colonies in 1833, those men and women who were newly free often refused to continue working on the sugar farms, where they were relegated to extremely low-paying roles. As a result, these plantations instituted indentured labor to fill their needs, transporting millions of Indian workers to nineteen different colonies across the British Empire—including Jamaica, Trinidad, Guyana, and Fiji—to work as "bonded laborers." While these workers were often promised careers, pay, and land ownership, in reality they often received none of those things and instead were treated very poorly—including facing the threat of violence.

HISTORIES OF RACISM IN THE UNITED STATES

For 250 years, starting when the first enslaved Africans were brought to Virginia in the seventeenth century, the legal institution of chattel slavery was part of everyday life in America. The forced unpaid labor of millions of African American people—as well as the theft from and genocide of Native Americans—was central to the economic development and wealth of the United States, and established the precedent for the exploitation of Black and Indigenous people, which continued long after slavery was legally banned. The institution also left a great impact on American society at large, cementing structures of racism and other forms of oppression that continue into the present.

South Asian Americans have felt the destructive legacy of these structures throughout our community's history and also, at times, attempted to benefit from them. For example, changing legal and scientific debates on race in the early twentieth century initially allowed South Asian Americans like Bhagat Singh Thind to claim to be white to gain American citizenship. Yet, as you will read in chapter 2, the strategy of claiming whiteness was ultimately a losing one. In fact, it was only in the 1960s, in the midst of the Civil Rights era led by Black Americans, that South Asians were finally allowed to enter the United States in larger numbers. Throughout this book, you will find examples of the ways that South Asian Americans have navigated the racial structures of the United States.

It is also important to note that structures of oppression extend beyond the legal and political sphere to impact intimate parts of our daily lives, including our speech. In a few stories in this book, you will read historical quotes that use words that we do not use today, such as outdated terms used to refer to Black Americans. Following the guidance of the educational organization, Facing History and Ourselves, we have chosen to let these words remain as they originally appeared, without any substitution. As they explain:

> The dehumanizing power of [these terms] and the ease with which some Americans have used [them] to describe their fellow human beings is central to understanding the themes of identity and human behavior at the heart of [our history].

American society. Keesar's petition is only one example of a slew of petitions filed by servants and lascars of South Asian origin, and illuminates a little-known history of the United States. The presence of South Asian servants and lascars adds to an alternative, more working-class vision of early South Asian America, and their presence on the East Coast adds another dimension to the more commonly known narrative of the early arrival of South Asians as farmers and lumbermen on the West Coast. Advertisements for runaway "East Indian" servants—and the petition for redress by a Bengali sailor—are part of a larger history of the South Asian presence in colonial America.

Rajender Kaur is a professor of English and director of the Asian Studies Program at William Paterson University.

JUMPING SHIP

Vivek Bald

In January 1918, in the dead of a severe New York winter, the SS *Khiva* docked on the West Side waterfront of Manhattan. The *Khiva* was a British steamship carrying goods from colonized India to the United States. A crew of laborers from what is now Pakistan and Bangladesh manned the ship. On the voyage, some of the men would have spent long days pushing wheelbarrows full of coal from the hold of the ship to the engine room; others would have hammered this coal into small pieces and piled them near the furnaces; still others would have shoveled the coal into the furnaces to feed the flames that made the steam that ran the turbines to propel the ship forward. Maritime work was some of the most arduous labor of the early industrial age, and in the case of British trade and transport ships, it was labor performed by men from the colonies. South Asians made up the largest group among colonial laborers on British steamships. They signed on to the ships in Calcutta and Bombay on contracts that were little better than indenture agreements and then toiled at the mercy of their British "masters" for months and years at a time.

That night in January, two young workers took leave from the *Khiva* to explore the docks of New York City. One, a Kashmiri named Amir Haider Khan, was just eighteen years old and already a four-year veteran of the maritime trade. He and his friend eventually wandered into a waterfront provisions store, whose Jewish proprietor put the idea into their heads of deserting their ship. He described the higher wages they could get on U.S. vessels and coached them on what to do. So one evening a few days later, Khan and his friend took shore leave again, "telling our shipmates we were going for a stroll," but they did not return. When they found themselves walking the streets of Manhattan in the middle of a cold winter night, "wrapping ourselves in whatever we had—an old pair of pants, a cotton shirt and a coat, a cheap cap and a coloured piece of cloth for our heads," it was an African American boardinghouse keeper in the predominantly Black Tenderloin district, along Seventh Avenue, who ultimately took them in and helped them hide. "[M]y companion had a talk with the Negro landlady," Khan wrote, "and explained to her that we had deserted a ship and did not want to return [and] it was necessary for us to remain indoors while the vessel was still in port, so that we would not be apprehended. [So s]he arranged for a young Negro girl who was living in a room on the same floor to [go] purchase our food [for us]—bread, butter, eggs etc. which she cooked for us in the house."

Amir Haider Khan was part of a population of early twentieth-century immigrants and sojourners from South Asia whose stories have remained largely hidden and untold. Beginning around the time of the First World War, hundreds of South Asian maritime workers, men who labored in the engine rooms and kitchens of British steamships, escaped into the crowded waterfronts of New York, Philadelphia, and Baltimore in search of less brutal work and better wages onshore. These men were predominantly Muslims from rural backgrounds. The largest number was from villages in East Bengal—a region that would later become the nation of Bangladesh. Others hailed from regions that are part of present-day Pakistan—Punjab, Kashmir, and the North-West Frontier. During the war, these men found that their labor was in demand in U.S. steel, shipbuilding, and munitions indus-tries, and they formed clandestine networks to help one another jump ship and make their way into the heart of New York City or travel inland to factory towns far from port. These secret networks helped sustain a presence of South Asian workers

---

ALADDIN ULLAH

Actor and writer Aladdin Ullah explored the story of his father, Habib Ullah, in his 2014 one-man show, *Dishwasher Dreams*. Habib Ullah was a steamship worker from the Noakhali region of East Bengal who jumped ship and made his way to New York's Lower East Side in the 1920s, settled in Harlem in the 1930s, worked for years as a dishwasher and line cook in downtown restaurants, and for a time in the late 1940s ran one of the city's earliest Indian restaurants, just off Broadway in Manhattan's theater district. In an interview with NPR, Aladdin discussed why, as a comedian, he became interested in delving into the history of the Indian laborers who arrived in early twenti-eth-century Harlem:

> How did these Bengali men come to America and how did they survive? In other words, if I'm in L.A. complaining about Hollywood, that's nothing compared to how these Bengali men arrived in New York. So I really wanted to explore what they went through, and the more I explored the more I realized I was connected to my father. And my father had already expe-rienced the frustration that I had, but I just took it for granted.

Aladdin is now collaborating with Vivek Bald on the upcoming documentary *In Search of Bengali Harlem*, which will further examine the lives of families like his.

---

in the United States even after the passage of the Immigration Act of 1917, so that by the 1920s, these men could be found throughout the New York area and across the industrial Midwest.

Only a handful of these men's stories remain—for the most part, passed down through their families. Amir Haider Khan spent an eventful seven years in the United States before returning to India to join the independence movement; he made several voyages as a member of the U.S. Merchant Marine, then worked in a steam engine yard in upstate New York and the Packard auto plant in Detroit. He got involved in Indian anti-colonial activities in New York City, helped smuggle pamphlets of the revolutionary Ghadar Party to Indian workers in port cities in Central America and East Asia, joined an early African American civil rights cam-paign in Detroit, and even learned to fly an early model airplane in rural Indiana.

John Ali was another ship worker, from a village in Sylhet, East Bengal, who

Bengali men with their African American and Puerto Rican wives at a banquet of the Pakistan League of America on the Lower East Side of Manhattan, 1952. In BengaliHarlem.com, courtesy of Laila Choudhury.

jumped ship in Baltimore in 1920. There, he learned English, in part, by listening to the radio. He married a local African American woman, Mamie Chase, and had three children, but moved from one factory job to another: from Columbus, Pennsylvania, to Chester, Pennsylvania, and finally to Detroit. Ibrahim Choudry was a student activist in East Bengal before working his way to New York on a steamship around 1923. He quickly became a leader among the community of escaped Muslim seamen in the New York area. He sheltered other ship jumpers, helped them with immigration issues, acted in the role of an imam during religious observances, and wrote letters back home for men who were not literate. In 1947, when East Bengal became part of a newly independent Pakistan, Choudry helped found the Pakistan League of America, a social and political organization headquartered on the Lower East Side of Manhattan, and in the 1950s, he built ties with African American Muslim groups in Harlem.

Habib Ullah, from Noakhali, and Eshad Ali, from Sylhet, were two of the first men to establish Indian restaurants in New York City. Ullah, who had spent years as a dishwasher and cook after jumping ship in the 1920s, opened the Bengal Garden Restaurant in Manhattan's theater district in 1946 and ran it with his Puerto Rican wife, Victoria. Eshad Ali opened the Bombay India restaurant in the center of

---

A NOTE TO THE READER ABOUT GEOPOLITICAL TERMS

Throughout the book, you will notice the use of various geopolitical terms—such as "South Asia," "India," and others—to mean different things at different times and to different people. Many of these terms have had their meanings defined and redefined throughout the nineteenth and twentieth centuries, as forces of colonialism and postcolonial movements have shifted borders and both constructed and deconstructed national identities. As Shweta Majumdar Adur summarizes in chapter 3:

> The modern-day countries of India, Pakistan, and Bangladesh were all a single colony of the British government until their independence in 1947. After independence, the subcontinent was partitioned into two nations, India and Pakistan; the latter consisted of two noncontiguous territories under one state's rule, West and East Pakistan. In 1971, East Pakistan declared a war of liberation and, with India's support, seceded from Pakistan. The newly independent nation is what we now know as Bangladesh.

As such, an individual from the 1920s may refer to a South Asian migrant as "Indian" even though, today, we may refer to that same migrant as "Pakistani" or "Bangladeshi." Please refer back to the introduction for a fuller exploration of the term "South Asia" and its history.

Harlem, on 125th Street, in the 1950s and ran it with the help of his African American wife, Ruth. These examples, along with Khan's story of holing up in a Black boardinghouse in 1918, point to the crucial role that African American and Puerto Rican women played in providing South Asian ship jumpers with the possibility of creating new lives in the United States. Indeed, it was African American and Caribbean communities in cities such as New York, Baltimore, and Detroit that took in South Asian Muslim migrants at a time when the United States itself sought only to exclude them.

Vivek Bald is a scholar, writer, and documentary filmmaker whose work focuses on histories of migration and diaspora, particularly from the South Asian subcontinent.

VISITORS & TRAVELERS

Anupama Arora

Tourists, students, and religious and political leaders made up a small but increasing number of South Asians who traveled to the United States in the late nineteenth century and the early decades of the twentieth century. Letters, memoirs, travelogues, and lectures document their time in the United States. While they marveled at modern technological advances, natural wonders such as Niagara Falls, and the kind and generous spirit of Americans, they also criticized racism against Black people and Native Americans. Traveling in this deeply divided society, they were themselves racialized as Black and seen as exotic objects through the Orientalist gaze directed at them. They were taken aback by Americans' "phenomenal" ignorance of the Indian subcontinent—seen primarily as a land of swamis, snakes, elephants, oppressed women, and strange religious and social practices—which they felt pressure to confront.

The 1893 World's Fair commemorated the four-hundredth anniversary of Columbus's arrival in America, and the World's Parliament of Religions was one of the auxiliary congresses held in conjunction with the fair. Two hundred representatives of twelve major world religions were invited to the parliament in a professed effort to showcase religious pluralism. Among the group of representatives that came from South Asia, Swami Vivekananda and Anagarika Dharmapala garnered the most attention.

Dharmapala, born Don David Hewavitarne in Colombo, Sri Lanka, and now considered a major Sinhala Buddhist nationalist and reformer, was twenty-nine years

---

SWAMI VIVEKANANDA

Swami Vivekananda, born Narendranath Datta, was a Hindu ascetic who played an important role in introducing Vedanta—a Hindu school of philosophy—and yoga to the West. His speech on India and Hinduism at the World's Parliament of Religions in 1893 led the *New York Herald* to remark, "Vivekananda is undoubtedly the greatest figure in the Parliament of Religions. After hearing him we feel how foolish it is to send missionaries to this learned nation." His 1896 book, *Raja Yoga*, was particularly influential and is often credited with laying the groundwork for the later spread of modern yoga.

---

old when he arrived in Chicago as a representative of Theosophical Buddhism. He not only used the parliament as a platform to criticize Christian missionaries for being "intolerant" and "selfish," but he also did so with the missionaries' own text, the Bible, since he had been educated in Christian missionary schools. This was startling to a large majority of American audiences, who found themselves encountering an intelligent and savvy "Oriental" instead of a heathen or a decorative object. In his speeches at the parliament and his lectures in the United States, Dharmapala emphasized similarities between Buddhism and Christianity. Such comparisons challenged Christianity's position as the superior or exceptional religion, something that especially irked the orthodox clergy. To their further annoyance, he noted that the parliament was not an exceptional event, but "simply the re-echo of a great consummation which the Indian Buddhists accomplished twenty-four centuries ago."

As Dharmapala became a minor celebrity during the parliament, reportage on him focused more on his physical and sartorial appearance as well as his oratorical performance—his "black, curly locks," "long brown fingers," "vibrant voice," and "pretty peroration"—than on his arguments. American white women especially flocked to the lectures of "th' Buddhist, in his robes of shinin' white." In fact,

---

THEOSOPHY

The word *theosophy* combines roots meaning "God" and "wisdom." It began appearing as far back as the seventeenth century, but Russian Helena Blavatsky helped start the religious movement under the name around 1875, in New York City. Blavatsky's version of theosophy took elements of philosophy, scientific theories, and Christian, Buddhist, and Hindu thought (including reincarnation) to create something new. Theosophy had a major influence worldwide, including in South Asia, yet its legacy is more than controversial. Blavatsky's 1888 book, *The Secret Doctrine*, includes dehumanizing ideas about racial hierarchies that echo the scientific racism of her time.

ORIENTALISM

Orientalism describes a way of seeing Middle Eastern and South, Southeast, and East Asian cultures that exaggerates and misrepresents differences between these cultures and those of Europe and the United States (or "the West"). Orientalist depictions, which often show up in writing, design, and visual art, tend to reduce "Eastern" cultures—and the people associated with those cultures—as backward, uncivilized, and even threatening. Edward W. Said, in his landmark book, *Orientalism*, emphasized the way that this biased view was used as a tool to affirm colonial rule and continues to be used to justify Western imperialism globally. As a result, Said notes, the understanding of countries like Egypt in places like the United States is always colored by that misinformed way of seeing.

---

one American woman, Mary Foster, a rich heiress and Theosophist from Hawaii, would go on to become Dharmapala's most generous benefactor, helping finance his mission globally. For her ardent support, Dharmapala referred to her as his "foster mother." In his subsequent visit to the United States, in 1896, Dharmapala did a lecture tour across the country, from New York to San Francisco. During his 1902–4 visit, he made connections with prominent American intellectual William James (novelist Henry James's brother), sitting in on his psychology class at Harvard, and also visited the Tuskegee and Carlisle training schools to learn about industrial and agricultural education.

In addition to religious leaders, prominent Indian sociopolitical figures such as Rabindranath Tagore, Dr. B. R. Ambedkar, and Lala Lajpat Rai came to the United States in the first two decades of the twentieth century. Tagore made several trips

From left to right: Virchand Gandhi (representing Jainism), Anagarika Dharmapala, and Swami Vivekananda at the 1893 World's Parliament of Religions in Chicago.

between 1912 and 1930, and his writing and pieces about him were published in magazines such as the *Atlantic Monthly* and the *Bookman*. Ambedkar was a student at Columbia University from 1913 to 1916 and wrote on the caste system and on the adverse impact of British colonialism on Indian economic development. Rai lived in New York City from 1914 to 1919, during which time he became friends with Dr. W. E. B. Du Bois, founded the India Home Rule League of America, and edited its publication, *Young India*, to rally American public opinion toward Indian independence. He also published *The United States of America: A Hindu's Impression and a Study* (1916).

While most travelers to the United States from South Asia in this time period tended to be men, there were also a few women—such as the pioneering Anandibai Joshee, Pandita Ramabai, and Parvatibai Athavale. Joshee became the first South Asian woman to earn a medical degree, from the Woman's Medical College

DR. ANANDIBAI JOSHEE

The Woman's Medical College of Pennsylvania (originally called the Female Medical College of Pennsylvania) was founded in Philadelphia in 1850 and was the first medical college for women in the world. In 1883, Anandibai Joshee applied to the school and was accepted. A few years later, she graduated as the first South Asian woman in the world to receive a degree in Western medicine.

Joshee was well aware of the historic nature of her pursuit. She wrote in her letter requesting admission to the college in 1883:

> . . . that determination which has brought me to your country against the combined opposition of my friends & caste ought to go along way towards helping me to carry out the purpose for which I came . . . to render to my poor suffering country women the true medical aid they so sadly stand in need of, and which they would rather die for than accept at the hands of a male physician. The voice of humanity is with me and I must not fail.

Joshee, who was only nineteen at the time, had personal experience with the difficulties of seeking treatment under British rule as a South Asian woman, having lost her own child while giving birth a few years earlier.

When she arrived in the U.S., there was concern here about how Joshee would assimilate into American culture. In a letter to the dean of the Woman's Medical College of Pennsylvania, a local woman said she would arrange "American" clothes for Joshee. However, when Joshee arrived, she was committed to wearing saris. In a stirring speech she gave before leaving Calcutta, she had said:

> I am determined to live there exactly as I do here. I propose to myself to make no change in my customs and manners, food or dress.

While she was in the U.S., Joshee would write letters to her husband back in India. The letters expose the daily difficulties Joshee faced, from feelings of loneliness to harsh accusations of abandonment from her husband. She also wrote her candid impressions about life in the United States. Though she praised the Americans for getting rid of political institutions like the monarchy and the aristocracy, she also thought they were arrogant, especially in their views of India and Indians. She wrote:

> It would not be really surprising if they conclude that we [Indians] are the missing link between ape and man . . . I had no idea that India is such a cruel and barbaric country! And until I met these people I had no idea, either, that it is such a heathen country!

October 10, 1885
Dr.Anandabai Joshee,Seranysore,India
Dr. Kei Okami, Tokio, Japan
Dr. Tabat M. Islambooly,Damascus,Syria

Dr. Anandibai Joshee, Dr. Kei Okami, and Dr. Tabat M. Islambooly at the Woman's Medical College of Pennsylvania on October 10, 1885. In SAADA, courtesy of the Legacy Center Archives at Drexel University.

PANDITA RAMABAI IN AMERICA

Born in 1858, Pandita Ramabai would become an important social reformer who worked to achieve better rights for women in India. The tragic events of her life guided her from an early age, beginning with the death of her parents in the 1877 famine to becoming a widow with a young daughter at the age of twenty-four. Soon after, Ramabai traveled across India, and eventually the globe, advocating for equal education and rights for women. In 1883, she was invited to Britain, where she began medical training and eventually converted to Christianity.

Pandita Ramabai honored on a postage stamp in India, 1989.

From Britain, Ramabai traveled to the United States, where she would reside for three years, lecturing and writing, including important criticisms of the treatment of women. During her stay, she also documented her observations of America in a Marathi travelogue published in 1889. The following excerpt is from Meera Kosambi's translation of Ramabai's book.

> When I arrived in the United States of America in March 1886, the winter was on the wane and the spring had started, so I could not see the winter in its true manifestation. It rained several times and snowed occasionally during the last part of March and in April. It is very hot here from May to September. Sometimes the mercury rises even to a hundred and ten degrees, but such days are few and far between. Normally the summer temperatures reach eighty to eighty-five degrees. The houses here, and their interiors, are designed for the winter, so that it is more difficult to endure the summer here than in our country. Moreover, the customs of these people are different from ours, which causes us a great deal of inconvenience.
>
> An amusing incident occurred in the house of the lady with whom I stayed as a lodger in Philadelphia. Although no one stopped me from doing anything I wanted in my room on the third floor, I had to be very cautious when I went downstairs and was in the company of others at mealtime. One particular day in June happened to be very hot, with hardly any breeze. In the afternoon the whole house was quiet, so, instead of being cautious as usual, I went down to the kitchen barefoot to fetch a glass of water. As ill luck would have it, the very thing that should not have happened, did happen. I was about to go upstairs with the water, when I ran into old Dr. B! Who knows what the old man thought at the sight of my bare feet, but his face fell and his expression showed chagrin and surprise as though at some shameless conduct. I rushed off to my room without looking at his face too long! A couple hours later I was reading in my room and had almost forgotten the incident, when there was a knock on my door. As soon as I said, "Please come in," a twelve-year-old boy, grandson of old Dr. B., entered and left me a short note which I opened and read as follows:
>
>> I know that it is the custom of your country to walk about barefoot without shoes and stockings; but it is considered immodest in our country. The members of my family are shocked to see you walking barefoot. Be kind enough to wear your shoes and stockings when you come down.
>>
>> Your friend,
>> Mrs. B.
>
> After this incident I vowed never to commit the offense of walking barefoot in anyone's presence as long as I was in the country.

A NOTE TO THE READER ABOUT CASTE

Throughout this book, you will notice that the term "caste" and related terms such as "Dalit," "Brahmin," "upper-caste," and others appear repeatedly. Caste is a system of religiously codified exclusion that has created entrenched structures of oppression that deeply and intimately impact the lives of over a billion individuals of South Asian origin. Structures of caste and casteism have been carried to and reinforced in South Asian diasporic communities across the globe—including in the United States. As Dhanya Addanki, a 2019–20 SAADA Archival Creators Fellow, wrote for *Tides*:

> . . . caste doesn't disappear when you take residence in the U.S. no matter how much you might try and ignore it, refuse to teach your children about it, or fail to recognize its presence, thick in the air in any South Asian circle and beyond.

Organizations like Equality Labs are working to ensure that any analysis of South Asian American history or the current South Asian American experience examines caste, and later essays and insets in this book share more detail as well. For a full report on caste in the United States, published by Equality Labs in 2018, please visit equalitylabs.org/castesurvey.

of Pennsylvania, in 1886, and Ramabai, a distant relative, attended Joshee's graduation. In a letter to her husband, Joshee wrote: "I think the Americans imagine anything [about India], no matter what the reality. . . . I did not know that India is such a barbaric and cruel country! Nor did I know, until I met these people, that it was so irreligious! . . . It would not be surprising if they imagine us to be the missing link between apes and humans."

In contrast to Joshee, Ramabai wrote a travelogue to celebrate the "greatness of the American nation" entitled *The People of the United States* (1889). Ramabai's three-year sojourn in the United States, from 1886 to 1889, led to the formation of associations called "Ramabai Circles," which collected funds for her mission to support upper-caste Hindu Indian widows. Almost three decades later, in 1918, another Brahmin Hindu widow, Athavale, traveled to the United States; in her autobiography, *My Story* (1928), she provides a glimpse into the kindness of Americans, the aggressive efforts

Pandita Ramabai and her daughter, Manorama.

of American missionaries to convert her, and her financial hardship as she worked as a maid in American households. The distinctive experiences of these three women highlight the class, caste, and gender dimensions of travel.

Whether they traveled for work or leisure, South Asian travelers found themselves taking on the role of intermediaries, as they sought to translate South Asia for Americans and, on the other hand, educate South Asians about the United States. Their travel writing offered a counterpoint to colonial Western travel writings on India saturated with Orientalist images. Using irony or humor or adopting the voice of a naive outsider, these travelers were able to critique aspects of American society while holding on to a romantic image of the United States as a young, anti-colonial, and democratic nation—in sharp contrast to imperial Britain.

OH NIAGARA!

A distinctive figure of Indian nationalism, Lala Lajpat Rai visited the United States twice. During the First World War, he spent four years in exile in the United States, where he formed the India Home Rule League of America in New York City. In those years, Rai continued working toward the cause of Indian Home Rule, publishing a monthly journal, *Young India*, and making contact with several people active in the American progressive and liberal circles, including Dr. W. E. B. Du Bois, Booker T. Washington, Margaret Sanger, and Walter Lippmann. His writings also included detailed descriptions of his travels, including several quintessential tourist sites, such as the U.S. Capitol, the Liberty Bell, and Niagara Falls. In the passage below, Rai writes about his train ride to Niagara and its "awe-inspiring" grandeur. More than a century later, Niagara Falls remains an iconic destination for South Asian Americans.

The last I wrote to you was from Boston. I left Boston on the evening of the 21st [Sept 1905] for the Niagara Falls by railroad. We reached the Niagara Falls at about 9 A.M. in the morning. The river consists of the volume of water that flows from Erie lake and then empties itself into Lake Ontario. Coming out of the Erie lake it divides itself into two currents, one passing the territory of the United States and the other that of British Canada. On the spot where these currents adopt different courses the water precipitates with great rush into a lower level. These currents are hence, on this spot, called the American and the Canadian rapids till they fall into the valley, at one place 167 feet lower and at another 158 feet. These are called Falls. There are two principal Falls on the Canadian side and two on the American side. The scenery here is magnificent, grand, and awe-inspiring. Here you see Nature in its naked majesty and are at once struck with its grandeur and beauty. But here, again, at the same time you are forcibly reminded of the equally great powers of man.

From "Oh Niagara!: Lala Lajpat Rai at Niagara Falls in 1905" for Tides, by Manan Desai.

Anupama Arora (she/her) is a professor of English and women's and gender studies at University of Massachusetts Dartmouth.

THE PARROT'S BEAK

Kartar Dhillon

Kartar Dhillon (or Kar, as she was known) was born on April 30, 1915, in California's Simi Valley. Her father, Bakhshish Singh, immigrated to the United States in 1897, and her mother, Rattan Kaur, arrived in 1910. One of the first South Asian families in the United States, the Dhillon family was involved in both the Ghadar Party, agitating for India's independence from British rule, and with labor organizing through the Industrial Workers of the World. When her brother Bud Dillon was just twelve years old, he volunteered to join a mission for India's freedom, which took him around the world. Kar was herself an activist and a writer who was engaged in India's freedom struggle, and she later supported organizations like the Black Panthers and helped organize farm workers in California. She passed away on June 15, 2008.

Here is an excerpt from Kar's autobiographical essay, "The Parrot's Beak":

I had dreams of becoming an artist; I planned to work actively for India's freedom from British rule. I looked upon marriage as a prison. But even though I abhorred the idea of marriage, the same year, right out of high school, I got married.

My oldest brother already planned to send me to India to marry the "right person." But the man I married, a political activist, born and raised in India, warned me, "You will have no rights in India. Your brother can force you to marry anyone he chooses. Marry me, then he will have no power over you."

I idolized this man, I had been impressed from the start by his fiery speeches at meetings of the Gadar Party, an organization formed to fight British rule in India. He already had a degree in political science from the University of California, Berkeley.

"But I want to go to the university," I said.

"You can do both," he insisted. "I will help you."

We got married secretly so that I could go on caring for my younger brothers and sister. But I did not keep my secret for long, because soon I had morning sickness and was frequently running out of the house to throw up behind the trees and bushes. "No children," I had said to my husband. "Political activism and babies don't go together." Though he had agreed with me, I found myself pregnant nonetheless.

My oldest brother was so furious when he found out that he kicked me out of the house. "Go live off your husband," he said, though he had bragged to people earlier about how much I did for the family. "Give her two empty bowls," he would say, "and she can produce a delicious dinner for the whole family."

I wanted to take the two youngest children with me, but my next oldest brother said, "You will have enough problems being married." A month later, all four of the younger children were brought to live with me and my husband—one of them had accidentally burned down the

The Dhillon family in Astoria, c. 1916. Seated second and third from left in middle row are: Rattan Kaur (mother) and Bakhshish Singh Dhillon (father). Children from left to right: Kapur, Karm, Katar, Budh. Courtesy of SikhPioneers.org.

house. Caring for the family was nothing new to me. When we were no more than seven and eight years old, my mother used to assign a baby apiece to me and my sister to watch for the day. At twelve, I was doing the entire family's wash on washboard by hand, and taking turns with my sister to cook meals. By high school, the job of milking thirty cows every morning and night was tacked onto my other duties.

When I was in my eighth month of pregnancy, I had no medical care. The clinics in the area where my husband leased land on a sharecrop basis refused me because I had not been in that county a full year. So in an effort to obtain care, all the children and I had moved back to the farm that my brothers sharecropped. We slept on large raisin boxes under the open sky, and I cooked meals on a grill placed over a hole in the ground for the wood fire.

A family friend was shocked to learn that I was not getting medical treatment and took me to the director of the same county hospital where my mother had died. But she also refused me admission, saying, "If these people can afford to farm, they can afford medical care." My friend pointed out that we did not have any money, that we could not even buy enough milk for all the children. "They buy one quarter of milk a day, and take turns drinking one cup every other day." She told her that my teeth were breaking off in pieces for lack of calcium, but the director remained adamant.

"She can't have her baby on the street," my friend said.

The hospital official fixed her eyes on my friend and asked, "Then why do these people have babies?"

As we walked out the door, a nurse who had been in the room whispered to us, "The hospital can't turn you away in an emergency. Come in when you are in labor."

And that is what I did. My joy was great at learning my baby was a girl. Because I was slipping in and out of the anesthesia, I asked three times to be assured I had heard right. I had indeed. I was so happy it was a girl because I wanted to prove to the world that she could be the equal of any boy ever born. Above all, I wanted a girl to give her the love and understanding that had been withheld from me.

"The Parrot's Beak" appears in Making Waves: An Anthology of Writings by and about Asian American Women *(1989) and* Growing Up Asian American: Stories of Childhood, Adolescence and Coming of Age in America, from the 1800s to the 1990s, *edited by Maria Hong (1993). Reprinted with permission.*

THE BELLINGHAM "ANTI-HINDU" RIOT

Paul Englesberg

The headlines on September 5, 1907, proclaimed a calamity: "HINDUS HOUNDED FROM CITY," "MOB LAW RULES CITY," "Mob Drives Foreigners from Lodging Houses and Mills," "Crowd Numbering 500 Drags Dusky Orientals From Their Homes."

In the early 1900s, Bellingham, Washington, situated on the shores of Puget Sound just south of the Canadian border, was a city with a rapidly growing population and a booming lumber industry employing thousands of workers. The influx of newly arrived workers, both domestic migrants from eastern parts of the country and foreign immigrants from Europe, China, Japan, the Philippines, and India, changed the demographics of this region, and the immigrants from Asia often drew the ire of local residents and, particularly, white workers. Chinese immigrants had been expelled from Bellingham and most other places along the

Pacific coast in the 1880s, although by the early 1900s salmon canneries employed many Asian workers on a seasonal basis. In 1906, immigrants from India who had recently arrived in Canada began to seek work in the United States, where mills were offering higher wages than in Canada, and many flocked to Bellingham due to its proximity and job market for laborers.

The immigrants from India came to Bellingham in small numbers in 1906, but by the summer of 1907, ships carrying hundreds of Punjabi immigrants were arriving at the docks of nearby Vancouver and Victoria, British Columbia. Before the

---

THE TERM "HINDU" / "HINDOO"

Throughout this chapter, you will see the term "Hindu" or "Hindoo" being used in historical newspapers or by historical figures. The term was at one time used as a broad racial classification, adopted officially by the U.S. government in the late nineteenth and early twentieth centuries, to describe all people of South Asian origin. It quickly came to carry a strong derogatory connotation, though, as it was frequently used by nativist groups to "other" South Asian immigrants, collapsing a community with a diverse range of religious, linguistic, cultural, and geographic origins to a single, non-American entity. The term was most frequently used in reference to the Punjabi, Sikh men who made up the majority of the early twentieth-century South Asian American community—resulting in headlines in Bellingham such as "Hindus Hounded from City" and "Hindu Hordes Invading the State."

---

outbreak of the riot on September 4, 1907, approximately one hundred Punjabis were employed in Bellingham lumber mills, and perhaps another two or three hundred had arrived in the city looking for work. They were commonly called "Hindus," meaning anyone from India or Hindustan, but most of these immigrants were in fact followers of the Sikh religion who could be distinguished by the turbans they wore, and perhaps 10 percent were Muslims. All were men and most were in their twenties or thirties. They were routinely discriminated against and harassed due to their appearance, their alleged willingness to work for low wages, and the fear that they were displacing white workers. Soon after their arrival, workers and community members began complaining about the presence of "Hindus" in Bellingham. Local newspapers often mixed negative opinion with factual accounts, describing them as "undesirable citizens," "brown men," and a "public nuisance."

A few days before the riot, during the massive Labor Day march on September 1,

1907, some labor leaders threatened violence against the Punjabi workers and the mills where they were working, and several attacks on Punjabi workers occurred in the days leading up to the riot. On the evening of September 4, mobs gathered in the streets, responding to a call to drive out the "Hindus." Police arrived after a large mob stormed the lodgings where thirty Punjabis were living. Other bands of rioters dragged immigrants from nearby rooming houses.

Bellingham's entire police force numbered only nine officers, and, fearing violent confrontation, the police chief accommodated the rioters and proposed a deal whereby the Punjabi workers would be held overnight in jail beneath the city hall and then be permitted to leave the city peacefully the following day. Seeing

---

THE MURDERS OF SRINIVAS KUCHIBHOTLA AND HARNAM SINGH

In February 2017, a white man shot two Indian immigrants, Srinivas Kuchibhotla and Alok Madasani, at a bar in Olathe, Kansas. Kuchibhotla was killed in the attack, and the perpetrator, who claimed to have mistaken his victims as Iranian, reportedly yelled, "Get out of my country" and "Terrorist" before shooting them. More than a century earlier, the April 23, 1908, edition of the *Oregonian* reported on the "Hindu murder trial," in which six white men were charged with the murder of Harnam Singh in Boring, Oregon. The article explained, "The state will seek to establish by evidence that the men went to Sandy [a neighboring town] and became partially intoxicated and then came down to the sawmill with guns, and, taking a position behind the cabin of the Hindu, fired shot after shot, until finally one of the bullets struck the unfortunate man." The article went on to suggest that "race prejudice" was the motivation for the men's actions, given that several "Hindus" were employed in the local sawmill at the time that the shooting occurred.

---

this as a victory, the rioters escorted the Punjabi workers to the jail and continued to round up others. By midnight, the streets were quiet, and at least one hundred Punjabi workers were huddled in the basement of the city hall. Many others either hid or fled the city on foot during the night.

The local press generally supported the police and reported no serious casualties; however, newspapers across the country, relying on an Associated Press dispatch from Bellingham, reported that six of the Punjabi workers had been badly beaten and hospitalized. The mayor and other local officials denounced these reports as false, but spokesmen for the Punjabi workers stated that they took the threats of violence seriously and indeed feared for their lives. The next day, under police and deputy protection, the Punjabi men who had been working in the lum-

Article from the September 16, 1906, Puget Sound American *describing recent "Hindu" immigration to Bellingham, Washington. In SAADA, courtesy of Paul Englesberg.*

ber mills claimed their pay and prepared to leave despite offers of continued work by some of the mill owners. Within days, most of the Punjabi workers had left, and word quickly spread to their compatriots in Canada and elsewhere to stay clear of Bellingham.

Although the numbers are not known, many of the Punjabi workers returned on foot across the border to Canada, and those with the money for tickets traveled south to Seattle, Oregon, or California by train or steamship. The last few Punjabi residents left on September 17, after their landlord warned them of hostile neighbors who wanted them evicted. The local prosecutor announced that charges were being dropped against the five men arrested for rioting because no one could be found to testify against them. Thus, within twelve days of the riot, the entire population of Punjabi workers—hundreds of men—had been expelled, but no one was brought to justice.

TULY SINGH JOHL (1878–1978)

The only documented story of the Bellingham exodus from the perspective of the Punjabi laborers is that of Thakar (Tuly) Singh Johl, who was interviewed in 1975 at the age of ninety-seven in Yuba City, California, by Joan Jensen for her book *Passage from India*. Tuly, the youngest of four sons, was born in 1878 in the village of Jundiala. He married, and in 1905, soon after his first baby was born, he left his wife and son to find work in Canada with six other men from his village (one was a Hindu, and the others, like Tuly, were Sikh farmers). They arrived in Victoria, but Tuly and the other five Sikh men of the group crossed the border to the United States and found work at a lumber mill in Bellingham. (Gurditta Mal, who was Hindu, stayed in Victoria, where he worked in labor and trucking jobs and had close ties to the Sikh community.) Although the lumber mill where Tuly and his fellow laborers worked was some distance from the riot, they left town within days out of fear of attacks, along with hundreds of others.

Unlike many Sikh immigrants who continued to wear the customary turban, Tuly was among those who cut his hair and wore a hat in order to find work and avoid harassment in North America. After working on a railroad construction crew, he settled in Yuba City, California, where he became a foreman on a fruit ranch and later purchased his own farmland. His wife and children later were able to immigrate and join him in California. His elder son studied agriculture and continued working as a farmer, and his second son became an ophthalmologist, one of the first Indian Americans to earn an MD and practice medicine.

I worked for seven months in a mill near Bellingham. Some of the men worked double shifts and white workers were being replaced as the East Indians were hired. They were dependable workers. I was working in the mill when the Bellingham riot occurred in September 1907. Police put many men in jail for their own safety. I kept working, but the next day the mill manager said they would have to leave or the white men would burn the mill.

Tuly Singh Johl, Yuba City Area, California. Courtesy of the Johl family and the Punjabi American Heritage Society.

ASIATIC EXCLUSION LEAGUE

In 1905, white labor leaders in San Francisco formed the Japanese and Korean Exclusion League with the primary goal of extending the Chinese Exclusion Act of 1882 to also ban Japanese and Korean immigration. Decrying the inclusion of Asian immigrant laborers in industries across the West Coast, the League lobbied U.S. congressmen for stricter immigration policies, tracked the arrival of new Asian immigrants to the Angel Island Immigration Station, petitioned local school systems to exclude the children of Asian immigrants, and engaged in other attempts to systematically exclude and terrorize Asian immigrants. In May of 1906, Congressman Hayes of the Fifth District wrote to the League's secretary congratulating him on the organization's successful efforts and highlighting the connections between the League and governmental officials. He wrote, "I have used many of the facts and figures gathered by the League, not only in the speech that I made in the House but in personal conferences with members of Congress, with the very best results, and I am glad to be able to report that the feeling in Congress is very much more favorable to the proposition to extend the Chinese Exclusion laws . . ."

Within a few years of its founding, the League grew its membership to form new chapters in cities and towns across Washington and California, and even expand internationally into Canada. In 1907, in response to the increased immigration of Punjabi laborers, the League renamed itself the Asiatic Exclusion League and expanded its goal to also exclude South Asian (derogatorily called "Hindu") immigration. In its meeting minutes from October 15, 1911, the League recorded:

> *The Hindu problem is the Chinese and the Japanese problem over again. The Hindu is in several ways more objectionable than either of the other Oriental races. He keeps his person as dirty as his quarters, and at the base of the danger from the Hindu is the danger faced in other Oriental immigration—the danger of lowering our civilization. . . . The Pacific Coast is united upon the broad principle of national law providing that peoples who cannot be assimilated without injury to the parent stock shall not be admitted here.*

In the days following the riot, the Bellingham Herald commented that "local citizens are rejoicing over the departure of the men and feel that a certain amount of good has been accomplished." Furthermore, the editor concluded that "the races will not mix and that the Bellingham incident will go a long way toward impressing this fact upon diplomats and lawmakers." The local press, claiming to speak for most citizens, generally deplored the rioters' methods but praised the riot's outcome as a blessing. City council members supported the actions of the police and mostly cast blame on the mill owners for employing the Punjabi workers. A few clergy were the only public voices to openly criticize the actions of the mob and the role of the police.

The Bellingham riot of 1907 was the first and probably the most devastating in a series of racially violent acts against Punjabi immigrants on the Pacific coast over the following months and years. Just a few days after the Bellingham incident, the largest race riot in Canada's history broke out in Vancouver, during which a large mob attacked residents and businesses in the Chinese and Japanese quarters. In November 1907, Punjabi immigrants were driven out of Everett, Washington, another mill city, sixty miles south of Bellingham. The Asiatic Exclusion League, a nativist organization based in San Francisco, and officials in the U.S. and Canada used these riots as evidence of popular opposition to Asian immigration as they pushed for stricter anti-Asian exclusion laws and policies.

Paul Englesberg (he/him) is a retired faculty member at the School of Education at Walden University. He is currently writing a book about immigrants, racism, and conflict in the Pacific Northwest.

NABHI RAM JOSHI

There will probably not be the same race prejudice against the prominent Hindu who is to attend the [State Normal School] as against his fellow countrymen who are working in the mills. And yet there is no such thing as caste in this democratic country of our[s]!

As the *Bellingham Herald* editor implied, it was remarkable that a student from India was welcomed with open arms during the period when "Hindu" was a term of revulsion and there was extreme prejudice in Bellingham and elsewhere in the Pacific Northwest against Indian immigrants. This young student from India, Nabhi Ram Joshi, arrived in Bellingham just before the 1907 riot broke out, and he lived in the home of a prominent Bellingham family, where he was treated with much kindness and as a member of the family.

Joshi was born in Ludhiana in the Punjab state of India. In the fall of 1907, at the age of nineteen, he enrolled at the Washington State Normal School in Bellingham, one of the few male students there and the second student from India to attend the school. He had worked at a mill across the border in New Westminster, British Columbia, where his older brother was foreman. During Joshi's year in Bellingham, he lived with the family of Dr. Edward Mathes, the school's principal. Joshi's arrival as a student in Bellingham was unusual enough to warrant the attention of the city's two newspapers, which made special note of his status in India as "representing the highest caste" and "a member of the Brahmin class." He was described in glowing language, in stark contrast to the way that "Hindu" immigrants were commonly described in these papers. He was "good looking," "well educated," "able to converse in several languages," and "well supplied with money."

After a year in Bellingham, Joshi transferred to the University of Washington, in Seattle, where he studied engineering. Due to his activism while he was a student, he was arrested upon returning to India in 1915, and he remained in custody for five years. Upon his release in 1920, he began his career in pharmacology. He kept up a correspondence with the Mathes family for much of his life, and as a result of their close relationship, a scholarship in his name was established to assist students from India who study at Western Washington University, which grew out of the State Normal School.

Nabhi Ram Joshi (far left, middle row) with State Normal School students in 1907. In SAADA, courtesy of Paul Englesberg.

GHADAR PARTY

Seema Sohi

In November 1913, a group of Indian revolutionaries gathered at their newly established headquarters on a San Francisco hilltop to raise a red, yellow, and green flag that represented freedom, brotherhood, and equality—the values of the free India they envisioned. These men were members of the Ghadar Party, a group of Indians who sought to overthrow the British Empire through armed revolution. On November 1, the party announced its emergence to the world by launching its first newspaper, *Ghadar*. In its inaugural issue, the paper boldly declared that "today there begins in foreign lands, but in our country's language, a war against the English Raj . . . What is our name? Ghadar. What is our work? Ghadar. Our name and our work are identical."

In less than a year, the party claimed to have thousands of members and dozens of branches across the world, including in Vancouver, Portland, Astoria, St. John,

Sacramento, Stockton, Panama, Manila, Hong Kong, and Shanghai. Additionally, the party began circulating twenty-five hundred copies of *Ghadar* in Gurumukhi and twenty-two hundred in Urdu each week. Within six months, the paper had reached India, China, Japan, Manila, Sumatra, Fiji, Java, Singapore, Egypt, Paris, South Africa, British East Africa, and Panama.

The Ghadar Party was a coalition of Punjabi migrant workers and Bengali and Punjabi intellectuals and students that emphasized secularism and unity despite linguistic, religious, and regional differences. Though its core leadership was Hindu, Sikh, and

Ghadar newspaper in Urdu, Vol. 1, No. 22, March 24, 1914. In SAADA.

Muslim, nearly 90 percent of its membership was Punjabi Sikh men, almost half of whom were veterans of the British Indian Army and whose loyalty and service to the empire was presumed by British officials. What united these seemingly disparate groups was their common belief that they had been pushed out of India because of colonialism and now experienced a shared sense of humiliation as degraded colonial subjects across the world. Racial discrimination and violence

---

GHADAR

The Ghadar Party gets its name from an Urdu word that derives from an Arabic word meaning "revolt" or "rebellion." Members primarily spelled their organization name as "Gadar Party" or "Ghadr Party."

---

in North America produced an anti-colonial consciousness among them, and the party's goal of an independent India was inseparable from attaining racial equality abroad.

Ghadar exhorted readers that it was their patriotic duty to circulate copies of the paper among as many Indians as possible. Indians across the diaspora who received copies of the paper were asked to send them on to friends in India after reading them in order to help spread the party's message. In spite of British efforts to prohibit the circulation of *Ghadar*, the paper continued to reach India from the Pacific coast of North America via Shanghai, Hong Kong, Nairobi, Johannesburg, Singapore, Manila, Bangkok, Tientsin, and Moji. When the first issue arrived in India on December 7, 1913, it was immediately banned, and officials in India began searching all luggage from the United States and East Asia and seizing any Ghadar Party publications. However, the contents of the paper still made their way

---

#DALITWOMENFIGHT

The Ghadar Party movement is part of a long history of transnational radical activism and organizing in the South Asian American community that continues to this day. One recent example is #DalitWomenFight, which began in 2015 as a campaign to "end caste apartheid," draw specific attention to the lack of protection for Dalit women and families in India, and stand in solidarity with other women who are victims of state violence in the United States. Inspired by the organizing of Dalit women in India, the U.S. campaign used social media and national tours to create marches and events in cities across the country, collaborating with other local radical South Asian American activists to achieve their goals.

---

into India. Once Indians became aware that authorities were on the lookout for the weekly periodical, they began hiding small cuttings and sending handwritten excerpts from the paper in private letters.

At the outbreak of the First World War, the Ghadar Party launched into action, heeding the call of their leaders, who proclaimed that the need for British troops in Europe presented an opportune moment to organize uprisings in both India and British imperial outposts. Between 1914 and 1918, the party mobilized nearly eight thousand Indians from North and South America and East Asia to return to India to overthrow British rule. Anticipating their return, British officials arrested hundreds of Ghadarites before they ever disembarked from the ships that carried them home, dealing a severe blow to the party's plans. Those who were not detained quickly made contact with Indian revolutionaries across the country and fixed February 21, 1915, as the day that simultaneous uprisings would erupt across

India. The uprisings would center on convincing Indian soldiers to strike against British officials first, thereby inspiring the masses to rise up and overthrow British rule. Ghadarites visited military cantonments to recruit soldiers, arguing that Indian military service perpetuated the status of Indians as slaves to the empire and as pawns used to slaughter the world's colonized peoples and reinforce the brutality of British rule. Party members also gathered arms, produced flags, and

---

BERKELEY SOUTH ASIAN RADICAL HISTORY WALKING TOUR

Anirvan Chatterjee and Barnali Ghosh spent years collecting stories, oral histories, readings, and archival materials before launching the Berkeley South Asian Radical History Walking Tour in 2012. The tour, which explores more than one hundred years of South Asians living in Berkeley, seeks to inform, ground, and inspire new activism, in the tradition of historians like Howard Zinn and Ronald Takaki. One of the stories featured in the walking tour is that of Kartar Singh Sarabha, an Indian student who came to the U.S. in 1912 to study chemistry at the University of California, Berkeley, and became a leading activist in the Ghadar Party. Sarabha returned to India in 1914 to fight for independence but was executed by the British for his role in the anti-colonial struggle. He was just nineteen years old when he was killed. Sarabha's poem "If They Ask You Who You Are" outlines his call to action.

If They Ask You Who You Are

If they ask you who you are
Tell them that your name is Rebel
That your occupation is to wipe out tyranny
That your work is to create ghadar
That this is your namaaz and your sandhya
That this is the way you worship
That this is your only true religion
That this is your khuda, that this is your Ram

Learn more at berkeleysouthasian.org.

Photo by Preeti Mangala Shekhar.

---

collected materials for destroying railways and telegraph wires, looting treasuries and distributing arms and ammunitions. Their plans, however, never came to fruition, due to the workings of British intelligence.

Although Ghadarites believed that their successful efforts in recruiting Indians in the United States would generate the same kind of enthusiasm in India, they discovered that India was not as ripe for revolution as they had hoped. Leaders of the Indian National Congress, priests of several important Sikh gurdwaras, and many nationalist leaders in India strongly denounced the party. While Ghadarites in North America successfully highlighted the interconnectedness of colonialism, racial subjugation, and economic exploitation to mobilize thousands along the Pacific coast, they were ultimately unable to convince their countrymen in India to join them.

Seema Sohi (she/her/hers) is an associate professor of ethnic studies at the University of Colorado Boulder.

THE KOMAGATA MARU

Seema Sohi

On May 23, 1914, the *Komagata Maru* sailed into the Vancouver harbor in British Columbia with 376 Indians aboard. They were challenging Canada's Continuous Journey Law, which prohibited any immigrant who did not arrive by "continuous journey" from his country of birth or citizenship to enter the country. Because there were no steamship lines sailing directly from India to the western Canadian provinces, the law made it nearly impossible for South Asians to enter Canada. The leader of the *Komagata Maru* was Gurdit Singh, a Sikh who over the course of two decades in Malaya, Singapore, and Hong Kong had become a successful businessman in the lumber industry. Singh was moved by the economic and political struggles of South Asians across East Asia, many of whom had heard of the economic opportunities in British Columbia but were stuck in cities like Hong Kong, Shanghai, and Yokohama after the passage of the Continuous Journey Law.

As Singh stated, "When I came to Hong Kong in January 1914 I could not bear the trouble of those who were in the gurdwara waiting to go to Vancouver. They were waiting there for years and living at their own expense.... I resolved to take them to Vancouver under any circumstances."

The *Komagata Maru* set sail for Canada from Hong Kong in April 1914 with 160 passengers on board, including Gurdit Singh's seven-year-old son. After making stops in Shanghai, Moji, and Yokohama to pick up additional passengers, the ship began its journey across the Pacific. When the *Komagata Maru* arrived in Vancouver, immigration inspectors ordered the ship to anchor offshore. Inspectors allowed the twenty of those on board who were returning to Canada to enter the country and issued deportation orders to the remaining passengers. While Canadian officials had hoped that their refusal to land the passengers would end the matter, the *Komagata Maru* remained in the Vancouver harbor for another eight

---

AN APOLOGY FROM THE CANADIAN GOVERNMENT

In Vancouver, along the city's waterfront, there is a stark monument to the *Komagata Maru* and the people who were turned away in 1914. Nearly 102 years after the incident, on May 18, 2016, Prime Minister Justin Trudeau finally issued a formal apology from Canada's House of Commons:

> *Today—while knowing that no words can fully erase the pain and suffering experienced by the passengers—I offer a sincere apology on behalf of the government for the laws in force at the time that allowed Canada to be indifferent to the plight of the passengers of the Komagata Maru.*

---

weeks. It quickly captured the attention of South Asians across North America, Africa, East Asia, and India, who saw the ship as a symbol and a rallying cry to South Asians all over the world to demand equality as British subjects and, later, to begin to challenge the British Raj itself.

When asked by Canadian reporters why he had chartered the ship, Gurdit Singh responded that the South Asian passengers on board were British subjects who considered it their right to travel to any part of the empire. Singh boldly warned Canadian officials that the passengers were determined to make the *Komagata Maru* a test case and that if they were denied entry to Canada, "other boats will be chartered and my people will continue to cross the Pacific until we secure what we

Passengers aboard the Komagata Maru *as it sits in Vancouver harbor in 1914. Courtesy of Vancouver Public Library.*

consider to be our just rights." Meanwhile, South Asians in British Columbia and the United States began organizing meetings and raising thousands of dollars on behalf of the passengers. Their goal was to take over the ship's charter in order to land the passengers. As leaders Hussain Rahim and Bhag Singh told an audience in Vancouver, the *Komagata Maru* was not only "about 376 Hindustanis on the ship but the fate of 330 million Indians."

After weeks of waiting, the passengers on the *Komagata Maru* grew increasingly hopeless. Many had staked everything they owned on the venture and had boarded the ship believing that they would gain entry to Canada as British subjects. Passengers sent telegrams to the Canadian governor-general pleading for water and food, as provisions on the ship were quickly running out. As the weeks wore on, communication from the passengers grew more distressed. Rats and flies were on the deck, the toilets were overflowing, and passengers were getting sick due to insufficient food, water, and exercise. They began making desperate appeals to be landed, claiming they did not "have enough physical strength to cross the Pacific again" and warning that the Canadian government would be held responsible for allowing them to die a "miserable death" off the Vancouver shore.

THE IMMIGRATION ACT OF 1917

The Immigration Act of 1917, along with existing immigration laws and agreements, prohibited immigrants from almost the entire Asian continent from entering the United States for more than three decades. The act created what was later known as the Asiatic Barred Zone: a precise geographic area of Asia, designated by Congress. All people who were residents of countries within this area, with few exceptions, were barred from entering the United States.

When it was passed, the 1917 Act constituted the most sweeping immigration law in U.S. history. In addition to a number of restrictions, the 1917 Act excluded from the United States all peoples living within a constructed geographic area referred to as the "Barred Zone." Situated south of the 20th parallel of latitude north, west of the 160th meridian of longitude east from Greenwich, and north of the 10th parallel of latitude south, the "Barred Zone" included almost all of Asia except Japan and the Philippines. Because Chinese and Japanese laborers were already excluded from the United States, and Filipinos were U.S. "nationals" as a consequence of American colonization of the Philippines, the "Barred Zone" Act was intended to prohibit the entry of migrants from India.

In addition to the "Barred Zone" provision, the 1917 Immigration Act increased the statute of limitations for deportation from three to five years for any "alien" deemed to have subversive or dangerous political beliefs or associations, namely those that could be construed as aligned with or advocating the principles of anarchism. . . .

The rationale behind the Immigration Act of 1917 and the nativism, exclusionism, and surveillance that it justified and reinforced are strikingly relevant today. Ultimately, the "Barred Zone" Act did not explicitly exclude South Asians by identity, but on the basis of geography. In this regard, it is akin to President Donald Trump's Executive Order 13769, "Protecting the Nation from Foreign Terrorist Entry into the United States," or the so-called Muslim ban. In addition to initially excluding migrants from seven predominantly Muslim countries, the order calls for the "extreme vetting" of all refugee applicants and enhanced "standards" for scrutinizing all persons seeking admission to the country. Much of the rhetoric behind this executive order is reminiscent of the 1917 Immigration Act, particularly in its appeals to national security.

Excerpt from an essay by Seema Sohi titled "From 1917 to 2017: Immigration, Exclusion, and 'National Security'" for Tides.

The Canadian government responded with military might. On the morning of July 21, the *Rainbow*, a thirty-six-hundred-ton Canadian naval cruiser that constituted the entire Canadian navy at the time, anchored near the *Komagata Maru* bearing twelve heavy-caliber guns and a number of machine guns aimed at the

---

BUDGE BUDGE MASSACRE

After being rejected in Vancouver, the *Komagata Maru* arrived back in Calcutta on September 26, 1914. Yet when it attempted to enter the Indian harbor, British officials forced it to stop and placed its passengers—who were still reeling from their experience in North America—under guard. Soon the ship was again diverted, this time to Budge Budge, about seventeen miles away. There the British intended to send the group to Punjab via train, but many of the passengers wanted to remain in the area and thus marched into the city to protest. British police met them there to force them to reboard the ship and attempted to arrest leader Gurdit Singh and others. The men resisted, with some refusing to reboard, and ultimately the police opened fire. At least twenty people were killed, and nine were wounded.

---

ship. By now it was clear to the passengers that Canada would not be swayed. Ultimately, the passengers felt they had no choice but to leave and agreed to do so only if provided with adequate provisions. The government agreed to the terms and loaded flour, curry powder, tea, and other provisions onto the ship. In the early morning hours of July 23, thousands of Vancouver residents gathered on the shore and the rooftops of the city, while Canadian police officers lined the wharf, to view the ship's departure after two months in the Vancouver harbor. Escorted by the *Rainbow*, whose first mission as a Canadian navy ship was to prevent British subjects from landing on British soil, the *Komagata Maru* lifted anchor and began its journey back across the Pacific.

Seema Sohi (she/her/hers) is an associate professor of ethnic studies at the University of Colorado Boulder.

45

Article from the November 18, 1906, San Francisco Call describing recent "Hindu and Mohammedan" immigration to San Jose, California. In SAADA, courtesy of Paul Englesberg.

CHAPTER 2

Forging Lives in Uncertain Times

1923–1965

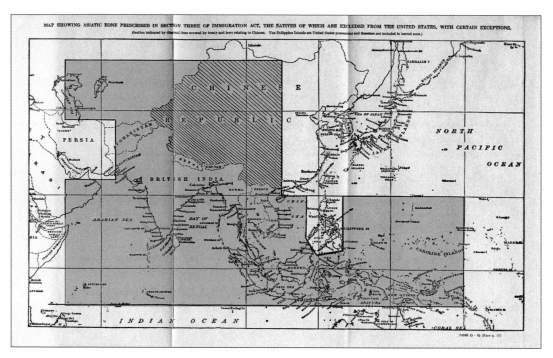

Map depicting the "Asiatic Barred Zone" created by the 1917 Immigration Act. The highlighted section illustrates the area of exclusion. In SAADA.

INTRODUCTION

Kritika Agarwal

"The recent decision of the Supreme Court of the United States that Hindus are not 'free white persons' has been hailed for the most part with delight by the California press and that of our Western seaboard, which we find has a Hindu problem . . ." This was how the *Literary Digest*, a popular weekly magazine, reported the 1923 Supreme Court decision in *United States v. Bhagat Singh Thind*, which denaturalized a South Asian immigrant for not being white. Titled "Hindus Too Brunette to Vote Here," the story featured an image of a turbaned South Asian laborer and quoted the California attorney general, U. S. Webb, as saying that the ruling would put an end to the "menacing spread of Hindus" in the state.

The Thind ruling came at a time of increasing xenophobia against Asian immigrants. It arrived on the heels of the 1917 Asiatic Barred Zone Act, which designated a geographic zone covering much of Asia, including South Asia, from which people could not migrate. It also preceded the Immigration Act of 1924, which set a quota that granted immigration visas to only 2 percent of the total number of people of each nationality in the United States as of the 1890 national census. Considering that the act barred entry of "aliens ineligible for citizenship"—a category that included South Asians as a result of the *Thind* decision—the trivial quota was largely for the benefit of non-Indians in India who sought to migrate to the United States.

Discriminatory immigration and naturalization laws had a profound impact on the then-fledgling South Asian community in the United States. The laws certainly had an impact both on the numbers of immigrants arriving and on the numbers of those who stayed. The 1900 census, for example, recorded 2,031 immigrants from India living in the continental United States. While statistics for the next few decades are hard to come by, the numbers of migrants from South Asia grew only marginally—especially when compared with the numbers of immigrants arriving from parts of Europe—and some scholarship suggests that the numbers actually declined during the 1930s.

Immigration and naturalization woes inevitably bled into almost every aspect of South Asian American life during these tumultuous years. The impassioned anti-colonial rhetoric of the early twentieth century calling for an armed revolution in India was replaced with political lobbying for immigration and naturalization reforms, and with nonviolent calls for allies in the United States to support Indian nationalism. As historian Joan M. Jensen writes, "After 1925, immigrants settled down to make the best of their restricted life in America."

Yet, as the following snapshots show, in addition to fighting against discrimination in the laws, South Asian Americans led multidimensional lives during these times. From Kala Bagai, one of the first South Asian women to land in San Francisco, who sowed the seeds of community for generations to come, to Rishi Singh Gherwal, who, like many other entrepreneurial South Asians, traveled the United States spreading the word about yoga, the South Asian American community during this time remained a dynamic one. And while visions of an exotic East full of men wearing turbans and young boys riding elephants animated the

U.S. imagination, South Asian Americans soldiered on in their quest for full acceptance as citizens. Some, recognizing the structural workings of racism, joined hands with African Americans in civil rights struggles.

And in these struggles, there were also moments of triumph. The passage of the 1946 Luce-Celler Act gave Indians the right to naturalize. One of the people to take advantage of this new law was Dalip Singh Saund, who had arrived in the United States in 1919, obtained a PhD in mathematics from the University of California, Berkeley, and then, because he could not find a job matching his education, settled as a farmer in California's Imperial Valley. In 1956, after decades of struggle, Saund became the first South Asian American (and first Asian American) elected to serve in the U.S. Congress. The Civil Rights movement in the 1960s eventually helped open the door for more South Asians to migrate to the United States, setting the stage for a more robust future.

Kritika Agarwal (she/her) is website editorial manager at the American Immigration Lawyers Association.

BHAGAT SINGH THIND

Kritika Agarwal

Born on October 3, 1892, in Amritsar, Punjab, Bhagat Singh Thind was among the earliest migrants to come from South Asia to the United States. Today, Thind is widely remembered as the subject of the famous case of *United States v. Bhagat Singh Thind* (1923), in which the U.S. Supreme Court found Indians to be ineligible for American citizenship because they were not white.

A graduate of Khalsa College in Amritsar, where he had studied American history and literature, Thind came to the United States via the Philippines at the age of twenty-one on the Fourth of July, 1913. Almost immediately after his arrival, Thind became involved in the Ghadar Party. Records from Thind's declaration of intention show that he was initially employed at the Hammond Lumber Company in St. Johns, Oregon, where mill workers and other Indian migrants had organized to form the Ghadar Party. In fact, Thind is often credited as one of the original members of the movement and, according to British surveillance records, performed various functions for the party in Oregon, including distributing literature, fundraising, and making speeches. In 1916, Thind left the Hammond Lumber Company and joined the Crossett Western Lumber Company, which, according to the British, had also become a "Ghadr centre under his influence." The British believed that Thind was "very active in distributing Ghadr propaganda," and by February 1918, they considered him to be the "leader of the revolutionary party in Oregon."

In 1918, Thind enlisted in the U.S. Army, served for six months at Camp Lewis, in Washington, and received an honorable discharge, with the discharging officer designating him as having an "excellent" character. Despite his service, when

---

THIND AND CASTE

Thind's argument for citizenship demonstrates the ways that early South Asian immigrants simultaneously navigated existing prejudices in the United States while exploiting and reinforcing those that they brought with them from South Asia. As Doug Coulson writes:

Thind emphasized the fact that Hindu religious law strictly prohibited marriage outside of one's caste. He cited the fact that the caste restrictions on intermarriage could be found in the Institutes of Manu, one of the oldest and most sacred Hindu religious texts. As a result of the strict observance of caste restrictions on intermarriage, he claimed, not only did high caste Hindus descend from primordial Aryan ancestors but they had remained a pure type of the race through the modern era. The fact that the caste system prevailed in India to a degree unsurpassed elsewhere and that it was "reprehensible for one of a higher caste to marry one of a lower caste," he claimed, provide an "effective barrier to prevent a mixture of the Aryan with the dark races of India." This argument invoked a familiar analogy between India's caste system and Western racial segregation and exclusion laws.

From "The Ghadr Party and the Indian Caste System in Thind" in Race, Nation, and Refuge: The Rhetoric of Race in Asian American Citizenship Cases *by Doug Coulson (SUNY Press, 2017).*

Thind filed for naturalization in a federal court in Portland in 1919, the examiner at his hearing expressed concerns regarding his national allegiance and racial qualifications. The examiner alleged that Thind's connections with the Ghadar Party and with "Germans, I.W.W's [Industrial Workers of the World] and anarchists" rendered him an "undesirable citizen." Thind denied any connections with the Ghadar movement but admitted that he had advocated for the "principle of India for the Indians, and would like to see India rid of British rule." Thind was ultimately granted U.S. citizenship in 1920 by Judge Charles E. Wolverton, who seemed impressed by his qualifications and believed that he had "modified somewhat his views" on the subject of British rule in India and had come to hold a "genuine affection for the Constitution, laws, customs, and privileges of this country."

Thind's citizenship was, however, quickly challenged by the Department of Labor and the Department of Justice, which instructed the U.S. attorney in Portland to file an appeal against his naturalization and to file a citizenship cancellation suit. The appeal was based on the question of whether Indians were racially eligible for naturalization in the United States. By the time Thind's case came before the Supreme Court in early 1923, the court had already ruled in *Takao Ozawa v. United States* that Japanese immigrants were not white based on "scientific" evidence, that "the words 'white person'" were "synonymous with the words 'a person of the Caucasian race,'" and that the Japanese, who were not Caucasians, but Mongolians, were ineligible for naturalization. As Ian Haney López notes in *White by Law*, "It must have seemed to Thind that he could not lose, for the Supreme Court itself had made Caucasian status the test for whether one was White, and every major anthropological study classified Asian Indians as Caucasians." In addition, "four lower courts had specifically ruled that Asian Indians were white, while only one had held to the contrary." Thind, however, could not count on the weight of these precedents.

In 1923, the Supreme Court, deciding solely on the question of whether a "high caste Hindu of full Indian blood" was a "white person," held that while Asian Indians might indeed be Caucasian per the prevailing scientific discourse, they were not white, and that the words "free white persons" must be interpreted as "words of common speech and not of scientific origins." Associate Supreme Court Justice George Sutherland, a naturalized citizen born in England, argued in his opinion that the conclusion made in *Ozawa* that "the phrase 'white persons' and the word 'Caucasian' are synonymous does not end the matter." He argued that what was more important than scientific reasoning was the intent of the original framers of the 1790 statute, for whom the word "Caucasian" would have probably been wholly unfamiliar: "It is in the popular sense of the word, therefore, that we employ it as

A. K. MOZUMDAR

Perhaps the first visitor from India to reside in Bellingham, Washington, was Akhoy Kumar Mozumdar, who attended the State Normal School as its first foreign student. Mozumdar, a Hindu mystic, studied for one term in order to polish his English and contributed an article to the school paper on education and cultures of India. In 1913, Mozumdar, then a resident of Spokane, became the first South Asian to obtain American citizenship, having convinced a federal judge that he met the criteria of being "white" by virtue of his "high-caste Hindu" status as a Brahmin. However, he and more than sixty other naturalized South Asians had their citizenship stripped in 1923 after the U.S. Supreme Court ruled unanimously in the *Thind* decision that South Asians were not "white," and therefore could not become citizens.

Courtesy of Mozumdar.org.

an aid to the construction of the statute." Sutherland continued, "It may be true that the blond Scandinavian and the brown Hindu have a common ancestor in the dim reaches of antiquity, but the average man knows perfectly well that there are unmistakable and profound differences between them today." Paying close attention to Thind's brown skin, Judge Sutherland argued that "it cannot be doubted that the children born in this country of Hindu parents would retain indefinitely the clear evidence of their ancestry" and that this would prevent them from merging into the "mass of our population," unlike the children of Europeans. The judge found Thind to be not only racially ineligible, but also unassimilable. Bhagat Singh Thind was denaturalized.

South Asians, both in the United States and abroad, responded to the Supreme Court's decision with widespread protest. Many believed that the decision was a direct result of Thind's anti-colonial activities. For example, an editorial in the *Modern Review*, a monthly magazine from Calcutta that frequently served as a platform for Indian nationalists, surmised that the Supreme Court justices were "old fogeys, all pro-British and open to the British Embassy's influence" and that the British embassy had "influenced the Supreme Court and got that decision to suit British interests." In another article appearing in the same

CHANGING DEFINITIONS OF WHITE

South Asian Americans like Bhagat Singh Thind were not the first nor the last to challenge the definition of whiteness in the United States. Though consistently used to exclude and oppress people of color, the meaning of "white" has always been in flux.

People who were once thought to be nonwhite, like Italian Americans and Irish Americans, are today considered white, but over the years U.S. courts have applied various legal definitions of whiteness—such as the "one-drop rule"—to specifically justify keeping Black Americans subjugated. Homer Plessy was a Louisiana man of mixed race who, in 1892, attempted to bring this inconsistency to light by challenging that state's Separate Car Act, which required separate seats for Black and white passengers on railway cars. Plessy, who was of seven-eighths European descent and one-eighth African descent, intentionally sat in the "whites only" section of a train as part of a plan devised by a local activist group. He was able to pass as white, but when asked by a conductor of the East Louisiana Railroad if he was Black, he said he was. Plessy and the other activists were hoping he would be arrested so that they could mount a case against the state, as they believed his relatively white skin would make him a more sympathetic figure in court.

Unfortunately, though he was arrested that day and his case did reach the Supreme Court in *Plessy v. Ferguson* (1896), Plessy's argument was rejected, and the judges did not agree that the railroad company was violating his rights. As a result, "separate but equal" laws were legitimized throughout the country and would remain intact until the Civil Rights Act of 1964.

magazine in 1927, Mary Das wrote: "It may be safely asserted that in the Thind case, the Supreme Court rendered a 'political decision' at the request of the Government of the United States and for other considerations involving foreign governments." Despite the protests, the Justice Department, using *Thind* as a precedent, moved to cancel the naturalization certificates of every Indian immigrant who had managed to obtain citizenship in the United States to that point.

Although he had lost his citizenship, Thind stayed in the United States and continued to work with

Photograph of Bhagat Singh Thind and Vivian Davies. In SAADA, courtesy of David Thind.

the Ghadar movement. He also began traveling across the country lecturing on spiritual science and religious philosophy. In 1936, despite remaining under British surveillance, Thind again applied for and obtained U.S. citizenship, under the

1935 Nye-Lea Act, which allowed World War I veterans to apply for naturalization regardless of race. This time, it appeared that Thind's citizenship was permanent. In 1940, he married Vivian Davies, and they eventually had two children. He died on September 15, 1967.

It is impossible to overestimate the significance of Thind's court case for the South Asian immigrant community in the United States. For more than two decades, the case determined the status and life opportunities for every South Asian immigrant in the country.

Kritika Agarwal (she/her) is website editorial manager at the American Immigration Lawyers Association.

DENATURALIZATION

Kritika Agarwal

The consequences of the Supreme Court ruling in *Thind* were devastating: immediately following the ruling that "Hindus" were not white and were therefore ineligible for citizenship, the Department of Labor directed the Department of Justice to ask federal attorneys around the United States to begin denaturalization proceedings against every U.S. citizen of South Asian origin who had gained citizenship in federal and local courts since 1908.

The word "Hindu," however, was not an accurate description for most South Asian immigrants at the time. In fact, one third of them were Muslim, and a majority of them were Sikh. When these immigrants were subject to denaturalization, one of the first tactics they used in the courts was to argue that they were not Hindu. For example, Qamar-ud-din Alexander, who had been granted U.S. citizenship in May 1916 in Mays Landing, New Jersey, argued in the courts that even though he was "born in Rawalpendie, Punjab, India, and for that reason might be termed a Hindu," he was "in reality and in fact . . . a Persian, tracing his Persian ancestry back some six or seven hundred years; his people having migrated from Persia to India about two hundred years ago."

John Mohammad Ali made a similar argument in 1925, when he claimed that even though he was a native of India, "originally his ancestors" had been "Arabians who invaded the territory now known as India, and settled and remained there." Ali argued that his ancestors had been "careful not to intermarry with the 'native stock of India' and . . . [had] kept their Arabian blood line clear and pure by intermarriage within

A pamphlet describing the lectures of Mohammad Ali, born in Punjab as the son of Dr. Sadiq Ali, the physician of the Maharaja of Kapurthala. The Maharaja, incidentally, attended the 1893 World's Fair in Chicago. According to the biography provided, Ali arrived in the U.S. in 1900, where he would found the headquarters for his company importing tea and cocoa in Detroit, Michigan. Courtesy of the University of Iowa's Redpath Chautauqua Collection.

the family." According to a story in the *Los Angeles Times* on Ali's case, "Features in the hearing in the United States District court of the case of John Mohammed Ali were a family tree extending backward through thirty-one generations to the Prophet himself, the spectacle of a University of Michigan professor measuring a swarty [sic] turbaned head for a sheik's characteristics and the briefly told story of the petitioner's love for his British wife." Ali also testified about his conversion to Christianity and, despite the turban on his head, insisted that he had "forsaken the Mohammedan religion" and that his love for his adopted country should not be "measured by a hat." The judge did not buy Ali's or his witnesses' testimony. Instead, recalling *Thind*, the judge applied the test of common knowledge, visual difference of skin color, and geographic origin to rule against Ali and his citizenship.

As these South Asian immigrants' strategies—which relied on abiding by "scientific" categories of race—failed in the courts, some of them began to change their approach. Sakharam Ganesh Pandit, an adept lawyer and one of the first South Asian immigrants to obtain naturalization in California, used an entirely

AMERICAN WIVES OF INDIA

In 1946, Gertrude Nasri formed the American Wives of India, a group of women in the Los Angeles area who intended to assist with famine relief for the Bengal region. The philanthropic society expanded into a robust organization with the mission of promoting "cultural and mutual understanding between the United States and Pakistan and India." In addition to providing relief and aid to refugees throughout South Asia, the nonprofit hosted lectures, benefits, and concerts in the United States. The group also published a biannual bulletin with articles and news items relevant to Indian and Pakistani women abroad.

Photograph of the American Wives of India that appeared in the February 15, 1949, issue of the Daily News *in Los Angeles. The caption reads: "ACTIVE MEMBERS of American Wives of India pictured in native saris, cholis and sandals (back row, left to right) Mrs. Abdul Hasson, Mrs. S.S. Dhillon, Mrs. Shiraj Uddin and Mrs. K. Sonkur. (Front row, left to right) Mrs. B. Bagai, Mrs. Gertrude Nasri, president, Mrs. Mohamed Tahir, Mrs. K.B. Chandra." In SAADA, courtesy of Rani Bagai.*

different strategy in the courts. In addition to putting forward an innovative legal argument that raised doubts about the state's ability to denaturalize citizens, Pandit also put on a racial performance of whiteness and model American citizenship. Emphasizing his education, class status, and marriage to a white woman, Pandit argued in court that U.S. citizenship and its attendant assumption of whiteness had bestowed certain social, cultural, and economic benefits on him, the loss of which would render his life meaningless. Pandit's multipronged strategy worked, as the district court judge ruled in his favor. Not pleased, the Justice Department immediately filed an appeal.

While Pandit fought his case in the courts, others used legislative and political means to protect their citizenship. Taraknath Das and his wife, Mary Keating Das, for example, took their fight to the U.S. Congress. Both met with several officials in the State, Labor, and Justice Departments and pleaded their case to Chief Justice William H. Taft. By 1926, Das and his wife had convinced Republican senator David Reed of Pennsylvania to introduce a "resolution to confirm the citizenship" of those Indian men who had naturalized before *Thind* and also to "affirm that no American women would lose their citizenship through marriage to any of them." In addition, Sailendranath Ghose, of the Friends of Freedom for India (FFI), managed to convince Senator Royal S. Copeland and Representative Emanuel Celler to introduce a much broader measure that would classify Indians as racially white and thus eligible for citizenship and future immigration.

In response to Senator Reed's resolution, the Senate Committee on Immigration finally held hearings in 1926 on the question of reconfirming the "naturalization of certain persons of the Hindu race." The committee heard testimony from several Indian immigrants as well as those who were opposed to the measure. Continuing with the performance of model American citizenship, the immigrants who testified were all well-educated, upwardly mobile, Christian, and, in many cases, married to white women. These included Shankar Laxman Gokhale, a magnetic engineer for General Electric; P. C. Mukerji, assistant chief chemist for Carnegie Steel; V. R. Kokatnur, a chemical engineer; and T. D. Sharman, a realtor. The resolution, however, faced stiff opposition from several Asian exclusionists who feared that extending citizenship to South Asians would raise similar demands from Japanese immigrants, and it ultimately died without ever reaching the floor.

Meanwhile, Sakharam Ganesh Pandit continued to fight his case, as well as those of several others. In 1926, relief finally came when the Ninth Circuit Court of Appeals upheld the decision of the district court and reconfirmed his citizenship. The judge noted that Pandit had "obtained his status legally" and was entitled to his citizenship and standing as a free white person. The Department of Justice ap-

---

DENATURALIZATION AND OPERATION JANUS

In early 2018, Baljinder Singh was stripped of his U.S. citizenship and faced deportation after federal officials argued that the forty-three-year-old had fraudulently obtained his citizenship more than a decade earlier. It was the first case to result from Operation Janus, a Department of Homeland Security investigation that identified 315,000 immigrants whose fingerprints were missing from government databases.

According to the prosecutors, Singh had originally entered the United States under a different name, in 1991, and faced deportation at the time, but he didn't disclose this information in his 2004 citizenship application. Though his denaturalization happened under the watch of President Donald Trump, Singh's case was the result of a broader and older process, as Masha Gessen pointed out in the *New Yorker*:

> Tempting as it may be to see this war as the creation of the Trump Administration—the outcome of electing the man who promised to build the Wall—this is not the case. . . . The denaturalization proceedings against Singh grew out of a 2016 report by the Department of Homeland Security's Office of Inspector General about an investigation into the fingerprint records of naturalized citizens; it found more than a hundred thousand records that had not been transferred from an older database to a current one, and identified more than eight hundred people who may have been naturalized in spite of being ineligible. In other words, the Trump Administration didn't start the hunt for "bad" immigrants but merely intensified it. It has revoked Obama-era guidelines for setting priorities in the deportation process, rendering it indiscriminate. . . . (though the number of deportations remains comparable to the Obama years).
>
> The apparent schizophrenia of Obama's policies, with a swelling wave of deportations on one hand and his attempt to secure an American future for Dreamers on the other, reflects a tension inherent in immigration policy. America claims the identity of a nation of immigrants, yet it often strives to keep out the immigrants it deems undesirable.

From "Trump, 'Shitholes,' and the Nature of 'Us'" for the New Yorker, by Masha Gessen.

---

pealed the case to the Supreme Court, which declined to review the lower court's decision and thus rendered Pandit's citizenship immune from further attack. Ultimately, on March 25, 1927, the Secretary of Labor recommended that in view of the

S. G. PANDIT, B. A.

(The Only Hindu Lawyer in the United States)

Attorney, Counselor, Proctor, Advocate and Solicitor
General practice of Law

All State and Federal Courts

917 Bank of Italy International Building   116 Temple Street,   Los Angeles, California
Telephones: Pico 1432 and Garvanza 752

An advertisement for Sakharam Ganesh Pandit, "The Only Hindu Lawyer in the United States," in the March 1921 issue of the Independent Hindustan. *In SAADA.*

Supreme Court's decision, "petitions then pending to cancel the naturalization of other Hindus on the ground of racial ineligibility be dismissed."

In the ensuing decades, South Asian activists in the United States continued lobbying Congress for naturalization relief for immigrants already present in the country. By the mid-1940s, however, Indian activists had expanded their efforts to make Indians as a group generally eligible for naturalization and to create a quota for them to immigrate to the country. India's participation in World War II especially allowed Indian immigrants in the United States to seek greater integration and a gradual opening of U.S. immigration and naturalization policies. In September 1944, representatives from the India Welfare League, the India Association for American Citizenship, and the National Committee for India's Freedom appeared before the Senate Committee on Immigration to lobby again for the passage of a bill, this time sponsored by Senator William Langer of North Dakota, to permit Indians who had entered the United States prior to 1924 to naturalize.

At the same time, Republican Clare Boothe Luce and Democrat Emanuel Celler introduced separate bills in the House to lift immigration and naturalization restrictions on both Indians and Filipinos. Once again, Indian activists insisted on the whiteness and cultural assimilability of Indians already in the United States, but their focus had also dramatically expanded—they now emphasized U.S. foreign policy, India's contributions to the war effort, and the urgency of establishing good relations with a country that was on the verge of independence and positioned to be an industrial powerhouse and a political world player. In 1946, Congress finally passed the Luce-Celler (Immigration) Act, which gave Indians the right to naturalize and also set an annual quota of one hundred immigrants from India.

Kritika Agarwal (she/her) is website editorial manager at the American Immigration Lawyers Association.

KALA BAGAI

Kritika Agarwal

TRIGGER WARNING: This story describes instances of self-harm and suicide.

In 1915, Kala Bagai, Vaishno Das Bagai, and their three children landed at Angel Island, off the coast of San Francisco, after a long journey from India. Arriving on a Saturday, the family spent an additional two days on their steamer, the *Korea*, before being taken to the Angel Island Immigration Station. Considering that few South Asian men came to the United States with their families, Kala's presence at Angel Island was an oddity. Her arrival was documented by the *San Francisco Call and Post*, which ran a picture of her holding her son Ram Mohan and described her as the "first Hindu woman" to enter San Francisco in a decade and credited her with introducing the city "to the latest thing in jewelry—the nose diamond." The Bagais were interrogated extensively at Angel Island, but upon demonstrating

Photograph of the Bagai family. In SAADA, courtesy of Rani Bagai.

that they had $25,000 in hand, the family was allowed entry into the United States and soon began their new lives in California.

Born in Amritsar, Punjab, Kala was only eleven years old when she was married to Vaishno, who was about six months older than her and from Peshawar. While studying in India, Vaishno became involved in the struggle for independence from the British and developed a desire to move to the United States, which his family initially opposed. Vaishno was only able to make the move after the death of his parents. In an oral history interview conducted by her grandson in 1982, Kala Bagai recalled her husband's rationale for moving: "The Ghadar movement wanted to take the British out of India. Mr. Bagai was in that movement. He said, 'I don't want to stay in this slave country; I want to go to America where there is no slavery.'"

Once in California, the Bagais moved into a furnished room and were eventually able to rent an apartment. Kala, who was twenty-one years old at the time of her arrival and unable to speak English, initially found life in the United States "strange." Providing childcare for three young children without assistance from her extended family or domestic help also proved to be a challenge. The Bagais eventually found a German family to take care of their three children while Kala lived with a local family in an attempt to learn English, but she left after a few months because she did not want to be away from her husband and children.

The Bagais' relative wealth did not shield them from racism. Soon after their arrival, they purchased their first home, in Berkeley. On moving day, however, they discovered that the neighbors had locked the house to prevent them from moving in. Kala recalled, "All of our luggage and everything was loaded on the trucks. I told Mr. Bagai, 'I don't want to live in this neighborhood. I don't want to live in this house, because they might hurt my children, and I don't want it.' He agreed. 'We paid for the house and they locked the doors? No.'" The family moved back to San Francisco and lived above Vaishno's general store on Fillmore Street.

In 1921, Vaishno naturalized as a U.S. citizen, but tragedy struck the family when he was stripped of his citizenship on the basis of not being white in the wake of the 1923 Supreme Court case of *United States v. Bhagat Singh Thind*. Vaishno was forced to liquidate his property, including his store in San Francisco. Furthermore, he was denied a U.S. passport to visit India and was told he should reapply for British citizenship (which he had renounced to become a U.S. citizen) and try to get a British passport. Increasingly disillusioned, Vaishno rented a room in San Jose and committed suicide by poisoning himself with gas in 1928.

Kala recalled being incredibly "lonesome" and "lost" after Vaishno's death, but eventually she managed to stand on her own two feet. Using detailed instructions that Vaishno had left behind regarding the multiple life insurance policies he had taken out prior to his death, which bankers to trust, and where to invest the money, Kala was able to send all three of her children to college. She learned English, and a few years after Vaishno's death, she married Mahesh Chandra, a close family friend and also a member of the Ghadar Party. But tragedy struck again when one of Kala's sons, Madan, who had graduated from MIT with a degree in engineering

Photograph of Kala Bagai in 1929, when she was thirty-six years old. In SAADA, courtesy of Rani Bagai.

VAISHNO DAS BAGAI'S LAST LETTER

In 1928, Vaishno Das Bagai, husband of Kala Bagai, wrote a letter to the *San Francisco Examiner*. In what was actually his suicide note, Bagai explained that his reason for taking his own life was a form of protest against the American naturalization laws that stripped him of citizenship, which he was originally granted in 1921. Part of Bagai's letter is excerpted below:

I have a good home, fine health, good family, nice and lovely wife, extra good children, few but best friends and a paying business. I came to America thinking, dreaming and hoping to make this land my home. Sold my properties and brought more than twenty-five thousand dollars (gold) to this country, established myself and tried my very best to give my children the best American education.

In [the] year 1921 the Federal court at San Francisco accepted me as a naturalized citizen of the United States and issued to my name the final certificate, giving therein the name and description of my wife and three sons. In last 12 or 13 years we all made ourselves as much Americanized as possible.

But they now come to me and say, I am no longer an American citizen. They will not permit me to buy my home and, lo, they even shall not issue me a passport to go back to India. Now what am I? What have I made of myself and my children? We cannot exercise our rights, we cannot leave this country. Humility and insults, who is responsible for all this? Myself and American government.

I do not choose to live the life of an interned person: yes, I am in a free country and can move about where and when I wish inside the country. Is life worth living in a gilded cage? Obstacles this way, blockades that way, and the bridges burnt behind.

Photograph of Vaishno Das Bagai. In SAADA, courtesy of Rani Bagai.

but couldn't find a job in the United States due to discrimination, returned to India and died soon after from an illness.

With the passage of the Luce-Celler Act in 1946, Kala and her two remaining sons were finally able to apply for naturalization and become U.S. citizens. Affectionately known as "Jhaiji," Kala died in 1983 in Los Angeles at the age of ninety. Her death was mourned both by her family and the wider South Asian community

---

AN ORAL HISTORY INTERVIEW WITH RANI BAGAI

Rani Bagai's father, Ram, was the son of Kala and Vaishno Das Bagai. In an oral history recorded for SAADA, Rani shares stories of her family's history, including insights into what it must have been like for her grandparents when they first arrived in California.

So my grandparents decided to come to San Francisco in 1915, about when my dad was just over a year old. They came to Angel Island, and the story is that immigration of course held them for a day or so. . . . My grandfather's main wish in coming here was to work for India's independence and to join the Ghadar Party to help fight for India's freedom. That was something my grandfather very strongly believed in and wanted, and he felt frustrated. As a young man he was pursued by the British and he was kind of a rabble-rouser. . . . He didn't feel like he could do anything from India, where he was constantly being oppressed. . . . He thought, "In the United States, I can do that. I can do what I can't do in India." So this was his goal. . . . And they bought a house in, I'm not sure if it was in Berkeley, but I think it was there. But they were the first Indians to buy property. And the story is that when they moved in . . . the neighbors realized they were Indian and they didn't want them living next to them. They would not let them in the house. . . . Of course my grandmother was scared; she was petrified. She told her husband, "No, I don't want to live here if they don't want us." . . . So I don't know exactly what they did with the house, if they sold it or what, but they couldn't live there.

Rani Bagai with her father, greeting Jawaharlal Nehru and Indira Gandhi at Los Angeles International Airport on November 15, 1961. In SAADA, courtesy of Rani Bagai.

in Southern California, which considered her one of its founding members. In an obituary, *India West* paid the following tribute to Kala:

> Armed with her personal philosophy expressed in the saying, "if you are good ... the whole world will love you," Mrs. Chandra radiated warmth, kindness, and good will to everyone. Her home became a "little India" to the community, and she became the symbol of "mother India."

As one of the first South Asian women to come to the United States in the early twentieth century, Kala's legacy lives on not just through her family, but also through the path she paved for generations of South Asian American women to come.

KALA BAGAI WAY

In 2020, using archival materials from SAADA, organizers in Berkeley campaigned for the city to rename a street in downtown in honor of Kala Bagai. In an oral history interview with Kala Bagai from 1982, she recounts the heartbreaking story of being denied entry into their family's new home in Berkeley by racist neighbors. Local organizers used this story to highlight the ways that, even in a city now known for its progressive values, racism and xenophobia have deeply impacted the lives of immigrant communities. In mid-September 2020, the Berkeley City Council voted unanimously to rename a section of Shattuck Avenue as Kala Bagai Way, and banners with her image now hang across downtown.

In SAADA, courtesy of Anirvan Chatterjee.

Kritika Agarwal (she/her) is website editorial manager at the American Immigration Lawyers Association.

RISHI SINGH GREWAL

Philip Deslippe

Yoga is often thought of as something ancient and Indian that only found a significant American audience in the last fifty years, but the familiar form of yoga as a physical practice, and its presence in the United States, are both a little more than a century old. Ideas about yoga were flexible in the United States at the turn of the twentieth century. It was usually thought of as mental and magical, not physical and postural, and it could include everything from positive affirmations and changes in diet to philosophy and psychology to occultism and contact with the spirits of the dead.

In the early twentieth century, dozens of well-educated immigrants from South Asia, limited by restrictive laws and prejudice in the United States, took advantage of the allure held by the imagined "mystic East" and traveled around the country presenting themselves as yogis, swamis, and metaphysical teachers to American

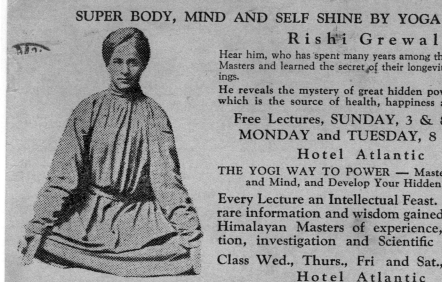

A 1940 postcard for Rishi Singh Gherwal's lectures and classes in Chicago, Illinois. Courtesy of Philip Deslippe.

audiences. Typically, they would travel from city to city giving free public lectures that would lead to smaller, private courses of instruction for a fee. A writer in 1934 estimated that 1 percent of all immigrants from South Asia made their living in this way.

One of these teachers was a Punjab-born Sikh named Rakha Singh Gherwal (1889–1964), who entered the United States in 1911 and began to teach yoga in 1925. By his own estimate, Gherwal traveled back and forth across the United States sixteen times and paid visits to most large cities. Newspaper advertisements show him everywhere from Los Angeles and New York to Utah and Montana during the interwar decades as he lectured on such topics as "Marvels of the Sub-Conscious Mind" and "What Becomes of Us after Death?" He was also an author and published several books and pamphlets, including *Great Masters of the Himalayas* (1927) and *Kundalini, the Mother of the Universe* (1930).

Unlike many of his peers in America, Gherwal had a deep interest in yoga that preceded his arrival. He published editions of classical yogic texts, wrote a commentary on the Yoga Sūtra of Patañjali, and was clearly influenced by the work

Portrait of Rishi Singh Gherwal in the 1950s. Courtesy of John Johnson.

of the yoga reformer and researcher Swami Kuvalayananda (1883–1966), who was instrumental in the modern hatha yoga revival in India. Gherwal can be considered the first person to openly teach yoga to the American public as we understand it today, a posture-based practice supported by medical science and practical benefit.

Gherwal was also a devout Sikh. He gave high-profile lectures on the Sikh tradition and regularly included stories of the life of its founder, Guru Nanak, and passages from the Siri Guru Granth Sahib, the living scripture of Sikhs, in the pages of his magazine, *India's Message*. Rishi Singh's brother, Jivan Singh, came to the United States in the early 1960s and served as the granthi in the gurdwara in El Centro, California.

Many South Asian–born yoga teachers in the United States during this time were active in the fight for Indian independence and would dedicate a lecture in each city they visited to the case against the British occupation. Gherwal was a member of the Ghadar Party in the 1910s and advocated for a free India from his platform as a yoga teacher in later decades. He not only discussed yogic matters in *India's Message*, but also reprinted speeches by Mahatma Gandhi and Rabindranath Tagore and provided his American readers with regular updates on the nationalist cause.

His most incredible political fight was for his own citizenship. Gherwal became a naturalized American in 1922, but only a few months later, when the Supreme Court decided that Bhagat Singh Thind was not a "free white person" and was therefore ineligible for American citizenship, the government moved swiftly to cancel Gherwal's citizenship and that of dozens of other South Asian Americans. As one newspaper said, Gherwal was left a man "without a country."

In 1934, after more than a decade of lawsuits and appeals, Gherwal literally took his case to the nation's capital. While lecturing on yoga in the evenings at a hotel in Washington, D.C., Gherwal personally lobbied members of the United States Senate during the day and convinced them to pass a special one-person bill that allowed his case for citizenship to be reheard. Gherwal was finally renaturalized as an American citizen in 1936 and had his name officially changed to Rishi Singh Grewal.

Once secure in his ability to travel, Grewal left for a trip to India in 1937, which he recounted in his 1939 book, *Lives and Teachings of the Yogis of India*. After the Second World War, his travel schedule slowed, and he began to settle in Southern California, dividing his time between Los Angeles and a retreat center in the Santa Barbara foothills. He married a German woman named Marian Besack who was a fashion designer and ran a fashion and textile company called Grewal Imports.

Rishi Singh Grewal died just a few months shy of his seventy-fifth birthday, in 1964. His wife brought his ashes back to India. His longtime student Ernst Haeckel, who accompanied him on the 1937 trip to India, continued to run Grewal's center in Santa Barbara. In the mid-1980s, the White Lotus Foundation, run by the American-born yoga teacher Ganga White and his partner, Tracey Rich, acquired the center, and they continue to hold retreats and yoga teacher training programs there.

Philip Deslippe (he/him/his) is a doctoral candidate in the Department of Religious Studies at the University of California, Santa Barbara.

"TURBANS DO THINGS FOR YOU"

Meenasarani Linde Murugan

"Turbans do things for you!" announces an advertisement from a 1940 Sears catalog. Depicting several types of turbans with different draping, shapes, and veils—all modeled by young white women—the ad states, "One of these ten is right for you! And all ten are right for 1940!"

In the 1940s, the turban was simultaneously an article of clothing for glamorous white women, a marker of religious and racial identity, a target for xenophobic exclusion (anti-immigrant discourse of the time often referred to "Hindoo" migrants from South Asia as a "tide of turbans"), and an object that played into exotic fantasies. It could be strategically deployed for a person's benefit or prove limiting, depending on your race and religion.

Examples of how the turban furthered fantastic depictions of South Asia in American popular culture can be seen in the Hollywood productions of *One

Thousand and One Nights and Rudyard Kipling's stories in the 1940s. While many of these films featured white actors in turbans and brownface, the first Indian to star in a Hollywood film, Sabu, also achieved fame at this time by playing into "Oriental" fantasies of turbaned boys who ride elephants and practice magic.

In the late 1940s, many musicians used visual gimmicks to book gigs on television and in nightclubs. Newspapers commenting on these performances would often refer to them as "funny hats routines." Within this context, the turban was literally one among many "funny hats," with the article of clothing being mined primarily for commercial gain. Black performers such as Rudy Ray Moore (who went by the name Prince DuMarr), Chuck Willis (who was often billed as the "Sheik of the Blues"), the doo-wop group the Turbans, saxophonists Lynn Hope and Louis Jordan, Screamin' Jay Hawkins, and even Dizzy Gillespie all adopted the turban.

These artists were not particularly invested in the sounds of the Middle East or South Asia but were rather drawn to the fantastic costuming.

Korla Pandit went a step further in embracing the exoticism of the turban. In February 1949, his *Adventures in Music* was first telecast on Los Angeles station KTLA. This program, like many that Pandit recorded into the 1950s, featured him playing a Hammond electric organ while wearing a jeweled turban. The announcer's voice-over described the music Pandit played as "an-

Publicity photo of Korla Pandit, circa 1949. Courtesy of the Hannibal Free Public Library (Hannibal, Missouri).

cient Eastern melodies," and promotional material for the show related Pandit's backstory of being born a Brahmin in India (making his jeweled turban an odd affectation). However, it has been recently noted that Pandit was not South Asian, but a Black man from St. Louis, Missouri, named John Roland Redd.

In nightclubs in the 1940s, a similar exoticism was taking place. R. J. Smith, in *The Great Black Way*, his history of Black music and nightlife in 1940s Los Angeles, describes one such nightclub on Central Avenue: "An after-hours lounge run by a large, amiable gay man, Brother's was a secret temple of exotica. You entered an alley just off Central, crossed a boardwalk that led up to a home, and you arrived at some other place. Ottomans and cushions lay low on the ground, and in every room people reclined in shadows." One nightclub critic lauded, "If you've never spent a night in Sudan, then by all means spend an evening at Brother's Rendez-vous." "Brother" himself complemented the exotic decor: "Henry 'Brother' Williams greeted people at the door dressed in a Chinese silk robe."

Aside from its more gimmicky uses for stage performances, the turban was also used at the time as a tool of "do-it-yourself desegregation," as *Ebony* magazine noted. For Black Americans, the turban could be mistaken as a sign of royalty or dignitary status in the Jim Crow South, marking those who wore one as foreign and outside binary racial codes. Yet, whether people who appeared to be Asian, Hindu, Indian, or Muslim were considered "colored" was often determined on a case-by-case basis. This was partly because there were few South Asians in the country at the time, as a result of various Asian-exclusion acts in effect. Even in their relative absence, however, the image of the South Asian allowed other people of color to take on parts of South Asian culture, and in turn adopt some of the racial indeterminacy afforded to South Asian people.

Meenasarani Linde Murugan (she/they) is an assistant professor in the Department of Communication and Media Studies at Fordham University.

CHANDRA GOONERATNE

Chandra Dharma Sena Gooneratne left Ceylon (now Sri Lanka) in the 1920s to get his doctorate at the University of Chicago. He began traveling around America giving lectures on a variety of topics, including abolishing the caste system and the movement for independence in India. As a result of his travels, and like other visiting scholars from Asia and Africa at the time, Gooneratne encountered anti-Black racism.

But he also began to realize that he could use his turban while traveling in the Jim Crow South to avoid harassment. At times he encouraged others to do the same, writing, "Any Asiatic . . . can evade the whole issue of color in America by winding a few yards of linen around his head. A turban makes anyone an Indian." Yet Manan Desai observes that Gooneratne's perspective changed over time:

> Gooneratne, however, later distanced himself from adopting the turban he was constantly pictured with in Chautauqua lecture pamphlets and in his photos from the University of Chicago: "With a turban . . . you fly unmistakable

Chandra Gooneratne during his time at the University of Chicago, where he was a member of the polo team. Circa 1926. Courtesy of University of Chicago Photographic Archive [apf4-00825], Special Collections Research Center, University of Chicago Library.

colors. 'But you miss,' he warns, 'the whole point of this game, which is to make the American know you and leave him as your friend for life.'" Gooneratne's commentary overlooks the different ways that the turban had also been a racial marker that has led to acts of violence against Sikh communities in North America from the 19th century onwards. But at some level, Gooneratne seemed to advise visitors to the U.S. to deliberately court confusion and misrecognition over their identities, if only to challenge the very premise of racial difference that governed the color line.

From "The 'Tan Stranger' from Ceylon" for Tides, *by Manan Desai.*

DALIP SINGH SAUND

Samip Mallick

"In November 1956, D. S. Saund, who everyone simply called 'Judge,' became the first person of Asian descent elected to serve as a United States Representative. He was a tireless champion of his southern California district and the farmers who called it home. But his unique backstory—born in India, naturalized U.S. citizen, successful businessman, county judge—also catapulted him to the international stage. During his career in the House of Representatives, at the height of the Cold War, Saund became something of a transcendent politician who had the singular ability to engage audiences abroad. Although he frequently confronted discrimination during his life in the United States, Saund maintained his belief in the promises of American democracy."

—U.S. House of Representatives Biography of Dalip Singh Saund

Dalip Singh Saund with John F. Kennedy and Lyndon Johnson, 1958. In SAADA, courtesy of Eric Saund.

The following first-person narratives from Saund demonstrate the challenges he faced on his path to Congress. From 1923 to 1946, South Asians were barred from becoming American citizens, a result of the Supreme Court decision in *United States v. Bhagat Singh Thind*. Because he could not become a citizen, Saund, who graduated from the University of California, Berkeley, in 1924 with a PhD in mathematics, had few professional options despite being highly qualified. Instead, he moved to Southern California and worked in farming and various other industries for the next twenty-five years. Finally, after the passage of the Luce-Celler Act in 1946, South Asians were returned the right to citizenship. Saund became a citizen a few years later and began his quest for political office, ultimately leading to his successful campaign for Congress.

The first excerpt is from a television interview with Congressman Saund con-

---

PRAMILA JAYAPAL

Pramila Jayapal was elected to the U.S. House of Representatives in 2016. She became the first Indian American woman to serve in the House, the first woman to represent Washington's Seventh Congressional District, and the first Asian American to represent the state of Washington in Congress.

Prior to becoming a politician, Jayapal was a longtime activist and writer. In 2001, she founded the nonprofit Hate Free Zone (now called OneAmerica) in response to the post-9/11 backlash against immigrant communities of color, and served as its executive director for eleven years. She is also the author of the book *Pilgrimage to India: A Woman Revisits Her Homeland.*

In an oral history from 2008, Jayapal reflected on the creation of Hate Free Zone:

> . . . there were so many things to do. The Somali grocery stores had been raided by the Feds— I mean the money-wiring businesses had been raided by the Feds. You know, people were being deported, Arab Americans, twelve hundred Arab Americans, and you know Muslim men had been picked up across the country. Sikhs were being attacked, and so there was so much to do! I mean, actually to respond to, you know, people who were not standing up to any of this. And I was watching the whole thing going, "This is . . . this is . . . how can we be doing this as a country? This is just crazy!" And I had become a citizen in 2000, and I thought, this is not what I became a citizen for. I became a citizen because I believe in these values of due process, and fairness, and justice. And so it was just like a moral imperative, and I think we operated that way.

---

ducted by "First Federal Presents" on WCKT Miami in 1959 during a family visit to Florida. The congressman is asked about how he went from such humble beginnings, growing up in a village in Punjab, to becoming the first South Asian elected to Congress. Here is his response:

> I had settled in Imperial County since 1926 as a farmer. I was a PhD in mathematics, but because I could not become a citizen of the United States, I could not find a teaching job. But I was satisfied as a farmer in the Imperial Valley, the only way I could make a living. While I was farming, I never let my interest in national and international affairs slow down. I was always interested in American political life.
>
> When I became a citizen of the United States on December 16, 1949, it was my ambition to run for public office. I ran for the office of judge of the justice court of the small town where I had lived for twenty-five years. Everyone thought that I had no chance. It was not possible for a

Hindoo to be elected judge. But I had faith in the American sense of justice and fair play. I campaigned hard and I won. Then I was not allowed to sit, because I had not been a citizen of the United States for more than one year. I ran again in 1952, and I served as judge of the justice court for four years.

In the meantime, in 1954, I had been elected as county chairman of the Democratic Central Committee of the county of Imperial. Then I had the opportunity to help in the campaign of the Democratic nominee for Congress in 1954. I became intrigued with that work. Then, in 1956, I amazed everybody when I announced my candidacy. Well, from then on the story is well known. I lived in Imperial County, which has only 20 percent of the population of the district. And the larger county, Riverside, has 80 percent of the population. And, to be frank with you, I did not know more than twelve persons in the Riverside County when I became a candidate. But it was simply amazing how scores of American men and women came over to help me by giving up their time and money. I had a very difficult campaign, but with the help of my American friends, and to the astonishment of everybody, I was elected to the Congress of the United States.

This second excerpt is from Saund's autobiographical memoir, *Congressman from India*, published in 1960. In the preface to the memoir, Saund writes: "This book is the simple story of the struggles, sorrows and joys, defeats and recoveries, of a twenty-year-old native of India who came to the United States and, nearly twoscore years later, became a United States congressman." In this excerpt, Saund describes the ways his political opponents attempted to cast him as an outsider in order to dissuade voters for supporting his campaign:

As election time neared, my Democratic opponent became increasingly violent in his attacks on me. He quoted passages from my book, *My Mother, India*, quite out of context, and ran a virulent full-page ad in

B. P. RAO'S FIRST DAYS

Interviewed by Sheila Shankar

B. P. Rao departed from Hyderabad, India, and arrived in New York City in 1959 at the age of 27.

In SAADA, courtesy of B. P. Rao.

One day three Indian graduate students and I went to Roanoke to go shopping. We went to a snack bar to have lunch. The four of us were sitting—the waitress was going back and forth, back and forth, and was not stopping to take our order. We asked her to take our order—she wouldn't stop or say anything. She was serving people but not us. Then one of my friends got mad and said, "They are discriminating against us." He wanted to argue with the waitress, but I said, "There is no point in arguing since this is an accepted fact in the area—let's just go out and eat somewhere else." So we just walked out without ordering anything and went to a grocery shop to buy bread and cheese and crackers and ate in the car. I felt bad. We never came across that kind of discrimination in India. It sort of affected me mentally. . . . I thought maybe we don't have any worth in this society.

the newspapers of both counties. In addition he attacked me severely in several radio broadcasts. I paid little attention to these attacks, and in fact refused to listen to the radio broadcasts. Indeed, the full-page ad was of such a nature that the three leading daily papers in the district refused to print it on grounds that it was libelous. My friends were angry and disturbed over all this, but I couldn't let it bother me in the least. I had positively and definitely made up my mind to present myself as a candidate for the high office of congressman on my own merits and not say a word against my opponent. I thus never felt the need nor the desire to answer his charges.

Later in the general election the Republican campaign also hit hard at my being born in India. Every effort was made to make it appear that I was an Indian, not an American. In newspaper ads I was not called D. S. Saund, but Dalip Singh in big letters and Saund in small letters. This sort of practice was widespread, but apparently it did not hurt my candidacy either in the primary or general election.

MOTHER INDIA

Historian Katherine Mayo's 1927 book, *Mother India*, had a major influence on American and British views of India at the time. Mayo, an American who supported the Asian exclusion acts of the late nineteenth century, was writing in opposition to Indian independence from British rule. In her guide to Indian society, she heavily criticized the country's treatment of women, its politicians, and the practice of child marriage, among other things.

The book sparked widespread outrage in India, with more than fifty responses published condemning Mayo's narrow view. Among these were Dalip Singh Saund's *My Mother India* (1930) and Dhan Gopal Mukerji's *A Son of Mother India Answers* (1928). The most famous response, though, came from Mahatma Gandhi, who called the book a "report of a drain inspector sent out with the one purpose of opening and examining the drains of the country to be reported upon."

The first woman legislator in India, Dr. Muthulakshmi Reddi, also spoke out against the book in a speech to the Women's Indian Association. Her words particularly highlighted Mayo's ignorance of the organizing work of Indian women:

Reformers of today do not deny there is the system of early marriage prevalent among the high-caste Hindus with all its attendant evils, but Miss Mayo—to be true to facts—instead of condemning the whole nation, might have added that it exists only among a certain section of Hindus, and a large section of the non-Brahmins and untouchables are not affected by it. Again, for the evils of early marriage, she goes for a list which was drawn up some thirty-three years back by the women surgeons of this country, when a bill for raising the age of consent was brought by one of our Hindu brethren in the assembly. Again, in 1925, when the question for further raising the age of consent came before the assembly, there were speakers both for and against such a measure—those for said there was no text in the Hindu religion to sanction early marriage, and those against affirmed that religion was in danger. Even at that period, the countless women's associations through India held meetings and asked for reform.

Samip Mallick (he/him) is the cofounder and executive director of SAADA.

THE CIVIL RIGHTS MOVEMENT

Nico Slate

In the summer of 1941, a team of nonviolent activists, Black and white, deseg-regated Cleveland's Garfield Park swimming pool. As the interracial bathers entered the pool, everyone else exited, and an angry crowd gathered. But the pro-testers remained calm. Several had trained in nonviolent activism while living at Ahimsa Farm, a small ashram founded by six students from Antioch College and their professor, an Indian sociologist named Manmatha Chatterjee. In addition to inspiring his students to apply Gandhian nonviolence against racism in the United States, Chatterjee had donated $5,000 to create Ahimsa Farm. Chatterjee was one of many South Asian Americans who helped bring Gandhian nonviolence into the Civil Rights movement.

Many people know that Mahatma Gandhi helped inspire Dr. Martin Luther King Jr., but the connections between South Asian and African American freedom

KAMALADEVI CHATTOPADHYAY

Kamaladevi Chattopadhyay was an Indian feminist, arts advocate, and freedom fighter who visited the American South in 1941. According to Nico Slate, author of *Colored Cosmopolitanism*, while in the United States she "made a point of staying only with African American families" and once identified herself to a demanding ticket collector as a person of color instead of as a prominent foreign figure who'd "only a few months before had tea with Franklin and Eleanor Roosevelt." Slate describes her in his book:

> For Kamaladevi Chattopadhyay, one of the most articulate champions of colored cosmopolitanism, being a woman, being a socialist, and being "colored" were all vital to her identity and her sense of purpose. Her nearly two years in the United States allowed her to reach out to African Americans as a "coloured woman" who had dedicated her life to opposing not only imperialism and racism but gender-based oppression as well.

In artist Shebani Rao's "Kamaladevi Comic," she shares the story of an incident in 1941 during Chattopadhyay's travels across the United States. Shebani writes: "I wanted to create a comic that brings Kamaladevi's work to life and gives South Asian kids a badass, desi feminist hero to look up to. I hope that sharing her story will inspire a new generation of desi activists in the U.S." Learn more at shebanirao.com.

For more, read Colored Cosmopolitanism: The Shared Struggle for Freedom in the United States and India, *by Nico Slate.*

struggles started long before Dr. King and involved the courage and creativity of hundreds of people, such as Krishnalal Shridharani, a veteran of Gandhi's Salt March who had studied sociology at Columbia University. Shridharani's dissertation, entitled *War without Violence*, inspired many Civil Rights activists to employ Gandhian tactics.

In 1960, the Civil Rights movement entered a new phase with the eruption of the sit-in movement, a series of student-led protests against whites-only lunch counters, restaurants, movie theaters, pools, beaches, and other places of public amusement. Two South Asian students at MIT, Jaswant Krishnayya and Ahmed Meer, decided to spend their summer vacation working with sit-in activists. Meer remembered, "We were both concerned with the plight of the American Blacks and found it inconsistent with the American image and ideals we had come to admire in the short time we had been in the U.S." Meer and Krishnayya planned to stay in a tent, surviving on peanut butter sandwiches and Tang. Fortunately, they established close connections with student activists throughout the South, who

---

DALIT PANTHERS

Formed by a group of writers and poets in 1972 Bombay in reaction to widespread violence against Dalits across India, Dalit Panthers was a liberation movement inspired by the Black Panther Party of the United States. The militant movement organized against the oppressive caste system in India and fought to eradicate the concept of "untouchability" in the country. The group led marches, rallies, and visits to "atrocity" sites to lend support to victims of caste violence.

The group's members also extensively used literature and art to confront traditional depictions of Indian society and religion, which included widespread publishing of Dr. B. R. Ambedkar's writings. They were also instrumental in popularizing the expanded use of the term "Dalit" to refer to lower-caste communities, previously often referred to as "untouchables." In 1977, five years after its founding, the group officially disbanded, but its legacy of resistance to the caste system is still felt today.

---

offered support and guidance. Back at MIT, Krishnayya published an editorial in the *Boston Globe* condemning violence in the South and encouraging sympathetic northerners to join the ongoing struggle.

Students were not the only South Asian Americans to participate in the struggle against racism. J. J. Singh, perhaps the most influential South Asian American in the 1930s and 1940s, developed close ties with Walter White, the executive

J. J. SINGH

After arriving in the United States in 1926, Sirdar J. J. Singh ran a successful Indian textile import store in Manhattan. Singh's involvement as a young man in the Gandhian noncooperation movement and the All India Congress Committee quickly shaped his political and social commitments in New York, and he soon became the high-profile leader of the India League of America (ILA). Established in the 1940s, the ILA was shaped by an anti-colonial nationalist outlook and published several political pamphlets and newsletters that sought to educate Americans on India's movement for independence. Aside from organizing around the cause of Indian independence, the ILA, along with the Pakistan League of America, supported legislation that would undo restrictions against immigrants from Asia. J. J. Singh and his peers were involved in the campaigning and lobbying that led to the eventual passing of the Luce-Celler Act of 1946, which allowed Indians in the United States to naturalize and accepted a quota of one hundred Indian immigrants per year into the United States. *Time* magazine described Singh as writing thousands of letters, making hundreds of phone calls, and tirelessly stalking Capitol Hill hallways to get the bill passed. Singh eventually returned to India in 1959.

J. J. Singh's granddaughter, Sabrina Singh, has continued her grandfather's legacy of civic engagement. In 2020, she was named as press secretary to Kamala Harris on the Biden-Harris campaign, and later transitioned into the role of White House deputy press secretary, following the presidential inauguration. In an interview with *Brown Girl Magazine* in October 2020, Singh reflected on her career as a public servant: "It was always drilled in me from my family to find ways to give back to your community. It can be anything from volunteering to what I'm doing now. . . . He [my grandfather] is someone who I think is very inspiring because the same hall in Congress he walked, I have worked in and walked through. It means a lot to follow in his footsteps."

secretary of the NAACP, and the two worked together to defend the rights of South Asian Americans and African Americans and to support the political independence and economic development of India. Another prominent South Asian American, Enuga Reddy, built ties with African Americans while working against South African apartheid as an official at the United Nations.

South Asian Americans continued to fight for their own rights as well. Their labors bore fruit in the 1965 Immigration Act, a dramatic change in the rules that governed who could enter the United States. Rather than enforcing racially based national quotas, the new law prioritized family ties and employment in certain fields. A response to decolonization as well as to the Civil Rights movement, the 1965 act aimed to make immigration reflect the country's long-standing promise of equality, a promise that Americans are still working to make a reality today.

Nico Slate (he/him) is a professor of history and head of the History Department at Carnegie Mellon University.

CHAPTER 3

Immigration after the Civil Rights Movement

1965–

Dr. Har Gobind Khorana, seen here conducting a DNA polymerase assay. Khorana was born in 1922, in the village of Raipur in what is now Pakistan. A biochemist, he immigrated to the United States in 1960 to serve as the codirector of the Enzyme Research Institute and a member of the Department of Biochemistry at the University of Wisconsin–Madison. In 1968, Khorana and two colleagues were awarded the Nobel Prize in Physiology or Medicine for their work deciphering the "genetic code" through which RNA codes for the synthesis of proteins. Khorana then joined the MIT faculty in 1970, where he discovered how to synthesize DNA and constructed the first artificial gene—a discovery that led to major advances in genetic engineering and the development of the biotechnology industry. Khorana retired from MIT in 2007 and passed away in Concord, Massachusetts, in 2011. Photo courtesy of the University of Wisconsin–Madison Archives (S04437).

INTRODUCTION

Fariha Khan

Pingali Mohan Rao, known as Mohan, came to the United States on January 23, 1968, after being accepted to the University of Wisconsin–Madison's Master of Structural Engineering program. The 1965 Immigration and Naturalization Act, signed by President Lyndon B. Johnson, marked a radical break with previous policy by eliminating quotas based on national origins. After this act was signed, universities saw a wave of students from India and other Asian countries pursuing graduate degrees in engineering and the sciences.

"My brother and sister-in-law, who lived in Beloit, Wisconsin, picked me up from O'Hare Airport [in Chicago], and we drove eighty miles to their place," remembers Mohan. "I stayed there for a few days to settle in." When asked if his brother had any advice for him, Mohan laughs. "Well, his advice for me was 'In America, everyone is on their own.' And I said, 'Fine, no problem!'"

Like many of his peers in the late 1960s and early 1970s, Mohan left South Asia to further his education and secure a financially solid future. His migration narrative reflects the desire of many South Asians at the time for education, family reunification, successful careers, and security. With opportunities in the United States for individuals with technical skills in the sciences, and the change in immigration policy from national-origins quotas to a preference system based on family relationships with U.S. citizens, the pull to migrate to the United States was strong for many South Asians. For others, there were factors that pushed them out of South Asia, and this diversified migration patterns. Nevertheless, the desire for a new life and a part of the "American Dream" connected these immigrants—as did their arrival in a new and changing country.

In the years immediately following the 1965 act, those migrating to the United States were primarily from India and West and East Pakistan. As Erika Lee writes in her essay in this chapter, most immigrants in this migration phase had the advantages of education, English-language skills, and middle- to upper-middle-class status. Many quickly established themselves in their careers and settled in the suburbs of major cities. They began families, built religious, cultural, political, and community organizations, and continued to travel back to see relatives.

By the 1980s and into the 1990s, South Asians were joining relatives who already had legal status in the United States. According to Diditi Mitra, family reunification allowed for individuals with varying skills and education levels to immigrate to the United States. At the same time, job-market needs in the United States grew from opportunities in healthcare and other science industries to include small-business opportunities and jobs in the nonprofessional sector. Work and family life remained key factors for immigrants creating new lives, but now the types of opportunities in work and education broadened.

As the computer and software-technology industries grew at a rapid pace in the 1990s, a new stream of technical workers was needed. Pawan Dhingra notes in this chapter that the H1-B visa allowed companies to attract skilled South Asians, particularly from India, to the United States for limited employment. For those who had the technical or educational qualifications, it was their only chance at possible permanent migration. The Diversity Immigrant Visa Program, often referred to as the Diversity Lottery, had no technical skills requirements. It drew new settlers and further diversified the immigrant population, as well as the types of work immigrants engaged in. As Shweta Majumdar Adur highlights in her essay, Bangladeshi Americans migrated through this program in the largest numbers, drawn by the possibility of financial stability and the chance for an education. This program established the Bangladeshi community as one of the fastest-growing immigrant communities in the United States until Bangladesh was deemed ineligible for the program in 2013. Both the H1-B visas and the Diversity Immigrant Visa Program expanded the South Asian immigrant population to allow entry to those who were previously not included.

The pull of financial security and education influenced the decision to migrate for many South Asians, but others were "pushed" out of their homelands and resettled in the United States. Retika Adhikari details the migration of the Nepali-speaking Bhutanese refugee community, offering a glimpse into the joys and difficulties of arriving in the United States at this time, with limited English skills and educational credentials. Political instability forced South Asian immigrants from countries such as Guyana and Uganda to arrive as "twice migrants," a term that describes immigrants who arrive at a country from a country other than their nation of origin. One example of the "twice migrants" group is Indo-Caribbeans, who have built lives for themselves along the East Coast, with the largest community in New York City. Nadia Misir writes in this chapter of the community's efforts to celebrate their multiple ethnic heritages through food, religion, and culture while facing discrimination in America.

While a specific group of South Asians arrived soon after the Immigration Act of 1965, with defined reasons, migration became more complex over time. Differentiating factors "pulled" various groups and "pushed" others to the United States. The community today is rich in religions, ethnic backgrounds, and nationalities, transforming what it means to be South Asian American. How they arrive or why they come may differ, but, like Mohan, each comes to the United States with a desire for opportunity, safety, and the possibility of achieving their dreams.

PINGALI MOHAN RAO'S FIRST DAYS

Interviewed by Mika Rao Kalapatapu

Pingali Mohan Rao immigrated to the United States from India in 1968, at the age of twenty-five. He had recently been admitted to an engineering master's program at the University of Wisconsin–Madison. Here is his story about his arrival and settling in his new country.

"My brother explained how to get to the university. I walked to the bus stop and paid two dollars for the Greyhound bus. When I arrived, I had no idea where to go—but I knew I needed to register at 'Bascom Hall.' It had snowed three to four inches. I had ordinary shoes, not snow shoes. . . . I had a jacket but not a heavy jacket."

After registration, next on the agenda was finding a place to live.

"I asked some people where to look—they suggested being as close to the engineering school as possible. When I went to Randall Street, the place of my department, I saw signs about accommodations. For $10 a week, I was able to stay there and was assigned a Korean roommate.

"I had never really cooked before, but I knew how to make potatoes and rice. For lunch, I would make a sandwich, and every night I would eat rice, with the potatoes and yogurt and some *avakaya* [spicy mango pickle] I brought from India."

Mohan had some money from his father, and the engineering department paid him $250 a month to work as a teaching assistant. These funds were enough to pay for the apartment and food. "I didn't have a car," he recalls.

"As far as winter clothes, the school knew students like us would come with nothing, so they had a charity place where we could go . . . and pick whatever we wanted. I got myself a big jacket and big boots, and I was all set.

"At first, I visited my brother every few weeks because I was homesick. . . . But after that, I didn't go as often, and he ended up moving to New Jersey that year. I didn't talk to my parents—it was too expensive to make international calls. We didn't have internet back then, of course. I would send postcards, and my father would write me back.

"I enjoyed my graduate studies. I was studying under the masters in my field and learned a lot. While I was in the program, I was interviewed by several firms, including Chicago and North Western Railway. They offered me the princely sum of $9,800 a year. That doesn't seem like much, but it was more than a lot of my friends. I moved to Chicago after graduating."

Mohan never considered returning to India.

"India was not as prosperous in those days," he recalls. "There were fewer jobs. After graduating, I was legally allowed to work in the U.S. for six-month increments and would have to check in with the immigration office after each period was complete." After his second check-in, the immigration officer suggested that Mohan apply for a green card, which he did and received within fifteen days. (Today, the wait period for a green card for an immigrant from India averages twelve years.)

"In 1972, I returned to India for a visit, and I was introduced to girls with the idea of getting married.

Pingali Mohan Rao with his wife, Anu Rao. In SAADA, courtesy of Mika Rao Kalapatapu.

I met a girl named Anu. We got engaged, and I returned a few months later for the wedding. She got her green card right away and we came back together."

Mohan and Anu made their home in Chicago for the next year, before moving to Ann Arbor and eventually settling in Philadelphia when they became parents. Mohan worked as a structural engineer at Southeastern Pennsylvania Transportation Authority (SEPTA) and the New York City Transit Authority until he retired in 2003 at the age of sixty. He was a vital part of the city response during the 9/11 crisis.

When asked if it was easier to be an immigrant in 1968, as one of the first wave of individuals to immigrate from India after the 1965 act, or now, Mohan does not hesitate: "It was much easier when I came. Back then, they were clamoring for people with our educational background to be part of American society. Back then, it was the easiest thing in the world for people like us."

Fariha Khan (she/her) is the associate director of the Asian American Studies Program at the University of Pennsylvania.

POST-1965 IMMIGRATION

Erika Lee

South Asians had been immigrating to the United States as early as 1820, but their numbers were small in comparison to other immigrant groups. Intense anti-Asian sentiment and discriminatory laws like the 1917 and 1924 Immigration Acts had closed the doors to most immigration from Asia. In 1960, there were only twelve thousand Indian immigrants in the country, representing just 0.5 percent of the foreign-born population at the time. Pakistanis were similarly small in number, with only 2,500 Pakistani immigrants entering the United States between 1947 and 1965.

But the 1965 Immigration Act opened up new immigration opportunities and transformed South Asian America. The law ended discriminatory national-origin quotas that had regulated immigration since the 1920s and established, in its place, a system that privileged families seeking to reunify and

THOMAS MATHEW'S FIRST DAYS

Interviewed by George Mathew

Thomas Mathew departed from Ernakulam, India, and arrived in Detroit, Michigan, in 1966 at the age of 28.

My wife, Remani, and I arrived at Detroit Metro Airport on December 23, 1966, a few months after we were married. We had flown from Ernakulam in Kerala, leaving our families behind, and stopped off in Rome—we'd thought it would be warm and sunny based on pictures we'd seen; instead it was thirty degrees and freezing cold!

From there, we flew into New York, and due to the heavy snow, we were delayed by a day at JFK; the airline kept us in a hotel overnight in Queens until the next day, when we boarded a Northwest Orient flight going to Detroit.

I wasn't worried—I had secured a good medical residency position in the U.S., and my parents said that before I went, I should get married, so I did. In those days, we were only allowed to bring eight dollars per person from India to the United States, so now I had sixteen dollars; in addition, I had brought some ivory pieces with me to trade or sell for extra money. Also, I had a friend, Koshy (he had been a few years ahead of me in medical school), who was going to pick us up from the airport.

When we finally did arrive, it was twenty to twenty-five degrees, and the entire place was covered in snow. We had never seen snow in our lives in Kerala, so it was shocking! We had kept our sweaters on since Rome, so it wasn't as bad as it would've been. Since we came a day later than we planned, my friend didn't know when we were coming and wasn't there to pick us up. I didn't have change for a phone, so I couldn't call him. I needed to find a place to sleep for us, and a way to get there.

I was expecting to start work in a few months at Mount Carmel Hospital, and they were offering accommodations for medical residents; I thought I could get in there. I found a cab to take Remani and me, and we headed towards Mount Carmel.

While we were going to the hospital, the meter went up to fifty to sixty dollars. I told the driver I didn't have enough money—I still only had sixteen dollars! Lucky for me, he laughed and turned off the meter! We arrived at Mount Carmel and asked for lodging—I didn't know it was a nun hospital. The nuns made me sleep on the third or fourth floor, while Remani had to share a room on the seventh floor with a nun.

The next day was better—Koshy was a resident at Mount Carmel, so he brought me back to his place, and we stayed with him for the next few nights until I found an apartment in Highland Park.

The thing is, I'd forgotten I had bought round-trip tickets for us—if I'd known how bad it was going to be that first day, I would have probably used the tickets to go back to India, but instead, I've stayed now for almost fifty years, built my practice, and had my kids. After that day, everything else seemed easy.

MINI PAUL'S FIRST DAYS

Interviewed by Merin Paul

Mini Paul departed from Trivandrum, India, and arrived in Chicago, Illinois, in 1993 at the age of 27.

I came to America on a job visa. I was received by my uncle and his wife. I stayed with them for two months while I was applying for my nursing licensure. Everything was new. The weather and all was different than India. It was warm but I saw that the weather was changing quickly. I also saw that it was different than India because you didn't see many people outside. Everyone has their own car and you hardly see any neighbors. The people I was staying with both worked and the kids were all in schools. Everyone was basically busy with their own lives. I saw that there was less social interaction between people compared to back home. But the kids and everyone in the home were all nice to me. They took me around wherever they went, for shopping, to friends' houses. They took me with them so I could see how the community was. I went to church and I met more Malayalee people there.

I started working in June. I had to apply for a temporary license to work as a "nurse–license pending." Working at the nursing home was not easy to start off. It was a totally different culture where I saw a lot of different ethnicities, different languages, and even the English was pronounced differently. All of a sudden, I was in charge of a unit of fifty patients, giving medications and taking care of them; it wasn't easy. I was staying with a lady who was an employee at the nursing home. She was also a Malayalee and would give me a ride in the morning. The coworkers were okay. Some of them were not okay. It was because I didn't know everything about the culture, or the community, so it took time to learn how things were. For example, the meals for the patients were different from what we ate back home. Like pancakes, syrup and butter for breakfast! Generally the staff was nice; some of them were picky. Some people were bossy, including non-nurses like housekeeping. I worked there a year and a half.

In order to get my license, I had to sit for the NCLEX exam. I took the exam after six months. The exam was hard but I prepared well. I think it was the last writing exam; after that it was computerized. I had to go to Chicago to take it. Pappa [husband] and Harsha [daughter] came in December. Raising Harsha was okay. She was so excited to be here. She went to school and made friends very quickly. We didn't have a babysitter and Pappa did not have a working visa, so he had to stay home and take care of her when she came home from preschool. One of my old friends from nursing school had twin kids here. Harsha and them were the same age, so we enrolled all three of them in the same preschool. My friend came maybe a year before me, so she also helped me to settle down. She helped me learn how to drive, learn how to shop and move to a new apartment. My uncle helped me buy a car in December. I learned how to drive right away because I had to go to work. Overall, it was very different than India. I was able to adapt to the new situation and I had people to support me. I found a way for stabilizing my job through getting my nursing license, but I got nervous because if didn't get my license, I would have to go back. But I was able to pass the exam the first time. So we started our life again as family in the United States.

"highly skilled" applicants in specific fields. Immigrants with expertise in the sciences and health fields were especially sought after to meet growing demands in these parts of the United States' postindustrial economy. South Asian immigrants started arriving in growing numbers. From 1980 to 2013, the Indian immigrant population doubled every decade, growing from 206,000 to 2.04 million. They now account for 4.7 percent of the foreign-born population. Pakistanis similarly experienced a growth in population. By 1990, there were about 100,000 Pakistani Americans, and there are now more than 409,000 Pakistanis in the country.

The 1965 Immigration Act also changed the type of immigrants who were able to come to the United States. The vast majority of South Asians who came before 1965

CANADIAN IMMIGRATION HISTORY

South Asian immigrants in Canada have faced similar issues to those in the United States, but their experiences have also diverged in many important ways. As early as 1903, people from South Asia—primarily Punjabi Sikhs—began settling in parts of British Columbia. As in the United States, anti–South Asian sentiments were high during this period (see "The Komagata Maru" in chapter 1), and they led to the 1908 Continuous Journey Law that sought to slow their entry.

These restrictions on immigration remained mostly in place until the 1960s, when changes in the law led to massive increases in the South Asian population of Canada. Today, South Asian Canadians make up nearly 5 percent of the country's population (in comparison to the United States, where South Asians make up nearly 2 percent of the population) and are thus the largest visible minority group in Canada.

---

were—like most immigrants from Asia, Latin America, and Europe at the time— classified as "unskilled laborers." South Asians (mostly young, single men) worked in lumber mills, railroads, and farms up and down the Pacific coasts of Canada and the United States and helped to expand and develop the economies in both countries. In contrast, those who arrived after 1965 were more likely to be young, educated professionals (both male and female) with highly sought-after technical skills.

Changes in both the United States and South Asia helped to fuel this new wave of immigration in the second half of the twentieth century. At the same time that the United States was opening the door wider to skilled and educated immigrants, countries like India were expanding their educational systems and producing

MADAN VASISHTA'S FIRST DAYS

Interviewed by Sarika Mehta

Madan Vasishta departed from Delhi, India, and arrived in Washington, D.C. in 1967 at the age of 26.

They asked me things like
"Do you ride an elephant to go to school?"

I was really shocked by the kind of questions people asked me about India—what little knowledge they had! They asked me things like "Do you ride an elephant to go to school?" "Do you live with monkeys?"—those kinds of questions. I had to just bear with it! "Do you find enough food in India?" "I've seen pictures of people starving." "People die in the streets. How do you look healthy? How do you find food?" They would ask me so many stupid questions back then! But even . . . I had the wrong idea of America—just what I had read in books. I assumed people rode horses and were cowboys like in the "Wild West." Just like in the movies. I was shocked when I arrived at Dulles Airport, taking the bus to Gallaudet University. I kept looking, but never saw any cowboys. I was so disappointed! It seemed there were only cars in America—no horses! So we all had our own misunderstandings about each other.

large numbers of well-educated and skilled workers who could compete in the new global marketplace. Because India's economy could not fully absorb all of these workers, however, many Indians looked abroad, including to the United States, for opportunities. The result of these factors is what sociologists call the "hyper-selectivity" of immigrants: those who come to the United States are more highly educated than their ethnic counterparts who do not immigrate.

Recent immigration laws have continued to facilitate the immigration of

A NOTE TO THE READER ON THE TERMINOLOGY OF LABOR

You may have noticed various terms related to labor being used throughout this book or, more broadly, in conversations about immigrants. These include terms such as "highly skilled," "low skilled," and "unskilled," which often reflect official United States governmental language associated with specific immigration pathways, such as the H-1B, H-2A, or H-2B visas. While these terms are often used to refer to specific forms of labor, they have also historically been used as ways to categorize the different groups of people performing those types of labor.

Writing about the British immigration system, but offering thoughts that resonate in the United States as well, Kate Ferguson notes the implicit judgments being offered through the use of such terms:

The second adjective: "low-skilled" is more complicated. Apart from being an insulting description of the essential, often backbreaking and emotionally draining work millions of people do, it has no clear definition.

Often, it suggests a kind of dispensability. Low-skilled work is work that anyone could do, given a few hours' training. Other definitions focus more on the lack of formal qualifications needed for the role. This, I should note, would put the prime minister in the same category as care-workers, hairdressers and garbage collectors.

But whatever way you choose to define it, we all have a sense of what is really meant by low-skilled work. It's a euphemism for "low-valued work."

Work that wouldn't impress at a certain kind of dinner party. Work that doesn't inspire envy. Work that is unglamorous.

Work that cleans your office during the night so your desk's not sticky when you get in. Work that takes care of your sick parents so you don't have to. Work that looks after your children so you don't have to. Work that serves you coffee when you desperately need a moment of human interaction. Work that puts food on your table. Work that cleans up the street outside your house. Work that builds cities.

From "There's No Such Thing as Low-Skilled Labor" for DW, by Kate Ferguson.

highly skilled workers. The 1990 Immigration and Nationality Act, for example, increased the flow of highly skilled "guest workers" from abroad with temporary visas known as H-1B visas. These allow companies to hire workers with at least a bachelor's degree for specialty occupations that require technical or theoretical expertise (scientists, engineers, and IT workers). As a result, U.S. companies, especially in the high-tech sector, have actively recruited highly skilled workers from Asia, who receive about three-quarters of these visas. Immigrants from India, which produces a large supply of information technology workers and software developers, received 70 percent of the 316,000 H-1B visas granted in 2014. South Asian immigrants and South Asian Americans have therefore played leading roles in emerging high-tech industries in the United States. For example, a number of Indian-born tech leaders now head up some of the country's most successful tech giants, including Google (Sundar Pichai), Microsoft (Satya Nadella), and Adobe (Shantanu Narayen).

What began in 1965 with a new immigration law has transformed South Asian immigration and South Asian American communities. The number of new immigrants arriving from the region is greater than ever before. These highly skilled workers retain privileges afforded to them by their educational and class status and simultaneously confront other forms of discrimination in America. Those who enter on H-1B visas are often paid less than their white peers, face limited upward mobility, and are sometimes exploited. In some extreme cases of abuse, these immigrant workers have been labeled "high-tech coolies" who are dependent on their employers to remain in the country. And racial, ethnic, and religious discrimination targeting South Asians affects all members of the community.

In short, skilled migrants are a central part of the new South Asian America that is transforming our country. While some have found a more welcoming United States than previous immigrants did, their American experience is a mix of both new opportunities and old discrimination.

Erika Lee (she/her/hers) is the author of several award-winning books, including, most recently, America for Americans: A History of Xenophobia in America *and* The Making of Asian America, *and is a Regents Professor and the director of the Immigration History Research Center at the University of Minnesota.*

FAMILIES BY LAW

Diditi Mitra

Those who resisted the 1965 Immigration Act, also known as the Hart-Celler Act, were concerned that it might result in an "un-whitening" of America. But despite these protests, the political environment of the 1960s, both domestic and international, favored the act's passage. The push for racial equality during the Civil Rights era made it difficult to maintain an immigration system that explicitly favored northern and western Europeans. Furthermore, America had emerged as the "leader of the free world," making it difficult for the nation to support overt forms of racism. Immigration policies needed to be equalized in order to maintain this standing in the eyes of other nations.

Interestingly, those who were against the 1965 act were eventually convinced that it should be passed by assurances that there would be a minimal rise in immigration from Asia. It was thought that the small number of Asian immigrants in the country at the time would mean that few would be able to take advantage of the act's family-reunification provision, which allowed nonworking "immediate family members" of U.S. citizens—spouses, minor children, and parents—to immigrate. It was also believed that those from "third world" countries lacked the necessary formal training to be able to immigrate through the skilled-labor provision. The underlying objective of the 1965 act was to increase immigration from eastern and southern Europe, which, like immigration from Asia, had been limited by the Immigration Act of 1924. The reality, however, is that immigration from Asian countries, including South Asia, increased considerably through the skilled-labor and family-reunification provisions of the 1965 act. Men typically immigrated first, later bringing wives and children, and eventually extended families.

One of the many South Asians who immigrated through the family-reunification provision of the Hart-Celler Act was Satnam Kaur. Kaur immigrated to New York from the Jalandhar district of Punjab in 1995, around the age of thirty-four. Her husband had arrived in the United States in the late 1980s and worked as a driver of yellow taxis in New York City. Because of the family-reunification provision, Kaur's husband was able to secure green cards for her and their two-year-old son so that they could live together in the United States as a family.

For a group of mostly Punjabi Sikh men, entering the United States with inadequate documentation, even without documentation, was not uncommon. Because the 1965 act allowed spouses of American citizens to get their green cards, marrying American citizens was one way that these immigrants legalized their status, became permanent residents, and eventually obtained their American citizenship. Once these men got their papers, they were also able to sponsor their immediate family members to immigrate to the United States.

The family-reunification provision of the 1965 act is an important factor in the diversification of the social-class background of immigrants from South Asia. Professional immigrants—scientists, doctors, and engineers—who had entered the United States through the skilled-worker category of the act were then able to sponsor family members who were not necessarily professionals themselves. Thus, beginning in the late 1970s, increasing numbers of immigrants from South Asia

THE TERMINOLOGY OF IMMIGRATION

Illegal vs. Undocumented

The following is excerpted from "Immigration Debate: The Problem with the Word Illegal," written by Jose Antonio Vargas for *Time* magazine (September 21, 2012):

[D]escribing an immigrant as illegal is legally inaccurate. Being in the U.S. without proper documents is a civil offense, not a criminal one. (Underscoring this reality, Justice Anthony Kennedy wrote for the majority opinion on SB 1070, Arizona's controversial immigration law: "As a general rule, it is not a crime for a movable alien to remain in the United States.") In a country that believes in due process of the law, calling an immigrant illegal is akin to calling a defendant awaiting trial a criminal. The term illegal is also imprecise. For many undocumented people—there are 11 million in the U.S. and most have immediate family members who are American citizens, either by birth or naturalization—their immigration status is fluid and, depending on individual circumstances, can be adjusted. . . .

And the term dehumanizes and marginalizes the people it seeks to describe. Think of it this way: In what other contexts do we call someone illegal? If someone is driving a car at 14, we say "underage driver," not "illegal driver." If someone is driving under the influence, we call them a "drunk driver," not an "illegal driver." Put another way: How would you feel if you—or your family members or friends—were referred to as illegal?

Chain Migration vs. Family Reunification

In 2017, in response to congressional and public debates about continuing Deferred Action for Childhood Arrivals (DACA)—which provides relief to young people who were brought to the United States without documentation as children—President Donald Trump began frequently demanding an end to what he called "chain migration."

The term has been used to describe the process of a green-card holder or U.S. citizen sponsoring a family member for immigration to the United States. Many immigration advocates believe that the phrase is demeaning and offensive, preferring "family reunification" instead. But the Trump administration and Republicans argue that "chain migration" is a useful shorthand that has been around for quite some time.

In a January 26, 2018, *New York Times* article by Linda Qiu, Leo Chavez, a professor at the University of California at Irvine and scholar of media representations of immigration, explained that "chain migration" was not a part of popular discourse until the ascension of Trump, and that it is indeed being used in a harmful way:

"It's an attempt to sway public opinion," Mr. Chavez said, adding that the once-scholarly term has taken on negative connotations as "if it's a conspiracy, a plot, a threat to the changing demographics."

It is not unlike "anchor baby," "the browning of America" or even "Dreamers," on the flip side, Mr. Chavez said. Such phrases have become more common in the ongoing debate about "how you talk about who are citizens, who are members of the nation and who can become Americans. It's never a settled question. It hasn't been for 200 years and it isn't now."

UNDOCUMENTED SOUTH ASIAN AMERICANS

According to the Migration Policy Institute, immigrants from Asian countries made up nearly 1.5 million of the 11 million undocumented immigrants living in the country in 2018—a figure that does not include undocumented immigrants from diasporic South Asian communities outside of Asia. Statistics for the exact number of undocumented South Asian immigrants living in the United States are lacking, but recent estimates suggest there are over half a million from India alone. Indeed, the fastest-growing group of undocumented Asian immigrants today is from India.

In an oral history interview with 2019–20 Archival Creators Fellow Gaiutra Bahadur, "Sherry Singh," an aide at a public school in Queens and an Indo-Caribbean immigrant, shared her story of coming to the United States "backtrack" from Guyana at the age of eight to reunite with her mother in 1996. In the excerpt below, Singh reflected on how her undocumented status deeply and intimately impacted her experiences growing up as a teenager in the Bronx:

> It wasn't until my high school years where I started noticing for Career Day . . . like they're asking questions and people are signing up and talking about what they want to do as a career or in the future. And it was like, okay, but in order for you to sign up for this—because originally I wanted to be a lawyer—and it was like if you want to sign up for this, okay, you need your social. If you need to sign up for this, you need this and you need that. And that actually put a fear in me, and it was like: why even bother, like, to push myself to accomplish something that I'm never going to get anywhere with? So I stopped. I started going off the edges, like I started not taking school serious. I started leaving. I would go for walks. And would just . . . what you would say, like, rebel against school and my family, because part of me was, like, so angry. Like why did . . . why everybody who lived their life and be able to do this and do this and I can't have that same chances?

In 2012, President Obama signed the Deferred Action for Childhood Arrivals (DACA) program into executive order. Under DACA, around eight hundred thousand undocumented young people who entered the United States as children, like "Sherry Singh" did, are eligible to apply for a driver's license, social security number, and work permit. DACA recipients are often referred to as "DREAMers." In a three-part series written for Sakhi for South Asian Women, Bangladeshi immigrant Caritas Doha reflected on the joy and relief she felt when she first became a DREAMer:

> . . . being undocumented is still a daily trauma; the anxiety is constant. I was driven to succeed, but imagining my future was painful. I had no solutions. So I will never forget the day DACA was announced. For years, I employed whatever agency and creativity I had, but my status was a looming cloud. DACA meant that I could actually realize my full potential.

> I wrote this the night I found out about my DACA approval:

>> One would think that after years of fantasizing about a moment, I would be armed with words to describe it; I am not. I have never felt happiness like this. Happiness without the latent worry that something about this moment will be taken away from me. But perhaps this is what ownership over one's life feels like. That such moments exist, when you are fortunate to experience them, which are Solid. Sturdy. Enduring.

>> Maybe that's naive. I just know that I am up writing this at 4am, for once jolted not by worry but by possibility.

> From "Part Three: New Beginnings" in the Documenting Dreams series for Sakhi, by Caritas Doha.

of lower socioeconomic status have immigrated to the United States. While the framers of the 1965 act did not foresee its usefulness to South Asians, the family-reunification and skilled-labor provisions have played a significant role in making the community what it is today.

Diditi Mitra is an associate professor of sociology at Brookdale Community College, in New Jersey.

Courtesy of Harmohan Sohi, owner of 7-Eleven franchises in Stockton, California, from 1978 to 1989.

THE H-1B VISA

Pawan Dhingra

"Every building is stuffed with Indians! . . . The whole building has only desis working. Except, the bosses are white and American."

An Indian immigrant IT worker made this observation about his workplace, an IT firm in the United States that contracted out immigrant workers to large business clients. Practically all of the workers were on H-1B visas. This visa has become a key means by which South Asians, and Indians in particular, migrate to the United States. The profile of Indian Americans as part of the so-called model minority results in part from this influx of migrants on the H-1B visa. Indians are the biggest beneficiaries of H-1B visas, even though the visa is not designated for any nationality or region of origin. As will be clear, central to understanding the H-1B visa is that it first and foremost frames these immigrants as workers.

108

THE LEAST WELL-KNOWN IMMIGRATION LAW

The H-1B visa is not a new legal means of immigration. It was written into the Immigration and Nationality Act of 1952, also known as the McCarran-Walter Act, and is part of a larger visa system meant for immigrant laborers. Certain industries—including agriculture, medicine, and engineering—have had labor shortages and have successfully lobbied the U.S. government for temporary workers. While IT workers may seem completely different from agricultural workers, they are understood by the U.S. government and their employing companies as laborers who are here to serve an industry due to a lack of U.S.-born personnel.

The Immigration and Nationality Act of 1990 should be recognized as a key chapter in Indian American history. It created the H-1B visa designation popularly used today by Indian immigrants and set the cap at sixty-five thousand H-1B immigrants a year, with more visas set aside for immigrants who received their secondary education in the United States. In addition, it allowed these visa holders to forge a path toward permanent residency and ultimately citizenship, with employer support and approval. H-1B visa holders can work in the United States for up to six years—some exceptions allow for even more—before they are required to get a green card. Since 1990, Congress has raised and lowered the cap on the number of H-1B visas per year, often in response to industry lobbying, from 65,000 to as high as 195,000. As of 2018, the cap is at 65,000 (with another 20,000 for graduates of U.S. universities with advanced degrees), with exceptions made for university, nonprofit, and government employees.

WORKING FOR A DREAM

While high-tech industries have pushed for more H-1B visas and generally have profited from them, the H-1B's broader impact on the nation and on immigrants themselves is more complex. On the one hand, a labor shortage in a growing, essential industry must be addressed in the short term, and immigration is an obvious solution. The growth of the IT industry in the United States is due in part to the influx of South Asian immigrants under this visa program. Immigrant

RITUJA INDAPURE'S FIRST DAYS

Interviewed by Isabella Nugent

Rituja Indapure departed from Mumbai, India, and arrived in Seattle, Washington, in 1997 at the age of 26.

In SAADA, courtesy of Rituja Indapure.

> *I had gotten married on December 3rd, and my husband was already here in the United States, so I was joining him. . . . I was traveling alone, and my departure was for 24th December. . . . I was very excited, but at the same time I was very sad, because I was leaving my parents behind. And this wasn't my first time I had ever stepped out of the country, but this was the first time after marriage, so I think it was emotionally kind of very stressful for all of us.*

> *But I got on the plane and somehow, because it was Christmas Eve or Christmas, I was expecting something spectacular or at least something different on the airplane. And it didn't happen, so I was very disappointed. . . . [When I landed in Seattle] I did not see any festivities at all. . . . Now it seems interesting that at the time I was like, "What? You don't have any Christmas decorations all around?" . . .*

> *I started looking for work because that was very important to me. I was practicing as a lawyer when in India, and I really wanted to start practicing and looking at opportunities. And unfortunately, you know, they weren't very forthcoming. I didn't have a chance to just take a bar exam and just start practice. I was told that I would have to either, you know, do a law clerk program or go back to school, which was not an option for me at that time. I started volunteering at the local library and I also volunteered as a case manager at a municipal court. So those were like some of my highlights that happened in the first year. . . .*

> *Even though I didn't pursue my law degree, I am involved in social justice and art and, you know, trying to elevate women's voices. [I] found an incredible community here, and I'm just very thankful.*

professionals often secure well-paying jobs and a comfortable lifestyle. A number become entrepreneurs over time.

Yet, on the other hand, any immigration law that frames immigrants as workers first and foremost limits their economic opportunities and their sense of belonging in the nation. Visa holders traditionally have had limited bargaining power relative to that of their employers. For instance, wages were set at below market value and have not increased as the labor supply has grown, in contrast to economic assumptions, which suggests that noneconomic factors—such as racial stereotypes about pliable South Asian workers—are at play. For many years, it was impossible for visa holders to change jobs without leaving the country, thereby giving employers extreme authority over them. A compliant workforce—one that does not protest against its pay or work conditions—is the result.

The visa program has evolved over time and places workers in an increasingly precarious position. Rather than working in the IT departments of major U.S. corporations, such as Google or Microsoft, immigrants more commonly find work with subcontracting firms, who hire them out to major corporations needing

---

CHANGES TO H-1B IN 2017

"I now feel I've got to be open to returning to India."

In 2017, following President Donald Trump's immigration initiatives and further restrictions on the H-1B visa program, this is what a frightened anonymous South Asian worker in Silicon Valley told the website *Scroll.in*. "From the point of view of knowledge and skills, I need to be abreast [of] all the latest developments in India so that I will be fully employable there. I am now focusing on two countries instead of one. . . . I feel there's an expiry date to my stay in America that I'm not aware of."

IT personnel. Nicknamed "body shops," these subcontracting firms pay limited wages and enable major industries to avoid investing in personnel and sponsoring immigrants for green cards. These immigrant workers can be laid off when business opportunities for the subcontracting firms run dry.

THE H-4 WIFE

Migrants often arrive with spouses, eager to build their lives. Yet because the H-1B visa holders are legal in the United States only as workers, their rights and opportunities as people are limited. Spouses of H-1B visa holders—who are often wives, given the gendered labor of the IT industry—must acquire an H-4 visa in order to live legally in the United States. Until 2015, however, this visa did not allow the visa holders to work. Because their legal status depends on their connection to the H-1B visa worker, a divorce means that the H-4 holder must return home. Wives with H-4 visas—often college-educated with English fluency and career ambitions—have been put at considerable risk and emotional toil as a result. Dominant patriarchal views portray an Indian American family where a wife must be dutiful and a divorce is viewed as her fault. Women on H-4 visas are more prone to suffer domestic abuse, whether physical, mental, and/or emotional, with often no recourse but to stay in the marriage or be forced to return home, where support from family and

---

THE "MODEL MINORITY" MYTH

The "model minority" myth refers to the harmful idea that certain groups are so successful that they are able to transcend their social status as minorities. This cultural expectation is often placed on Asian Americans, including South Asians, and creates a false narrative that all Asians are smart, wealthy, and hardworking—which in turn is used to argue that Asians are less in need of government assistance and are more deserving of praise than other communities of color.

The myth creates an incorrect perception that Asians not only primarily have jobs as doctors, lawyers, and engineers, but also are "docile" and nonconfrontational people, thus examples of the "model" way to assimilate into American culture. In popular culture and political discourse, this myth is used as a wedge to separate Asian Americans from others, especially Black Americans.

It also ultimately paints a monolithic, easily dismissible portrait of all Asian Americans. In reality, there is no single story of Asian Americans, or even South Asians, since these categories include such a wide variety of people and experiences. In fact, according to a 2018 Pew report, Asian Americans now have the widest income gap of any group in the country: "From 1970 to 2016, the gap in the standard of living between Asians near the top and the bottom of the income ladder nearly doubled, and the distribution of income among Asians transformed from being one of the most equal to being the most unequal among America's major racial and ethnic groups" ("Income Inequality in the U.S. Is Rising Most Rapidly Among Asians").

---

community cannot be taken for granted. As of 2015, H-4 visa holders can seek employment in the United States, but they still must pass through various hoops to do so and, of course, depend on the employer to pursue the proper paperwork.

WHOSE JOB WAS IT?

"Send me your husband's résumé," President Barack Obama said to a middle-aged white woman during a virtual town hall meeting in 2012. She had expressed to him that her U.S.-born and educated (and presumably white) husband could not find employment as a semiconductor engineer, and yet firms were employing immigrants on H-1B visas. The visa program is only to be used when U.S.-born workers cannot be found for the same wages, and a shortage of such talented workers arguably continues to exist.

H-1B visa holders have contributed significantly to the U.S. economy and job growth, and yet, U.S. workers have routinely complained to politicians that employers are undercutting workers and bringing in immigrants at below-market wages. The firms that recently have received the most H-1B visas—like Tata and Infosys—are actually based in India and have offices in the United States. Employees of these firms are contracted out to U.S. companies but rarely become permanent workers. Major corporations benefit handedly from this system.

Moreover, corporations have been caught training H-1B visa workers in the jobs of U.S. workers, with the goal of outsourcing jobs to them in India when they return home—in contrast to the national goals of the H-1B program. Yet, the fact that so many IT positions go unfilled indicates a labor shortage, making the visa program still essential. Politicians are taking notice. Changes and limits to the H-1B visa program have bipartisan political support. Nationalist rhetoric targets undocumented immigration and this visa program as "taking jobs" from U.S. workers. The H-1B has been nicknamed by its critics as the "outsourcing visa."

Capital moves in anticipation of the politics surrounding H-1B visas. Indian-based IT contracting firms with offices in the United States are ready for shrinkages in visa allotments. As capital moves, so do people. Indians are now migrating to Monterrey, Mexico, for instance, as Indian corporations set up shop in locations near the United States. The level of immigration and the rights of those here will continue to fluctuate depending on the (sometimes conflicting) needs of capital and the laws of the United States.

Pawan Dhingra is associate provost and associate dean of the faculty at Amherst College and a professor of American studies.

BANGLADESHI IMMIGRATION

Shweta Majumdar Adur

The modern-day countries of India, Pakistan, and Bangladesh were all a single colony of the British government until their independence in 1947. After independence, the subcontinent was partitioned into two nations, India and Pakistan; the latter consisted of two noncontiguous territories under one state's rule, West and East Pakistan. In 1971, East Pakistan declared a war of liberation and, with India's support, seceded from Pakistan. The newly independent nation is what we now know as Bangladesh.

Therefore, until 1971, there was no separate category in U.S. immigration records to account for migration from Bangladesh. Migrants of Bangladeshi origin were subsumed under the category of "Indian" before 1947 and then "Pakistani" until 1971. There was only a small number of South Asians in the United States before 1965 due to nativist legislations, discriminatory race-based quotas, and explicit bans on migration. For example, the Immigration Act of 1917, alternatively known as the Asiatic Barred Zone Act, excluded all Asians. Yet today, South Asians are among the fastest-growing group of immigrants, and the United States reportedly has the seventh-largest emigrant population from Bangladesh.

Two major acts—the Hart-Celler Act of 1965 and the Diversity Immigrant Visa Program of 1990—reversed the restrictions placed on South Asians, and the two were largely responsible for the migration of Bangladeshis to the United States. The Hart-Celler Act played a decisive role by rescinding race-based bans on migration. The Civil Rights movement that challenged racist policies and the acute

---

A NOTE TO THE READER ABOUT IMMIGRANT GENERATIONS

Terms related to "generations"—from "first generation" to "second generation" to "1.5," "1.25," and even "1.75 generation"—are commonly used in discussions about immigrants and immigrant families. Yet, these terms do not have clear-cut or universally set definitions, and individuals often face much confusion and debate about which term best applies to them. Below, we offer some of the popularly used definitions for these terms, but it is important to remember that no one definition can fully capture an individual's specific life circumstances and experiences. As you read these terms, you may connect with and choose to identify with one or the other, or you may choose not to.

First generation may refer to individuals who were born and raised outside of the United States and who immigrated to the country as adults. Alternatively, it may refer to any foreign-born individual in the United States, regardless of the age they were when they immigrated. Or it may refer more specifically to the first members of a family to acquire citizenship or permanent residency status.

Second generation may refer to individuals who were born in the United States to foreign-born parents and raised within the U.S. Alternatively, it may refer to individuals who were born outside the U.S., but who immigrated with their families when they were young children. Or it may refer to individuals who were born in the country to one foreign-born and one U.S.-born parent.

1.5 generation may refer to individuals who were born and spent a significant amount of time outside of the U.S. before immigrating over as older children or young adults. Other decimal-related terms, such as 1.25 or 1.75 generation, are sometimes used to further specify the amount of time an individual spent living outside of the United States.

---

labor shortage in STEM fields anteceded the landmark act. The first waves of immigrants from Bangladesh were affluent and highly educated professionals, and many among their ranks were fleeing the political turmoil that marked Bangladesh's war of liberation in the seventies. However, their numbers were small, and in 1973, only 154 Bangladeshi immigrants arrived in the United States. It wasn't

IT'S A DAY TO KEEP THE GLASSES ON

Mehrin Masud-Elias departed from Dhaka, Bangladesh, and arrived in Los Angeles, California, in 1993 at the age of 17.

She writes:

> It's been many years, but
> I haven't forgotten the two bags,
> 23 kg each, with dimensions of
> 90cm x 75cm x 43cm,
> including the handle, pockets and wheels.
> What I don't remember are the
> minute choices that decided
> what parts of a young life
> to pack into those bags
> and what to discard on a
> one-way ticket out of home.
> What if I forgot to pack the essentials
> all those years ago?

In SAADA, courtesy of Mehrin Masud-Elias.

until the 1980s that Bangladeshi migration to the United States finally took off; recorded numbers soared to a little more than 5,880, and between 1980 and 2000, the population grew by an impressive 1,469 percent.

The Diversity Immigrant Visa Program of 1990, also called the Diversity Lottery or the Green Card Lottery, has been pivotal in increasing the number of Bangladeshi immigrants in the United States. Established with the aim of diversifying the country's immigrant population, the act annually sanctions fifty-five thousand permanent-resident visas for natives of countries that have low rates of immigration to the United States. It is estimated that between 1996 and 2002, the diversity program accounted for 30.5 percent of Bangladeshi immigrant admission to the United States. Scholars argue that the program was also key to diversifying the demographic profile of Bangladeshi immigrants—while the employment-based provisions for migration had largely favored "highly skilled" professionals, the diversity program enabled migration from less-privileged backgrounds. Along with professional diversity, there was also regional diversity among the Bangladeshis who arrived in the United States, with significant groups from Sylhet, Chittagong, and other parts of Bangladesh. In 2013, however, Bangladesh was deemed ineligible for the Diversity Immigrant Visa Program.

While the Green Card Lottery and employer and family sponsorship have served as the main legal mechanisms propelling Bangladeshi migration to the United States, more recent accounts show the presence of a small but growing group of undocumented migrants from Bangladesh. Due to the recent nature of migration, the overwhelming majority of the Bangladeshi population in the United States is foreign-born, and first-generation immigrants outnumber second-generation. Geographically, they are concentrated in the metropolitan New York area. In New York City, the Bangladeshi population grew dramatically by 42 percent between 2008 and 2011, from 34,237 to 48,677. Bangladeshis are the fastest growing among Asian groups in the city, and immigrants account for 74 percent of this Bangladeshi population. Other large enclaves of Bangladeshis can be found in Detroit, Los Angeles, Miami, Atlanta, and Washington, D.C.

In areas where Bangladeshis have settled, they have created Bengali civic organizations and clubs. The Bangladeshi American Foundation, the Bangladesh Association of America, and the New England Bangladeshi American Foundation are among the notable examples. The majority of Bangladeshis are Muslims, while a small number belong to other religions, such as Hinduism and Buddhism.

Shweta Majumdar Adur (she/her/hers) is an assistant professor of sociology at California State University, Los Angeles.

BHUTANESE REFUGEES

Retika Adhikari

S apana and Khem, with their fifteen-month-old daughter, Lily, landed at Syracuse Hancock International Airport in New York one frigid evening in December 2014. They had flown out of Kathmandu's Tribhuvan International Airport in Nepal approximately thirty-two hours earlier to start their new lives in upstate New York. The couple had tried to fit their entire life's belongings in two black duffle bags weighing exactly twenty kilograms apiece, which was all they were allowed per the luggage policy of the International Organization for Migration (IOM), the organization responsible for bringing refugees to the United States. Children under two were allowed nothing. While packing her bags in Nepal, Sapana wished her daughter Lily was at least two years old.

Sapana and Khem are among the nearly 117,000 Bhutanese refugees who have been resettled in eight countries in the global North, including the United States, by the United Nations Refugee Agency (UNHCR), after almost two decades spent living in refugee camps in Nepal.

Bhutanese nationals from southern Bhutan who have Nepali ancestry and are native Nepali speakers fled Bhutan in the early 1990s as the Bhutanese government implemented policies to create a homogeneous Bhutan. Changes in citizenship laws between 1977 and 1985 made it difficult for Nepali-speaking southern Bhutanese and their families to obtain citizenship in Bhutan. The 1989 cultural policy of "One Nation, One People" promoted the majoritarian Drukpa-Buddhist

Leela Kuikel, a leader of the Bhutanese American Organization–Philadelphia, holds up the flag of Bhutan while sharing the story of his community's exile from that country. Photograph from a SAADA Community Forum event at the Philadelphia History Museum on May 29, 2014; photo by Vivek G. Bharathan.

culture, Dzongkha language, and Drukpa dress code, targeting Nepali-speaking Bhutanese to assimilate; they refused to conform to these new policies, so they were forced to flee. Approximately one hundred thousand Bhutanese refugees temporarily settled in seven refugee camps in eastern Nepal with the hope that they would soon return to Bhutan. But Nepal was embroiled in a decade-long civil war, so the situation was not addressed in a significant way until 2007.

With relative political stability in the country, Nepal appealed to the UNHCR in 2006 to facilitate permanent resettlement of Bhutanese refugees. Several countries in Europe, Australia, New Zealand, and Canada agreed to take in refugees in limited numbers. But the U.S. government offered an unlimited quota for Bhutanese refugee resettlement, and the U.S. emerged as the most popular resettlement destination since 2008. The decade-long resettlement project ended in 2019 with the

United States resettling over ninety-six thousand Bhutanese refugees throughout the country, including the state of Alaska.

Although the U.S. government provides public assistance to refugees for up to eight months from the time of arrival, Bhutanese refugees are encouraged to be self-reliant as soon as possible. Khem, who worked as an elementary school teacher in Nepal, now has a job as an assembly-line worker at a packaging company in up-state New York. He started the job in his fourth month in the U.S. and works night shifts, which start at 11:00 p.m. and end at 7:30 in the morning. He shares that getting adjusted to his new work environment was a challenge. Not only did he have to train himself to stay awake at work, but he also had to endure standing on his feet for eight hours straight. For families who have just arrived, however, working night shifts is more convenient: it frees up their weekdays so they can get to government offices for immigration-related appointments, such as for a thorough medical examination that can take up to several months to complete.

With limited English-language skills and educational credentials that are not recognized in the United States, the majority of Bhutanese refugees, like Khem, start with low-paying jobs. Unlike the popular image of the highly skilled post-1965 South Asian immigrant, Bhutanese refugees are typically low-wage workers who live in urban neighborhoods with few resources. Sapana and Khem experience the United States primarily through interactions with their neighbors who are refugees from Burma, Iraq, and Somalia. The America these families see on TV is not the America they finally inhabit. As Rita, another newly arrived Bhutanese refugee put it, "Landing at New York City's airport really felt like we had arrived. I got goose bumps seeing the jam-packed skyscrapers from above. It looked just like those images we see on TV. But then taking the next plane to Syracuse and driving to the apartment, glitzy New York became remote, worse than the town next to our camp."

The growing Bhutanese refugee community not only signals a shift in the demographic makeup of South Asian America along ethnic and class lines, but also presents a complicated understanding of what it means to be a South Asian immigrant in the United States at this moment.

HARI BHANDARI'S FIRST DAYS

Interviewed by L. D. Dieckmeyer

Hari Bhandari departed from Chandragadhi, Nepal, and arrived in St. Louis, Missouri, in 2011 at the age of 19.

Hari Bhandari (left) in a photo taken in Kathmandu on October 18, 2011. In SAADA, courtesy of Hari Bhandari.

I came from Jhapa, in the east of Nepal. I had been there for twenty years. My entire childhood was spent in one of the seven UN camps for Bhutanese refugees. We came here because we are Bhutanese Nepalis, and the Nepali government didn't give us citizenship, so we came to the USA to work, get an education, and have citizenship for the first time in our lives. I traveled with my mother and my older sister. From our camp to Kathmandu to Paris and New Jersey, we were in a group of nearly 150 other refugees coming for resettlement in the U.S.

The very last thing I did in Nepal was talk to my friends—some of whom went to Australia, Canada, and other cities in the U.S. after I left. Even still, some are waiting in the camps for third-country resettlement. The most important things I brought are my education and my memories. There were so many good and bad things there that let me be grateful now that I am here.

We flew from Paris to New Jersey. In New Jersey, our flight to St. Louis was canceled. We cried a lot, because no one was looking after us to help us make our flight and we didn't know what to do. After waiting for a short time, we got on another flight and finally made it to our destination, St. Louis. When we arrived in St. Louis's Lambert Airport, the first thing I wanted was to meet my family. My uncle was supposed to be at the airport to receive the three of us, but because of catching another flight, no relatives were there. Again I was sad. A caseworker from the International Institute, a refugee resettlement agency, fetched us from the airport. Finally we went to our uncle's house. After three years, we laughed and talked until five in the morning.

When we first came to St. Louis, all the Nepali refugees were celebrating Dashain and Tihar. We went to the park our first Sunday. I was so happy and excited to see all those Nepali people. I never thought that we would meet in the United States. Since I came here from Nepal, I have realized a lot of things. When I first came, traveling was scary and I felt American people did not care for us. Now I know some American people are good and some people aren't, just like all people. Nowadays, I like to be friends with both Nepali and American people. At first, speaking and understanding English here was difficult, though I had studied English in Nepal. Now I am a student and I'm very excited to get my first citizenship in my life. Even though I have to wait for three years, I already finished the citizenship book!

Retika Adhikari (she/her) is the Chancellor's Postdoctoral Research Fellow in the Department of Asian American Studies at the University of Illinois at Urbana-Champaign.

INDO-CARIBBEAN COMMUNITIES AND TWICE MIGRANTS

Nadia Misir

"I was the only Brown guy who walked into the bar. I just wanted to watch the game, but I was told to leave," Edmond Tiwari remembers. He experienced a similar situation at City College when his peers barred him from joining a cultural club for South Asian students. Edmond was not "Indian enough," according to the club's members, because he migrated from Guyana.

Edmond, an Indo-Guyanese, came to the United States to attend college in 1987, when he was eighteen years old. He settled in Richmond Hill, Queens, home to mostly Italian American and Irish Catholic families at the time. Edmond's story provides a window into the history and experiences of the Indo-Caribbean community in the United States.

Indo-Caribbeans trace their ancestry—usually at least four or five generations—back to India. European colonialism and a global appetite for sugar triggered the

Aleah Ranjitsingh shares photos and stories from her family at a SAADA storytelling event at the Queens Public Library in Richmond Hill on October 27, 2018. Photo by Suzanne Mahadeo.

creation of many Indian diasporas across the globe. Britain abolished the slave trade in 1833 and recruited indentured servants from India to work on sugar plantations in the Caribbean. Between 1838 and 1917, more than one million Indian indentured servants traveled by ship to British Guiana, Suriname, Jamaica, Trinidad, Fiji, Mauritius, and other colonies to cut sugarcane. Today, Guyana, Trinidad and Tobago, and Suriname are home to the Caribbean's largest groups of ethnic East Indians. (It is important to remember that East Indians are just one of many ethnic groups in the Caribbean.)

Indo-Caribbeans living in the United States are twice migrants. Though they are of Indian descent, they have migrated from countries other than India. In 1965, the United States passed the Hart-Celler Act, which abolished quotas and allowed immigrants from a wider variety of countries to migrate to the United States. Many Indo-Caribbeans left their homes to permanently settle abroad. This sparked a double diaspora within the Indo-Caribbean community: twice displaced, from India and the Caribbean.

Indo-Caribbeans have settled all over the United States, and there are sizable Indo-Caribbean communities in Florida, Georgia, and Virginia. New York City, however, is home to the largest population of Indo-Caribbeans outside of the Caribbean. Today, Guyanese make up the largest Indo-Caribbean population in New York City. Many Indo-Guyanese left their homes in the 1970s and 1980s, when political and economic conditions in their country worsened. The majority of these migrants and their American-born children, like Edmond Tiwari, live in the Richmond Hill neighborhood of Queens, New York.

Richmond Hill is known to most as Little Guyana. The bustling neighborhood is also home to immigrants from Trinidad and Tobago, India, Ecuador, and the Dominican Republic. Residents pray at Hindu temples, Christian churches, mosques, and gurdwaras. Food and religious and cultural celebrations, such as the annual Phagwah Parade, are important ways members of the community keep in touch with their heritage. Residents can enjoy Caribbean foods and beverages at one of the neighborhood's many roti shops, which have their roots in Indian, African, Chinese, Portuguese, and British cuisine and food culture. Those who practice Hinduism can buy material and cultural attire for religious ceremonies at pooja shops. These shops line Liberty Avenue, the hub of the neighborhood, along with West Indian grocery markets selling fresh fish imported from Guyana, fruits, and vegetables and many restaurants specializing in Guyanese-Chinese cuisine. Cultural organizations, such as the Rajkumari Cultural Center, foster Indo-Caribbean cultural and artistic life in the neighborhood.

Indo-Caribbean migrants and their families have often been misrepresented

---

QUEENS GIRLS

Writing about her experience growing up in Queens in the 1990s, Odessa Despot shares:

> I grew up in Jamaica, Queens, with some of the bravest girls to walk this planet. The girls I knew were quietly fierce and pioneers of the urban landscape. Most lived in heavily populated West Indian communities in Queens (South Ozone, Jamaica, and Richmond Hill), and self-identified as Trinidadian, Guyanese, and, on occasion, East Indian. Most of us knew each other from high school or friends of friends and bonded over the traumas of adolescence, girlhood, boys, parents, immigrant life, becoming American, and a shared experience of marginalization. We came of age together, and redefined teenage rebellion in a quiet, yet powerful way.

From "Queens Girls" for Tides, by Odessa Despot.

In SAADA, courtesy of Odessa Despot.

BERNARD DESPOT'S AND ROSHNI DESPOT'S FIRST DAYS

Interviewed by Odessa Despot

Bernard Despot departed from Port of Spain, Trinidad and Tobago, and arrived in Queens, New York, in 2011 at the age of 36.

My name is Bernard Despot, and I am sixty years old. I am also a citizen of the United States. And I have to say that this did not come easily. I came here in 1989, and I was thirty-eight years old. And I worked very, very hard for everything that I have. But the U.S. has given me that opportunity. I am a resident of Queens, where I have lived all my time here. I have achieved a lot, I have seen my three children go to college, and I myself have gotten my GED. It's all a challenging process, and it's very tough. I worked as a dishwasher, a parking attendant, a bus driver, and now I'm working as a shuttle driver for the Hilton Hotel. I've worked a lot of places to achieve the things that I want, and the successes that I got came with hard work.

When I first came to this country, one of my first memories was of the street vendors selling souvlaki and the gyros. Every Christmas when I get that smell, it brings me right back to my first time in the U.S. I'm about where I should be, I've seen all my children grow up, and I am indebted to a lot of people for the support that has made me who I am. It's really, really wonderful. Some of the bad experiences that I may have had, I have overcome. I remember it snowed, and the snow was very difficult when you have to work. There were times that I missed work and been disciplined because I was not familiar with this climate. Now I can call here home. I still think of Trinidad, but this is where I am, and I'm happy.

—

Roshni Despot departed from Port of Spain, Trinidad and Tobago, and arrived in Queens, New York, in 2011 at the age of 33.

My name is Roshni Despot. I live here in New York City, and I came from Trinidad and Tobago with my three children and my husband. The first few days living in New York was very difficult. . . . We decided to find a job to work and help ourselves and the three children. Having them all here was very hard, and we were doing good as time passed by. New York City, America as a whole, has given us so much. . . . We are very proud to be here in the U.S., very grateful.

There was lots of traffic, and lots of cars, trucks, and buses. A lot to see and a lot to take in. It's totally different from where we came from, but beautiful. We were loving ourselves so much. It was beautiful but a challenge. Those first couple of days, people cooked all the time. I don't think there was as much time to prepare food like back home, but we had lots of pizza and Chinese food, and in between we tried to make home food, like curry chicken, rice, and other things. But then we got used to American dishes. My kids love American food.

I miss our family in Trinidad—we have so much family—and our home that we had to leave behind. It was very, very hard, but we had to leave. I think the kids did very good for themselves. They have accomplished a lot.

COOLIE WOMAN

In 2013, Gaiutra Bahadur published *Coolie Woman: The Odyssey of Indenture*, which tells the story of a young woman who sailed from India to Guiana as a "coolie"— the pejorative British term for indentured laborers who replaced the newly freed slaves on sugar plantations all over the world. That woman, pregnant and alone, thousands of miles from home, was Bahadur's great-grandmother. Bahadur's book not only uncovers her ancestor's story but also paints a picture of the lives of hundreds of thousands of other "coolie women" whose stories had gone largely untold.

In a 2013 interview with the *New York Times' India Ink* blog, Bahadur explained her reasoning for using the term "coolie" in the title of her book.

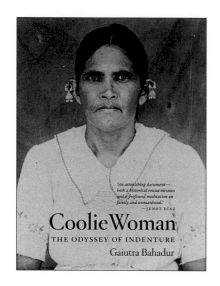

Q. You've chosen a term some might consider pejorative as the title of your book. Why did you take that risk?

A. I took the risk because I think the title captures perfectly the burdens shouldered by the women whose stories I tell. The word "coolie," coming from the Tamil for "wages," was originally a neutral term for porters paid to carry loads at docks or baggage at railway stations in the subcontinent. Then it gained the stigma of a new form of slavery, when the British imperial bureaucracy used it as their term for the indentured laborers on plantations across the globe. In the West Indies, it became even sharper edged, an ethnic slur really, used to describe any Indian, indentured or not, plantation worker or not. The word "coolie" is the right one to use because it carries the history of colonialism on its shoulders, and the title "coolie woman" is the right one because Indian women in the Caribbean did too. They had to fulfill the needs and desires of both Indian men and British men. They carried the weight of expectations: that they maintain a transplanted culture, that they represent its honor, that they hold families together.

in the media. Ray Cavanaugh, in an article for the *Washington Post*, described how he stumbled upon Little Guyana after falling asleep on the A train and missing his stop: "Nobody told me about Little Guyana, a mile-plus-long stretch in the Richmond Hill neighborhood of Queens where the residents are Indian but sound like Bob Marley when they speak." His words are indicative of a certain ignorance surrounding Indo-Caribbean culture and the community's visibility in popular culture today. The physical and psychological distance Indo-Caribbeans experience in regard to their Indian heritage and roots continues to influence members of this community and how they choose to identify.

THE STATE OF STATELESSNESS

In August 1972, General Idi Amin Dada, then president of Uganda, completely transformed the lives of Ugandan Asians with a single pronouncement. Claiming to have been inspired by a godly directive in a dream, Amin ordered the expulsion of the Asian minority in Uganda. Made stateless, Ugandan Asians traveled to the United Kingdom, Australia, Canada, and the United States in search of new homes. Days before Amin's edict, Peter Nazareth published In a Brown Mantle *(1972), a novel that predicted with striking accuracy the rise of an Amin-like figure and his decision to expel the Asian minority. While this expulsion remains one of the most dramatic illustrations of anti-Indian sentiment, it was not by any means the only one for its time or the last one in recorded history.*

Almost ten thousand miles away, the expulsion of Ugandan Asians created tremors for the Indian community on the island of Fiji, where the Fiji Times published letters from readers applauding Amin's actions. That very year, Viliame Savu's Fijian Independent Party insisted that indigenous Fijians alone should "decide the destiny of their land." Three years later, the founder of the Fijian Nationalist Party, Sakiasi Butadroka, made a motion in Parliament for the repatriation of Indo-Fijians to India. Since then, Fiji has experienced four separate coups, all of which have been connected, explicitly or implicitly, to the fault line between Indo-Fijians and indigenous Fijians.

Slightly more than five thousand miles away, the nativist language of the Fijian political landscape and the statelessness of Ugandan Asians had already coalesced in the condition of Malaysian Indians. In 1969, in the aftermath of its most violent race riots, the Malaysian government, dominated by ethnic Malays, announced that all noncitizens would have to apply for work permits. However, according to Chandra Muzaffar, this announcement largely "affected Indians in the main, since thousands of them, especially plantation laborers, were actually stateless." Sequestered away on self-contained rubber and oil plantations, many Indians had simply failed to become citizens although they were born and raised on Malaysian soil.

These are only three of several examples in which diasporic Indians in former British colonies found themselves grappling with the realities of being on the verge of statelessness, or being excised from the postcolonial nation-state.

From "The State of Statelessness" for Tides, *by Dashini Jeyathurai.*

"I'm predominantly Indian, but also mixed from being from the Caribbean. I'm proud of my mixes. I tell people the best way I can explain myself is by my food: rice, beans, curry, dhalpuri, plantain," says Padmini Naidu, a podcast host and Guyanese American living in New York. Naidu's words illuminate the nature of living between multiple histories, places, and cultures.

Nadia Misir is a writer from South Ozone Park, Queens.

CHAPTER 4

Post-9/11

Courtesy of Desis Rising Up and Moving (DRUM).

INTRODUCTION

Rajini Srikanth

Following the attacks on the World Trade Center buildings on September 11, 2001, the United States went to war—with groups inside, and outside, its borders. And it is still at war, perpetually on high alert, refusing to trust particular communities within the country and refusing to take in others fleeing the horrors of violence and poverty in various parts of the world. The six contributors in this section expose the painful experiences of those groups in the United States who became the target of the country's suspicion and misplaced wrath following the attacks of September 11. At this moment, it is hard not to feel that the United States is becoming a more hostile nation, a crueler nation, and an increasingly arrogant and self-righteous nation. However, if we read carefully the pieces in this section, if we respond to the powerful emotions expressed in them, and if we open our hearts to the experiences they portray, we may gain the insights that will enable us to rescue the United States from being a country filled with anger and hate.

Like all democracies, the United States is a work in progress, undergoing revision, still in the process of moving toward its envisioned ideal form. In Valarie Kaur's essay, she offers a compelling image of the United States as still waiting to be born. The nation is pushing and straining to emerge, she says. A democracy, by its very nature, is an imperfect and messy endeavor. Ideas and desires are continuously being examined, contested, evaluated, and considered for how they may affect the lives of people of different ages, abilities, genders, sexual orientations, races, and religions. To be a true democracy, a country must see itself as continually moving toward "perfection," desiring its achievement but knowing that it can never be reached.

There is danger in a country that feels it has achieved perfection or come close to it, because this sentiment stops a country from examining itself and being alert to its mistakes. Paradoxically, a nation that believes itself to be "the best" is seldom so, because such a country ceases to consider whether its policies are harmful to particular groups inside and outside its borders. Typically the groups within a country who have power, who have institutions and laws organized for their benefit, see no reason to question whether these arrangements are good or bad for other, less powerful groups.

The historian Gary Y. Okihiro, in his book *Margins and Mainstreams: Asians in American History and Culture*, eloquently points out that it is the marginalized groups within the United States who have forced it to live up to its own self-proclaimed ideals. He observes:

> The core values and ideals of the nation emanate not from the mainstream but from the margins—from among Asian and African Americans, Latinos and American Indians, women, and gays and lesbians. In their struggles for equality, these groups have helped preserve and advance the principles and ideals of democracy and have thereby made America a freer place for all.

The challenges and resistances mounted by marginalized groups throughout the history of the United States have saved the country from its own ethical destruction. These groups have courageously refused to succumb to unjust power, unjust laws, unjust practices; they have refused to be defeated by despair; they have refused to become victims. The deep promise that is "America" lives in the fierce resilience exhibited by the people described in the essays of this section.

After the horrific attacks of September 11, 2001, individuals of Arab and South Asian descent and those who are Muslim were kept under constant watch. The excerpt from Marina Budhos's novel *Watched* reminds us of the psychological toll that state surveillance can take on individuals and communities. Groups under scrutiny are expected to be perfect citizens and residents, threatened with dire consequences if they stray from this prescribed path. There is no script for how you should behave, and even when you follow what you think might be the script, the person or the institution in power can suddenly change the expectations or misinterpret your performance.

We get a glimpse of this danger in Imran Siddiquee's narration of their encounter with law enforcement soon after the attacks of September 11, 2001. Will Imran and their brother, who is sleeping in the back seat of the car when they are pulled over, lose their lives? What is the tone Imran should adopt? How slowly should they move to get out their license? Should they make eye contact or not? Should they smile or not? Just what are the rules of engagement on this highway, a place that could be as dangerous as a battle zone, where you could become a statistic—killed for resisting arrest, killed for making a quick move, killed because your sleeping brother in the back seat wakes up and, disoriented, makes a move that the police officer outside your car construes as dangerous? The power lies completely with the police officer; he can do with it what he wishes.

As we have seen for the past several years with sickening regularity, agents of the state have full latitude to construct narratives that present them as threatened and therefore justified in using deadly force. From the streets of cities like Sacramento, Minneapolis, Ferguson, and New York to the mountains of Afghanistan, soldiers and other figures who are portrayed as working for the nation's safety and security can wield their force indiscriminately upon those whom they suspect of being dangerous. The flimsiest fragment of information can become indisputable evidence of guilt, as Anant Raut's essay reveals. Innocent shepherds and merchants from Afghanistan became decades-long prisoners at one of the harshest prison facilities run by the United States: the prison camp at Guantánamo Bay, Cuba. Were it not for lawyers like Raut, the majority of the 750-plus Muslim men who were brought there from Afghanistan would have died there. Several of them did take their own lives by refusing food. Despite the seemingly insurmountable legal and political difficulties faced by the detainees, their lawyers would not give up and secured the release or transfer of several hundreds of detainees. These lawyers were determined that the United States would live up to the principles of its own Constitution. By February 2018, the number of detainees at Guantánamo was down to forty-one.

In 1968, the Third World Liberation Front strikes by California students put education at the center of creating a consciousness of liberation and solidarity. The students, inspired by the education minister of the Black Panther Party, George Murray, demanded a curriculum that highlighted their experiences as Black, Chicano, Asian, and Native peoples in the United States. Education, they underscored, was a significant instrument of social justice and social change. The upheavals unleashed by the Civil Rights movement and the anti-war protests against the U.S. involvement in Vietnam created the unstable terrain for the students to reimagine the conditions under which national and global society could be organized. Thus, the classroom, at least at the college level, became seen as a space where a person could dismantle traditional modes of conceiving their role within the body politic of the nation and the global community. Students demanded the rejection of old master narratives; they called for new narratives of solidarity, anti-racism, and anti-imperialism. In Samina Najmi's essay, we read how, in the post-9/11 period, an elementary school teacher passed up a rich opportunity to teach her students about the vibrant mix of religious faiths in the United States. Knowledge for this teacher had to come safely packaged. She was not prepared to help her students understand its transformative power.

Deepa Iyer's essay reminds us that we are all part of the fabric of the United States. Though skin color, religious affiliation, and comfort with languages other than English might mark South Asians as potential threats, Iyer states emphatically that there is a richer, more expansive vision of the United States. And it is up to those groups who are profiled, targeted, and surveilled to counter the xenophobic practices that diminish the idea of America.

Thus far, the United States has written only one apology letter—to the surviving internees of the shameful period of Japanese American incarceration. The unwritten letters of apology are many: for Native American genocide; for slavery; for lynchings; for Hiroshima and Nagasaki; for segregation; for McCarthyism; for the existence of the prison facility at Guantánamo Bay; for the invasion of Iraq; for the victims of gun violence; for the unjustly imprisoned; for drone attacks; for unconditional support of Israel; for turning back children from Central America seeking asylum; for refusing to take in Syrian refugees. How does a nation seek forgiveness, and how does a nation begin to repair the many wrongs it has done? The essays in this section describe the injuries committed by the United States after the attacks of 9/11, and they gesture to the impressive ways in which the injured and the wronged, through the depths of despair, challenge the country to work toward its noblest aspirations.

Rajini Srikanth (she/her) is a professor of English and dean of the Honors College at UMass Boston.

THE POST-9/11 BACKLASH
AND RESPONSE

Deepa Iyer

O n September 11, 2001, our nation witnessed devastating acts of terrorism, which resulted in the deaths of more than three thousand people. In the hours and days that followed, Americans around the country grieved for the innocent lives that had so cruelly been cut short. But South Asians, Arabs, Muslims, Hindus, and Sikhs endured a double grieving after 9/11, as community members began to experience acts of discrimination, violence, and profiling. This post-9/11 backlash occurred because some members of the American public, the media, and government agencies assumed that we are more likely to commit terrorist acts simply because we come from countries in the Middle East and South Asia, or because we are Muslim or perceived to be Muslim.

Unfortunately, the backlash was not limited to the years immediately after 9/11. In 2012, the Sikh Temple of Wisconsin became a site of horrific violence when a

A candlelight vigil held on August 6, 2012, at the Palatine Gurdwara in Illinois in remembrance of the victims of the mass shooting at the Sikh Temple of Wisconsin. Photo by Ramona Gupta.

white supremacist killed six worshippers on a Sunday morning. In 2015, a young Black Muslim boy by the name of Ahmed Mohamed was placed in juvenile detention after school administrators in Irving, Texas, assumed that a homemade clock Ahmed had made as a science experiment was a bomb. In 2016, South Asian, Arab, and Muslim passengers reported being removed from airplanes because airline personnel or fellow travelers complained that they behaved "suspiciously" by speaking in Arabic on the phone or wearing a hijab and asking to change seats. And in the time since Donald Trump was elected, hate crimes against these groups have continued to grow.

This climate of fear and suspicion has been worsened by government policies and practices that target our communities. For example, the Associated Press reported in 2009 that the New York Police Department's Demographics Unit sent undercover police officers to monitor activities at mosques, cricket and soccer games played by South Asians and Arabs in public parks, and restaurants owned or frequented by members of South Asian, Muslim, and Arab communities. These practices of surveillance and profiling (assuming that people are inclined to commit criminal activity simply based on their race, faith, or immigration status) have taken a heavy toll on our communities and damaged relationships with law enforcement agencies.

But the post-9/11 backlash also mobilized our communities to speak up, to organize, and to build our power. For example, many individuals decided to assert their civil rights—such as Sikh and Muslim students who face routine harassment and bullying in schools, like being called "terrorist" or "ISIS" and even having their turbans or hijabs pulled off. In addition, many activists and community members began building organizations to respond to the crises facing South Asians, Muslims, Arabs, and Sikhs. In the wake of 9/11, organizations such as South Asian Americans Leading Together (SAALT), the Sikh Coalition, and Muslim Advocates

---

DRUM AND THE NCSO

Founded in 2000, DRUM (also known as "Desis Rising Up and Moving") is a membership-led organization made up of low-wage South Asian and Indo-Caribbean immigrant workers and youth in New York City. DRUM focuses on mobilizing and building the leadership of its membership to lead social and policy change that impacts their own lives—from immigrant rights and education reform to civil rights and workers' justice. DRUM is multigenerational and aims to represent the diaspora of the South Asian community—Afghanistan, Bangladesh, Bhutan, Guyana, India, Nepal, Pakistan, Sri Lanka, Suriname, Trinidad and Tobago, and beyond.

DRUM is also a member of the National Coalition of South Asian Organizations (NCSO), a network of community-based organizations that believe in common principles related to social change and that provide services to, work with, convene, organize, and advocate for South Asians in the United States. South Asian Americans Leading Together (SAALT) currently coordinates the NCSO.

DRUM (Desis Rising Up and Moving) newsletter, published July 2001. Articles include "Race Riots in Britain," "When Rich Bhatia Exploits, Domestic Workers Organize," and other articles related to organizing in the South Asian diaspora. Courtesy of Desis Rising Up and Moving (DRUM).

LAVAAN BY ZAIN ALAM

In 2017, musician Zain Alam participated in SAADA's "Where We Belong: Artists in the Archive" project, an initiative where artists used SAADA's collections—photographs, videos, letters, and publications that date all the way back to the late 1800s—to create works that bring to life histories often overlooked by other cultural heritage institutions. As one of five artists selected for the project, Alam chose to edit together the silent home videos of Sharanjit Singh Dhillonn, which show him and his family living in Norman, Oklahoma, in the 1950s and '60s. Alam also composed a new song to go along with the footage, and in an interview with Public Radio International, he described how the videos, including one that shows Dhillonn's 1959 wedding to a white woman named Dorothy, inspired the creation of *Lavaan*.

Zain Alam presents Lavaan *at SAADA's "Where We Belong: Artists in the Archive" symposium at the Historical Society of Pennsylvania on April 8, 2017. Photo by Mohammad Azim Siddiqui.*

Alam researched Sikh wedding traditions and learned about the prayers and songs, called lavaan, that are recited at Sikh ceremonies. . . .

"Like many people with home videos, once they had kids, [Sharanjit] took lots of footage of his children learning to walk for the first time, falling down and getting back up," says Alam. "And at first, I thought, 'Oh God, why are they recording this so many times? Why isn't there more footage of the wedding?'"

But eventually, Alam grew fond of these everyday scenes. He juxtaposed the images of the kids falling with images of television headlines reporting hate crimes against the Sikhs in America that keep coming back in the news, again and again.

"There's a moment in the video where the footage goes from color to black and white, the Sikh prayer fades out, there are these sorrowful bells, and you see that the father's hair has been cut off," says Alam. "And it turned out that [Sharanjit] got rid of his hair and beard because he was attacked at a gas station in Oklahoma."

According to an oral history from Dorothy and Bibi Dhillonn, the gas station owner refused to help Sharanjit or call the police after the attack. The biographical sketch accompanying the footage donated to SAADA describes how Sharanjit cried when he cut off his hair. He did it only because he felt unsafe and that his turban was making it difficult for him to find work.

"To me, the greater narrative of learning to walk, getting up and falling back down again connected heavily with present moments where the Sikh community has been targeted since 9/11," says Alam.

From "Why This Musician Wants to Understand Xenophobia Today by Remembering the Past" for The World, *by Ada Tseng.*

began taking shape to be leading national voices on issues ranging from discrimination to profiling. At the local level, organizers and advocates at DRUM–South Asian Organizing Center (New York City), Chhaya CDC (New York City), the Arab American Association of New York, the South Asian Network (Los Angeles), the Arab American Action Network (Chicago), and many others sprang into action to address the evolving needs of community members.

For many years after 9/11, South Asian, Arab, Muslim, and Sikh nonprofit organizations have existed in a cycle of crisis response, pivoting to the range of needs presented by clients and community members while also advocating against harmful government policies and divisive public narratives. And while our communities are no longer just "post-9/11 communities," we continue to face hate violence, surveillance, and xenophobic political rhetoric. How we unite to confront these challenges and create more inclusive and multiracial communities will shape our future in the years ahead.

Deepa Iyer is a South Asian American writer, strategist, lawyer, and racial justice advocate.

WATCHED

Marina Budhos

In 2006, I published *Ask Me No Questions*, a novel about an undocumented Bangladeshi family snared in a post-9/11 crackdown. Many asked me if I was going to write a sequel to the novel. Yet I didn't want to; I wanted to leave the story open-ended, much like the lives of many undocumented immigrants. I didn't want to give answers; I wanted to prompt questions and conversations.

I then began to see the next beat in the story: surveillance. If *Ask Me No Questions* was about being invisible in the immediate aftermath of 9/11, *Watched* is about being too visible in a world saturated in watching. And I wanted to explore this issue close-up, seen through the eyes of a teenager. *Watched* follows the story of Naeem, a Bangladeshi high schooler in Jackson Heights, Queens. He's an eternal procrastinator, hoping he can charm his way through life, until mistakes catch up with him and the cops offer a dark deal.

A HISTORY OF SURVEILLANCE

In his 2018 essay for *Tides* magazine, "Bhagat Singh Thind in Jail," Philip Deslippe explores the life of Thind beyond his famous battle for citizenship in the Supreme Court, which included being surveilled for the rest of his life, leading up to his 1942 arrest in Nebraska for "operating as an unregistered spiritualist minister."

Almost as soon as South Asians arrived in the United States in significant numbers at the turn of the century, the British were concerned with the threat that their political organizing in America posed to colonial rule in India. Coordinated efforts between the British, Canadian, and American governments across three continents covertly monitored Indians in the United States, tightened borders and immigration, and repressed political activity. British surveillance of South Asians in the United States continued through the interwar decades and was not limited to political activists and organizers. Swamis, yogis, and metaphysical teachers were also a surprisingly serious concern for British Intelligence, who gathered information and kept files on many of them, and noted with uneasiness that these charismatic figures exercised a significant form of soft power as they spoke to American audiences in one city after another and generated sympathy for India and Indian self-rule.

Thind was a combination of each kind of figure that worried the British: he was involved with the political movement for Indian independence, he led the most visible case for South Asians to gain American citizenship, and he was one of the dozens of travelling lecturers that crisscrossed the country. Perhaps more than nearly anyone else, Thind was aware of the extent to which the British government monitored South Asians in the United States. There are existing records of over a quarter-century of covert British surveillance of Thind by the time of his arrest in Nebraska, starting with his involvement with the Ghadar Party in Oregon in 1916. He consistently appears in British Intelligence lists of "Indian Extremists" and he was referred to in one letter as "the notorious Indian seditionist." There are reports from agents who provided detailed

Dr. B. S. Thind . . . Towel for a turban, mush for breakfast.

Fruitarian Spirit Teacher Dines on Bologna in Jail

Thind in prison, from the Omaha World-Herald, July 2, 1942.

descriptions of Thind's movements and associations, attended his speeches, and dutifully collected his promotional materials in cities such as Detroit, St. Louis, and, in 1926, sixteen years before his arrest, Omaha, Nebraska.

From "Bhagat Singh Thind in Jail" for Tides, *by Philip Deslippe.*

I'm fascinated with how surveillance feels from the inside: how does a young man, searching for his identity, for heroes, learn how to be in the world, when he senses that his every move is tracked? What does it mean to always be watched? How, as a young person, does he make an identity for himself when he is often seen as a suspect? And what happens when he's offered a chance to remake his life and be on the other side—to become the watcher, someone who has the power to see into other lives, and perhaps change his own?

The writing of the book proved to be more challenging than I anticipated, as I

THE WEEK AFTER 9/11

According to a 2001 SAALT report, there were 645 bias incidents between September 12 and September 17, 2001, directed at South Asians and Arab Americans. This included the September 15 hate-crime killing of Balbir Singh Sodhi at a gas station in Arizona. The report states:

The backlash took the form of racial jokes made in the workplace, verbal harassment in the streets, phone threats to individuals in their homes, property damage and violence at places of worship, and tragically, the shooting deaths of several individuals.

As a result, many members of Middle Eastern and South Asian communities reported that they were frightened to leave their homes, attend work or school, or practice their religions for fear that they would be the targets of discrimination or attacks.

America became less free.

Find the full report, "American Backlash: Terrorists Bring War Home in More Ways than One," at saalt.org.

---

was buffeted by painful headlines—the terrorist attacks in Paris, sting operations and further attacks in the United States, and the rise of ISIS and its slick recruitment of young people. In the end, though, my aim is to tell the human story behind the headlines: the complicated choices and pressures teenagers—especially Muslim teenagers—face when their world is so riven and made precarious by violence, extremism, intolerance, and mistrust.

Here is an excerpt from *Watched*:

The watching, it seeps into everything in our neighborhood. It's like weather, the barometric pressure lowering. Before the monsoons came in Bangladesh, you could feel the air thicken and squat on your head. A constant ache behind your eyeballs.

For the past few years there's been another kind of pressure: a vibration around us, the air pressing down, muffling our mouths. We see the men, coming down the metal stairs from the elevated subway, or parked in cars for hours on end: clean-cut guys, creased khakis, rolled-up sleeves. The breath of Manhattan steaming off their clothes. They aren't from around here—that we can tell. Not like the young couples with their big padded strollers. Or the girls with peacoats and holes in their black tights, who moved to the nice part of Jackson Heights, carry yoga mats in cloth bags from stores I've never heard of. No, these people are different. They stroll into stores, finger the edges of the newspapers in their racks, check out flyers taped to the side of the fridge.

One day two of them came into my parents' store, pretended to buy some gum, and then asked a few questions about the travel agency upstairs. *Where is the man who runs the place? Mr. Ahmed? How often does he come in? Does he stay after hours?*

Abba shook his head. "I do not watch my neighbor so much. He is from Pakistan, that is all I know."

"Yet you hold packages for him?"

"Yes, but that is because they are not open all the time. It is favor."

The man consulted a tiny notebook. "You attend the same mosque? Al-Noor Masjid?"

At this, Abba froze, fingers resting light on the register, staring at the door. "No, we are praying at different place." It hurt my heart, hearing this. Abba's English, when he spoke to strangers, was halting, yet proper. He'd studied some English in Bangladesh and hated sounding uneducated to Americans.

"Abba?" I whispered after the detectives left, and touched his arm. "You okay?"

He stirred and blinked. "I am fine." But his voice was rough at the edges.

It's his accepting, his hemmed-in air, his giving up that makes me crazy. The way he makes that sad gargling noise at the back of his throat, just stands here, rocking on his shoes. Or shuffles to the back of the store to pray. Lets those men scare him. *It's in Allah's hands. Nothing more to do,* he says.

Fight them! I want to cry. *Fight me!*

But he doesn't. He's too tired. Tired of his own years, first doing construction in Dubai, then in Brooklyn, long days up on the scaffolding scraping cement, a new wife and son, now the store, where every month he and my stepmother lean their heads together, write the rent check. *One more month*, he sighs. *Then maybe we close up.*

"I gotta go, Abba," I said, standing beside him now. I pointed to my backpack, as if to prove myself.

He just turned his face away.

Marina Budhos (she/her) is an author of several books of fiction and nonfiction and a professor of English at William Paterson University.

HIDING OSAMA BIN LADEN

Samina Najmi

"Mama," says eleven-year-old Maya one evening in May 2011, "some kids in my class asked me if my family had helped to hide Osama bin Laden."

Hmmmm.

It's true that I'm from Pakistan and that my parents still live there—not way up north among the frosty mountains in Abbottabad, where bin Laden has just been killed, but way down south by the balmy Indian Ocean, in Karachi. I also realize that given the scant distinction that elementary school children make between public and personal conversation, my background and my parents' whereabouts must be common knowledge among Maya's classmates. But playing host to Osama bin Laden—*really?*

Maya looks up from her social studies homework with tentative eyes. Ten years flash by me in one indistinguishable moment. Maya was a toddler when the terrorist attacks of September 11 happened. She had learned to walk the earth in Taunton, Massachusetts, barely three months earlier. I mourned the deaths and destruction at Ground Zero while she rummaged through the kitchen cupboards and built towers out of Tupperware. Then I mourned the backlash against people of Muslim background, like me, while she closed her dark, pondering eyes to lullabies my grandmother once sang to me in Urdu. My childhood a spliced narrative of Pakistan and England, I thought I had finally found belonging in America. But the backlash told me that 9/11 was not my tragedy to grieve. It rendered me homeless in the world, even as Taunton gave Maya gravity, and introduced her to the cloud shapes above and the woodbine below.

And while the world seemed to take leave of its senses, while we razed Afghanistan that October in order to kill one Saudi man responsible for our national tragedy, I was about to bring an American boy-child into the world.

Cyrus was born five months after 9/11, when Maya was twenty-one months old. He learned to roll over on the rug, then crawl, and speak his own first words as the official rhetoric regarding Saddam Hussein's weapons of mass destruction gathered momentum and spread like a pernicious gas. The week Cyrus took his first independent steps in Taunton, we invaded Iraq.

By August of that year, I had bowed out of adjunct teaching as an English professor, scooped up my two young children, and left for Pakistan. Five months later, I returned with them to Taunton with the knowledge that the only text I could hold sacred was the American Constitution—that I could trust it in a way that I couldn't trust governments or public opinion anywhere. Even if we warred with two Muslim countries simultaneously, America would give me the space to raise my children as I wished: as secular Americans, invested in civil rights for all.

And secular they most certainly have been—for the most part. We began to celebrate the Muslim holiday of Eid when we realized that we would be decorating Christmas trees and conducting Easter egg hunts because our children enjoyed them. That was when our secularity took the form of embracing a plurality of holidays. Other than that, my children's lack of religious indoctrination has taken even me by surprise. One year, shortly after our move to Fresno, California, Eid

coincided with Rosh Hashanah, so
a Jewish friend, Toni, and I made a
joint presentation on the two holidays for the children in Maya and
Cyrus's elementary school.

"Who knows the story of Adam
and Eve?" Toni asked.

All the children raised their
hands—all except Maya and Cyrus.
My children had never heard of
Adam and Eve! That was the point
at which we decided to include
creation stories and diverse rituals
of prayer and fasting in our reper-
toire of narratives aimed at raising
our children as culturally literate
Americans.

Courtesy of Desis Rising Up and Moving (DRUM).

Yet, for all our attempts to provide our children with a multiplicity of narratives
to grow up on, the years since 9/11 have presented them with narrow choices that
render our own parental philosophies irrelevant. Today, I realize with a shock what
I thought I knew: that Maya and Cyrus have no memory of a pre-9/11 America. This
means they have never lived in a world in which Muslims have not been hypervis-
ible. They are growing up in an age that makes no distinction between "Muslim"
(follower of a faith) and "Islamist" (adherent of a political ideology) but collapses
fundamentalist, moderate, and secular "Muslims" into one undifferentiated mass.
Perhaps it is because Maya takes such a world for granted—as I who do have memory of a pre-9/11 America cannot—that she appears so uncannily vigilant for her
years. In 2008, during the heady time of hope in Barack Obama's candidacy, my
children had planted "Obama for President" signs among the cypress trees of our
front yard in Fresno. But when, during a televised presidential debate with John
McCain in early 2008, Obama asserted the need for greater military intervention

in Afghanistan and Pakistan, Maya—not quite eight years old, and flitting within earshot—stormed out of the room, exclaiming: "He wants to terrorize Pakistan! I'm voting for McCain."

Fresno, where Maya has been living since she was six years old, forms a pocket of Christian conservatism smack-dab in the center of California. In 2010, at the beginning of Maya's fifth-grade year, the repeated attacks on a mosque in nearby

---

BULLYING IN SCHOOLS

According to the federal government, 28 percent of students in sixth through twelfth grade have experienced bullying. But the Sikh Coalition reported that up to two-thirds, or 67 percent, of Sikh American students report being bullied. The playground has always been a more fraught place in America for students of color, but in the week after September 11, the cloud of fear in the country engulfed South Asian, Muslim, and Arab American youth in new ways.

For instance, on the same day that Balbir Singh Sodhi was killed in Arizona, California's *North County Times* reported that a sixteen-year-old Pakistani student at Escondido High School was told by her classmate that she looked "like a terrorist," while multiple schools in Jefferson Parish, Louisiana, were shut down after students of Middle Eastern origin were heavily taunted by classmates. A 2001 report by SAALT features dozens of these stories of bullying and hate in schools that week.

Read the reports "Hate Crimes: A Community-Wide Impact" and "American Backlash: Terrorists Bring War Home in More Ways than One" at saalt.org. Read "Go Home, Terrorist: A Report on Bullying against Sikh American School Children" at sikhcoalition.org.

Madera led to conversations in her classroom. Some explained the attacks as a reaction to the ill-advised plan to build a mosque two blocks from Ground Zero. Maya, finding herself a lone "representative Muslim" in class, asserted that the 9/11 terrorists were not really Muslims, only pretending to be. (She had heard my devout father say that the hijackers were not "true" Muslims and took that literally to mean that they were imposters.) Before the conversation could go any further, her teacher, a reasonable woman with brilliant blue eyes, declared: "I live in California, not New York, and school is not the place to discuss politics." And so the shiny gold coin of a potential learning moment, in which thirty-two young people might have pondered the sanctity of civil rights for all Americans, rolled away and was buried in the cracks of the fifth-grade curriculum.

"Hiding Osama bin Laden, huh? So what did you tell them?" I ask my daughter.

Maya chews on her pencil. "I told them that just because Osama bin Laden was found in Pakistan doesn't mean he was Pakistani," she says, her eyes soft with amusement.

Whew, I think. She doesn't seem ruffled. She isn't about to conflate her love of Pakistan, and of her grandparents' home, with religious affiliation. I imagine my parents rolling out the red carpet for Osama bin Laden, on and on for five years, and chuckle.

A week later, I've tucked Maya and Cyrus into bed, made myself a ritual cup of Ovaltine, and turned on the reading lamp by my night table when I notice Maya's slender body framed in the doorway to my room.

"Not sleepy, honey?" I ask.

Maya walks across the room and sits on the bed beside me. Her small hand rests on mine.

"Mama," she says, gentle as a baby bird, "I'd like to keep the Muslim fast this Ramadan."

Samina Najmi (she/her/hers) is a professor of English at California State University, Fresno.

THE PAIN OF OTHERS

Imran Siddiquee

Soon after a few brown-skinned men attacked the Twin Towers in 2001, my brother and I were sitting in a white Mazda 626, pulled over on the side of the road. I was in the driver's seat. We had been out that morning because it was the day after Thanksgiving, and we had an annual tradition of waking up very early to try and snag a deal at one of the electronic megastores. Waiting in line for a DVD, a video game, or maybe a CD—it was one of the highlights of what was then my favorite holiday of the year in Springfield, Illinois.

We were headed home from Best Buy, empty-handed, after dropping off two other Bangladeshi American kids who had accompanied us at the crack of dawn. The excitement had dissipated a bit, and the reality of all the food we had eaten the night before was making me long for bed. In fact, my brother was actually lying down in the back seat of the car. He stayed asleep even after the officer knocked on my window.

Ironically, he had pulled us over on the road directly in front of Best Buy. I could still see it from where we were stopped. The whole morning started to feel like a huge waste. In addition to not sleeping much the night before, I hadn't trimmed my beard in a few days, and I felt the weight of both of those decisions as I rolled the window down. Did I look scary? Should I make sure to smile?

The officer eyed me for a moment before gesturing toward the back seat. "What's with him?" I explained that my brother was asleep and that we had been up early, but he wasn't really listening to me and abruptly demanded that I wake him up.

So I carefully turned and nudged my brother. He didn't respond. I perhaps never hated and loved him more at the same time. I was afraid of what the cop might

---

BLACK LIVES MATTER

Watching grainy videos of police officers pulling over Black Americans, often resulting in life-ending violence, is a fixture of modern American life. Raising public awareness of this kind of police brutality directed at Black Americans and other people of color is a goal Black activists have been organizing toward for decades. The heightened awareness seen in the last decade can be credited to the work of the Black Lives Matter movement, which sprang up in 2013 to "eradicate white supremacy and build local power to intervene in violence inflicted on Black communities by the state and vigilantes."

According to the movement's official website in 2021:

> In 2013, three radical Black organizers—Alicia Garza, Patrisse Cullors, and Opal Tometi—created a Black-centered political will and movement building project called #BlackLives-Matter. It was in response to the acquittal of Trayvon Martin's murderer, George Zimmerman.

> The project is now a member-led global network of more than 40 chapters. Our members organize and build local power to intervene in violence inflicted on Black communities by the state and vigilantes.

> Black Lives Matter is an ideological and political intervention in a world where Black lives are systematically and intentionally targeted for demise. It is an affirmation of Black folks' humanity, our contributions to this society, and our resilience in the face of deadly oppression.

The murder of George Floyd by a Minneapolis police officer on May 25, 2020, further forced Americans to confront systemic anti-Blackness and sparked protests in cities across the United States and around the globe.

---

do if I couldn't wake him quickly, and just as afraid of what might happen after I did. In that moment I recalled all the stories of racism in America that I'd heard since I was a kid, but especially the stories of growing anti-Muslim sentiment in the country. I thought about the bullies at school when I was younger, and the one who recently called me "Osama."

Eventually my brother did rattle awake, and I told him to sit up straight. The officer gave me a ticket for a seat belt violation, and then warned me to "be more careful." I'll never know if we were targeted because of my beard, or if it was just a regular

---

ISLAMOPHOBIA

The targeting of South Asian, Arab American, Sikh, and Muslim communities did not begin or end with the post-9/11 backlash. In 1995, after the Oklahoma City bombing, mosques across the country—including the Springfield mosque in Imran Siddiquee's story—experienced a wave of arson attacks. Much of this Islamophobia was the result of early news reports speculating that "Islamic fundamentalists" had carried out the Oklahoma City bombing, even though Timothy J. McVeigh and Terry L. Nichols, the perpetrators, were both white non-Muslims. According to a *New York Times* article from August 28, 1995, "In the three days after the Oklahoma City bombing in April, an anti-defamation group recorded 222 attacks against Muslims—ranging from spitting on women wearing shawls to death threats to shots fired at mosques to a fake bomb thrown at a Muslim day care center."

That same article cites the taking of American hostages in Tehran in 1979 and the 1993 World Trade Center bombing as when anti-Muslim hostility in the United States started to grow. Yet, as the stories in this book demonstrate, suspicion and hatred directed at "othered" communities is much older than that.

SURESHBHAI PATEL

On February 6, 2015, Sureshbhai Patel, a fifty-seven-year-old Hindu Indian man who was visiting his son in Madison, Alabama, was assaulted by local police officers in an apparent hate crime. Patel did not speak English, and a resident of his son's neighborhood had called the police on him for "suspicious" behavior, identifying Patel as a "skinny black man wearing a toboggan." The police used excessive force, including slamming Patel to the ground, causing him to be paralyzed from the waist down.

Video footage from a police car's dashboard camera resulted in the firing of one police officer and a subsequent charge of third-degree assault. Yet in 2016, that same officer was reinstated by the Madison Police Department.

---

traffic stop, but it didn't matter. After that, I stopped wanting to go shopping on the day after Thanksgiving. I thought more about the colonizing roots of the holiday. Some fantasy of American life began to break—and that was for the best.

Years later, I recounted this story to one of my sisters, who is a year older than I am. I asked her what she remembered about being Bangladeshi American in the time after 9/11. I realized it was the first time we had ever spoken about it. As my own gender identity shifted, I started to think about how little I knew of what it was like for women, queer, and/or gender nonconforming Muslims in this country after that morning in September. So many of the stories I'd heard—and told—were like my story of being pulled over: focused on the Islamophobia that non-Black Muslims assumed to be men have faced.

My sister was in college at the time of the attacks, and what she remembers is a climate of fear developing on her New England campus. There was the time a classmate hung an American flag upside down outside a window in protest of the

---

LOVE, INSHALLAH

The introduction to *Love, InshAllah: The Secret Love Lives of American Muslim Women*, edited by Ayesha Mattu and Nura Maznavi, says:

Muslim women—we just can't seem to catch a break. We're oppressed, submissive, and forced into arranged marriages by big-bearded men.

Oh, and let's not forget—we're also all hiding explosives under our clothes.

The truth is—like most women—we're independent and opinionated. And the only things hiding under our clothes are hearts yearning for love.

Everyone seems to have an opinion about Muslim women, even those—especially those—who have never met one. As American Muslim women, we decided this was an opportunity to raise our voices and tell our own stories.

---

government's actions, which led to a crew of mostly white men walking up to her complex with two-by-fours in their hands, demanding that she take it down.

But she also mentioned our local mosque being burned down in 1995, and how that feeling of being "othered" had been around for much longer. When I ask my mom, who wears a hijab, she reiterates this, that she had felt uneasy going to the grocery store on certain days before too—a feeling that hasn't stopped her from enjoying life in this country, but one that she has sadly grown accustomed to, and that came roaring back in the months after the 2016 presidential election.

Always looking over my shoulder, worried who might be at my back, I had often overlooked experiences like this: the pain of others. Which is exactly how this racist patriarchal system of surveillance is designed to work.

INDEX OF THE DISAPPEARED

In an interview for *Tides*, Brooklyn-based visual artist Chitra Ganesh shared a reflection on *Index of the Disappeared*, a collaboration with fellow artist Mariam Ghani that serves (in the words of Ghani) as "both a physical archive of post-9/11 disappearances and a mobile platform for public dialogue."

Index of the Disappeared, my long-term collaboration with Mariam Ghani active since 2004, is rooted in the notion of archiving around absence and erasure. In the weeks and months after 9/11, we were confronted daily with missing flyers and commemorative tributes all over New York City to those who lost their lives in the attack. As time went on, developments such as the Patriot Act, the institutionalization of American exceptionalism, and a rise in Islamophobia began to crystallize. This happened in conjunction with my own experience of hearing in parallel about disappearances of people within our community. Arabs, Muslims, South Asians, the lawyers and activists who were supporting them, and neighboring communities being detained, profiled, interrogated, deported, and in some cases permanently disappeared through

How Do We See the Disappeared, Index of the Disappeared *by Chitra Ganesh + Mariam Ghani, 2004. Window installation and video, dimensions variable, White Box, New York.*

death via neglect in detention and holding facilities. Of course, these threats of erasure continue in our current political environment with the resurgence of a much more aggressive ICE presence and mass deportations in immigrant neighborhoods throughout the country.

We realized that there was a story around 9/11 that was absent from the official record, erasures which we felt urgently needed to be probed and explored via our art practice. Bodies were being obscured from public view—physically disappeared via unlawful detentions, special registration, surveillance and mass deportation, and then disappeared once again in the language of the law, through practices like redaction.

It is through fragments of conversations and the prisoners' voices that allowed the architectural plan seen above to surface. It was visualized not from blueprints, or legal documents, but through the call-and-response communication between prisoners who listened for the number and distance of voices within absolute darkness and constant solitary confinement.

From "Between, Beneath, and Beyond" for Tides, *by Jaret Vadera.*

Imran Siddiquee (they/them) is a filmmaker, writer, and speaker challenging systems of domination.

GUANTÁNAMO BAY

Anant Raut

> "The laws and Constitution are designed to survive, and remain in force, in extraordinary times."
>
> —Justice Anthony Kennedy, *Boumediene v. Bush* (2008)

There is the America before that Tuesday. And there is the America after that Tuesday.

After the Twin Towers fell, the American response was swift. American forces were dispatched to Afghanistan to find Osama bin Laden and, more broadly, to root out al-Qaeda and terrorists. By January, hundreds of accused terrorists had been picked up, cycled through various transit points, and deposited in the U.S. Naval Station at Guantánamo Bay, Cuba.

In the U.S. justice system, they would have had a chance to go before a judge, hear why they were being imprisoned, and challenge the allegations and evidence against them. But by bringing these foreign nationals to a U.S. military base on the southern tip of Cuba, the Bush administration had assumed that U.S. law wouldn't apply. The U.S. government planned to hold them indefinitely as part of its "war on terror," arguing that they were too dangerous to let go. Under these circumstances, imprisonment in Guantánamo could effectively become a life sentence.

A group of human-rights lawyers at the Center for Constitutional Rights (CCR) decided to challenge the detention of these foreign nationals by invoking the legal right of habeas corpus in 2002. The concept of habeas corpus—that the state can't indefinitely hold a person but must present them to a court to justify their detention (habeas corpus translates literally as "you have the body")—came to the United States from English common law, where it has existed for centuries, predating the Magna Carta. Representing a small group of Kuwaiti prisoners, CCR's lawyers took their case all the way to the Supreme Court, which held that the terror suspects in Guantánamo Bay had a statutory right to challenge the basis for their detention in federal court.

In 2004, I was a junior associate when my law firm, along with others, decided that indefinite imprisonment without trial went against everything that made our justice system an example for the rest of the world. The firms partnered with CCR to represent many of the prisoners. I was assigned five Saudi prisoners, and quickly undertook to coordinate the representation of all one-hundred-plus Saudi prisoners across various other law firms so that we could defend them as a bloc.

As we dug into our cases, we soon found that many of the prisoners had arrived at Guantánamo with little or no supporting evidence for the terrorism charge—no facts, no paperwork, no corroborating evidence, no witnesses whom we could interview. In capturing these prisoners, the United States had adopted a market-based approach, dropping flyers offering bounties to locals for turning over "terrorists" to U.S. forces. You see the problem with the incentives. In a region where extended clans have feuded for generations, locals were in many cases being offered more money than they could make in a lifetime by simply handing someone over to American forces.

THE CASE OF THE TWENTY-TWO HINDUS

On July 29, 1913, thirteen men, all from the Punjab province in British India, alighted at the Angel Island Immigration Station in San Francisco Bay, seeking entry into the United States. The group, comprising twelve Sikhs and one Muslim, had sailed on SS Persia *from Manila, Philippines, then an insular territory of America. . . .*

The arrival of the "Hindus"—as natives of British India were generically called in the U.S., regardless of their religious affiliations—made news in local dailies the next day. This was for two reasons: one, because traveling aboard the Pacific Mail Steamship Company–owned SS Persia, *they had been part of a benchmark voyage. While the Persia was a veteran of transpacific journeys, this particular trip had seen it ferry the largest-ever number of "steerage passengers" from Asia to the U.S. . . .*

The second reason why their arrival made news in the West Coast dailies was because all of them were detained at the station immediately after disembarking, pending arrest.

The ground on which the thirteen Hindus were held was the most common one forwarded by the Immigration Bureau to keep "undesirable aliens" from Asia out of the U.S.—that they were "likely to become public charges," burdens on the American taxpayer. And the stated reason why they were deemed liable by immigration officers to become such was "that they are of the laboring class, that there is no demand for such labor and there exists a strong prejudice against them in this locality." This despite the fact that in Manila, each detainee had been issued a form Five Forty-Six—an "Alien Certificate—Insular Territory"—by the U.S. Immigration Service. . . . This document certified that its bearer had been "duly inspected and registered, and [would] be admitted into the United States upon proper identification, and surrender of [the] certificate to any immigration officer at a designated port of entry."

From "The Case of the Twenty-Two Hindus" for Tides, *by Sharmadip Basu.*

Composite photograph created using images from the Immigration Arrival Investigation Case Files collection. In SAADA, courtesy of the National Archives at San Francisco.

Some of these prisoners had been routed through so-called black sites, CIA-controlled locations in foreign countries where prisoners were interrogated, often brutally and in violation of human rights law and the Geneva Conventions. Those interrogation tactics, developed by a pair of contractors for the CIA, resulted in no useful intelligence but yielded the kinds of false claims and affirmations that led to, for example, the United States' invasion of Iraq in 2003.

So the individuals that ended up in Guantánamo Bay ranged immensely. Some were indeed orchestrating terror attacks, while others were entirely innocent of terrorism charges, but were mistakenly caught up in the broad sweep of the terrorist net.

But the lack of due process for the imprisoned individuals made it nearly impossible to determine who was guilty of those charges and who was not.

The Department of Defense had created military tribunals and given them exclusive jurisdiction to hear challenges to the prisoners' detention. The tribunals operated under a lesser standard of evidence, where the judge, prosecutor, and defense counsel were all military, and the prisoners were given a Kafkaesque opportunity to defend themselves against allegations they lacked the security clearance to hear.

For example, Mustafa Ait Idir was asked to respond to an accusation that he had associated with a known al-Qaeda operative while living in Bosnia. Quite reasonably, Idir asked for the name of the person he was suspected of associating with.

> *Tribunal president:* I do not know.
> *Idir:* How can I respond to this?
> *Tribunal president:* Did you know of anyone that was a member of al-Qaeda?
> *Idir:* No, no.... This is something the interrogators told me a long while ago. I asked the interrogators to tell me who this person was.... Maybe I knew this person as a friend. Maybe it was a person that worked with me. Maybe it was a person that was on my team. But I do not know if this person is Bosnian, Indian, or whatever. If you tell me the name, then I

can respond and defend myself against this accusation.

Tribunal president: We are asking you the questions, and we need you to respond to what is on the unclassified summary.

So we got to work, chipping away at the government's legal arguments. We won steadily in court. But for all of our paper victories, the situation of our clients, sitting in the heat of Guantánamo for years at this point, remained unchanged.

I began to realize that the ultimate solution would have to be diplomatic, not legal. The federal government was never going to allow these individuals to get a trial in a U.S. court, but maybe they could be persuaded to turn them back over to their own governments. To that end, I helped arrange the first-ever meeting between the Saudi ambassador to the United States and counsel for the prisoners. We dispelled some myths about the types of people being held there and discussed what could be accomplished by the Saudi government working directly with our own.

Like a tributary winding its way to a river, the painstaking diplomatic process began to yield results. Foreign governments began negotiating to bring their citizens back. In the meantime, we continued our fight in the courts. With respect to the military tribunals, we were finally vindicated in 2008. The Supreme Court,

---

"T5" BY SWET SHOP BOYS

On June 29, 2017, Swet Shop Boys made their TV debut by performing this song, written by Himanshu Suri and Riz Ahmed, on *The Late Show with Stephen Colbert.*

Chorus:
Oh no, we're in trouble
TSA always wanna burst my bubble
Always get a random check when I rock the stubble

Terminal 5, Terminal One
Think we're termites, wanna terminate us
Terminal 5, Terminal One
Think we're termites, wanna terminate us
Terminal 5, Terminal One
Think we're termites, wanna terminate us

From the 2016 Swet Shop Boys album, Cashmere.

in *Boumediene v. Bush* (2008), held that the prisoners had a constitutional right to habeas, and that the tribunals were an inadequate substitute for that right.

The federal government, rather than face the prospect of defending their years-long detention of these prisoners before a federal judge, transferred the bulk of the prisoners to their home countries in the months that followed. Some remained because of the instability of their home countries or substantial evidence of their guilt. Still, because of the haphazard, poorly documented way that many of these prisoners were obtained, fully shutting down the terrorism detention program there has eluded successive administrations. Even now, fifteen years later as of this writing, prisoners remain.

We took these cases fully prepared for our clients to be anti-American terrorists; we couldn't have known that many of them would turn out to be innocent. We did it for the same reason that John Adams vigorously defended the British soldiers who had committed the Boston Massacre of 1770, when the public, thirsting for retribution, would have accepted a show trial and quick sentencing: because the truest test of a nation's commitment to liberty occurs not when freedoms are most easily given, but when they are most readily taken away.

Anant Raut (he/him) is an antitrust law and policy expert, particularly at its intersection with consumer privacy, and previously served as Democratic counsel to both the House and Senate Judiciary Committees.

BREATHE

Valarie Kaur

Valarie Kaur delivered the following address during a watch night service (late-night service) at the Metropolitan AME Church in Washington, D.C., on December 31, 2016.

Waheguru Ji Ka Khalsa, Waheguru Ji Ki Fateh.

On Christmas Eve 103 years ago, my grandfather waited in a dark and dank cell. He had sailed by steamship across the Pacific Ocean from India to America, leaving behind colonial rule. But when he landed on American shores, immigration officials saw his dark skin, his tall turban worn as part of his Sikh faith, and saw him not as a brother, but as foreign, as suspect, and threw him behind bars, where he languished for months. Until a single man, a white man, a lawyer named Henry Marshall, filed a writ of habeas corpus that released him on Christmas Eve

1913. My grandfather K. R. Singh became a farmer, free to practice the heart of his Sikh faith—love and oneness. And so, when his Japanese American neighbors were rounded up and taken to their own detention camps in the deserts of America, he went out to see them when no one else would. He looked after their farms until they returned home. He refused to stand down.

In the aftermath of September 11, when hate violence exploded in these United States, a man that I called uncle was murdered. I tried to stand up. I became a lawyer like the man who freed my grandfather, and I joined a generation of activists

ON SHIMA FARM

Produced in 1914, this fifteen-minute black-and-white film captures the California estate of George Shima (born Kinji Ushijima, 1864–1924), one of the wealthiest Japanese American farmers of the time. The film is unique in that it contains footage of several South Asian laborers on the farm, in two sections: "Migrant Laborers from India" (1:09–1:20) and "Onion Fields" (1:21–1:44). Shima's farms were located in the Stockton–Sacramento delta, and his home (also captured in the film) was located at 2601 College Avenue in Berkeley.

Courtesy of San Joaquin Delta College.

fighting detentions and deportations, surveillance and special registration, hate crimes and racial profiling. And after fifteen years, with every film, with every lawsuit, with every campaign, I thought we were making the nation safer for the next generation.

And then my son was born. On Christmas Eve, I watched him ceremoniously put the milk and cookies by the fire for Santa Claus. And after he went to sleep, I then drank the milk and ate the cookies. I wanted him to wake up and see them gone in the morning. I wanted him to believe in a world that was magical. But I am leaving

---

ECKSHATE

The Desis Rising Up and Moving official website writes about Eckshate:

DRUM's leadership development program for young working-class South Asian & Indocaribbean women. Eckshate *means "together" in Bengali, and the program was developed by a young woman leader who sought to bring young women together to fight the isolation they experience, build relationships as they heal from oppression, and work together on creating a campaign for gender justice in their communities. . . .*

Since 2016, Eckshate has spearheaded a new model of engaging working-class communities around issues of gender justice—through the annual Dhaba. Dhaba *is a Punjabi term for a roadside cafe in India and Pakistan, a public space usually dominated by men. The Eckshate Dhaba flips the male-dominated public space on its head; it's a neighborhood-wide young-women-led initiative to reclaim public space for working-class women by engaging different sectors of our communities around women's liberation, and building community through art and culture.*

---

my son a world that is more dangerous than the one I was given. I am raising, we are raising, a Brown boy in America. A Brown boy who may someday wear a turban as part of his faith. And in America today, as we enter an era of enormous rage, as white nationalists hail this moment as their "great awakening," as hate acts against Sikhs and our Muslim brothers and sisters are at an all-time high, I know that there will be moments, whether on the streets or in the schoolyard, where my son will be seen as foreign, as suspect, as a terrorist. Just as Black bodies are still seen as criminal. Just as Brown bodies are still seen as illegal. Just as trans bodies are still seen as immoral. Just as Indigenous bodies are still seen as savage. Just as the bodies of women and girls are still seen as someone else's property. When we see these bodies not as brothers and sisters, then it becomes easier to bully them, to rape them, to allow policies that neglect them, that incarcerate them, that kill them.

Yes, rabbi, the future is dark. On this New Year's Eve, this watched night, I close my eyes and I see the darkness of my grandfather's cell, and I can feel the spirit of ever-rising optimism, in the Sikh tradition Chardi Kala, within him. And so the mother in me asks: what if? What if this darkness is not the darkness of the tomb, but the darkness of the womb? What if our America is not dead, but a country that is waiting to be born? What if the story of America is one long labor? What if all of our grandfathers and grandmothers are standing behind us now? Those who survived occupation and genocide, slavery and Jim Crow, detentions and political assaults. What if they are whispering in our ears, today, tonight: "You are brave!" What if this is our nation's great transition?

What does the midwife tell us to do? Breathe! And then? Push! Because if we don't push, we will die. If we don't push, our nation will die. Tonight we will breathe. Tomorrow we will labor in love, through love. And your revolutionary love is the magic we will show our children.

Waheguru Ji Ka Khalsa, Waheguru Ji Ki Fateh.

Valarie Kaur (she/her) is a renowned civil rights leader, lawyer, innovator, and award-winning filmmaker.

Courtesy of Desis Rising Up and Moving (DRUM).

CHAPTER 5

*Identity &
Equality*

origin
south asian?

gay lesbian **bi**

or simply

q u e e r ?

support / ? / social group forming
now !

blade personals

for details call **1.900.370.2117**

box **6288**· **$1.50/minute**

thru the end of August

go on... *call*

sri lanka

india

bhutan

maldives

tibet

pakistan

nepal

bangladesh

Ardhanarishwara
0.5 male, 0.5 female
form of Lord Shiva
embodies the male and
female principle
in **one**·
·Trikone

Flyer for the first meeting of LGBTQ South Asians in Washington D.C. Courtesy of Yassir Islam.

INTRODUCTION

Radha Modi

South Asian identity represents a diverse collective of ethnicities, religions, and ancestries in the United States. The goal of this chapter is to begin the process of showcasing narratives from community activists, scholars, and educators that highlight the complexity of South Asian identities and struggles for justice. These narratives show that South Asian identities are in flux as issues of intersectionality, visibility, discrimination, and resistance arise.

Intersectionality, with its origins in Black feminist thought, is the understanding that a person's life experiences and various identities (race, class, gender, etc.) overlap and are not isolated, and collectively contribute to how a person experiences prejudice and discrimination. Often, stories of South Asian Americans are limited to their nationality, which results in narrow and homogenous depictions of the community. Intersectionality resists the idea that one identity—

ethnicity, in this case—is more important than others. The intersections of race, gender, religion, caste, and sexuality weave together a fuller and more textured representation of lived South Asian experience. In this chapter, queer, transgender, and gender-nonconforming South Asian hxstories* by Sasha Wijeyeratne and Mala Nagarajan and a poem by Mashuq Mushtaq Deen show the urgency around lifting intersectional South Asian voices and the challenging pressures to remain hidden.

The theme of visibility also runs throughout the stories in this chapter. Typically, the experiences of Indian, heterosexual, Hindu, middle-class men eclipse the diverse voices of the South Asian community. The push for visibility counteracts this erasure. In her story, Suzanne C. Persard describes the formation of Jahajee Sisters, a collective that works to bring attention to and address the gender-based violence experienced by Indo-Caribbean women. Further, V. V. Ganeshananthan challenges the use of the "South Asian" descriptor and discusses the potential loss of visibility of her Sri Lankan background due to the centering of Indian identity over others.

Another prominent theme in this chapter is the discrimination faced by the South Asian community. Discrimination occurs in covert and overt ways—microaggressions, racial profiling, hate crimes. I demonstrate in my essay how skin color preferences and gender often work together to perpetuate colorism in South Asian communities. South Asian women are pressured to lighten their skin and pass on this perceived advantage to the next generation. In larger American society, South Asians are treated with suspicion in part due to their brown skin color and assumptions about their religious beliefs, and as a result, the community has witnessed a rise in hate crimes since 9/11. Moreover, a timeline of queer hxstory by Sasha Wijeyeratne and Mala Nagarajan demonstrates intersectional discrimination of queer and genderqueer South Asians, from homophobic legislation in South Asia to the exclusion of queer groups in the India Day Parade in New York City.

A final central theme in this chapter is resistance. As South Asians experience invisibility and discrimination because of their intersectional identities, they are simultaneously making efforts to resist and fight for justice. Much of this resistance has been raising awareness and building coalitions with other communities facing oppression. As Manan Desai writes, as early as 1913, Dr. B. R. Ambedkar, a Dalit rights leader, connected the common struggle of caste oppression in India to race oppression in the United States in his letter to civil rights scholar W. E. B. Du Bois. Most recently, South Asians have strived to be in solidarity with the Black Lives Matter movement and continued to forge connections between various intersectional issues.

Ultimately, while this chapter is partly about the past, it is also an opportunity to see the potential for South Asian identity and the pursuit of equality. How is skin color integral to the South Asian American racial experience at home and in other spaces? What does it mean to be South Asian, queer, and trans? Whose narratives are marginalized when the focus is on Indian, straight, cisgender, Hindu men? How do we build coalitions within the South Asian community as well as with other communities of color to work toward justice? The answers to these questions span the six narratives in this chapter, with each story offering a piece in illuminating the lives of South Asians in the United States.

* *Hxstory,* here, is deployed to counteract the normative gendered use of *history.*

Radha Modi (she/her/hers) is an assistant teaching professor at Florida State University.

BROWN

Radha Modi

In 2013, Nina Davuluri, a second-generation South Asian daughter of immi-grants, won the Miss America contest. There were two notable responses to her win: first, she experienced backlash for her brown skin, and thus her supposed links to "terrorism." Second, the South Asian community wondered what her winning meant for skin color politics in the diaspora. Many came to the conclu-sion that she would never win a similar contest in South Asia because of her dark skin color.

"Don't Play in the Sun!"

Skin color is an integral part of the South Asian experience in the United States. During colonial rule, the British cemented the use of skin color to stratify South Asians. Now, popular culture and media (such as Bollywood) perpetuate the saliency of skin color. Dark skin tones have consistently been associated with negative or villainous traits. Advertisements for skin-bleaching creams are common and rarely contested. The persistent and systemic equating of dark skin to evil and of light skin to good within the South Asian community has resulted in darker skin being the marker of undesirability and inferiority (which is also linked to anti-Black attitudes).

"Don't play in the sun!" South Asian youth living in the United States grow up hearing these words. The booming directive often comes from first-generation parents, relatives, and community members wanting to maintain proximity to whiteness and thus status. With lighter skin comes privilege in society, such as access to higher-paying jobs and high-status marriage proposals. While both boys and girls are encouraged to "stay out of the sun," girls are the typical target of these messages, even into their adulthood. Women grow up in households where routine direct and indirect comments are made about their skin color and their bodies.

The larger South Asian–specific ethnic/religious communities often echo these

---

BODY IMAGE

Ushshi Rahman is a writer, dissident, and creative working to dismantle anti-fatness. In an interview with the Body Pos Project, Ushshi talks about how being a Bangladeshi woman plays into their body identity:

> When I talk about fat politics and body politics, it's really important to acknowledge that when you stand at multiple margins and identities, it's impossible to separate them all as through individual lenses. You experience it all together; it's multidimensional and multifaceted, much like the human experience at large. I can feel good in my body and size and feel really prideful of my skin color, ethnicity, and my nationality and, at the same time, have huge issues with how we're treated here in America. And I can have huge issues with how our government and society treats us back in Bangladesh as well, sometimes for the same reasons, sometimes for diametrically different ones.

> I have a muslim [sic] last name and am from a predominantly muslim country, I am visibly a person of color. I'm also tattooed and hypervisible in my aesthetic choices and generally look like the anti-authoritarian that I very much am. Guess how often I get flagged at airports? Hah. It's impossible to not be aware of how my body identity and presence factors into all of this. As a large person, as a brown person, and as a woman, in no particular order of importance, I sometimes lament and feel like there is nowhere in the world that is really safe to just exist and truly be free. That's a conundrum that I have to negotiate daily, and I would be lying to you if I didn't say it is a heavy load I am always unpacking, always attempting to cast off, always heaped back upon.

sentiments about skin color. These peers reinforce South Asian ideologies around skin color and, with it, links to gender norms. South Asian women across class and religious backgrounds are encouraged to stay indoors while boys play outside. Young women are also advised to use skin-lightening creams—the same creams that are sold all over South Asia and are part of a multibillion-dollar beauty industry. The recommendations are the same across skin tones: lighter-skinned women are told to protect their light skin, and darker-skinned women are encouraged to prevent more darkening of their skin.

UNFAIR AND LOVELY

Unfair and Lovely, a response to the widely promoted skin-lightening cream Fair and Lovely, is a 2015 photo series featuring South Asian sisters Mirusha and Yanusha Yogarajah, created by Black American artist Pax Jones to combat "colorism on a global scale by highlighting its intersectionality." In 2016, it sparked an online campaign, in collaboration with *Reclaim the Bindi*, featuring women of color around the world posting photos of themselves with the hashtag #UnfairAndLovely.

"Go Back to Your Country"

The experiences around skin color are not limited to the home. South Asians also experience skin color–related discrimination in the larger United States. Bhagat Singh Thind, a Sikh Indian, argued in the early 1920s in an Oregon court that since he was anthropologically Caucasian, he should have a right to American citizenship. The case was appealed and ultimately reached the U.S. Supreme Court. In 1923, the Supreme Court ruled in favor of the United States in *United States v. Bhagat Singh Thind* by clarifying the definition of "Caucasian" as "common understanding" of white and thus denying Bhagat Singh Thind and other subsequent South Asians citizenship at that time.

In the post-9/11 atmosphere, Brown bodies are marked as "terrorist" and suspect of anti-American behavior. South Asians are profiled and subjected to harassment due to their religious markers and skin color. Over the past decade, there have been numerous accounts of Sikhs, Hindus, Christians, and Muslims with South Asian ancestry who have experienced various forms of threats and assaults.

Photograph from DRUM's first-ever public action, on April 2, 2000, in Jackson Heights, Queens. The event was part of "41 Days of Action," organized in response to the acquittals of four police officers who shot and killed Amadou Diallo, a twenty-two-year-old immigrant from Guinea. Courtesy of Desis Rising Up and Moving (DRUM). Photo by Kristine Samms.

Recent cases include the murders of Satwant Singh Kaleka, Paramjit Kaur, Suveg Singh Khattra, Prakash Singh, Ranjit Singh, and Sita Singh in a mass shooting by a white supremacist at the Oak Creek Gurdwara in 2012; the murder of a Hindu Indian man, Sunando Sen, in the New York City subway, also in 2012; and the profiling, beating, and subsequent paralysis of Sureshbhai Patel in Alabama by police in 2015. In 2017, Srinivas Kuchibhotla was killed in a hate crime in Kansas, and a Sikh man, Deep Rai, was shot just a month later in Kent, Washington.

These, however, are not singular occurrences in the South Asian community. Most South Asian Americans have experienced some discrimination related to their skin color, religion, and immigration status especially since 9/11 and the election of Donald Trump.

FIGHTING FOR SOCIAL JUSTICE

Having experienced skin color policing in the home or skin color discrimination outside, South Asians are fighting back for racial justice, immigrant rights, and gender empowerment. Organizations such as South Asian Americans Leading Together (SAALT), Desis Rising Up and Moving (DRUM), and South Asian American Policy & Research Institute (SAAPRI) are pushing for immigration reform, local and national policy on hate crimes, and regulation of racial profiling by the police. In addition, community groups offer regional South Asian youth retreats and summits to raise political consciousness and build leadership skills. South Asian youth are blogging about colorism in the community and empowering young girls to be body positive. Skin color serves as a salient part of the racial experience for all people of color in the United States, including South Asian Americans, and links the struggles across our communities fighting for justice.

Radha Modi (she/her/hers) is an assistant teaching professor at Florida State University.

WHAT DR. B. R. AMBEDKAR WROTE TO DR. W. E. B. DU BOIS

Manan Desai

In 1913, B. R. Ambedkar arrived in New York City from Bombay at the age of twenty-two, on a scholarship to attend Columbia University that fall and pursue a master's in economics. After returning to India (and completing a PhD in London), Dr. Ambedkar would go on to become the most influential Dalit leader in India in the twentieth century, the chairman of the constituent assembly that drafted the Indian constitution, and one of the most incisive theorists of caste and greatest intellectuals of modern India. From the perspective of a researcher, Ambedkar's proximity to Harlem during his years of study at Columbia has always raised several questions about his experience in the United States. How might have his experiences in New York affected his thinking? Aside from his influential mentors at the university (John Dewey, Edwin Seligman, James Shotwell, and James Harvey Robinson), who were his personal acquaintances in the United States? And did his

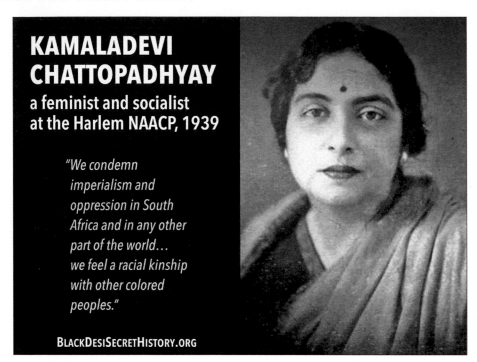

BLACK-DESI SECRET HISTORY

KAMALADEVI CHATTOPADHYAY

a feminist and socialist at the Harlem NAACP, 1939

"We condemn imperialism and oppression in South Africa and in any other part of the world… we feel a racial kinship with other colored peoples."

BlackDesiSecretHistory.org

Anirvan Chatterjee's website, *Black Desi Secret History*, provides a glimpse into the way "South Asians and African Americans have been standing up for each other for over a century." From feminist Kamaladevi Chattopadhyay connecting with the NAACP in 1939 to Black civil rights leader Bayard Rustin founding the Free India Committee in 1945, the site features a number of stories that emphasize the ways various Black and Brown people have recognized our shared struggle against racism, colonialism, and other forms of oppression.

experience witnessing anti-Black racism in America influence his thinking on the caste question in India? Despite the many allusions to race in the United States in his writings, Ambedkar—as far as I know—left no firsthand account of his time in New York to answer such questions.

An interesting record appears in the papers of Dr. W. E. B. Du Bois, the prominent African American intellectual and activist, whose archive is housed at the University of Massachusetts. In the 1940s, Ambedkar contacted Du Bois to inquire about the National Negro Congress's petition to the United Nation (UN), which attempted to secure minority rights through the UN Economic and Social

Dr. W. E. B. Du Bois (left) and Dr. B. R. Ambedkar (right).

Council. Ambedkar explained that he had been a "student of the Negro problem" and that "[t]here is so much similarity between the position of the Untouchables in India and of the position of the Negroes in America that the study of the latter is not only natural but necessary." In a letter dated July 31, 1946, Du Bois responded by telling Ambedkar he was familiar with his name, and that he had "every sympathy with the Untouchables of India."

Du Bois had long been fascinated with India's role as a harbinger of anti-colonialism. He had befriended India Home Rule League nationalist Lajpat Rai during the latter's exile in the United States, between 1914 and 1919. Du Bois's interest in India turned up in editorials of the NAACP-issued magazine *The Crisis* over the decades, as well as in the novel *Dark Princess*, published in 1928. For Du Bois, the cause for Indian independence was one facet of a larger movement to undo the color line that belted the world. Du Bois's correspondence with Ambedkar, however, does not appear to extend beyond this letter.

The analogy between the caste system in India and racism in the United States, on the other hand, has a much longer and sustained history. In 1873, Jotirao Phule,

RESPONDING TO A LETTER IN THE CHICAGO DEFENDER

In 1930, K. Romola, an Indian immigrant, published a vicious letter in the *Chicago Defender* that dismissed any similarities between the conditions of African Americans and those of Indians. "Too much has been written by the Negro papers, magazines, and fourth rate writers like Du Bois, about the darker races," Romola wrote, "but who in the hell wants to join the caravan with the black ones? Our caste system in India excludes those who do not belong to the Aryan (white) race and we even here exclude any Indians who live and socialize with the Negro." Romola signed off with the self-anointed title "Director of the Aryan propaganda society." The term "Aryan" was a racial categorization that was sometimes applied to South Asians, and several Indians had used the category for the basis for their right to citizenship.

H. G. Mudgal (seen above), who was editor of Marcus Garvey's *Negro World* at the time, authored a ferocious response to Romola's casteist and racist claims, describing his fellow Indian as an "out of touch" snob and self-hating "victim of the white propagandists." Mudgal suggested that Romola, in criticizing African Americans, had "utterly forgotten the political, social, and economical oppression that India has been subjected to under the British." Mudgal's writing often stressed the interconnected nature of the African American struggle and worldwide anti-imperialist movements, including in India. The question of whose struggles the South Asian American community chooses to identify with has echoed throughout its history.

Adapted from "H. G. Mudgal, Harlem Editor" for Tides, *by Tizarat Gill and Manan Desai.*

DALITS AND THE PERSISTENCE OF CASTE

The word *Dalit* can mean "broken," "scattered," or "downtrodden." It is used today by those formerly called "untouchables" (and the *adivasis*, or indigenous peoples of South Asia) under the caste system, a religiously codified system of oppression. The term may have first been used in relation to caste oppression by the nineteenth-century reformer Jotirao Phule, but it was popularized by the economist and Dalit leader Dr. B. R. Ambedkar in the 1930s, and revived in the 1970s by the radical Dalit Panthers.

The oppression of Dalits has not been limited to India or South Asia. According to a 2018 Equality Labs study, "Caste in the United States," 25 percent of Dalits in the U.S. report facing "verbal or physical assault" based on their caste. And one in two of all Dalit respondents said they lived in fear of their caste being outed. Read more at equalitylabs.org/castesurvey.

---

an important social reformer in Maharashtra, began his polemical *Gulamgiri* (*Slavery*) with a dedication to American abolitionists "with an earnest desire, that my countrymen may take their noble example as their guide in the emancipation of their Sudra Brethren from the trammels of Brahmin thraldom [enslavement]." Nearly a hundred years later, an organization led by Dalit artists and activists named themselves the "Dalit Panthers," in reference to the Black Panthers in the United States. In their manifesto, issued in 1971, the Dalit Panthers wrote: "From the Black Panthers, Black Power was established. We claim a close relationship with this struggle."

Manan Desai is an associate professor of Asian/Pacific Islander American studies in the American Culture Department at the University of Michigan.

QUEER SOUTH ASIANS IN AMERICA

Mala Nagarajan and Sasha Wijeyeratne

Queer South Asians have existed for millennia. However, organizing around this identity in the United States is newer. Queer South Asians have made an impact by creating safer spaces for our community. We have made visible and vocal an alternative South Asian narrative informed by queerness. We have organized to promote social justice and equality inside and outside our communities.

For the vast majority of us, being queer, transgender, bisexual, lesbian, or gay *and* being South Asian was unthinkable. Our identities were separated into silos. At home, we hid our queerness. At school or work, we were outsiders because of our race and ethnicity. In queer spaces, we often felt invisible or exoticized. We craved a space where all of our identities of race, gender, and sexuality could coexist.

In the mid- to late 1980s, queer South Asians started organizing and creating community spaces. These spaces strengthened our sense of identity, built community, and inspired visibility and activism. The first queer South Asian organization in the world, Trikone, started in 1986 in San Francisco with a call to South Asians on a piece of paper pinned to a community board at an LGBT community center.

Like this, we made connections through the community grapevine. We published newsletters and magazines to reach others. We organized cultural festivals like *Desh Pardesh* that fused art, film, and activism. Around this time, Urvashi Vaid

---

QUEER

"Queer" is a multifaceted and complex term.

One definition of queer is abnormal or strange. Historically, queer has been used as an epithet/slur against people whose gender, gender expression and/or sexuality do not conform to dominant expectations. Some people have reclaimed the word queer and self identify as such. For some, this reclamation is a celebration of not fitting into norms/being "abnormal." Manifestations of oppression within gay and lesbian movements such as racism, sizeism, ableism, cissexism, transmisogyny as well as assimilation politics, resulted in many people being marginalized, thus, for some, queer is a radical and anti-assimilationist stance that captures multiple aspects of identities.

Definition from the Lesbian, Gay, Bisexual, Transgender, Queer, Intersex, Asexual Resource Center at the University of California, Davis.

---

became the head of the National Gay and Lesbian Task Force, bringing visibility to queer South Asian experience.

Despite our efforts, mainstream South Asian communities denied our existence. This kind of societal stigma made life difficult, resulting in many of us feeling isolated, depressed, and suicidal. We created support groups to help each other. These spaces and increased visibility gave the community hope. As a result, more of us came out, connected to others, and found community.

FIGHTING OPPRESSION

South Asian queer communities are powerful, but they also can replicate cultures of oppression. Prejudice and unconscious biases often privileged gay, upper-middle-class, cisgender male, Hindu Indians. Many failed to acknowledge or advocate for issues affecting queer South Asians with other identities, such as women, trans people, Muslims, and working-class people. In response, new groups, like SA-Grrls and Al-Fatiha, formed to address the needs of communities who are marginalized within queer South Asian spaces.

As we worked to build community spaces and elevate our visibility, we also organized against state violence in the United States and South Asia. From 1992 to 2009, the South Asian Lesbian and Gay Association of New York City (SALGA-NYC) demanded entry to N.Y.C.'s India Day

SALGA MARCHES IN THE NYC PRIDE '95 PARADE

WHERE: The Northwest corner of 5th Avenue and E. 54th Street (at 11:30 we will move to our position on 5th Ave. between E. 54th and E. 55th Street.)

WHEN: Sunday, June 25, 11:00am–6:00pm

WHAT TO WEAR: *Saris* for the queens, *salwar kameez* for the kings, *dupattas* for the ambivalent, and shorts/t-shirts for those who don't know what we're talking about.

▲ ▲ ▲ ▲ ▲ ▲ ▲ ▲ ▲ ▲ ▲ ▲ ▲ ▲ ▲

SALGA dances its way through the NYC Pride '95 Parade. DJ Geeta will take her act on the road via the SALGA Dance Mobile spinning raucous bhangra, reggae and tribal house. We will be marching with other queer people of color groups. The parade begins at noon sharp—arrive by 11:30 or you may not be able to find us. The parade ends in the West Village where we will watch the rest of the parade and hang out at the piers afterwards. We encourage everyone who supports us and the work we do to march with us. **Refreshments will be provided.**

▼ ▼ ▼ ▼ ▼ ▼ ▼ ▼ ▼ ▼ ▼ ▼ ▼ ▼ ▼

Courtesy of South Asian Lesbian and Gay Association (SALGA).

Parade. The parade organizers rejected SALGA, refusing to accept that queerness and gender nonconformity have always been part of South Asian cultures. In fact, homophobic laws, such as section 377 of India's constitution, were enacted and imposed by the British during India's colonization. The fight for inclusion now became about something more than queer South Asian visibility. Participation in N.Y.C.'s India Day Parade was also about recognizing India's long legacy of queerness and drawing attention to British colonial legacies of oppression. As queer South Asians, our identities disrupt narratives that portray queerness as a Western aberration and South Asia as a "pure," "exotic," and homogenous place. In 2010, after years of protest, the India Day Parade organizers finally granted SALGA-NYC entry.

FORGING SOLIDARITY

Along with organizing for our own communities and survival, we also organized in solidarity with other movements. In August 2014, Michael Brown was shot and killed by a police officer in Ferguson, Missouri. The response to this murder made #BlackLivesMatter visible as a national movement. Many queer non-Black South Asians recognized that our fight for justice is intimately tied to Black liberation. Queer South Asians started and joined #APIs4BlackLives collectives, organized solidarity actions, raised money for the movement, and marched in the streets with Black friends, family, and communities.

We also recognized the immediate need to educate our own communities. Organizers with the Queer South Asian National Network (QSANN) developed a workshop, "It Starts at Home: Confronting Anti-Blackness in South Asian Communities." The workshop, building on years of work by South Asian youth educators in East Coast Solidarity Summer, asked queer South Asians to confront anti-Black oppression in our own communities and home spaces. Queer South Asians ran the workshop in at least six different cities.

While "queer South Asian" as an identity is new, gender-nonconforming people and nonheterosexual relationships are timeless. For millennia, we have existed. Embedded in our histories, cultures, and mythologies, we emerge from darkness. We refuse to remain invisible or navigate separated lives. We embrace and celebrate South Asian as a full spectrum of identities. We fight in solidarity with other communities of color. As we seek to live as our full selves, we know that we will not be free until all queer and trans people, and all people of color, are free.

Mala Nagarajan (she/he), cofounder of the Seattle-based Trikone-Northwest, is a caregiver and nonprofit consultant.

Sasha Wijeyeratne (any pronouns) is currently the executive director of CAAAV: Organizing Asian Communities, organizing working-class Chinese, Bangladeshi, and Korean immigrants in Chinatown and Queens in New York City.

SALGA AND THE INDIA DAY PARADE

**TAKE A STAND AGAINST
HOMOPHOBIA, SEXISM, AND CLASS BIAS**

The South Asian Lesbian and Gay Association (SALGA) will hold a press conference/community education panel to address the Federation of Indian Association's (FIA) refusal to allow SALGA to participate in the 1997 India Day Parade. Panelists will include members of SALGA, Workers Awaaz (a women's organization working on domestic violence and domestic workers issues), Asian and Pacific Islander Coalition on HIV/AIDS, Inc. (APICHA), and the South Asian Women's Creative Collective.

Since 1993, the FIA has excluded SALGA from participating in the India Day Parade. Over the years, FIA has used various spurious excuses to disguise their homophobic exclusionary policies. Despite the official positions that SALGA cannot march because it is not an FIA member organizations or because it is South Asian and not specifically Indian identified, the FIA's underlying homophobia is evident in the inconsistency of their stance. While refusing SALGA permission, FIA made allowances for other South Asian Identified and non-FIA member groups. Over the years, the FIA's ban has expanded to exclude feminist and HIV/AIDS activist groups that have supported SALGA's right to march.

Join the South Asian Progressive task force, a coalition of South Asian activists countering the FIA's perpetuation of homophobia, sexism and class bias by attending the press conference/community education panel at:

**The Brecht Forum
122 W27th St, 10th Flr (btwn 6th and 7th Ave.)
Saturday August 16th, 6:30pm.
The panel will be followed by an alternative celebration/protest
at the India Day Parade on Sunday, August 17th.**

SALGA-NY is a social and political group for lesbians, gay men, bisexual and transgendered people who trace their origin from countries such as Afghanistan, Bangladesh, Bhutan, Burma, India, Nepal, Pakistan, Sri Lanka, and Tibet. For more info call: 212-358-5132

Courtesy of South Asian Lesbian and Gay Association (SALGA).

The flyer pictured here is for a press conference/community-education panel addressing the Federation of Indian Associations' refusal to allow the South Asian Lesbian and Gay Association (SALGA) to participate in the 1997 India Day Parade in New York City. The conference was held at the Brecht Forum and was followed by a protest organized by SALGA and the South Asian Progressive Task Force.

Though SALGA would eventually be included in the parade, it would subsequently be excluded as well. In 2010, Arun Venugopal wrote about the issue for WNYC News in an article titled "South Asian LGBT Community Marches in India Day Parade":

> Ten years after they were last allowed to march, members of the LGBT community re-joined New York City's India Day parade on Sunday. Led by openly gay City Councilman Danny Dromm and Council Speaker Christine Quinn, a small contingent of gay and lesbian marchers made their way down Madison Avenue, past tens of thousands of spectators.

> As with the St. Patrick's Day parade, an annual showdown between parade organizers and the LGBT community has been a guaranteed feature of India Day, which commemorates the country's independence from Britain in 1947. The last time the South Asian Lesbian and Gay Association was allowed to march was in 2000.

LGBTQ people of color—especially transgender women of color—continue to face exclusion and violence in the United States. At the same time, these groups have made great strides in protecting their communities and securing their rights. Beyond the decades-long battle to legalize same-sex marriage, culminating in the 2015 U.S. Supreme Court decision in *Obergefell v. Hodges* lifting bans on it in all fifty states, groups like SALGA have continued to fight for the representation of people of color outside of and within LGBTQ communities.

TIMELINE OF IMPORTANT EVENTS IN QUEER SOUTH ASIAN HXSTORY

400–200 BCE — Tamil Sangam literature refers to relationships between two men and explores the lives of trans women in the Aravan cult in Koovagam village in Tamil Nadu.

300 BCE — Vatsyayana's *Kama Sutra* devotes an entire chapter to homosexuality.

1015 — Sultan Mahmud of Ghazni, the first Muslim ruler of the Indian subcontinent, has a relationship with his slave, Malik Ayaz.

1590 — Shah Hussain, a Punjabi Sufi poet regarded as a saint, falls in love with a Brahmin boy named Madho Lal. They are often referred to as a single person with the composite name Madho Lal Hussain.

1861 — The British Empire's Offences Against the Person Act of 1861 includes an anti-sodomy section, which is later credited with giving birth to Section 377 of the Indian Penal Code and similar anti-sodomy laws across the Indian subcontinent.

1918 — Tara Singh and Jamil Singh are separately arrested for interracial sodomy in Sacramento, California, the earliest-known records of South Asian men who have sex with men (MSM) in North America.

1985 — *Anamika*, a newsletter for South Asian lesbians, publishes the first of three issues.

1986 — The first queer South Asian organization in the world, Trikon (later renamed Trikone), is founded in San Francisco by Arvind Kumar and Suvir Das. An associated print newsletter is also established.

Late 1980s — Other queer South Asian organizations form in cities around the U.S. and the world, including Chicago, Los Angeles, Bangalore, Bombay, London, and Toronto.

1989 — Urvashi Vaid, an Indian American, becomes executive director of the National Gay and Lesbian Task Force, a national LGBTQ advocacy and community-building organization.

1989–2001 — *Desh Pardesh*, a lesbian- and gay-positive, feminist, anti-racist, anti-imperialist, and anti-caste/classist community forum, highlights arts, culture, and politics and the voices and expressions of systematically silenced South Asian community constituencies.

1995 — Pride Utsav (San Francisco) is the first queer South Asian conference in the U.S. (followed by conferences in 2000, 2006, and 2013).

2007 — The Supreme Court of Nepal issues orders to end discrimination against sexual and gender minorities.

2009 — The Delhi High Court decriminalizes all consensual same-sex activity among adults (later overturned by India's Supreme Court on December 11, 2013). Pakistan's Supreme Court declares a third gender for the trans/hijra population.

2010 — SALGA is admitted into the New York India Day Parade after a ten-year exclusion.

2011 — Gautam Raghavan, a gay Indian American, is appointed the LGBT liaison for the White House Office of Public Engagement, the highest U.S. government position held by a queer South Asian.

2012 — The Desi Queer Helpline (DeQH) forms.

2014 — The Supreme Court of India rules that transgender people have all the rights granted by the Indian constitution.

2014 — The Queer South Asian National Network (QSANN) forms.

A VERY, VERY BRIEF HISTORY OF A DESI TRANSGENDER MAN

Mashuq Mushtaq Deen

TRIGGER WARNING: This story describes instances of self-harm and sexual assault.

AT THE AGE OF ZERO, I am born. I appear to be a baby girl. My parents do not question what appears to be. I am named Shireen.

AT THE AGE OF FOUR (or perhaps younger), my best friend in nursery school—Daniel, an Asian American boy—gives me a toy truck. I love this truck for about a day and a half before my parents make me give it back to him. I never completely forgive them for this.

AT THE AGE OF TWELVE, I am an only child at home, my brother off at college. I am terrified that I will someday soon get my period. My mother, a pediatrician, mentions that she has some very athletic patients who don't get their periods until they're nineteen. I play basketball, soccer, tae kwon do, and tennis—I hope it's enough. I start to ask questions about the possibility of getting a preventive hysterectomy. With the approach of puberty, my parents get suddenly strict about EVERYTHING. When I go to an overnight summer camp (to study algebra, of course), I scare my best friend there by walking on the high stadium wall of the football field. I don't tell her that I've contemplated suicide and have been talking to God about it.

AT THE AGE OF FOURTEEN, I get my period. It is as devastating as I fear. It's harder to play sports. I wear two pads end-to-end and spandex shorts to keep everything in place. I hate it.

AT THE AGE OF SIXTEEN, I'm fighting with my parents all the time, it seems. They take a break from the fighting to throw me a surprise sweet-sixteen birthday party, but I can't seem to enjoy it. This is the year I experiment with cutting for the first time. I also discover the power of the miniskirt and flirting with boys. I like the power, so I try to wear skirts for a year. And sexy underwear. All my friends are doing it.

AT THE AGE OF SEVENTEEN, I decide that I was right the first time—skirts are not for me. Also, sexy underwear gives me a wedgie. I am eager to get the hell away from home and go to college. I am accepted to Columbia University in New York City.

AT THE AGE OF EIGHTEEN, my composition professor, Alexandra, reads my writing and thinks it would be a good idea for me to see a therapist. I have a platonic crush on her and will do anything she asks me to do, so I go. (This is also the year I read *Stone Butch Blues* for the first time and discover boy's underwear. I LOVE boy's underwear.)

AT THE AGE OF NINETEEN, I shave my head. My parents are totally freaked out. My brother thinks I'm being difficult. Shortly thereafter, I realize my crush on Alexandra is not entirely platonic, and I come out as bisexual. My parents are totally freaked out (again) and in denial. They want me to see a psychiatrist. I go, reluctantly, and am given a prescription for Prozac. I am cutting more often. I feel like my personality is fragmenting.

AT THE AGE OF TWENTY, I drop out of college, to my parents' utter dismay. I live at home and see a therapist. One afternoon, I pop a handful of pills and go to the hospital to get my stomach pumped. I am admitted to a psych ward for the first time. Within a few months, I am admitted again. And then again—this time at a long-term facility for a year.

AT THE AGE OF TWENTY-ONE, I check myself into a Super 8 Motel and attempt to end my life by slitting my wrists with a broken piece of glass. I just cannot handle the emotional pain and self-loathing anymore. As I'm sawing away at my wrists (killing yourself is not as easy as one might think), I have a conversation with God, who says things I cannot put into words here, and I realize that there is a part of me that wants to live. I am surprised.

Everything about my life changes in that moment.

AT THE AGE OF TWENTY-TWO, because life is not a linear trajectory, I am raped while traveling in Costa Rica. I am unprepared—can one ever be prepared for something like that?—because I don't understand that men look at me (an old-school butch) and see a girl.

AT THE AGE OF TWENTY-THREE, I go back to college, this time a state university in Massachusetts.

AT THE AGE OF TWENTY-FOUR, I meet my partner, Elizabeth, while rehearsing the play *The Lion in Winter*. She's nothing I was looking for and she is the love of my life.

AT THE AGE OF TWENTY-EIGHT, I read *Stone Butch Blues* for the second time and realize it's not just about being butch—it's also about being transgender. I am confused about what I am. I go to India to do volunteer work and meet a transgender man for the first time. The ground falls out from under me.

AT THE AGE OF TWENTY-NINE, I begin to transition from female to male, first with pronouns, then with hormones. I am terrified.

AT THE AGE OF THIRTY-ONE, my parents see my beard and stop talking to me for two years.

AT THE AGE OF THIRTY-SEVEN, I am invited to a cousin's wedding in India, and then I am suddenly disinvited. My parents and I fight about this, and they stop talking to me for a year and a half.

AT THE AGE OF THIRTY-NINE, all the cats are out of the bag, I think. I hope. My parents and I talk every weekend now. They are happy to see me. (They have become Obama Democrats after the debacle that is George W. Bush's presidency, and so we can even talk about politics. We still skirt queer issues.) My partner and I go on our first vacation with my parents—to Yellowstone National Park! To the surprise of all my American friends, who seem to think that traveling with your parents is a horrible way to spend nine days, we have a wonderful time.

AT THE AGE OF FORTY—so NOW, in other words—I am painfully aware of the time we have lost fighting with each other. None of us are getting any younger, and I want to spend as much time with them as possible, while we still can. Maybe at one time, they wanted a different sort of child than they got with me, but, to be fair, there was a time when I wanted different parents than they were, so we're probably even. I like who I am and they helped me to become this person, sometimes by comfort, sometimes by crucible. For my part, I am still learning how to be an adult with them. I tell them "I love you"—such an American thing to do—so much it makes them uncomfortable, but, nevertheless, they now say it back.

Mashuq Mushtaq Deen (he or they) is an award-winning playwright and published author.

Deen on a road trip to Oklahoma in 2016. In SAADA, courtesy of Mashuq Mushtaq Deen.

ALOK VAID-MENON AND A "TRANSFEMININE FUTURE"

Alok Vaid-Menon is a gender-nonconforming South Asian American writer, educator, activist, and community organizer. Their work transcends any one medium; they use everything from fashion to social media to poetry to explore themes like diaspora, loneliness, race, gender, and street harassment.

I am constantly devastated by the fact that the things that are most dear to us are often the things we are not supposed to talk about in public. I don't know how to compartmentalize myself into binaries—male/female, public/private, happy/sad—in order to make myself easily digestible. I am deeply curious and disheartened when people aren't able to express their full selves with one another. I notice that the things that they tell us to relegate to the private—our femininity, our gender nonconformity, our emotionality, our struggle—are often the things that are most powerful precisely when they are in public. For me, stories transcend the myth of private/public. They are a way of flirting around boundaries and borders.

From *"Alok Vaid-Menon on Building a Transfeminine Future"* for Broadly, by Vrinda Jagota.

HELPLINES FOR LGBTQ YOUTH

If you are a young person in crisis, feeling suicidal, or in need of a safe and judgment-free place to talk, there is help and you are not alone.

The Trevor Project's Trevor Lifeline offers around-the-clock support with trained counselors: **thetrevorproject.org**; **1-866-488-7386**

The Desi LGBTQ Helpline for South Asians—DeQH—is volunteer run and available on certain days: **deqh.org**; **908-367-3374**

JAHAJEE SISTERS

Suzanne C. Persard

In March 2007, a group of four Indo-Caribbean women gathered in Queens, New York, frustrated by gender-based violence and oppression and their community's silence over it. Wanting to create a space for dialogue for the women in their community, they began planning the first-ever Indo-Caribbean Women's Empowerment Summit. As they planned, news spread about the death of Natasha Ramen, a twenty-year-old Indo-Caribbean woman who was murdered in Queens by her rapist. In the women's devastation and indignation over the lack of response to this heinous crime, they pushed forward with their plan to counter silence with outrage and action.

Not even two months after the summit, another Indo-Caribbean woman was murdered: twenty-three-year-old Guiatree Hardat, who was killed by her ex-fiancée, an Indo-Caribbean NYPD officer, after she called off their engagement

Courtesy of Jahajee Sisters.

because of violence. Again, this death was met with absolute silence from the Indo-Caribbean community of New York City. The summit organizers saw a need for sustainable organizing in Indo-Caribbean women communities, and the Indo-Caribbean Women's Empowerment Group was born. The second summit, in 2008, was held in partnership with Sakhi for South Asian Women, an anti–domestic violence organization.

The collective silence surrounding the deaths of these two Indo-Caribbean women echoed the legacy of gender-based violence during the period of indentureship. Between 1838 and 1917, Indians—primarily from Uttar Pradesh and Bihar—supplanted the labor provided by African slaves, now freed, on plantations in countries including Jamaica, Guyana, Trinidad, Suriname, and Mauritius, as well as South Africa and Fiji. On the ships that sailed from Calcutta to ports of indenture, Indians on board referred to each other as *jahaji bhai* and *jahaji bahen,* "ship brother" and "ship sister." Although the descendants of indentureship have been obscured from the pages of South Asian and South Asian American history, the Indian indentured diaspora survives a deliberate legacy of marginalization. One organization leading the effort is Jahajee Sisters, which grew out of the work of those early organizers of the Women's Empowerment Summit.

The name Jahajee Sisters was chosen to honor our ancestral legacy. Conversations from a kitchen table in Queens transformed into a collective effort to create and sustain a space for organizing Indo-Caribbean women. Launching the

---

BOLO BAHEN! SPEAK, SISTER!

We were once caterpillars
emerging from cocoons
now butterflies with iron wings
soaring to new heights.

~~~

The reshaping of community
is like blowing glass
molded in the fire of violence
dipped in waters of reflection
creating priceless gifts
holding the beauty of unity.

From Taij Kumarie Moteelall's "Walking Our New Road into Being: Women of the South Asian Diaspora on Self-Awareness and Empowerment," the introduction to Bolo Bahen! Speak, Sister!

---

first arts-and-activism community program for Indo-Caribbean women, Jahajee Sisters partnered again with Sakhi for South Asian Women, and together they produced *Bolo Bahen! Speak, Sister!,* a chapbook of poetry written by survivors of domestic, sexual, and intimate partner violence culminating with a performance at the Queens Museum of Art.

Jahajee Sisters emerged as the first movement-building organization for Indo-Caribbean women in the United States calling for an end to gender-based violence and advocating for reproductive justice and LGBT rights. As a community made invisible, we knew that returning to the legacy of our ancestors was a critical part of building a movement. Recognizing that our great-grandmothers sailing on ships from Calcutta were resilient and the embodiment of strength—although they might not have called themselves "feminists"—Jahajee Sisters sought to evoke their spirit, fundamental to our movement and our name. As organizers and activists, we've inherited a powerful legacy from Indo-Caribbean women whose own narratives must be centralized and celebrated despite generational trauma and inherited legacies of violence.

Suzanne C. Persard (she/they) is a scholar, writer, and activist who was born and raised in Bronx, New York, to parents from Kingston, Jamaica.

MARGINS, OR ON NOT BEING WITH MOST OF YOU, MOST OF THE TIME

V. V. Ganeshananthan

I am South Asian. This identification means choosing to acknowledge the common ground I share with people who trace their origins to Afghanistan, Bangladesh, Bhutan, India, the Maldives, Nepal, Pakistan, and Sri Lanka. When I meet someone from one of these communities and they also elect to use this term, I know that they identify with me. Sometimes this exchange feels like a kind of secret handshake—one I wish wasn't such a big secret. In the United States, at least, being South Asian and not being of Indian origin can be a battle—one that leaves me feeling torn between working in solidarity with Indian American communities and challenging their dominance in South Asian political and cultural spaces.

I am of Tamil and Sri Lankan origin. But I am often misidentified, in the United States, as a person of Indian origin. Because of many factors—history, nationalism, immigration policy, geopolitics, geography, population sizes—most people are

Artwork by Chamindika Wanduragala, a Sri Lankan American artist combining puppetry, visual art, stop-motion animation, and sound design, and also a DJ (DJ Chamun). Chamindika is the founder and executive/artistic director of Monkeybear's Harmolodic Workshop, which supports Native, Black, IPOC in developing creative and technical skills in contemporary puppetry. Her work can be seen at chamindika.com.

more familiar with India than with any other South Asian country. And most South Asians in the United States are Indian. It's not unusual for media outlets, schools, and even casual conversations to reinforce the perception that *all* South Asians are Indian. (The census, for example, has a box labeled "Asian Indian." I don't check it.) But I am *not* Indian, and I am also connected to a country where Indian imperialism has done real damage. How then to navigate being taken for Indian? How to explain to my Indian American friends how I feel about this erasure of my identity, or about their country's problematic histories in Nepal, Sri Lanka, and other places? How to explain to non-Asians, who may be hard-pressed to care about the finer points of others' identities? How to tend to where my interests *do* overlap with those of my Indian American friends, as they frequently do? Many South Asians still don't use the term "South Asian." Perhaps it's unfamiliar; perhaps they resist it as the construction of outsiders; perhaps they prefer to identify with their country of origin, and to make others identify with it too. Some people of Indian origin are slow to correct the assumption that all South Asians are Indian, and every time one of these statements is made and passes without comment, I notice.

The centrality of Indian American identity in South Asian America exerts a huge pressure on our conversations. I first learned to understand the effect of majoritarian influence from Sri Lankan political discourse. Just as my status as a

---

LEAH LAKSHMI PIEPZNA-SAMARASINHA

Poet, performance artist, and social activist Leah Lakshmi Piepzna-Samarasinha is the author of the poetry collections *Consensual Genocide* (2006), *Love Cake* (2011)—winner of a Lambda Literary Award for Lesbian Poetry—and *Bodymap* (2015) and the memoir *Dirty River* (2015). Their writing often reflects their identity as a queer, disabled writer of Sri Lankan heritage. In an interview with Usman Mushtak, Piepzna-Samarasinha said, "Stories create the world. Seeing stories that look like your own, that you've never read written down before, or that are stories you've never thought of before that change your whole idea of what is possible, are a big revolutionary deal. . . . My poems are my stories of the freedom dreams I want for me and us."

Adapted from the Poetry Foundation's biography for Leah Lakshmi Piepzna-Samarasinha.

South Asian American of Sri Lankan origin puts me on the margins of South Asian America, my status as a member of the Tamil Lankan diaspora puts me at odds with conventionally named Sri Lankan groups, many of whom prioritize Sinhala Buddhist nationalism. It's not uncommon to find diasporic organizations with Sri Lanka in their names that have little interest in critically engaging the country's treatment of its minorities. I can find little refuge in many Sri Lankan Tamil diaspora groups, which all too often fail to address—or even promote—the brutal history and effects of Tamil militancy.

Where's a Tamil Lankan to go? I want to be part of multiethnic conversations, dialogues critical of Indian cultural hegemony, the Sri Lankan state, Tamil militancy and other non-state actors, and the international community (and myself as part of that). When I feel little room for my identities in discussions, I try to collaborate with others to make new spaces (including Lanka Solidarity, for example, a small multiethnic network of activists based in North America and interested in critical takes on Sri Lankan politics).

As an activist in the larger South Asian community, I have sought out spaces that have chosen to label themselves South Asian, and not Indian. The latter would, no doubt, be expedient in a variety of ways—India and Sri Lanka are both easier for people to recognize. But South Asia is a concept that lies beyond nation or ethnicity; it's a collective idea rooted in cross-border solidarities. To elect South Asia bespeaks a generosity of vision and a desire to be inclusive. It's an invention and a reclamation of space. So when the South Asian American Digital Archive asked me to write about Sri Lankan American identity, and I thought about why I was willing, I returned to the idea of South Asia. It's true—it might be something that doesn't exist, something made after the fact to try to contain an odd mishmash of pasts. But perhaps that is not a mistake, but a victory. Perhaps this is what the South Asian diaspora has in common, regardless of national or ethnic origin—our relentless ability to rename and invent ways to belong to each other.

V. V. Ganeshananthan (she/her/hers) teaches fiction and nonfiction writing in the MFA program at the University of Minnesota, and is the author of a novel, Love Marriage.

SAADA'S ARCHIVAL CREATORS FELLOWSHIP PROGRAM

In any community, no matter how narrowly defined, power and marginalization are a factor in whose voices are heard and whose are silenced, in whose stories are preserved and whose are ignored. Groups within the South Asian American community that have been traditionally marginalized and excluded are the most challenging to include in SAADA because of the uniquely vulnerable status of these communities. For example, there is practically no information available to the public about the more than half a million undocumented South Asians in the country today. At a time of increased deportation and heightened uncertainty around immigration status, collecting stories and materials from these populations is only possible through partnership with those from within and with deep existing relationships in these communities. SAADA's Archival Creators Fellowship Program, launched in 2019 with a grant from the Andrew W. Mellon Foundation, supports community members in becoming active participants in proposing, designing, appraising, curating, and creating archival collections that reflect the histories and perspectives of the most marginalized groups within the South Asian American community.

The three fellows for the inaugural cycle of the fellowship in 2019–20 were:

Dhanya Addanki (she/her) is a journalist, writer, and photographer, and formerly an editor at *Sojourners*. Dhanya spent most of her career working in the human rights journalism space, ensuring people from the most silenced and marginalized communities have the power to shape their own narratives and have the platform to hold oppressive powers accountable. Dhanya's project is uncovering the stories of Dalit people—specifically Dalit women—in the U.S. This project's main goals are to unearth the history of the people in this community, people who have often not had the privilege to know their past, and to showcase the nuance, dignity, and power in Dalit communities in the U.S. Because of her strong belief that communities cannot heal from historic, intergenerational trauma without knowing their history, with this project, Dhanya is catalyzing collective healing and liberation through story.

Gaiutra Bahadur (she/her) is a Guyanese American writer and the author of *Coolie Woman*, a personal history of indenture in the West Indies that was shortlisted for Britain's Orwell Prize for artful political writing. Her work as a journalist, essayist, and creative writer has appeared in a wide range of anthologies, magazines, and newspapers across the globe, including the *New York Times Book Review*, the *New York Review of Books*, the *New Republic*, the *Nation*, *Lapham's Quarterly*, the *Guardian*, *History Today*, the *Griffith Review*, the *Boston Review*, and *Dissent*. Gaiutra teaches journalism as an assistant professor in the Department of Arts, Culture, and Media at Rutgers University–Newark. For her project, Gaiutra is gathering stories and material objects that bear witness to the tales and textures of departures and arrivals for Guyanese immigrants in the New York metro area.

Mustafa Saifuddin (they/them) recently completed a PhD in soil ecology from Boston University and works in the field of environmental justice. Mustafa's family is from India, but they were born in Saudi Arabia before growing up in Texas. They are working to build an ongoing archive of South Asian American queer and trans stories as a fellow for SAADA. Mustafa's project is uncovering stories of inspiration, resistance, and resilience, and finding creative and authentic ways of storytelling that allow for community building while maintaining privacy and resisting surveillance.

The following excerpts are from oral history interviews conducted by SAADA's 2019–20 Archival Creators Fellows.

—

AN ORAL HISTORY INTERVIEW WITH ANJALI R.

Conducted by Mustafa Saifuddin

Anjali R. is the founder of Parivar, a trans and queer South Asian space in the San Francisco Bay Area. In the oral history, Anjali describes growing up in India, exploring different permutations of gender expression while moving throughout the U.S. and Canada, and navigating transphobia within queer South Asian spaces.

AR: (30:14)

I think from Seattle I was getting involved . . . I was involved in the Houston community, but I really felt the need . . . I think it was the point where I felt, I am settled, I have privilege, I have access, I need to give back to the community. And if I can do that, and another trans woman, another South Asian doesn't have to go through what I had to go through in my life, I'll feel good about that. And the way I got involved was I came back into the same group, which was very cis, South Asian male–driven from back then, but I immediately realized that I wasn't welcome. Later I tried to get on their board, they wouldn't let me get on their board. . . . It still is run by men who are intimidated by a very strong woman like me.

And then an incident happened where the community leader in their personal private business had hired a trans woman—a South Asian trans woman that I knew from Houston—much older to work in their restaurant, didn't pay her, she was uneducated. She reached out to me, and it . . . just snowballed into this big, big thing that almost went to the newspapers, where I threatened to sue them if they didn't pay her. She was homeless, she lost her apartment, she had to come stay with me. So I think that really catapulted me into believing that discrimination happened a lot more, and I did not know a lot of these things. So many words. I did not know a lot of these words and activism. But that really told me that I need to be involved because I have something that most people don't in my identity, which is I can speak, and . . . I know how to manage and work through the system and really support folks like me.

And I think that catapulted me and I [*laughs*], I guess again I was exterminated from the community in such a big way that, for example, two days after all this meltdown happened, and she was finally paid, you know, by them, I . . . ended up . . . going to a birthday party in Dublin, of a kid whose parents were, you know, in the community, and they had known me . . . since when I lived here in the early 2000s before my transition. The door opened, and they said, "We're so sorry, but can you please leave?" And they shut the door. And that broke my heart into another million pieces, but it also told me this is what happens on a regular basis, and I have to stop it.

And so I continued to get involved, I continued to learn, because I'm coming from a world of very much privilege where I don't know what it means to be on the street, I don't know what it means to be in sex work, I don't have the same narrative. So a lot of the community, my trans community—especially not simply South Asian, because I have not met many, many South Asian trans people to begin with anywhere, leave alone the Bay Area. I was more involved in the overall trans community and, you know, learning a lot about what it means to be a Black trans woman, the anti-Blackness that exists in the South Asian community.

A lot of those aspects really brought me to a point where I learned a lot, and then I would execute a lot more, and then I realized that I had the strength, the power, and the ability to be in a leadership role. I started getting involved and being on a lot of boards. . . . About a year and a half ago, you know, SF State Foundation reached out, saying, "Can you do a South Asian performance for 139?" And while that seemed great, it was also very difficult for me to say, "You know we're just going to do a performance and we're going to go home." And when we did the performance, and the second time we did it, it was just so big. The response from female South Asians in the community—in the South Asian community, the trans, anybody who was not the more cookie-cutter mold wanted this to continue, and that's how Parivar came about. And I've invested so many hours and time in it, more than my regular job, and I wouldn't do anything different in how I grew the organization to where now we are fiscally sponsored, we have a board, and I'm at peace that I'm able to make a difference.

—

AN ORAL HISTORY INTERVIEW WITH JOHN BOOPALAN

Conducted by Dhanya Addanki

John Boopalan is a Dalit theologian and pastor and the author of the book Memory, Grief, and Agency: A Political Theological Account of Wrongs and Rite.

JB: (28:32)

Dalit. Dalit is a political term. Even the government of India doesn't recognize the word *Dalit*. [*Laughs*] The government of India would rather say, "SC." "Scheduled caste." "Scheduled for affirmative action." "You're a historically marginalized caste, sure, and we've scheduled you for affirmative action." "You're scheduled caste." So my father has always been open about his scheduled caste identity.

And because my father's marriage was intercaste, he told us a story from our very young childhood days that when he got married, he told my mother's side of the family that he was SC, and that they should know that.

DA: How did they react to that?

It's a . . . that's a big question. Yeah. This is actually such a fascinating topic. Because today I'm a big believer in intersectionality . . . which means that we can't talk about one particular wrong without talking about something else. So I can't talk about caste without talking also about gender, without also talking about religion, without also talking about class, without also talking about sexuality, right? That's just what needs to be done. That's the responsible thing to do. And I think it's a natural outflow of any liberationist impulse. So, I say that kind of at the outset to answer you, to respond to your question, because . . . my mother's Naidu, my father's Paraiyar. Those are the particular caste identities, right? My mother's mother, so grandmother from my mother's side, her Naidu husband left her for another Naidu woman very early on in their marriage. So really he married out of necessity. He loved another Naidu woman. He married my grandmother because his family said he should. He never loved her and he deserted her right from the very beginning. So my grandmother raised my mother and my mother's sister, two daughters she had, on her own without her husband. So in some sense, my reading of it is she saw through the lie of caste.

Caste is a lie. It continues. It was a lie, it always was a lie, and is a lie even today. And the lie is basically if you protect your caste identity, things will be well for you. Right? That's . . . that's the lie. That's the lie. It's partly true . . . if you see it in terms of power and control, it's true. But in terms of a good life, it's not true.

DA: Say more about that. What do you mean by that?

In terms of power . . . see, most people today marry within their caste. It's because of power. If you're from a dominant caste, it means that somewhere in your history, you have some land. That's what it amounts to in the Indian context. You have land, you have gold, and stuff like that. You have wealth, you have accumulated wealth that has often been accumulated at the cost of unpaid slave labor, almost . . . of Dalits, and tribals, and other oppressed communities in India, right? It's accumulated wealth. Wrongly accumulated wealth [*laughs*] . . . but still accumulated wealth. Often land, often gold, and other kinds of things. So people marry within their own caste at the end of the day, even if they don't phrase it in such a way for precisely that. They'll get a piece of the pie, they'll get a piece of the land, they'll get some gold. Who doesn't want a pot of gold? And in India, a pot of gold is not like a metaphor. It's a thing. You literally have a pot of gold waiting for you if you're dominant caste that will be given to you at the time of your marriage. Doesn't matter if you're a man or a woman or whatever. When you get married, you will get a pot of gold, you probably get a piece of land, you'll get other stuff. Who doesn't want that? It's power. It's control, that way. But in terms of a good life . . . no.

. . . One last thing, right? I have had and continue to have friends from all across the caste spectrum. And I know several of my dominant caste friends who will date across caste. And they really love these partners of theirs. They truly genuinely love them up until the point of marriage. Really, that's it. Most often when it comes to marriage, that's it. They would have dated for two years, three years, four years, five, six, ten! They are, truly, madly, deeply in love. And they say bye. And they marry from their own caste at the end of the day. Why? Power. Power.

—

AN ORAL HISTORY INTERVIEW WITH "SHERRY SINGH"

Conducted by Gaiutra Bahadur

"Sherry Singh," a DACA recipient, is an aide at a public school in Queens. Here, she tells her story of coming to the United States "backtrack" from Guyana at the age of eight to reunite with her mother in 1996.

SS: (28:11)

. . . I started, like, getting this anger towards my mom because I said I wanted to come, but not in this way where it's like I can't live my life. You know, I don't know who's who. I don't know where I go, what I sign up for.

It took . . . a while before I even got a passport, a Guyana passport at that, because in order for me to get a passport, I needed to file a report for a missing passport. I never got a passport because I didn't come with my own passport. So . . . I needed to go to the precinct and make a report. I went to the precinct. You need an ID to make the report. So it was like it was so long that I couldn't even get a proper identification because of this situation.

And you go to the doctor, and . . . it's like, okay, do you have an ID? . . . Then, at nineteen I was pregnant and then my husband and I started going to the doctor's appointments. In order for you to do this, where's your ID, where's your address. And it was constant fear because it's like, at this point, you don't know where that information is going, who's who.

After 9/11, it got even crazier, where it became more strict . . . where not even a regular ID could work. You need a New York State ID, and you need all these things. So even now, like, when my family was coming over here, I wanted to tell them, "Don't do it, because it's not an easy life to live in the U.S. undocumented." Because if you were to look at it, it would be way better off to be in

Guyana. Because I understand it's a struggle, because it's a terrible country. But coming over here, it's not as easy as people think.

And because of living in that constant fear of you never know who's gonna, what's gonna be your time, it was even more stressful and fearful the fact that I became a mother. And my kids, like, it went from not being all about me anymore. . . . What if I'm walking on the street one day with my kids and they come and take me? Or go to a doctor's appointment and they're there waiting for me because now I'm in all these systems and doctors.

Because I think . . . even now people that live here documented [try not to do] certain things that could . . . jeopardize themselves. And I see that on a day-to-day basis, where it's like kids are hurt at school and their parents don't want to take them to the doctor or don't want the ambulance being called because of their situation. Or something as basic as right now [in] the pandemic: to go online 311 and sign up to get groceries as much as they need it. They have that fear, like, where is this information going?

. . . even the census. You know, I did volunteer work for the River Fund pantry to fill out the census. And people fear where, like, I don't have a social. Where's this information going? Who's getting this information? And some of them will tell you straight up. They trust you enough to say, "I don't have my papers," or "I don't want to do it." And you could tell already it is because of—some of them even call me over, it's like, do you need a Social Security number or something to fill this out? And . . . it's sad to see people to have to live this way, because right now with the pandemic, you have . . . people that was already undocumented . . . was already living paycheck to paycheck. And now that the pandemic is happening and they work at bars and restaurants and grocery stores, and these things are closed, like, how are these families supposed to live? How are they supposed to get by on a day-to-day basis?

So it's like . . . it's hard, not only for yourself, but see to . . . live that life of being in that situation that you could relate and you know, these families and their fear and what they have and things like that. So it's definitely, definitely fearful, even with DACA, obviously not safe still.

—

Learn more about SAADA's Archival Creators Fellowship Program at saada.org/acfp.

CHAPTER 6

Faith & Religion

A booklet published by the San Francisco Vedanta Society shortly after the temple's opening reported: "THE FIRST HINDU TEMPLE in the Whole Western World. S.W. corner Webster and Filbert Streets. Erected August 21, 1905, by the San Francisco Vedanta Society, San Francisco, Calif., U.S.A., under the Auspices of The Ramakrishna Mission, Belur-Math, Calcutta, India." Courtesy of the University of California, Berkeley.

INTRODUCTION

Khyati Y. Joshi and Bandana Purkayastha

South Asian Americans practice many religious traditions—including Hinduism, Islam, Christianity, Sikhism, Buddhism, Jainism, Judaism, and Zoroastrianism—or practice none of these, and are atheist or agnostic. In this chapter, we focus on Hinduism, Islam, and Sikhism, the three largest religions in South Asia. Beginning with a brief account of the historical presence and development of these religions in the United States over the last two centuries, we then discuss how South Asian Americans live these religions and acquire their knowledge of them in the United States. Finally, we consider the contemporary challenges of practicing these religions in the United States.

But here is what we don't do: We do not provide a comprehensive view of South Asian American religious beliefs. We do not explain the philosophies, scriptures, or tenets of the religions we do discuss—topics you might encounter when studying a religion itself.

In describing how South Asian Americans *live* certain religions, we go beyond texts, traditions, and rituals to examine how religion and spirituality are manifested in the everyday lives of Hindu, Sikh, and Muslim South Asian Americans. Our focus is not, for example, on the question "How Sikh is she?" Instead, we aim to answer the more important question "How is she Sikh?" Through this focus on lived religion, we can understand how religion shapes identity, even for those who do not consider themselves religious or see religion as a dominant part of who they are. We illustrate how experiences vary, and how encounters in the public space can reveal the gaps between how mainstream American culture understands religion and the acceptance of the practices of South Asian Americans.

Khyati Y. Joshi (she/her) is a professor of education at Fairleigh Dickinson University and a social science researcher whose work focuses on the intersections of race and religion in the United States.

Bandana Purkayastha (she/her) is a professor of sociology and Asian & Asian American studies at the University of Connecticut.

BEGINNINGS

Khyati Y. Joshi and Bandana Purkayastha

South Asians began arriving in the United States in larger numbers beginning in the late nineteenth and early twentieth centuries. They were mostly Muslims from the Bengal region of present-day India and Bangladesh, along with Sikhs from the Punjab region of present-day India and Pakistan. The Bengali Muslims were peddlers who arrived on the East Coast; the Sikhs were mostly laborers who were most visible on the West Coast. Whatever their actual religious affiliations, these early South Asian migrants were identified as "Hindoos" by the government and in the popular language of the late nineteenth and early twentieth centuries.

These Muslim, Sikh, and Hindu migrants arrived in a country where they were religious minorities. As they settled in the United States and created their communities, they started establishing their own houses of worship. The first gurdwara in the United States was established in Stockton, California, in 1912, primarily through the efforts of Sikh pioneers who had become successful farmers in the region. The first Hindu place of worship in the country, the Vedanta Society of New York, was established in 1894 in two rented rooms after the influential visit of Swami Vivekananda to the World's Parliament of Religions; it moved to its current location on the Upper West Side in 1934. Muslims also began setting up houses of worship: Mufti Muhammad Sadiq, an Ahmadiyya community leader born in Bhera, Punjab, established a headquarters for the Ahmadiyya mission in Chicago in 1920. After the period from 1917 to 1965, when immigration from Asia was heavily restricted (a limited number of Indians immigrated to the United States under the

STOCKTON GURDWARA

The Stockton Gurdwara Sahib, the first gurdwara built in the United States, held its first prayers and rituals on October 24, 1912. In its early years, the Stockton Gurdwara was the meeting place for Sikhs who were involved in the Ghadar Party, an organization that was eager to establish India's independence through an armed revolution against British rule. Until 1947, the Stockton Gurdwara functioned as the only religious institution in the state of California where Sikhs from the greater area could gather for religious worship. Congressman Dalip Singh Saund, the first Asian American, Indian American, and Sikh American to be elected to the U.S. Congress, was a member of the Stockton Gurdwara community.

Photograph of members of the Pacific Coast Khalsa Diwan Society in front of the Sikh Temple in Stockton at dedicatory services. November 21, 1915. Courtesy of Holt-Atherton Special Collections, University of the Pacific Library.

1946 Luce-Celler Act), immigration from South Asia increased substantially with the passage of the 1965 Immigration Act. With the exception of some gurdwaras and mandirs (Hindu temples) on the West Coast, there were virtually no houses of worship for newly arrived Sikhs and Hindus to join. So these communities soon began constructing their own houses of worship—or, in many cases, taking over vacant churches and making those religious spaces their own. By contrast, South Asian Christians and Muslims found numerous churches and a few mosques (built by Arab or African American Muslim communities) in the United States, although they soon wanted their own spaces for religious and cultural practice and started establishing churches and congregations, such as the Indian-origin Christians who established the Malankara Archdiocese of the Syrian Orthodox Church in North America.

Today, South Asian American religions are visible because we see mosques, temples, and gurdwaras across our nation. In many cases, these houses of worship are the hubs of ethnic and religious communities—even though worship, prayer, and ritual are also often done at home. Despite the existence of strong ethno-religious communities in many places, South Asian Americans of all ages also continue to be a minority in the workplace, at school, and in other public spaces. This combination of experiences—worshipping communally and taking part in cultural

---

RELIGIOUS AFFILIATIONS OF INDIAN AMERICANS

According to the Pew Research Center, only about half (51 percent) of Indian Americans are Hindu. In a 2012 Pew study, 18 percent of Indian Americans identified themselves as Christians, and 10 percent said they were Muslim. In fact, the religious makeup of the Indian American population differs quite a bit from that in India—where only 2.5 percent of the population is Christian, and nearly 80 percent is Hindu—and instead reflects varying histories of migration.

Adapted from "5 Facts about Indian Americans" from Pew Research.

---

activities, practicing religion as an individual or within a family, and existing in a society where the majority is white and Christian—shapes how South Asian Americans live their religion from day to day and across their life spans.

MUFTI MUHAMMAD SADIQ AND THE MUSLIM SUNRISE

Founded in Detroit in 1921 by Mufti Muhammad Sadiq, the *Muslim Sunrise* (formerly the *Moslem Sunrise*) is the earliest Muslim publication originating in the United States. Now a quarterly magazine published by the Ahmadiyya Muslim Community, it took its name from a saying of the prophet Muhammad (suggesting that "the sun shall rise from the west") and continues to serve as a platform for Islamic and interfaith discussion.

Sadiq was born in Punjab and sailed from England to Philadelphia in 1920. During his three years in the United States, he reportedly converted more than seven hundred people to Ahmadiyya, emphasizing racial tolerance. The Al Sadiq Mosque (Wabash Mosque) in Chicago, built in 1922, is the oldest-standing mosque in the country today and was funded primarily by African American Ahmadi Muslim converts.

Courtesy of muslimsunrise.com.

Khyati Y. Joshi (she/her) is a professor of education at Fairleigh Dickinson University and a social science researcher whose work focuses on the intersections of race and religion in the United States.

Bandana Purkayastha (she/her) is a professor of sociology and Asian & Asian American studies at the University of Connecticut.

LIVED RELIGION

Khyati Y. Joshi and Bandana Purkayastha

Contrary to certain stereotypes in American popular culture, South Asian Americans organize their religious practices in a variety of ways. Some South Asian Americans worship as a group, while others practice on their own or with their family. Some people worship in mosques, gurdwaras, churches, or temples; others, either because they have no house of worship nearby or simply by personal choice, practice at home. Practicing one's faith can involve celebrating specific religious events and performing rituals, or simply understanding and living according to a set of values that can be practiced quietly during the course of one's daily life or as part of a community.

EXPERIENCES

Unlike Muslims and Sikhs, Hindus do not have a single sacred book. The diversity of Hindu religious authorities, doctrines, and traditions leads to a diversity of practices and beliefs.

Hindus are the numerically largest group among South Asian Americans. Even though the number of temples in the United States has grown from a handful in the 1960s to hundreds or thousands today, many Hindus do not go to temples regularly. Some do not go because their way of living their religion never included temples; others cannot go because there are no temples nearby. Many Hindus have a variety of home-based practices, ranging from conducting pujas (prayer and other worship practices) to engaging in meditation and practicing yoga. For those whose practice never included temples, their spirituality is reflected through a set of values they associate with their religion.

Sulochana is a first-generation immigrant from southern India. Her house, in an affluent suburb, has an alcove with a few statues of gods and goddesses (representations of Hindu principles) that her parents gave her. She has taught her children about the statues, and her children have each chosen a personal god or goddess and taken those statues to college and, later, to their own homes. Each morning and evening, Sulochana lights a *nanda deepa* (a "lamp of bliss," often a flame in a shallow, cup-shaped, carved bronze holder) as part of her daily ritual. She also goes to a temple in her state during the celebration of some of the pujas she knows; the temple is far from her home, so she can't go there more often.

Like Sulochana, Juthika, who emigrated from eastern India, has an alcove in her home devoted to pictures of gods and goddesses. She also keeps pictures of her ancestors in this alcove. When she cleans it or decorates it with flowers or *alpona* (freehand designs created with a mixture of rice powder and water), she thinks of her links to her gods and goddesses and to her ancestors. She rarely goes to temples, but she tries to go to her regional religious celebrations when they are on weekends.

Anjali, a second-generation Hindu of Indian origin, does not keep any statues or other religious images in her apartment, nor does she attend a temple. For her, knowing and practicing dharma (fulfilling one's obligation as a human being through thought and everyday practice) in whatever she does throughout the day is the core of her religion.

AN ALTAR TO DALIT HONOR

In 2020, Dhanya Addanki created "An Altar to Dalit Honor" as a fellow for SAADA, showcasing the nuance, dignity, and power in Dalit communities in the U.S.

As part of her project, Addanki conducted an oral history interview with Rev. Evangeline Anderson-Rajkumar, a Dalit woman, feminist, activist, and ecumenical theologian, who reflected on the connections between Christianity and Dalit identity:

From a Christian perspective, this is so real that we hold on to this utter equality, utter grace, as kind of the grounding principles, because we are talking about the giver of life, the author of life, also as the one who embraces you back. And there I connect the earth and God. The earth as that which embraces you again, as you entering the womb again. And therefore burying of bodies, for me, is like the mother earth taking you back. You know, that kind of common religiosity, spirituality—that's possible. And that which really does not need a brand name, like those that exist today. It doesn't need a brand name. It doesn't need . . . yeah, how popular the name of a religion is. It's possible to be human beings. It's so critical.

And when I reflect on the Dalit perspective, and my Dalit identity, and Dalit theology, if I hold on to those three Bs—body, blood, and our being. The question of body and blood, especially these two, if they were used as the basis to keep people away from life, dignity, and livelihood, the answer lies in the same body and blood. You cannot search for some answer outside this realm. Affirmation of Dalit identity and their power lies in affirmation of their bodies, affirmation of their blood. So much so that it is not untouchability. Liberation lies only when they touch you. When you make Dalit bodies as so powerful and strong that there is no liberation without the Dalit touch. That's the kind of affirmation that we need to arrive at.

Artwork by Mon M.

Geeta, a Hindu Nepali American who lives in the suburbs, cannot reach other people in her religious community easily, so she misses most of the celebrations. She fasts on special days to remind herself about her role as a sister, wife, and mother; her fasts are a kind of prayer for the well-being of her family. Mukta, also a Hindu from Nepal, cannot create an appropriate atmosphere for worship in her rented apartment; she has to abide by the rules about fire hazards so cannot keep her incense sticks or *deepas* lit as part of her daily worship rituals. (Sulochana's children face the same problem in their college dorm rooms, so they don't observe

---

HINDU TEMPLE JOINS SANCTUARY MOVEMENT

In 2017, the Shaanti Bhavan Mandir in Queens became the first Hindu temple in the nation to publicly declare itself a sanctuary congregation, part of a network of houses of worship that will support and shelter undocumented immigrants.

Davanie Singhroy, who helped lead the temple's efforts, described the decision:

"We are a community largely comprised of immigrants and undocumented immigrants, and we were worried that this step would bring attention to our congregants who are undocumented," said Ms. Singhroy, 22, a temple and Sadhana member. "But in the end we decided those are the very people we were going to help by taking this step."

From "Hindu Temple in Queens Joins Sanctuary Movement" for the New York Times, by Sharon Otterman.

---

some of their family rituals there.) Following the custom of her grandmother and mother, Mukta makes sure she spends some time each day in meditation. She considers this practice the essence of becoming a good person—that is, someone who lets go of all ill feelings toward others and focuses on their goodness and humanity.

These snapshots reflect two important points. First, since Hinduism is extremely diverse and there are few celebrations that all Hindus celebrate on the same day or for the same reason, lived Hinduism varies a great deal depending on the family and the South Asian cultural region to which a family traces its roots. Hindus who trace their lineage to different parts of India or Nepal or Bangladesh or Sri Lanka are likely to have different types of practice. Second, unlike in public spaces of worship, where men are typically the priests or heads of the religious community, in most homes, women are the keepers of these rituals. They teach their children about daily reflection and practice.

Hindus are not the only group that engages in home-based practice. Supreet Kaur, a Sikh American, describes how, in her home, "We do prayers in the morning. . . . And every evening we read from Guru Granth Sahib. The Golden Temple streams online, webcast of the Delhi . . . so we would often read that together in the morning or in the evening. We never talked about it, just read it. We've done that together."

Sikhs live their religion in the United States in many ways beyond home-based worship. Among the second generation, summer camps play an important role in making a connection to one's faith. "My household is very religious. . . . Though I didn't have a community as much around me, . . . [family] made me feel connected to be Sikh," said one second-generation Sikh woman. "We did certain things—we didn't cut our hair, we went to gurdwara, we followed certain traditions, and the [summer] camps were a big factor. [In the camps,] that was the first time I really got exposed to a community [of] young people at my age in the area. That I did enjoy very much. I think there were points in camp that I felt very connected" to a Sikh community and identity.

Salma, a second-generation Pakistani American of the Muslim faith, describes her home-based practice: "I would pray every night with my mother before I went to sleep. When I was a child, I would mimic my mother as she bowed down in prayer and recited *surahs* [chapters from the Quran]. My mother would help me memorize *surahs*. . . . She would recite each line and I would repeat it until I could recite them."

For Muslims, despite having a common book—the Quran—and a common core of values that everyone learns, the actual practicing of rituals and symbolism can vary a great deal depending on the culture a family follows. Many Muslim women wear coverings—from headscarves (hijabs) to those that cover the whole body—and the types and styles of these coverings may vary based on the culture of the country of origin. Other Muslim women do not interpret their faith this way or cover their hair at all. Many adult men and women fast during Ramadan, but who

MASJID AL-RABIA

"A lot of us were both nervous and excited," said Zaynab Shahar, speaking to *Teen Vogue* about the opening of Masjid al-Rabia, a women-centered, LGBTQ-inclusive, sect-diverse masjid in Chicago. Shahar, a PhD student in religion at the Chicago Theological Seminary, a queer woman, and a board member of the masjid, gave the khutbah (sermon) during the first Jummah (Friday) prayers at the masjid.

According to *Teen Vogue*, "At Masjid al-Rabia, women compose the majority of the board and are usually the ones calling the azan, giving the khutbah, or leading prayers."

From "Masjid al-Rabia Is a Mosque for All Muslims" for Teen Vogue*, by Aviva Stahl.*

Artwork by Fabiha Ahmed, courtesy of Masjid Al-Rabia.

they gather with or who they invite for the evening feasts to break this fast—and, of course, what they eat there—can vary, depending on who they consider to be close friends and family. Many families will invite people of different religions to share the feast, which inevitably reflects the best foods of their own culture.

Knowledge

Most South Asian immigrants arrive in the United States with knowledge of how to practice their religion, their understanding based on what they know from the places and communities they come from. Many second-generation South Asian Americans want to similarly understand the tenets of their faith. But the children of immigrants have sometimes struggled with this, because their parents could not always explain the meaning of rituals that were "just done" in their home

---

BASDEO MANGAL'S FIRST DAYS

Interviewed by Kamal Badhey

Basdeo Mangal departed from Fyrish Village, Guyana, and arrived in New York City in 1996 at the age of 53.

In SAADA, courtesy of Kamal Badhey.

My name is Basdeo Mangal.

When I arrived in America . . . I said to myself that I'm finished with this type of worshiping. But I went to the school to pick up my grandson, and [a] lady had her granddaughter [who was] sick. Very sick. . . . She went to all the doctors, hospitals, and she couldn't get help. So when she see me at the school, she asked me when I come to this country. I tell her I only came last week into this country. And she started praying and asked me that we can go to her house and see her granddaughter. And when I go, I see her granddaughter sick, and she's on the bed. I prayed to mother and I put my hand on her forehead, and she opened her eye, and after she opened her eyes I tell the lady that your granddaughter is going to live.

When I arrived in this country, I wanted to go back next two days or three days, because I don't know anybody over here, I don't know who to talk to, how to go, and my daughter didn't have a place for me to pray and do pujas every morning. When I wake up I bathe, I pick my flowers, I go to my altar, and I pray. Well then, when I said I want to go back, she cleared out her attic and make her attic a room of prayer place for me, and I went and I buy pictures and I put them there and I started praying.

country. Still, the first place where most children of immigrants learn to live their religion is at home. They also learn lived religion through visits to their parents' home countries, from other community members, and in houses of worship, where they are available.

When the children of immigrants visit the countries from which their ancestors emigrated, they encounter different ways in which religion is organized there. A young person who returns to Kathmandu, Nepal, witnesses the daily walk many

---

GOOD MUSLIM, BAD MUSLIM

Tanzila "Taz" Ahmed and Zahra Noorbakhsh started the monthly podcast *#GoodMuslimBadMuslim* in 2015. The show explores "the good and the bad of the American Muslim female experience" in a satirical manner and has been featured in national media, including *WIRED*, *Forbes*, and *Cosmopolitan*. In 2016, the duo recorded an episode from inside the White House.

The following is an excerpt from a 2015 interview on NPR's *All Things Considered*:

Zahra Noorbakhsh and Tanzila "Taz" Ahmed host the podcast #GoodMuslimBadMuslim. But they don't have a shtick where one of them is good and the other is bad. It's more complicated than that.

Noorbakhsh, an Iranian-American comedian, and Ahmed, a Bengali-American writer and activist, say this podcast was born out of conversations about just what it means to be a "good Muslim."

"In the Muslim community we're looked at as the bad Muslims because, you know, Zahra drinks, I go to punk shows," Ahmed tells All Things Considered *host Arun Rath. "Externally, in the American community, we're looked at as bad Muslims just by default of being brown-skinned and being Muslim, so we kind of are in this gray zone."*

"To complicate matters even further," Noorbakhsh adds, "many times because I identify myself as a 'pork-eating, alcohol-drinking, premarital-sex-having Muslim,' then I'll have audience members say, 'Oh, you're the good kind of Muslim,' because to them . . . I am less Muslim."

From "What Is a 'Good Muslim' Anyway? A Podcast Disrupts the Narrative" for NPR.

Hindus and Newars (who practice an "inseparable" mix of Hinduism and Buddhism) take to different Hindu and Buddhist temples in the city. People who go to Pakistan, Bangladesh, or certain areas in India are likely to remark on how many Muslim rituals are held in public places. Those who go to India may note that the tombs of the Sufi saints attract people of different religions and that most major religions are practiced all over the country.

As one young person notes: "My extended family in India always insisted that the value of connecting with others and a wider universe respectfully [was] far more important than learning specific rituals. But to do this meant understanding the values and objectives of other religions and finding the commonalities that make us human while rejecting the bigotry of zealous practitioners. The best way to acquire the knowledge is through observing other people's everyday behaviors— understanding what makes some more kind, generous, humane—and acting on that knowledge. Many members of my extended family teach us not to waste things. Every bit of extra food is given to someone else; extra clothes, extra books are sent to others regularly. Some family members have home alcoves where some of them say their prayers, but all of them don't, and they do not sit together to worship unless they are having a puja at home. They occasionally go to temples, churches, and tombs of Sufi saints. They would take me along with them. I learned when and where I had to take off my shoes, when and where I had to keep them on, when I could serve food and when I could eat with a community of other people, what I had to wear or do to show respect for the religion. Each time I visited my extended family, I also learned from many of the older neighbors. After they retired from their jobs they seem to have visited places of pilgrimage; I learned about the Shiva lingam in the Amarnath cave, about the hajj, about the Golden Temple, about Sarnath, and about Lourdes, because they visited those places."

Second-generation South Asian Americans also learn about their religions from weekend religious instruction or summer camps, or from college courses. Sometimes those camps and weekend courses provide a broad overview of the religion that may not be the same as a particular family's practice of living their religion. This discrepancy between descriptions of the faith provided by one authority figure (a professor or teacher) and those of another (a parent or grandparent) can cause confusion or frustration.

In the United States, Hindus, Sikhs, and Muslims often have to explain to others what they believe, why they perform certain rituals, and the significance of religious markers, such as the hijab for Muslim women or the turban for Sikh men. Sikh males are required to keep long hair, along with four other markers,

A MUSLIM-HINDU MARRIAGE

The following is an excerpt of "Multicultural Love in the Time of Polarization," written by Suman Guha Mozumder for *India Abroad* (September 29, 2017):

> *When Indian-American actor Aasif Hakim Mandviwala, professionally known as Aasif Mandvi, married Shaifali Puri, CEO of the poverty aid nonprofit Uplift, in a Hindu-Muslim ceremony in Atlanta in August, it was more than the celebration of their 4-year romance—it sent a message as well.*
>
> *"Obviously, our wedding was not primarily a political or social statement; it was first and foremost a declaration of our love in celebration with our family and friends. However, the optics of it are what they are, and if it sends a message to the larger Indian community and the American community, then we are both more than happy for that," Mumbai-born Mandvi told* India Abroad.
>
> *Although interfaith marriages are nothing new, the wedding of Mandvi, a Daily Show correspondent, and Puri was one of the first such celebrity marriages involving a Hindu and a Muslim from India, performed with the blessings of both families.*
>
> *Puri, who described herself as a proud wife, said she and her new husband were both fortunate that their families supported the union wholeheartedly. "The act of intermingling our faith and our traditions was something our parents and siblings also embraced and actively helped us figure out how to do in the most beautiful way possible," said Puri.*
>
> *"I know that too often, this kind of unconditional support is not offered within our community to interfaith/cross-cultural/interracial couples, not to mention same-sex couples," Puri said.*
> *. . .*
>
> *In the current political climate in the U.S., the marriage between a Hindu and Muslim like that of Mandvi and Shaifali may also have a larger and more important connotation.*
>
> *"We are living in a divided time," Mandvi told* India Abroad. *"Our president has led the charge with divisive and hate-filled rhetoric and others continue to follow his example often with deadly outcomes. I hope that in some small way mine and Shaifali's wedding symbolized inclusion, in every way, whether it be the ceremony itself, the food, the clothes or even the fact that the first image when you walked in to the venue was a statue of Ganesh next to a quote from the Koran."*

to symbolize their commitment to their religion. But for young Sikh men in the United States, their long hair often becomes a challenge, because most other males do not grow their hair in the same way. To cut or not cut their hair is something that is often on the minds of young Sikh men.

As a young Sikh male, Amardeep, says: "I was a little different than most of the [non-Sikh] kids, because a lot of the kids struggled with, 'Oh, should [I] keep my hair—like keeping your hair, keeping uncut hair, was the key tension in the Sikh religion. In history many people had given their lives just to keep their hair. . . . You

THE KERALA CATHOLIC ASSOCIATION NEWSLETTER

The Kerala Catholic Association of Detroit was a nonprofit religious organization that existed from 1980 to 1995. The KCA was renamed Kerala Catholic Community and then, at its official dissolution in 1995, the St. Thomas India Catholic Mission. The KCA was a community of Detroit metropolitan-area Catholics and composed of followers of the Latin, Syro-Malabar, and Syro-Malankara Rites.

The inaugural issue of the *Kerala Catholic* newsletter from March 1981 included news about upcoming community events, such as an Easter celebration at St. Patrick's Church with a Malayalam mass and reception.

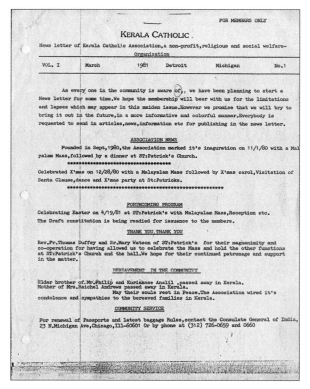

In SAADA, courtesy of Paul Dolfus.

know, when you were fourteen years old, you're growing up, so it's like, 'Hey, what's the big deal, do I really need to keep my hair?' And I remember being at . . . [a Sikh summer] camp and being fourteen years old, [and] one of the teachers asked me, like, 'Hey, have you guys ever thought about cutting your hair? Raise your hand if you ever thought about cutting your hair.' And I still remember this moment where I was the only kid that didn't raise my hand."

Sikh women also traditionally do not cut their hair, but women's long hair is not always considered a religious marker by outsiders, so Sikh women are not as pressured to explain their long hair.

In college, young people often organize clubs that bring people of their religions together to celebrate their major religious events. Thus, celebrations of Diwali, a holiday for many Hindus (and Jains and Sikhs), or Eid, the ceremonial end of the holy month of Ramadan in Islam, become a focal point of activity and an opportunity to build bridges with other young people. Since many South Asian Americans grow up in places where there are few others with similar backgrounds in their neighborhoods, these religious camps, schools, and clubs at colleges and universities become places to gather and discover others like themselves.

CHALLENGES

While freedom of religion is enshrined in the First Amendment of the Constitution, and while we often hear that the United States "welcomes people of all religions," having the freedom to practice your religion doesn't always mean that your religion is accepted and respected—or that your rights are truly equal compared to those of the majority. The United States may strive for religious pluralism, which in its ideal state accepts and affirms all the religions present in the country, but in reality, South Asian Americans face challenges in practicing their religion here. For example, in towns across the country, when communities attempt to build gurdwaras, mandirs, and mosques, local officials or residents have objected to these structures, and have used pretexts like zoning or parking regulations to prevent them. And while many religious celebrations, like Hindu Diwali and Muslim Muharram processions, take place in public spaces in South Asian countries, they often cannot be celebrated in the same way in the United States.

Conflicts between religious holidays and school obligations are an issue for most students. Whereas Sundays, Christmas, and other Christian holidays are typically days off from school, Hindu, Muslim, and Sikh holidays may fall during the week, and Muslims' traditional weekly day of worship is Friday. So in most places, students still have to attend school on their family's major holidays. Even if the school district allows children to take an excused absence, the students still have to make up the work, so they do not really get the day "off" to celebrate. Some decide they don't want to miss school, because making up the work is much harder. This puts these students and their families in the position of having to

---

A CALL TO PRAYER IN HAMTRAMCK, MICHIGAN

The following is an excerpt from "Tension in a Michigan City Over Muslims' Call to Prayer," written by John Leland for the *New York Times* (May 5, 2004):

To hear people in this blue-collar city tell it, things were fine until the al-Islah Islamic Center petitioned to broadcast its call to prayer, or azan, over an outdoor loudspeaker.

Masud Khan, the mosque's secretary, sat on the carpeted floor on Wednesday and reflected on what he had learned about some of his neighbors in the last few months. "How much they hate us," he said softly.

Jackie Rutherford, a librarian and youth-care worker, sat on her front stoop watching three men in Islamic shirt-dresses and tupi caps at the house across the street. "I don't know what's going to happen to our little town," said Ms. Rutherford, 39.

"I used to say I wasn't prejudiced against anyone, but then I realized I had a problem with them putting Allah above everyone else," she said, of the plan to amplify the call to prayer, which mosques announce five times a day. "It's throwing salt in a wound. I feel they've come to our country, infiltrated it, and they sit there looking at us, laughing, calling us fools."

For the population of Hamtramck, a city of 23,000 surrounded by Detroit, the battle of the loudspeaker, which the City Council approved on Tuesday, has revealed a crossfire of religious, ethnic and lifestyle grievances, aggravated by the lingering memories of Sept. 11, 2001, which left many Muslims here feeling they were under suspicion.

---

choose between attending school, or participating in weekend sports and other practices, and observing their holiday or prayer obligations (and then still having to make up their work).

Similar challenges can emerge in the workplace. Those who are in white-collar jobs can take personal days off and make up the work later, or trade work with supportive coworkers. But those who work in jobs that pay by the hour cannot afford that luxury; in order to take a day off, they must forfeit that day's pay. And Muslims who pray five times a day face challenges in getting time to pray at work.

In addition to home-based worship and temple-centered community activities, lived religion for South Asian Americans includes civic engagement—such

as inviting local elected officials to attend religious and cultural programs
at their houses of worship. These in-
vitations act as an introduction to or
an affirmation of their presence in
the locality, state, or nation. Having
built these relationships, many communities with substantial Muslim
or Hindu populations have begun
to lobby for including Eid or Diwali
among recognized school holidays.
Some communities even have full-
time Islamic schools.

Another example of asserting one's
right to religion is Sikh men going
to court to assert their right to wear
turbans. For observant Sikh men who
wear a turban and work a job that requires wearing a helmet—such as the
military or police force—they must

*Bhagat Singh Thind in his U.S. Army uniform at Camp Lewis in
1918. In SAADA, courtesy of David Thind.*

choose between wearing the required uniform and observing a central expectation of their religion. Recently, the United States military has begun to allow some
freedom for individuals to wear religious attire, including turbans, headscarves,
and yarmulkes, in noncombat military jobs.

Another major concern for and risk to South Asian Americans is the rise of hate
crimes against Muslims, or those perceived to be Muslim, in the United States since
September 11, 2001. Sikhs have often been the targets of post-9/11 hate crimes, because of misrepresentations about their religion by the media and politicians and
misunderstandings about "Muslim attire." Most South Asian Muslim men do not
wear turbans; turbans are a cultural (not religious) expression in a few countries
in the world, such as Afghanistan, where Muslims happen to be the majority. How-

ever, the assumption that all turban-wearing people are Muslims means Sikh males are often targeted for hate acts, since they wear turbans as a requirement of their religion. Some Sikh men have even been killed because they were seen as Muslims.

Turban-wearing males are not the only targets. South Asian American Hindus, Christians, and Muslims have also been targeted, often because they are assumed to be Muslim based on their skin color or appearance; in other cases, they are targeted simply because they are seen as foreign. In recent years, anti-Muslim rhetoric has been on the rise, and Americans who are Muslim (or are assumed to be

---

FACING HATE AND VIOLENCE

The Sikh Temple of Wisconsin in Oak Creek is one of the two largest gurdwaras in the United States. In August 2012, a gunman with ties to a white-supremacist group entered the gurdwara around 11 a.m. and started shooting at the people inside. The people inside the gurdwara were preparing *langar*, a communal meal that is free for everyone. Most of the community members had not yet arrived for the services scheduled for later in the morning. Six people—Paramjit Kaur, Satwant Singh Kaleka, Prakash Singh, Sita Singh, Ranjit Singh, and Suveg Singh Khattra—were killed in the attack, and four others, including a police officer, were severely injured. The echoes of this hate crime continue to reverberate among the Sikh American community, and many young Sikhs have written about their ongoing fear about the possibility of being targeted as they pray in their gurdwara.

Muslim) live in fear of violence. Families are afraid for their children in schools and of random targeting in public places, especially as some politicians—including former President Trump—escalate the feelings against Muslims.

Living their religion also requires South Asian Americans to create spaces for their religions and identities in civic life, and it is here where Hindus, Sikhs, and Muslims face another challenge: their religions are often not perceived as legitimately "American." In 2007, Christian protestors interrupted a Hindu priest who had been invited to offer a Hindu prayer in the Senate chamber; they claimed that the legislative body was allowing "false prayer." Protests like these often portray Hinduism, Islam, and Sikhism as antithetical or antagonistic to Christianity. Because these religions are seen as "foreign" and "un-American," people try to foster hate against them. Thus, Hindus, Sikhs, and Muslims face challenges in finding spaces to build their gurdwaras, mosques, and temples so they can practice their religions with members of their community, or even make choices about something as important as what happens to their bodies after they die.

While these challenges to living one's religion exist, American Hindu, Sikh, and Muslim communities continue to become more engaged in American politics and civic life to ensure their faiths are represented in their country. For example, Sikhs have begun celebrating the birthday of Guru Nanak, the founder of Sikhism, at the White House, which has also recognized, and hosted celebrations of, both Diwali and Eid (although this tradition was questioned by the Trump administration). Many South Asian American groups have used traditional and social media to counter derogatory views about their religions; they have formed human-rights advocacy groups to assert their rights and have joined in the efforts of groups working to protect the civil liberties of all Americans. So the work of gaining widespread acceptance also becomes a part of lived religion.

Khyati Y. Joshi (she/her) is a professor of education at Fairleigh Dickinson University and a social science researcher whose work focuses on the intersections of race and religion in the United States.

Bandana Purkayastha (she/her) is a professor of sociology and Asian & Asian American studies at the University of Connecticut.

CHAPTER 7

Civic Engagement

Photograph from the Lease Drivers Coalition's first-ever action in August 1997, where members formed a motorcade from 14th Street to City Hall in New York City. Their banner reads "Justice Respect Dignity For Yellow Cab [hidden]." Courtesy of the New York Taxi Workers Alliance (NYTWA).

INTRODUCTION

Monisha Das Gupta

Ghazala Khan and Khizr Khan, U.S. citizens who were born and raised in Pakistan, seared the nation's conscience when they appeared onstage at the 2016 Democratic National Convention to decry Republican presidential candidate Donald Trump's open war on immigrants and Muslims in the United States. They spoke as Gold Star parents, those recognized for having a loved one die in service of their nation during war. Their middle son, Captain Humayun Khan, had died in 2004 in Iraq when he put his body in front of a vehicle carrying explosives at a checkpoint in Baqubah, averting a massacre. Khizr Khan's words, spoken directly at Trump—"You have sacrificed nothing and no one"—rang out at the convention center in Philadelphia and circulated with great speed on social media.

My South Asian friends and I repeated those words with wonder. Those were fightin' words. Those were grievin' words. They cracked open the stereotypical image of model-minority South Asian Americans who keep their heads down, stay away from politics, and mind their own business. We frequently inscribe passivity and compliance on Khizr and Ghazala's generation.

When Donald Trump reacted by portraying Ghazala as the silenced and oppressed Muslim woman, she spoke out in a *Washington Post* op-ed, also widely shared on social media, and rejected that characterization. In doing so, she pushed back against an enduring culturally racist representation that has justified colonialism and, most recently, the post-9/11 war in Afghanistan. She is a Brown Muslim woman. But she did not need to be rescued from her religion or her husband.

For the South Asian American community, something momentous had happened. Ghazala and Khizr Khan publicly identified as American Muslims. They stepped into the light of blazing cameras for weeks to make public their commitment to core principles of U.S. democracy. They made their private grief public as well. They sent out the message that they were not willing to be silent in face of the constant attacks on and vilification of Muslims. They communicated their solidarity with all immigrants by denouncing Trump's talk of walling off Mexico from the United States and banning refugees.

We were hearing a somewhat different South Asian immigrant story than the ones that circulate in mainstream media. As the stories in this chapter demonstrate, Khizr and Ghazala Khan's actions are part of our long refusal to accept the flat and racist portrayals of our communities as uniformly affluent and politically disengaged, objects of rescue, or terroristic. Post-1965 South Asian communities in the United States have been building a political culture in the form of activist and advocacy organizations to respond to the erasure of our multiple and complex experiences as South Asian Americans.

The stories gathered in this chapter cover a wide range of political engagements. Discover, for example, the cross-racial efforts in 1971 Baltimore to support the Bangladesh Liberation War: protestors sailed dinghies out into the harbor to block a Pakistani ship that, with the backing of the United States government, was going to restock Pakistan's war supplies. We see evidence of Bangladeshi Americans' political experience garnered during the Bangladesh freedom struggle of 1971 in an unexpected location—Hamtramck, Michigan—where, in 2015, a Muslim-majority city council was elected. Alisa Perkins brings us the story of Banglatown, where Bangladeshi councilmen played a key role in fighting for the right of Muslims to amplify calls to prayer. Sangay Mishra's analysis captures the trends in South Asian Americans' participation in the electoral process locally and nationally.

But what about migrants like Nayek, a construction worker brought into the United States under false pretexts to work in the oil industry? SaunJuhi Verma tells Nayek's story of acute exploitation, his escape from a Mississippi labor camp with the help of African American and Latino allies, and his demand for rights against conditions that turned him into the "walking dead." Hamid Khan, a longtime activist in the Los Angeles area and the former executive director of the South Asian Network (SAN), established in 1990, recounts the ground-up pan–South Asian organizing to challenge the marginalization of South Asian working-class immigrants, many of whom were undocumented, while also calling into question the community's policing of gender and sexuality. This explains why SAN was the first responder in 2003 to the distress caused by the Department of Homeland Security's "Special Registration" program that targeted Los Angeles's adult men from Muslim-majority countries.

Soniya Munshi's bittersweet story about an undocumented Bangladeshi high school student, Amna, who was able to escape her parents' control, brings us back to the dangers of perpetuating the trope of an oppressive and misogynist South Asian culture. In light of the deepening Islamophobia, racial profiling, and fears of deportation with which our communities are struggling, Amna's story provokes us to think broadly about legal remedies when addressing gender violence.

These engagements go well beyond the restrictive definition of civic engagement to include local and national electoral politics and commitments to liberal democracy. They underline the sustained efforts within our communities to build collective power and voice, often through cross-racial and cross-border solidarities, to transform structures that perpetuate various forms of violence.

Monisha Das Gupta (she/her) is a professor of ethnic studies and women's gender and sexuality studies at the University of Hawai'i at Mānoa.

BLOCKADE FOR BANGLADESH

Hasan Ferdous

In 1971, during Bangladesh's Liberation War, while much of the action was confined to the territory of Bangladesh, there were battles being fought in locations many oceans away.

In Britain, Action Bangladesh brought together numerous international organizations to rally support for Bangladesh. In France, septuagenarian statesman and public intellectual André Malraux announced his readiness to take up arms alongside Bengali guerrilla fighters. More than sixty international luminaries, among them Mother Teresa and Senator Edward Kennedy, signed an Oxfam petition calling for international intervention. The "Concert for Bangladesh" at New York's Madison Square Garden, the first of its kind, drew global attention to the ongoing strife in Bangladesh. Even the government of South Yemen said it was ready to coordinate the collection and distribution of arms for Bangladeshi soldiers.

Courtesy of Arif Yousuf.

The most spectacular intervention was by a small group of peace activists in the United States, who stopped a Pakistani ship from docking at the Baltimore harbor to collect weapons by offering their own bodies as "mines." It sounds unreal, and yet this is exactly what happened on July 14, 1971. It all started on July 2, at the monthly meeting of the American Friends Service Committee (AFSC), an organization involving mostly Quakers, who are committed to social justice and peace through nonviolent means. Many of the AFSC members were veterans of anti–Vietnam War protests who had courted arrest and police harassment. Soon after news broke of the Pakistani crackdown in Dhaka and elsewhere in Bangladesh, the AFSC formed Friends of Bengal to mobilize public support for Bangladesh. They also established contacts with the Bangladesh Information Center, a Washington support group that was already involved in lobbying congressional leaders to oppose U.S. support for Pakistan. Through a contact from the office of Senator Edward Kennedy, then chair of the Senate subcommittee on refugees, they learned about the arrival of the *Padma*, a Pakistani ship, at the Baltimore port to collect war supplies. Could they do something to stop the ship from docking?

They came up with an idea: how about mining the port? Of course, they did not think of using actual mines; they wanted to use their own bodies as "mines." Sailing in small dinghies, they would surround the ship and stop it from proceeding.

Richard Taylor and his wife, Phyllis, led the group of activists. The Taylors had long been involved in nonviolent protests, often using the tactics Gandhi used in South Africa and India. They quickly got in touch with Friends of East Bengal, a support group in Philadelphia that included mostly Bengali academics teaching

---

BLOCKADE

Blockade, an award-winning 2016 documentary produced and directed by Bangladeshi American Arif Yousuf, has brought international attention to the 1971 protest. The film has been described as "show[ing] how a group of American and Bengali activists protested against the U.S. government's military and economic support for Pakistan's army during the war by staging a non-violent blockade of Pakistani ships in East Coast ports. . . . Drawing upon rare archival images of the protests and interviews with key activists [including Richard Taylor], *Blockade* offers a powerful reminder of the lengths that ordinary people around the world go in order to stop violence."

From "Film Screening: Blockade" for IIAS.

---

at various U.S. universities. Among them was Dr. Sultana Krippendorf, a young professor who had just become a mother. She was assigned to contact the dockworkers in Baltimore and convince them to support the peace activists. Passionate about the cause and dogged in her persuasion, Krippendorf was able to sway the president of the local trade union. Soon, the media was notified of the big event.

The group first learned that the ship would arrive on July 11, three days ahead of schedule. At the appointed time, everybody gathered at the port, anxiously waiting for the ship to make its way to the shore. But it turned out to be a false alarm. The media was furious, berating Taylor and his friends for wasting their time.

Disappointed but still determined, the Friends of Bengal soon regrouped. Now definite about the date, several hundred people gathered at the harbor on July 14. As the sun dipped in the west, casting its long shadow on the gathered crowd, somebody noticed in the distance the mammoth ship. With its propeller shafts creating huge waves, it was cruising its way to the port. The protestors had collected several small dinghies and were ready to set sail. But the harbor police told them in no uncertain terms that it was too dangerous to take such small dinghies so close to the ocean-going vessel: "You will all drown in the blink of an eye."

Undaunted, Taylor went behind the police barricade and found a small marina that seemed unguarded. Quickly, he and his friends lowered several dinghies into the water. No sooner had the peace flotilla begun its slow journey than the port

---

THE CONCERT FOR BANGLADESH

On August 1, 1971, Ravi Shankar and the Beatles' George Harrison organized two massive concerts for "Bangla Desh" at Madison Square Garden in New York City, constituting the first-ever benefit concert on such a scale. Shankar had approached Harrison with the idea for the fundraiser after millions of Bengalis were forced out of East Pakistan (now Bangladesh) by the West Pakistani army's genocidal war effort, and after East Pakistan had already endured wide-scale devastation in the wake of 1970's Bhola cyclone.

The concert, which featured performances by Ali Akbar Khan, Bob Dylan, and Ringo Starr, raised close to $250,000, and subsequent album and film sales of *Concert for Bangladesh* reportedly raised another $12 million. Yet controversy surrounded the administering of the funds, since the concert organizers had not obtained tax-exempt status through UNICEF beforehand. A majority of the initial money raised was held by the IRS and did not go to Bangladesh for a decade.

Even so, Shankar, who was Bengali himself, would say later of the event's success, "In one day, the whole world knew the name of Bangladesh. It was a fantastic occasion."

---

police surrounded them. The police lifted the peace activists one by one onto their vessels and arrested them for violating police order. The hundreds of people who had gathered at the harbor clapped joyfully as they courted arrest.

The next day, after spending a night at the police station, the protestors were produced before a local judge. Issuing a stern warning, the presiding judge let them go. Later, he took Taylor aside and told him that his son, too, was among those arrested.

I met Richard Taylor several times. I couldn't believe that these people, who seemed completely unconnected to Bangladesh and its people, would risk their lives to register a protest. What had prompted them to this drastic act? Taylor, his demeanor always calm, told me that there are times when people must listen to their inner voice and do the right thing. Protesting against genocide and denouncing the U.S. government for its alliance with the marauders was the right thing to do.

MOLLA ANAM'S FIRST DAYS

Interviewed by Nasia Anam

Molla Anam departed from Dhaka, Bangladesh, and arrived in Washington, D.C., in 1974 at the age of 34.

In SAADA, courtesy of Nasia Anam.

When I arrived, Bangladesh had just achieved independence. And most of the countries of the world, they did not even recognize Bangladesh. . . . Only two countries recognized Bangladesh: India and Soviet Russia, because they were allies. . . . Aeroflot, Soviet Russian airlines, [was] the only airline in the world that would accept Bangladesh Taka [Bangladeshi currency]. But they didn't fly from Dhaka, only New Delhi. So I had to fly to India first, and I stayed a week with my parents in Calcutta. From Calcutta, I flew to Delhi on Indian Airlines. From Delhi, I took the Aeroflot flight.

It was April. It was spring in Bangladesh. I had one suit, which I was wearing, . . . that was given to me by my in-laws for a wedding present. The Aeroflot flight flew from Delhi to Moscow. . . . When I got to Moscow, I had a completely different experience, because the whole airport was full of police. And it was like almost everybody was a convict. I had to submit my passport to the police. After about an hour and a half, they arranged a hotel for me. I was very hungry, but I couldn't buy anything because everything I wanted to do had to be accompanied by a police officer. I think there were maybe three times more police officers than passengers in the airport.

The following day, I flew to New York, but the plane could not land there because of dense fog. All the planes were diverted to other cities. My wife's friends were supposed to pick me up in New York, and they were waiting for me there, but I was diverted to Dulles Airport. Since I was diverted there, I had to go through immigration in Washington, D.C. There they handed me my green card and said, "Welcome to the United States." I spent my first night in America in a beautiful Marriott hotel.

Hasan Ferdous is a writer and journalist from Bangladesh, now based in New York.

ORGANIZING FOR IMMIGRANT RIGHTS IN LOS ANGELES

Hamid Khan

I came to Los Angeles in 1979 as an immigrant from Pakistan. Being undocumented, a person of color, and Pakistani, I quickly started experiencing and living my "otherness." Very early on, I started to look at the state of other members of the South Asian community and saw that there was not a whole lot of work going on in L.A. around building solidarity with other marginalized communities and building power within the South Asian community. My earliest experience with organizing against structural racism stemmed from the experience of a couple of young Pakistani men who had been verbally harassed and denied entry to a nightclub. We reached out to young Latinos and African Americans who were being treated in the same way. The group organized and publicly exposed racist practices at a chain of restaurants in the area and eventually won a lawsuit in 1985. This experience informed and broadened my understanding about organizing across racial, cultural, and ethnic lines.

Beginning in the 1980s, I noticed the rapid demographic change in the South Asian community in the L.A. area. Fractures appeared between the newly arrived working-class and working-poor individuals, who didn't have the language facility and the education or immigration status, and those highly educated individuals who had migrated through the 1960s and 1970s. At the same time, the Reagan years marked a sharp rise in Islamophobic language and a broader anti-immigrant narrative. For me, the issues that affected us were not just about the Pakistani community; they cut across all communities of color.

During this time, I was also building relationships with people from India and Bangladesh. It became clear to us that any organizing would have to be pan–South Asian and would require building relationships with other local communities that were experiencing racism, poverty, and other forms of marginalization. Our conversations led to the creation of the South Asian Network (SAN) in 1990. I initially served on the board of SAN and later as the executive director until 2010. Surprisingly, I experienced resistance from my close social circles for this kind of pan–South Asian organizing. Some of my friends questioned my reaching out to Indians and Bangladeshis in a manifestation of how Partition and the liberation of Bangladesh plays out in people's imaginations.

From its earliest days, SAN's engagement was not limited to how policies and programs affect the South Asian American community. The main architects of SAN recognized that we also needed to examine gender, class, and ethnic inequalities *within* the community. We began holding town halls in the greater L.A. area to create a participatory space in which community members could share their experiences, enabling us to collectively develop solutions. At the town halls, divisions within the community emerged. Working-class people spoke about issues of racial and economic injustice, while those who were "well settled" were avoiding those conversations. Young South Asian women were speaking up about their marginalization within their families, and the restrictions placed on them as a result of being seen as repositories of homeland cultural values. Around 1996, issues of sexual orientation surfaced. We supported the efforts of the South Asian LGBTQ

In SAADA, courtesy of Hamid Khan.

organization Trikone, which later became Satrang, and invited them to use SAN's office space to help them organize.

The town halls counteracted the disengagement fostered by those members who were deeply entrenched in our communities and were involved in building mosques and temples but not invested in community empowerment. Based on the complex day-to-day issues that were emerging at these town halls, we realized that we needed to push for an intersectional approach in our organizing, a novel idea at that time.

As we were linking people with providers, we adopted a case-management model that helped us not only understand the inequities and injustices within the system but also build relationships with community members and other social justice organizations, beginning with Asian and Pacific Islander groups. *Service* is a dirty word in grassroots organizing, but for SAN it had the cultural resonance of collective caring. It was also anchored in our understanding of the Black Panther

245

model of service and defense as a form of addressing and confronting white supremacy and state violence. These different layers of immigrant existence led to
SAN's holistic approach to South Asian immigrants' struggles. We came to see that
a single incident, whether it was wage theft, sexual harassment, domestic violence,
the city's denial of health services and public assistance, or racial violence, represented a multitude of human-rights violations.

In the process, we developed an analysis of the impacts of state violence on our
communities. We pushed our allies to publicly confront it, not just in the media
but also on the street. Consequently, we were well positioned to respond to the
escalation of racial attacks, state surveillance, and deportations after 9/11, because
we were already working on hate crimes against South Asians and confronting
the national security surveillance apparatus put in place after the 1995 Oklahoma
City bombing and the secret evidence rules and secret detention authorized by the
Antiterrorism and Effective Death Penalty Act of 1996.

In response to the Department of Homeland Security's "Special Registration"
program, between January and April 2003, SAN volunteers conducted intakes and
know-your-rights education with more than seven hundred people who had been
served notices to appear. We organized individuals who were at risk of deportation and tracked the way in which this program, which instituted racial profiling
as a policy, was being used to deport community members.

In the years that followed, SAN became a strong voice in the immigrant-rights
movement in the city. We helped organize and participated in rallies and large-
scale marches for immigrant rights and, as desis, made ourselves integral to the
conversations and organizing around "immigration reform." Our organizing also
exposed the compromises and false representations that local and national non-
profits made on behalf of the community, thus leaving communities to fight oppressive and racist enforcement policies. Based on our long experience with being
racially profiled, surveilled, and targeted by the state, we continuously educated
the South Asian community and our allies on the need to formulate transformative narratives and organizing, which we laid out in a statement written with five
other groups that worked on human rights, deportation, and youth empower-

Hamid Khan (right) of the Stop LAPD Spying Coalition. Photo by Paulo Freire Lopez.

ment. We reinforced the need to fight measures in proposed legislation that further criminalized our communities.

I now coordinate the Stop LAPD Spying Coalition, founded in 2011 and based in the L.A. Community Action Network, which is a veritable voice of L.A.'s low-income and homeless population to fight the criminalization of poverty. The coalition is engaged in community outreach and organizing against the massive architecture of surveillance, spying, and infiltration being built by local law enforcement, and the codification of counterterrorism and counterinsurgency tactics in daily policing.

My experience with SAN continues to inform my current organizing. SAN provided a unique opportunity to understand movement building guided by the key principle of intersectionality. The ongoing assault on South Asians, Muslims, and Arabs is yet another chapter in the United States' long history of demonizing the "other." It also creates opportunities to build solidarity and collective action with communities whose current and historic realities guide us in preserving dignity and celebrating a strong culture of resistance.

Hamid Khan (he/him) is an organizer and coordinator with the Stop LAPD Spying Coalition.

FEMINIST ENGAGEMENTS

Soniya Munshi

Late one Friday afternoon, when I was an advocate at Manavi, an organization for South Asian women, I received a phone call from a worried guidance counselor at a high school in Brooklyn. Amna, an undocumented Pakistani teenager, was in trouble. Her parents had found out that she was dating a young man in her class, and they were planning to take her back to Pakistan to get married. Amna was afraid to go home. I was able to speak with her directly, and within hours, we helped to transport her to a transitional home specifically for South Asian women.

We were able to quickly respond to Amna's needs because of the difficult social-change work that South Asian women's organizations like Manavi have engaged in over the past thirty years. Beginning in the mid-1980s, South Asian women in the United States began to organize to address the various forms of gendered violence—from sex-selective feticide to child sexual abuse to domestic violence to worker abuse to widow maltreatment—we may experience over the course of our lifetimes. These community-based organizations, almost always led by middle-class immigrant Indian women, understood gendered violence to be shaped by patriarchy, racism, xenophobia, capitalism, homophobia, and other structures of oppression. South Asian women's experiences are located in these intersections.

To do this work, South Asian women's organizations challenged the cultural racism of the mainstream women's movement, which viewed our cultures as backwards, static, and impossibly patriarchal. These organizations also challenged the

---

XENOPHOBIA AND "OTHERING"

Xenophobia is the intense dislike of foreigners, or the fear and distrust of what is perceived to be foreign and strange. This can involve demeaning people through negative stereotypes or exalting a culture in a way that gives it an "exotic" quality. In either case, the result is "othering," or the placement of a culture or group of people in opposition to—and below—that which is dominant.

---

silence in our communities that protected the model-minority illusion that we have no problems. Through neighborhood marches, silent vigils, protests, legal services, support groups, community education, policy advocacy, and many other activities, South Asian women's organizations have been providing survivors of violence with culturally and linguistically specific support as well as engaging communities to take a stand against gendered violence. Informed by an intersectional analysis and a commitment to multi-issue organizing, many South Asian women's organizations have become a central space in their communities.

Amna's story illustrates some of the everyday dilemmas of South Asian organizing around gendered violence and where we have more work to do. First, Amna was under eighteen and needed to become an emancipated minor to obtain a restraining order against her parents, which would prohibit them from communicating with her. She was lucky: we found a lawyer to take her case pro bono. It is going to be easy, he said. We just have to explain to the judge that her parents are giving her a "death sentence": if she goes to Pakistan, she will surely be abused and likely killed. Stereotypes that portray South Asia as a dangerous and violent place with no regard for women's lives worked in her favor. The judge granted her request.

A week later, we came back to court for the final restraining-order hearing. Amna's working-class immigrant parents were in the courtroom without legal representation because their attorney was running late. (He never showed up). They were having a hard time communicating with the interpreter due to a difference in dialect. Yet several things quickly became clear: they wanted to talk to their daughter but understood that they were now legally prohibited from doing so; they did not want their daughter to date one of her classmates, especially because he was

Artwork by Margarita Korol, courtesy of Manavi.

not Pakistani; and, yes, they were going to arrange her marriage, as was the family tradition. The final restraining order was granted. Amna was relieved. She felt safe, and in many ways, this was a simple and successful case.

Months later, Amna moved from the transitional home to an apartment with her best friend's family. Her friend's mother called the police one night when Amna's father showed up to convince her to come home. He was arrested for violating the restraining order. He was undocumented, and this was right after 9/11. It is possible that he was swept into the heightened crisis of detention and deportation of migrants—those who had encounters with law enforcement were particularly vulnerable. Amna worried about him, and about her mother, who was disabled

---

MULTI-ISSUE, INTERSECTIONAL ORGANIZING

The term "intersectionality" was coined by Columbia law professor Kimberlé Crenshaw in 1989, referring to the interconnecting and often overlapping systems of oppression that people face in our society. But the idea has been around for much longer. It's reflected in the words of Black women- like Sojourner Truth as far back as 1827. In 1984, Black feminist pioneer Audre Lorde wrote on the topic, "Those of us who stand outside the circle of this society's definition of acceptable women; those of us who have been forged in the crucibles of difference—those of us who are poor, who are lesbians, who are Black, who are older—know that survival is not an academic skill. . . . It is learning how to take our differences and make them strengths. For the master's tools will never dismantle the master's house."

As evidenced in many of the stories in this book, South Asian Americans have embraced intersec- tional feminism in their work as well. This includes the organizing that Manavi, an organization for South Asian American women whose mission is to end violence against all women, did in leading protests against the xenophobic hate group Dotbusters in the late 1980s, and the alliances that Sakhi for South Asian Women formed with SALGA-NYC, particularly around the latter's exclusion from New York City's India Day Parade. Since 9/11, multiple organizations that are primarily focused on assisting South Asian survivors of domestic violence have expanded their work in response to community needs, such as the Georgia-based nonprofit Raksha organizing against immigration enforcement in Atlanta, API Chaya in Seattle responding to xenophobic incidents in the area, and Daya Houston responding to the Hurricane Katrina crisis in New Orleans.

---

and depended on her husband's income. To my knowledge, Amna never found out what happened to her father after that arrest.

Amna's story shows us that when the law works for survivors, which it does not always, they may be able to find safety, which they deserve. But even when we see the outcome we are hoping for, there can be consequences we do not necessarily want or need. Were there ways that we could have supported Amna in staying safe without criminalizing her family, especially her mother, who may herself have been living in fear? Did the family have friends, neighbors, religious leaders, or relatives who may have been able to intervene to advocate for Amna? We did not ask these questions at that time. We assumed that going to court for legal protec- tion was the best and only strategy.

Reliance on the legal system to respond to gendered violence involves other types of risks and impacts on survivors from communities that have an uneasy relationship with the state, because of their immigration status, vulnerability to racial or religious profiling, class status, or other issues. Amna was comfortable moving through the legal process. Another survivor in a similar position may be

---

A QUIET PERSISTENCE: TURNING POINT FOR WOMEN AND FAMILIES

In the aftermath of 9/11, anti-war activist Robina Niaz identified an urgent community issue that was not being addressed: the safety and well-being of Muslim survivors of domestic violence. South Asian women's organizations were usually secular, and Muslim women's groups were not adequately addressing domestic violence. In response, Niaz founded Turning Point for Women and Families, a pan-Muslim community-based organization that offers culturally and religiously sensitive services for women and children.

Based in Queens, one of the most diverse areas in the United States, and where the majority of Muslim New Yorkers reside, Turning Point raises awareness of the needs of Muslim communities while also working in Muslim communities to challenge gendered violence. Niaz has seen change in the community over the years: more conversations about domestic violence, awareness of elder abuse, emerging women's leadership, young girls practicing self-defense. Although support from within the community is an ongoing challenge, Turning Point practices a quiet persistence, such as regularly conducting Friday evening outreach in local mosques. As Niaz states, Turning Point "is not going away. These are issues the community has to tackle."

---

deterred by the possibility of exposing herself or her family to the risks of arrest or deportation. To end gendered violence, our work must respond to the needs of those who are most marginalized within South Asian communities, particularly those survivors who may not want to or be able to rely on the criminal legal system. We must focus on community-based responses that build our knowledge and skills in order to collectively support the safety and self-determination of survivors, while also transforming our families and communities.

Soniya Munshi (she/her/they) is an associate professor in the Department of Ethnic and Race Studies at the Borough of Manhattan Community College/CUNY.

BANGLATOWN, USA

Alisa Perkins

"First U.S. Town with a Majority Muslim City Council Unites around Diversity," reported *Russia Today*. "What's Life Like in America's First City with a Muslim-Majority City Council?" queried the *Nation*. The news spread rapidly in local, national, and international channels: on November 3, 2015, Hamtramck, Michigan, had elected a city council composed mainly of Muslim Americans. Some reporters heralded the election as another experiment with diversity for Hamtramck. In contrast, other reporters portrayed the vote as an alarming precedent. They played upon Islamophobic rhetoric to predict disastrous results.

Hamtramck, Michigan, may claim the highest percentage of Muslim Americans of any American city. Hamtramck was once home to bustling auto factories and was famous as a center for Polish American life. Now, Muslims make up about 40 percent of the city's total population. Many Hamtramck Muslims trace their

Parade to celebrate Bangladesh Avenue, June 28, 2008. Photo by Alisa Perkins.

lineages to Bangladesh, Yemen, and Bosnia. Others are African American. The city's Muslims contribute just one part to its eclectic mix—at least twenty-seven different languages are spoken at Hamtramck public schools. The prominence of Bangladeshi Americans among them has prompted some residents to playfully dub the city, or at least certain sections of it, "Banglatown." Bangladeshi Americans represent about 15 percent of the city's population. They have often led the way in bringing changes to a municipality known for breaking the mold.

In 2015, Hamtramck residents reelected two Bangladeshi Americans to the city council: Abu Musa and Anam Miah. They would serve alongside incumbent Bangladeshi American Mohammed Hassan. In the same year, Yemeni American Saad Almasmari became a fourth Muslim member of the city's six-person council. These men joined a robust tradition of Muslim American municipal leadership in Hamtramck that began in 2003 with the election of Bangladeshi businessman Shahab Ahmed to the city council. Several other Bangladeshi American leaders

SOUTH ASIAN ENCLAVES

In the northeast corner of Staten Island, near the terminal for the Staten Island Ferry, you can dine on roti and sambols in "Little Sri Lanka." In nearby Richmond Hill, Queens, you'll find the offices of the Indo-Caribbean Alliance, serving a community sometimes referred to as "Little Guyana." Across the country, in Northern California's Bay Area, more than three hundred thousand Indian Americans—the largest Indian population in the United States outside of New York—work in and out of Silicon Valley. And in Chicago, along Devon Avenue, there are dozens and dozens of sari stores, halal restaurants, and grocery stores serving a diverse group of South Asian American families. These are just a few of the many enclaves that immigrants from South Asia have set up in the United States in the last century, building communities that feel a little bit more like home and have subsequently served as the most common entry point into the country for generations of South Asian Americans.

also took the spotlight in Hamtramck that year. In 2003, Al-Islah Mosque leaders Abdul Motlib and Masud Khan made international headlines when they asked the city to recognize the legality of their mosque's amplified call to prayer (*adhan*). In the post-9/11 climate, some protesters represented the sound of a call to prayer in the street as a sign of a Muslim "takeover" of the city. Muslim American leaders worked closely with diverse groups of Hamtramck residents to support the call to prayer as a civil rights issue and an interfaith concern. Due in part to this cooperation, in 2004 Hamtramck became the first U.S. city to officially script the Islamic call to prayer into a municipal ordinance.

Aside from participating in these headline-making events, many Bangladeshi Americans take an active role in the everyday politics of the municipality. One way they do so is through the Bangladeshi American Public Affairs Committee (BAPAC). BAPAC regularly organizes voter drives and hosts forums introducing the city's elected officials to the community. I asked BAPAC leader Kamal Rahman to explain why he thinks Bangladeshis are so politically active in Hamtramck. He explained that it partly has to do with the political consciousness of this community that began to develop with the partition of India and Pakistan (1947) and with other regional events in the latter half of the century:

> Bangladeshi Americans realize the power of politics. This goes back
> to our history. In 1947, when India was partitioned, Muslims realized
> that they had fallen a bit behind. Then there was the 1952 movement to

recognize Bengali as the official language of what was then East Bengal. We also have the 1971 struggles for independence from Pakistan. Our successes in these two moments had to do with the political participation of everyday people. Voting in Bangladesh, and more recently in the United States, for us has become a celebration. Men and women alike stand in long lines to participate in the political process. We are happy to do it because we recognize our power as individuals to create change.

The Bangladeshis who make such an impact in Hamtramck hail mainly from Sylhet, a northeastern agricultural region. Sylhetis have a long history of migration to western countries, beginning with those who served as seamen for British colonists and then "jumped ship" to establish themselves in various cities across the globe. Significant communities of Bangladeshis settled in the United Kingdom as early as the twentieth century. In contrast, Bangladeshis did not begin to arrive

Inaugural ceremony of Bangladesh Avenue, November 8, 2008. Left to right, holding the sign, are Hamtramck mayor Karen Majewski (center), Bangladesh ambassador M. Humayun Kabir (immediate right), and Hamtramck's first Bangladeshi American city council member, Shahab Ahmed (far right, with balloons). Photo by Alisa Perkins.

in the United States in appreciable numbers until after the 1971 independence from Pakistan. At that point, a trickle of students and professionals were finally able to begin their U.S. journeys. America's Bangladeshi population began to climb in 1980, based on a number of mechanisms, including the Diversity Lottery, in addition to employer and family sponsorships. Most of them settled in New York City. In recent years, Bangladeshis have spread out to southern cities like Atlanta and midwestern cities like Hamtramck.

Since the mid-1990s, Bangladeshi Americans have established dozens of businesses in Hamtramck, significantly boosting the city's economic health and vibrancy. The community annually hosts the large revenue-generating Bangladeshi Festival, bringing Bangladeshi culture, foods, and crafts into the streets. In 2008, the Hamtramck City Council honorarily designated a stretch of Conant Avenue as "Bangladesh Avenue"—only the second street to be named after Bangladeshis in the United States (see "Fazlur Rahman Khan" in chapter 8 to learn about the first). The designation of Bangladesh Avenue in Hamtramck recognizes the rapid growth and substantial contribution made to the city by one of its most energetic, dynamic, and civically minded groups.

Alisa Perkins (she/her/hers) is an associate professor in the Department of Comparative Religion at Western Michigan University.

SOUTH ASIAN GUEST WORKERS

SaunJuhi Verma

> "I don't know where it was worse, being treated like a slave in the Gulf or here in America, where they pretend you are an equal. . . . How can I go back now—I have no papers, no money. I have become a walking corpse. I'm neither here nor there. I can't live here and I can't go back home. I have become the walking dead."
>
> —NAYEK, U.S. GUEST WORKER

In 2006, U.S. employers began recruiting South Asian guest workers in greater numbers into the southern states. They served as construction workers in the building of oil refineries, drilling rigs, and other necessary structures of the booming oil-extraction industry. Nayek was among these Indian construction workers; his experience offers a glimpse into the worksite practices of the U.S. guest-worker program.

Nayek was kept at a fenced and guarded labor camp in Mississippi by his sponsoring employer and forced to work in construction sites. He worked twelve-hour shifts with minimal breaks and was given undrinkable water from the local swamps, all the while paying fees of nearly $1,100 per month for his residence in a trailer (shared with sixteen other workers), daily meals, and safety equipment. Nayek had paid Indian labor recruiters $20,000 for the promise of citizenship, permanent employment, and a chance to settle with his family in the United States. Instead, he found himself in debt prior to and during his foreign employment. He eventually escaped from the labor camp and from the employer who had kept him in those conditions.

While such labor practices may be considered egregious and unjust, numerous governments—including those of the United States and India—indirectly authorize them. The U.S. guest-worker program was initiated under the presidency of George W. Bush; it authorized foreign laborers to enter the United States for short-term work so as to eventually return to their countries of origin. One of its many objectives was to provide legal protection for workers like Nayek at their employment sites and to prevent undocumented residence in the United States. In practice, however, labor abuses continue to be the norm rather than the exception for guest workers across industries.

Amid these difficult circumstances, South Asian migrants have navigated a path to demanding their rights in the United States. Their journey toward holding employers accountable, specifically for fraudulent recruitment and exploitative employment, began by making connections with Latino and African American men at their worksites. In Nayek's case, after entering the United States as a guest worker, he often felt a lack of respect from his white peers and experienced double standards in the enforcement of rules by white foremen and managers. It wasn't until he developed a friendship with Bill, an African American steelworker at the same worksite, that Nayek was able to put into words his experiences of being racially excluded at work—he identified the legacy of racial exclusion in the southern part of the country as informing these contemporary practices of discrimination against male laborers.

The burgeoning racial consciousness of South Asian migrants, combined with the financial and physical duress of laboring in the U.S. guest-worker program, motivated their desire to escape from their exploitative conditions. However, the prospect of escaping a sponsoring employer was daunting and risky for migrant

NATIONAL GUESTWORKER ALLIANCE & SAKET SONI

The National Guestworker Alliance (NGA) is a membership organization founded by guest workers who were trafficked to the Gulf Coast after Hurricane Katrina. Today, the NGA organizes contingent workers in critical sectors of the economy across the United States.

Saket Soni is the executive director of the NGA and the New Orleans Workers' Center for Racial Justice. Soni also coauthored "And Injustice for All: Workers' Lives in the Reconstruction of New Orleans," the most comprehensive report on race in the reconstruction of the post-Katrina Gulf Coast, and "Never Again: Lessons of the Gustav Evacuation," an account of the treatment of African Americans in the sheltering process during Hurricane Gustav.

Saket Soni speaks at a Jobs with Justice conference in 2011. Courtesy of Jobs with Justice.

workers. Again, building relationships with fellow workers helped pave a path: Latino friends offered shelter, knowledge about navigating the terrain outside of labor camps, and introductions to migrant-advocacy agencies. These initial multi-racial bonds and knowledge sharing were critical for South Asian men in traversing exclusionary labor markets.

In particular, access to migrant-advocacy organizations allowed South Asian workers to build on their existing political fluency. A significant number of them had experience with labor organizing and resistance strategies from having worked in the Gulf Cooperation Council (GCC) countries, which bore similarities to their experience in the United States. Migrant workers identified how their labor contributed to economic growth in their origin countries of South Asia, to the building of oil economies in the Middle East, and now to the formation of the U.S. energy industry infrastructure. Yet in return, they found themselves in a state of unbelonging in all three places, of being denied full recognition of their basic rights. While they were a critical link in the global economy, they experienced exclusion from formal rights. As such, these workers frame their demands for legal recognition as linked to their exploitation within migrant markets and as central to the process of fully belonging in a nation-state. South Asian construction workers in the U.S. oil industry are but one of many examples of how the law becomes complicit in marginalizing recent migrants.

SaunJuhi Verma is an assistant professor in the School of Management and Labor Relations at Rutgers University.

ELECTORAL PATTERNS AND DILEMMAS

Sangay Mishra

The South Asian American community is one of the fastest-growing immigrant communities in the United States, and it is gradually becoming an important electoral group in the mosaic of ethno-racial minorities who have started playing a noteworthy role in both national and local elections. However, there is very little discussion of the electoral participation and preferences of this newly emerging group.

A few surveys of Asian Americans in recent years have provided a glimpse into the participation patterns of South Asian Americans in the electoral arena. One of the important findings to emerge from these surveys is that, despite having the highest median household income in the country and a high proportion of college graduates, Indian Americans have a relatively low rate of voting. This goes against the conventional understanding that high levels of economic and educational resources lead to greater participation in the electoral process. For instance, the percentages of white and African American college graduates are 30 percent and 17 percent, respectively, and their rates of voting are 74 and 77 percent. In comparison, 74 percent of Indian Americans are college graduates, but their voting percentage is relatively low, at 66 percent.

SUMI KAILASAPATHY TAKES A KNEE

Photo by Ryan J. Stanton.

In 2017, in solidarity with National Football League star Colin Kaepernick—who began kneeling during the national anthem as a way of protesting racism and other injustices, and ultimately launched a national debate that included a demeaning response from former president Donald Trump—a city council member in Ann Arbor, Michigan, launched her own protest. *CNN* reported:

> *Four of the 11 Ann Arbor, Michigan City Council members were inspired by NFL players and took a knee during the Pledge of Allegiance in a council meeting to protest inequality.*

> *Sumi Kailasapathy, a third-term council member, came to the idea after following the NFL protests, in which players have taken a knee during the National Anthem to protest social injustice throughout the nation.*

> *To the councilwoman, this is a subject that hits close to home; she came to this country as a refugee after losing her home during the Sri Lankan civil war, which took place from 1983 to 2009.*

> *"People tell me to go back to my country, and I don't know how to tell them that this is my country, this is my home and I work very hard to take care of and support my community. If I leave, where am I going to go?" Kailasapathy said.*

From *"Take a Knee Protests Go from the Sidelines to City Council Chambers" for* CNN, *by Andrea Diaz.*

This voting pattern among Indian Americans is commensurate with that of other immigrant communities and points to a lack of political integration in immigrant communities in general. This gap is even more pronounced for smaller groups, such as South Asians, who do not constitute a very large electoral block. The South Asian experience points to a trend in which political parties are reluctant to expend effort on mobilizing new immigrants. A number of South Asian community leaders have pointed out that political parties— both Democratic and Republican—do not reach out to new immigrants, even while

Door hangers created by SAAVY (South Asian American Voting Youth) for the 2004 presidential election. In SAADA, courtesy of Tanzila Ahmed.

they are open to people from these communities who approach them. An Indian community activist based in New York City explained it this way: "I don't think [political parties] are going around and asking for us to participate, because the system is well established and they don't see any reason to bring anybody new into the fold." Political parties and candidates are generally reluctant to bring new constituencies into the electoral arena out of fear that it might upset the existing electoral balance. A Bangladeshi community leader who unsuccessfully contested a state assembly seat in Queens, New York, stated, "Political parties are afraid; they do not want to see [new immigrants] registered. . . . If they will become registered [voters], the power equation will be changed, so they don't want it." These concerns expressed by South Asians about political parties and candidates find resonance among other immigrant communities as well.

Despite a relatively low level of electoral participation, South Asian Americans do have political preferences, as revealed in recent surveys. Analysis of national voting patterns suggests that Indian Americans voted overwhelmingly for the Democratic presidential candidate in 2008 and again in 2012 and 2016. Findings from the 2012 National Asian American Survey (NAAS) indicated that Indian Americans are most supportive of the Democratic candidate, even in comparison to other Asian American groups. An overwhelming percentage of Indian Americans voted for President Obama (84 percent), which was far higher than Japanese Americans (70 percent), Chinese Americans (69 percent), Korean Americans (66 percent), Filipino Americans (62 percent), and Vietnamese Americans (61 percent). Furthermore, a survey conducted during the midterm elections in 2014 showed that 58 percent of Indian American voters—the highest among Asian American groups—

HINDUS FOR TRUMP

Rashmee Kumar, writing for the *Guardian*, described a particularly dissonant moment in the weeks leading up to the 2016 presidential election:

To a South Asian onlooker, this could have been a scene from any other Desi function on a Saturday night. The booming Bollywood music beckoned a stream of families, wearing ornate saris and sharp kurtas, fragrant plates of samosa chaat in hand, toward the stage, replete with an extravagant display of lights and visuals.

But among the convivial crowds also stood a white man wearing a baseball cap and shirt that read "Hillary for Prison." The placards waiting on empty seats called out "Trump for Hindu Americans" and "Trump Great for India." Everyone was waiting for Donald Trump.

Three weeks before the election, Trump made a brief but rousing appearance at the Republican Hindu Coalition's (RHC) Humanity United Against Terror charity concert, an event framed around raising money to combat "radical Islamic terrorism," particularly for Hindus from Bangladesh and Kashmir.

"I'm a big fan of Hindu, and I'm a big fan of India," Trump told hundreds of enthusiastic attendees in Edison, New Jersey, a town known for its sizable South Asian population.

From "Hindus for Trump: Behind the Uneasy Alliance with Rightwing U.S. Politics" for the Guardian, *by Rashmee Kumar.*

---

indicated their preference for a Democratic candidate on a generic House ballot. The survey also reported that Democratic Party favorability was highest among Indian Americans (68 percent), in comparison with other Asian American groups.

The increasing support among Indian Americans for Democratic candidates, however, is coupled with the fact that a majority of Indian Americans—approximately 55 percent—do not identify themselves as either Democratic or Republican. This pattern suggests that even as they vote solidly Democratic, Indian Americans, along with other Asian Americans, remain a politically volatile group in terms of party identification, and consequently in their long-term voting loyalties.

It is important to note the caveat that most recent surveys have only included Indian Americans as part of their sample, making it difficult to generalize the findings to other South Asian Americans. However, other sources identify individuals through additional criteria, such as data on the voting patterns of different religious groups, including Muslim Americans. By extrapolating from these sources, one can identify emerging political preferences of South Asian groups beyond Indian Americans. The data indicate a pattern of Muslim Americans voting overwhelmingly for the Democratic Party, similar to that of Indian Americans and Asian Americans. Former President Trump's comments against immigration and minorities are expected to contribute to the continuation of this trend.

POLITICAL ENGAGEMENT

In addition to serving as an important electoral group, South Asian Americans have also stepped into roles of public service and become powerful political voices in their own rights. In 2021, Kamala Harris achieved a series of firsts as she became the first woman, the first Black American, and the first South Asian American to serve as the vice president of the United States. Prior to her historic election to the White House, Vice President Harris also served as the first South Asian American U.S. senator, elected in 2016 to represent her home state of California. In Congress, Harris was joined by fellow South Asian Americans in the U.S. House of Representatives. Pramila Jayapal of Washington's Seventh District, Ro Khanna of California's Seventeenth District, and Raja Krishnamoorthi of Illinois's Eighth District were all also elected in 2016. Ami Bera of California's Seventh District was elected in 2012.

Beyond serving as politicians, South Asian Americans have also made their voices heard in our democracy by building political-advocacy organizations such as South Asians for America, Desis for Progress, and IMPACT. These organizations serve as sites of community, creating spaces where South Asian Americans can come together to engage, educate, and mobilize to build collective political power.

Sangay Mishra is an assistant professor of political science and international relations at Drew University.

CHAPTER 8

Arts & Popular Culture

Ravi Shankar and Alla Rakha perform at the Massachusetts Institute of Technology in 1976, at a concert organized by Sangam, the Indian students' association. In SAADA, courtesy of Waris Warsi.

INTRODUCTION

Nilanjana Bhattacharjya and Shilpa Davé

South Asians and South Asian Americans have had an enduring influence on American arts and popular culture in many fields, including literature, sports, cinema, theater, fashion, music, and architecture. The stories in this chapter reveal this engagement: how certain American cultural movements have unexpected South Asian origins, how South Asian cultural productions in America demonstrate the variety and multiple dimensions of the South Asian experience, and how South Asians and South Asian Americans have forged solidarities across political and cultural lines that disrupt conventional understandings of South Asian American identity.

The chapter begins with Neelanjana Banerjee's account of the rise of South Asian American literature in the 1990s, which she locates alongside the *New Yorker's* special fiction double issue in 1997, the fiftieth anniversary of India's independence.

Banerjee identifies a new wave of popularity in the United States for South Asian and South Asian American writers during the 1990s through the mid-2000s and explores how a more recent generation of South Asian American writers have introduced additional perspectives to address the political and cultural shift for South Asian Americans since 9/11.

The chapter's next selections convey how South Asian Americans have managed to transcend traditional divisions within and outside the South Asian diaspora. Vivek Bald recounts how "hype man" Bardu Ali collaborated with Chick Webb, Harlem's king of swing jazz during the 1930s, and introduced Ella Fitzgerald to the world; at the same time, Bald situates Ali within a longer history of Bengali immigrant merchants in the United States from the 1880s onward. As Bald notes, these immigrants' and their descendants' intermarriage with African Americans across the United States connects strands of a collective history with roots in the American South, the Caribbean, and the Indian subcontinent, as well as in both colonialism and slavery. Stanley Thangaraj, Akshat Tewary, and Vasef Sajid look at the rise of South Asian American men's basketball leagues since the 1980s and how these men's participation in these leagues—across cultural and linguistic barriers—both defines a new South Asian diasporic identity and establishes a means of assimilation.

The stories that follow, by Jigna Desai and Neilesh Bose, describe how South Asian Americans, who were once only the topics of others' films and plays, have risen to create films and plays of their own, redefining South Asian American identity and South Asian culture on their terms. Desai remarks on how South Asian Americans' filmmaking since the late 1980s has countered previous exoticized and Orientalist depictions of South Asia and South Asian Americans, has made South Asian Americans visible, and has engaged with racism, multiculturalism, and the meaning of home. Bose begins his history of South Asian and South Asian American theater in the United States in its earliest forms in the mid- to late nineteenth century, with European Americans' staging of classical Indian plays in translation and plays about South Asia. He then discusses more recent integration of South Asian plays into mainstream professional theater "*by* South Asian American people, *and about* South Asian American lives," including Ayad Akhtar's *Disgraced*, which was awarded the Pulitzer Prize in 2013.

Our last four stories focus on South Asian culture's lasting influence on mainstream American culture. Meenasarani Linde Murugan explores how Indian prime minister Jawaharlal Nehru's visits to the United States during the 1950s and 1960s inspired French designer Pierre Cardin to introduce his own version of the Nehru jacket, which became so popular that the Beatles, the Monkees, and Johnny Carson were wearing them by the late 1960s. J. Daniel Elam writes about one of the earliest South Asian American authors, Dhan Gopal Mukerji, who won the prestigious Newbery Medal in 1928 for his children's book *Gay-Neck: The Story of a Pigeon*, and whose many other books raised his American readers' consciousness about India's anti-colonial movement, casteism, and India's inequities related to those in the United States. Sarah Morelli writes on the founding of the Ali Akbar College of Music in San Rafael, California, during the 1960s and how its renowned master teachers over multiple generations have now introduced tens of thousands of students in the United States to north Indian classical music and dance. Finally, Yasmin Sabina Khan recalls the fascinating life of her father, the structural engineer Fazlur Rahman Khan, whose innovative designs resulted in such famous skyscrapers as Chicago's Sears Tower, the world's tallest building from its completion in 1974 until more than two decades later.

These individual histories illuminate just a few of the many contributions and impacts South Asian Americans have achieved in the twentieth and early twenty-first centuries.

Nilanjana Bhattacharjya (she/her/hers) is a principal lecturer and Honors Faculty Fellow at Barrett, the Honors College at Arizona State University, where she teaches interdisciplinary courses on the humanities, Asian studies, music, and film.

Shilpa Davé (she/her/hers) is an assistant dean in the College of Arts and Sciences and an assistant professor in the Department of Media Studies at the University of Virginia.

SOUTH ASIAN AMERICAN LITERATURE

Neelanjana Banerjee

In 1997, the *New Yorker*'s special fiction double issue featured an illustration of khaki-clad white explorers pushing back a tangle of vines to find a statue of the elephant-headed Hindu god Ganesh reading a book. The image, by Owen Smith, resembles the artist's other pulp-inspired covers for the magazine. The two explorers appear both amazed and exhausted by the revelation of another cultural literary trend—this one centering on South Asian writers.

The issue was jam-packed with short stories, critical pieces, long essays, poems, and more, all written by or about South Asians—including a piece about where to get a Nehru-style jacket like the one Knopf president Sonny Mehta wore. If there was ever a moment when the mainstream popularity of writing by South Asian Americans was at its peak, this was it. One piece in the magazine was an early review of Arundhati Roy's international best seller *The God of Small Things* by none other than John Updike, one of America's great novelists, full of backhanded compliments like this one:

> Her novel provides one more example of William Faulkner's powerful influence upon Third World writers; his method of torturing a story—mangling it, coming at it roundabout after portentous detours and delays—presumably strikes a chord in stratified, unevenly developed societies that feel a shame and defeat in their histories.

But aside from soliciting a white writer to give a South Asian writer legitimacy, the magazine mostly filled its pages with original pieces by South Asian writers who would go on to earn great acclaim, like Kiran Desai, who would win the Man Booker Prize in 2006 for her novel *The Inheritance of Loss*. There was poetry by Vijay Seshadri, who would win a Pulitzer Prize for his collection *3 Sections* in 2014. And though she was nowhere in its pages, the issue seemed to pave the way for the enormous debut of Jhumpa Lahiri, whose short-story collection *Interpreter of*

JHUMPA LAHIRI

Jhumpa Lahiri is an award-winning writer of short stories, novels, and essays who often focuses on the inner lives of Indian American immigrants in the United States. She received the Pulitzer Prize in 2000 for *Interpreter of Maladies*, her debut short-story collection, and her novel *The Namesake* was turned into a popular film directed by Mira Nair and starring Kal Penn. Her other works include *Unaccustomed Earth* and *The Lowland*, which was shortlisted for the Man Booker Prize and a finalist for the National Book Award in Fiction.

Lahiri, who grew up in Rhode Island in the 1970s, reflected on some of the common themes in her writing in a 2006 piece for *Newsweek* magazine:

When I first started writing I was not conscious that my subject was the Indian-American experience. What drew me to my craft was the desire to force the two worlds I occupied to mingle on the page as I was not brave enough, or mature enough, to allow in life. My first book was published in 1999, and around then, on the cusp of a new century, the term "Indian-American" has become part of this country's vocabulary. I've heard it so often that these days, if asked about my background, I use the term myself, pleasantly surprised that I do not have to explain further. What a difference from my early life, when there was no such way to describe me, when the most I could do was to clumsily and ineffectually explain.

From "My Two Lives" for Newsweek, *by Jhumpa Lahiri.*

Maladies would win the Pulitzer Prize in Fiction just a few years later, in 2000—an unbelievable honor for a first book of short fiction. Lahiri is one of the first and most

CHITRA BANERJEE DIVAKARUNI AT MOUNT RAINIER IN 1984

In SAADA, courtesy of Chitra Divakaruni.

About thirty-three years back, my husband, Murthy, and I made a road trip to Washington State. We lived in Northern California then. I was a student. Murthy had recently started working. We rented a car because our regular car was too beat-up to withstand a road trip. I remember the feeling of adventure and excitement. We felt so American! It was a great trip where we met fellow travelers of many ethnic backgrounds. The highlight for me was our visit to Mount Rainier. I remember that some of the waterfalls and peaks had been given Indian names by the transcendentalists, from our Vedas—that was so amazing. It made me feel we were living in a culture that embraced many people from many countries. I hope that this wonderful aspect of America's diversity never changes.

From SAADA's Road Trips Project, which aims to reframe a major American tradition by sharing stories of South Asian Americans traveling across the country.

well-known writers of the second generation of South Asian Americans, though her work continues to mostly address the first generation trauma of immigration and assimilation.

The mid-1990s to mid-2000s was the pinnacle of popularity for South Asian American writing, which rode in on the coattails of the "multicultural" boom of that time, when the work of writers like Amy Tan—who wrote stories of "model minority" immigrant life—were being gobbled up greedily by the masses. But a careful look at the South Asian American writers who were being heralded shines a light on the particularities of colonization and immigration. These writers, like Bharati Mukherjee and Chitra Banerjee Divakaruni—and others featured in that *New Yorker* issue, like Amitav Ghosh and Amit Chaudhuri—were born in India, hailed from upper-middle-class Bengali Indian backgrounds, were educated in English-medium schools, and immigrated to the West as academics before focusing solely on writing. Their writings dealt with issues of immigration and assimilation, or looking back on the homeland, as Ghosh does in his novel *The Hungry Tide* and his Ibis trilogy, which is set in nineteenth-century India.

After September 11, much shifted for South Asian Americans, especially for South Asian Muslims, and writers strove to address these issues. H. M. Naqvi's novel *Home Boy* follows three friends—AC, Jimbo, and Chuck—twentysomething Pakistani dudes out for a weekend of fun that turns ugly in post-9/11 New York; with an homage to *The Great Gatsby* and an unnerving time spent in a detention center, this novel really captures the energy and devastation of that time. Ali Eteraz wrote *Native Believer*, a satirical picaresque novel that follows his protagonist—a non-believing Muslim American who gets fired from his job due to his "beliefs"—on a dark journey into the underbelly of Philadelphia's nightlife. Though there seems to be a glut of narratives about Muslim American men and their issues with their faith and becoming a target, there are also writers like Bushra Rehman, whose novel *Corona* takes us through a Pakistani American girl's upbringing in Corona, Queens, and follows her when she has to leave her tight-knit community because she no longer fits the mold. This is a lively coming-of-age narrative plus road trip comedy that draws attention to the need for including more Muslim American female voices.

As more second-generation South Asian American writers come into their own, they seem to show a desire for intersectionality in their work and to want to tackle large transnational issues. If the first-generation writers focused on the hardships of immigration, the second generation seems to want to reach back and look at the traumas of the homeland—especially by imagining themselves into those moments. Bangladeshi American poet Tarfia Faizullah's *Seam* centers on interviews she conducted with Birangonas, women who were raped in the Bangladesh Liberation War. Not wanting to make the poems only about these women, Faizullah puts herself into the poems as "the interviewer," pulling the

---

NAYOMI MUNAWEERA'S FIRST DAYS

Nayomi Munaweera departed from Lagos, Nigeria, and arrived in Los Angeles, California, in 1984.

In SAADA, courtesy of Nayomi Munaweera.

Nayomi Munaweera, author of *Island of a Thousand Mirrors*, was born in Sri Lanka in 1973, but a brewing civil war pushed her family to move to Nigeria when she was three. When a military coup hit Nigeria in 1984, the family was uprooted again—this time to Los Angeles.

In this excerpt, adapted from from SAADA's First Days Project, Munaweera discusses her initial impressions and experiences upon arriving in the United States.

When Munaweera came to the United States at age twelve, she remembers feeling confused about the basics. "I remember being at a party and another Sri Lankan girl saying, 'So, are you from L.A.?' And I literally didn't know that L.A. meant Los Angeles, so I said, 'No. Uh, I don't know?' I was very confused, and all of the other kids started laughing. But I literally did not understand, really, where I was, or the greater geography of the state or the country."

During her family's first days in the country, things were scarce. "I remember specifically I had two pairs of jeans, a green sweater, a pink sweater, and, I think, two shirts. Those were my choices," she says. "And these other girls were showing up in school with a new outfit every day."

Then there was hairspray. "That was new to me!" Munaweera says. "We didn't have that at the time in Nigeria. We lived in a really rural area there." But the demands were clear: "It was the '80s, so you learned about Aqua Net."

Also unacceptable: hairy legs. "In neither Nigeria nor Sri Lanka at that time would it have been something to remark upon," she says. "But in an American high school or junior high school, this was a big deal. You had to shave your legs; you had to shave your armpits—so there was much more attention on the body in a certain way. And these are just lessons you learn and just watch and you learn how to emulate."

---

reader into her process. Nayomi Munaweera's novel *Island of a Thousand Mirrors* follows both a Sinhalese girl as her family deals with the Sri Lankan civil war and a Tamil girl, raped by soldiers, who becomes a freedom fighter and intersects tragically with the narrator's family. At first, Munaweera had a hard time finding a publisher in the United States, so her book was published in Sri Lanka, and then India. When it started winning international awards, Munaweera finally found a publisher in the United States and continues to publish here today.

Twenty years after the *New Yorker*'s India fiction issue hit the stands, the landscape of South Asian American literature has grown more diverse, with writers achieving great acclaim across genres. In the summer of 2016, Bangladeshi American writer Rumaan Alam published the novel *Rich and Pretty*, much touted as a "summer read" by major media. Alam's book focuses on two white women in New York City and their complicated friendship. Perhaps this is the true sign of our success—that we are no longer pigeonholed to write about a certain subject.

Neelanjana Banerjee is the managing editor of Kaya Press and teaches writing and literature in the Asian American Studies Departments of UCLA and Loyola Marymount University in Los Angeles.

FROM HOOGHLY TO MISSISSIPPI TO HARLEM

Vivek Bald

Legend has it that sometime in 1935, a teenaged Ella Fitzgerald was introduced to Chick Webb, the reigning king of Harlem swing jazz. The person doing the introducing was Webb's charismatic hype man and emcee, Bardu Ali. Ali had heard Miss Fitzgerald sing and was insisting that his boss hire the young singer to front the Chick Webb Orchestra. Webb was reluctant at first, but with Ali's prodding, he gave Fitzgerald a chance and soon took her on.

Fitzgerald would become perhaps the most famous female jazz vocalist of the twentieth century. But who was this Bardu Ali? According to press reports of the day, Ali was originally from New Orleans. He was described as "Negro" or "Creole" on his mother's side and, variously, as Turkish, Egyptian, or "Arab" on his father's.

In fact, Bardu Ali's father, Moksad, was from the Hooghly district, just north of Calcutta, in British colonial West Bengal. The Harlem performer was tied to a little-known history of Bengali Muslim work and settlement in the American South that stretched back to the 1880s.

In that decade, small merchants connected to a series of villages in Hooghly started making trips to the working- and middle-class summer beach resorts of New Jersey: Atlantic City and Asbury Park. The Bengalis were catering to a late-nineteenth-century U.S. fashion for "Oriental goods." They brought with them silks and cottons—tablecloths, wall hangings, bedspreads, pillowcases—embroidered by women in Hooghly in a style known as *chikan*.

BENGALI HARLEM AND THE LOST HISTORIES OF SOUTH ASIAN AMERICA

In 2015, academic and filmmaker Vivek Bald published *Bengali Harlem and the Lost Histories of South Asian America*, a book about the historical migration of Bengali Muslims from South Asia to the United States. Bald is currently working on the documentary film *In Search of Bengali Harlem*, which will continue to look at the lasting legacy of the "hundreds of Indian Muslim merchant sailors from the region that is now Bangladesh [who] were either left in port or abandoned their ships in New York City" between World War I and the 1940s.

The Hooghly traders ultimately branched out from New Jersey's boardwalks, moving southward at the end of each summer season to winter tourist sites such as New Orleans and Charleston, South Carolina. After establishing a foothold in these cities, the traders continued to expand; by the early twentieth century, they had built a peddling network that stretched throughout the South, into the Caribbean and Central America, and as far south as Panama.

Although hundreds of men from Hooghly and Calcutta circulated through this network between the 1880s and the 1910s and then returned to their towns and villages in West Bengal, a smaller number settled in southern U.S. cities and married local African American and Afro-Creole women. This was the case with Bardu Ali's father. Moksad Ali was one of the earliest Bengali traders to settle in New Orleans in the 1880s. There, he married a young woman named Ella Blackman.

Moksad and Ella Blackman Ali had three children in New Orleans between 1895 and 1900, then moved across the Mississippi Delta to Waveland, Mississippi, where they had five more children over the next decade, including Bardu (whose given name was Bahadour). Moksad dropped out of the public record by the mid-1910s, but by 1920, Ella Blackman Ali and five of her children had become part of the Great Migration; they traveled northward along with thousands of African Americans from the southern states to New York City and eventually settled in Harlem.

The Ali family's story demonstrates just how entwined the lives of some early South Asian migrants became with those of members of the African diaspora. The U.S. census shows that in 1900,

Bardu Ali. Courtesy of Baltimore Afro-American Archives.

Moksad and Ella Blackman Ali were living in New Orleans's Lower Ninth Ward as heads of a large family. Their household included their first three children, Monzure, Karamouth, and Roheamon; Ella's younger sister, Fanny; Fanny's husband, John Brooks—who was from Georgia, and was of Haitian and Jamaican descent—and Fanny and Ella's eighty-year-old grandmother, Hannah Judah. Judah was a freed slave from Virginia who had come to New Orleans in the 1840s and had supported Ella, Fanny, and their mother in earlier years, working as a housekeeper. It was a heterogeneous extended family, spanning four generations with roots in multiple southern states, the Caribbean, and the Indian subcontinent, as well as in at least two religious traditions, and in experiences of both colonialism and slavery.

In turn, Bardu Ali—one of the earliest second-generation South Asian Americans—spent a lifetime in Black show business. Bardu began his career performing as a dancer on the Black vaudeville circuit of the 1920s, partnering with a young woman, possibly his wife, Thelma, as the team "Baby and Bardu Ali," and with his younger brother, Abdeen, as "The Ali Brothers." Bardu quickly made a name for himself in theatrical and musical circles as a suave and crowd-pleasing emcee, and in the 1930s was recruited by the swing jazz bandleader Chick Webb.

After Webb's death in 1939, Bardu Ali moved to Los Angeles, where he became an instrumental part of the city's Central Avenue music scene in the 1940s. Here he

VIJAY IYER AND RUDRESH MAHANTHAPPA

Rudresh Mahanthappa performs at SAADA's "Revolution Remix" concert on August 24, 2019. Photo by Justin L. Chiu.

Vijay Iyer and Rudresh Mahanthappa are world-renowned jazz artists and among the very first South Asian Americans to find success and acclaim in a genre of music that originated in, and is still closely associated with, African American communities. As *Pitchfork* put it in 2016, "Nobody knew what to make of" the pianist Iyer and alto saxophonist Mahanthappa "when they began barnstorming the jazz world in the late 1990s." But the two started performing together regularly, including during the period directly after the 9/11 attacks in New York City. Iyer reflected on that moment:

When Rudresh and I teamed up, that was political. Not in the sense that we were going to run for office, but it was a community-building move. Through the fact of us working together and the details of how we worked together, what we did was political. So if you look at my collaborations, it is very much in line with all these others in the sense that it is a building of community, particularly among artists of color. This is what I learned from the example of elder African-American artists, which is where it is all coming from; to refuse to be silenced.

Excerpted from "Dual Identities: A Conversation with Jazz Soulmates Vijay Iyer and Rudresh Mahanthappa" for Pitchfork, *by Britt Robson.*

teamed up with the drummer Johnny Otis to open the Barrelhouse, the country's first nightclub devoted to the emerging style of rhythm and blues (the direct precursor to 1950s rock 'n' roll). Ali closed out his career in the 1970s as the business manager for the comedian Redd Foxx, when Foxx was the lead actor in one of the United States' first Black situation comedies, *Sanford and Son*.

Bardu Ali was not the only person in the family to make a name for himself in entertainment. One hundred years after Moksad Ali and Ella Blackman married in New Orleans, one of their fourth-generation descendants, Rozonda Thomas, aka "Chilli," became an internationally known pop star as one-third of the all-female R & B group TLC.

Vivek Bald is a scholar, writer, and documentary filmmaker whose work focuses on histories of migration and diaspora, particularly from the South Asian subcontinent.

DESI BASKETBALL DIARIES

Stanley Thangaraj, with Akshat Tewary and Vasef Sajid

A number of South Asian American men's basketball leagues have flourished over the last thirty years in North America, allowing league participants to subvert stereotypes of South Asians and, in the process, redefine South Asian cultural identities through sport. One of these leagues, the North American Indo-Pak basketball circuit, originated in the mid-1980s in Canada and expanded to the United States in 1989. With the popularity of basketball in the country over the last three decades, it was hard for young South Asian American men not to take to the sport. Although several South Asian American athletes had played soccer, American football, or baseball, the rise in basketball's popularity made it the logical choice for expressing, and redefining, what it means to be a South American man—cool and athletic.

After playing basketball with several young, mostly Pakistani Muslim American men I had met at Al-Farooq Masjid in Atlanta, I decided to participate with them in a North American Indo-Pak tournament. Mustafa, Qamar, Malik, Kumrain, and I formed the team Atlanta Outkasts and would play in our very first tournament as a team in Greenville, South Carolina. We decided on yellow jerseys with red lines, in a way matching the colors of Atlanta's NBA team, the Hawks.

In preparation for the tournament, we spent a few days practicing as a team—at Mustafa's parents' home, at Emory University's gym (where I'd bought guest passes for the men), and at the J. M. Tull–Gwinnett Family YMCA, where we dominated

---

SONIA RAMAN

In 2020, Sonia Raman was hired as assistant coach for the Memphis Grizzlies, making her the first South Asian American woman to serve as a coach in the National Basketball Association (NBA). The daughter of Indian immigrants, Raman grew up an avid basketball fan. She played basketball in her hometown of Framingham, Massachusetts, rooted for the Boston Celtics, and joined the college basketball team as an undergraduate at Tufts University.

After graduating from Boston College Law School, Raman began a career in law but maintained a connection to basketball by volunteering as assistant coach for the Wellesley College team. In 2008, she decided to leave the legal field and pursue coaching full-time when she joined MIT as the Division III women's basketball team's head coach. There, Raman led her team from its previous five-consecutive losing seasons to back-to-back victories at the 2018 and 2019 New England Women's and Men's Athletic Conference championships. Her impressive coaching record and dedication to basketball eventually led Raman to an offer from the NBA.

In an interview with the *New York Times*, Raman remarked on her career, "It's a very nontraditional career path for someone of South Asian descent. My parents are both immigrants from India, so coming here and working hard and providing me with so much opportunity—I don't think it was on their radar that their daughter was going to become a basketball coach. But I think they saw where my passion was all along."

---

the pickup basketball scene. All these practices were geared toward creating rapport, understanding and synchronizing our movements on the court, finding out strengths and weaknesses as a team, going over some offensive and defensive strategies, and etching out roles for each team member.

What we accomplished athletically on the basketball court is not often associated with South Asian American men; the popular misconception about our athletic prowess is that we are "nerds" and that "Brown men can't jump." Mustafa's smooth, high-release left-handed shoot and great dribbling skills were on show. Malik, standing at 6' 2", demonstrated his jumping and blocking abilities and pulled down key rebounds. Kumrain added ball-handling skills and a strong shooting stroke. Qamar brought his sense of toughness and street cred to our team.

At tournament time, we drove from Atlanta to Greenville along Highway 85 North. After checking into our rooms, Malik, Mustafa, and I drove to get a bite to

---

VIVEK RANADIVÉ AND SHAHID KHAN

Indian American businessman Vivek Ranadivé is the co-owner of the National Basketball Association team the Sacramento Kings. He had previously been a co-owner of the Golden State Warriors, making him the first person of Indian descent to own an NBA franchise.

Shahid Khan, a Pakistani American businessman, is the owner of the National Football League team the Jacksonville Jaguars. According to *Forbes*, Khan was the "first ethnic-minority owner" in the NFL.

In both the NBA and the NFL, owners of color are exceedingly rare, despite the fact that a majority of players in both leagues are Black Americans. In 2017, Khan made national headlines when he stood arm-in-arm with Jaguar football players during the national anthem, an act of solidarity with those, like Colin Kaepernick, who were protesting the continued killing of Black Americans by the police in the United States. Though Khan did not take a knee as Kaepernick famously did, the *Washington Post* described his action as "the first time an NFL team owner had taken such a public stand on the side of his players during a national anthem demonstration."

---

eat at Wendy's, where I ordered my favorite burger, the Big Bacon Classic. A burst of laughter bounced off the walls—Mustafa and Malik were laughing their hearts out.

Totally confused, I gave them the stink eye and asked what was so funny. They could barely contain themselves. Mustafa finally muttered, both humorously and seriously, "What the hell are you?" Malik joined in: "Seriously, what are you?" This made no sense to me; I asked for more, and Malik, with great enthusiasm, said, "Man, we thought you were Hindu, but then you order a burger." Of course, the stereotypical perception of Indians is that they are all upper-caste Hindus who do not eat beef. He added, "Then we thought you must be Muslim. [And] you ordered bacon!" His laughter seeped out. "Really, what are you?" I explained to them that I was a Tamil Christian with roots in southern India. Suddenly, our friendship forged on the basketball court became an opportunity to challenge the dominant understandings of South Asian Americans and our ancestral ties.

This instance at Wendy's was not an isolated event of confronting South Asian

WILMETH SIDAT-SINGH

Poster from the Office for Emergency Management, Office of War Information News Bureau, 1943. Artwork by Charles Henry Alston.

Wilmeth Sidat-Singh was an African American collegiate and professional basketball and football star in the segregated United States of the 1930s. His parents, Elias and Pauline Webb, were both Black. After his father died, his mother married Samuel Sidat-Singh, a medical student from India who adopted Wilmeth, giving him his family name. Because of his name and lighter skin, people would often assume that Sidat-Singh was a "Hindu."

But when a Black sportswriter wrote an article revealing that Sidat-Singh was indeed Black, the Syracuse University football star was benched for the next game, as the University of Maryland refused to take the field against a Black man. After college, Sidat-Singh's athletic career did not last long, because both the NBA and the NFL had unofficial bans on Black athletes at the time. He eventually served in the Tuskegee Airmen unit of the U.S. Army Air Corps during World War II, dying in 1943 during a training mission.

In 2013, the University of Maryland offered an official apology to the family of Wilmeth Sidat-Singh.

American stereotypes. At the 2006 Indo-Pak national basketball tournament in Chicago, I met with one of the key players from the Houston Boys, Karthik, who identifies religiously as Jain. Through basketball networks in Houston, he had become friends with some Malayalee Christians and Hindus. Their team, the Houston Boys, is a religiously and ethnically heterogeneous group that includes

---

SOUTH ASIAN AMERICAN OLYMPIC GYMNASTS

Young South Asian Americans have enjoyed and excelled in a variety of sports, including gymnastics. Mohini Bhardwaj de Freitas is a member of the USA Gymnastics Hall of Fame and was the first South Asian American gymnast—and the second South Asian American athlete in any sport—to win a medal at the Olympics. She earned a silver on the uneven bars at the 2004 Summer Olympics in Athens, and prior to that competed at the 1997 and 2001 World Championships. Today, Bhardwaj owns the OOA Gymnastics gym in Bend, Oregon, where she also coaches.

The early legacy Bhardwaj built as a South Asian American in gymnastics has since been expanded by several others. Raj Bhavsar earned a bronze medal as a member of the 2008 U.S. Olympic team for men's gymnastics and silver medals as a member of the U.S. team at both the 2001 and 2003 World Championships. Bhavsar's cousin and 2021 Olympics hopeful Akash Modi represented the United States at the 2018 and 2019 World Championships, served as an alternate for the 2016 U.S. Olympic team, and, in 2017, became the first South Asian American to win the prestigious Nissen-Emery Award, an honor given to the best male collegiate gymnast in the United States. Syque Caesar, a former captain of the University of Michigan's men's gymnastics team and current assistant coach for the Stanford team, represented Bangladesh at the 2012 Summer Olympics. And Asad Jooma, a 2021 Olympics hopeful and member of the University of California, Berkeley, men's gymnastics team, represented Pakistan at the 2018 Asian Games.

In an interview with the *Juggernaut*, Jooma reflected on the growing community of South Asian American gymnasts: "Growing up in Tennessee, I was the only person who looked like me in gymnastics. But now, I know people from my own community back home who are doing gymnastics in high school. And I've met and become friends with South Asian Americans across the country doing gymnastics. In a way, we are building our own community."

---

people who are often neglected and dismissed from the stories of South Asian diasporas. This experience of socialization across ethnic and religious lines in basketball is not as common in U.S. cricket teams. In fact, the recently deceased West Indian cricketer legend Desmond Lewis intimated that the religious tension and nationalistic posturing by Indian Americans, Pakistani Americans, Hindus, and Muslims in Atlanta's cricket league made the experience conflict-ridden and unenjoyable for Atlanta's Caribbean cricket teams.

At the Indo-Pak basketball games and tournaments, teams with different ethnic, religious, national, migration, and racial backgrounds occupied the courts. Spouses, girlfriends, sisters, mothers, fathers, uncles, and aunties were sometimes in the stands cheering for them. Some of the dominant teams included Ahmadi Muslims from Washington, D.C., and their Hindu teammates; Sikhs from the northeastern United States and Canada; ethnic Punjabis, Telugus, Gujaratis, Biharis, Tamils, and Malayalees; players from the Bangladeshi diaspora; South Asians with Caribbean backgrounds, such as Indo-Guyanese and Trinidadians; Sri Lankans and, at times, Tibetans. Most of the players were born and raised in the United States, with some being mixed race.

All these points of ethnic, religious, and national difference play a part in team formation, but they do not affect the kinds of friendships and politics that emerge on the basketball court. The sense of community that grows out of playing together and respecting each other goes beyond the Hindu-Muslim, India-Pakistan divide. A no-look pass, a crossover dribble, a shot block, and a dunk were all things highly valued and celebrated in this basketball community. As a result, these young South Asian American basketball players define what it means to be South Asian in an expansive way while also celebrating each other's skills, bodies, abilities, and competitive desires. In the process, the spectacular basketball on the Indo-Pak basketball courts helped expand, challenge, and reimagine the very contours of belonging and citizenship in the United States.

Stanley Thangaraj (he/him/his) is an associate professor of anthropology, gender studies, and international studies at the City College of New York.

Akshat Tewary (he/him/his) is a PhD student in the Media and Communications Department at University of Leicester, UK, and an immigration lawyer.

Vasef Sajid (he/him/his) is a design sales manager for Best Buy.

FILM AND CINEMA

Jigna Desai

In Canadian Srinivas Krishna's film *Masala* (1991), the sassy grandmother, played by the late and exuberant Zohra Sehgal, talks back to the god Krishna through her VCR. She demands that Krishna help pay the mortgage, take care of her family, and generally make life better in her immigrant community. This imaginative trope emphasizes the important and sometimes contentious relationship between South Asians in North America and cinema. *Masala* captures how these communities use media to tell their stories as well as to talk back when what media offers them is inadequate.

Since its inception, film has been significant to how we imagine ourselves as people. And South Asians, in particular, have a rich and long history with cinema. One could argue, then, that film is one of the primary mediums of South Asian American identity. Yet South Asian Americans haven't always been provided

D'LO

D'Lo is a queer/transgender Tamil Sri Lankan American actor, writer, activist, poet, and comedian who has appeared in Netflix's *Sense8*, HBO's *Looking*, and the Emmy-winning Amazon series *Transparent*. He has performed his comedy around the world and coproduces DisOriented Comedy, a nationally touring stand-up showcase of "mostly female" Asian Americans.

Imran Siddiquee interviews D'Lo for SAADA at the twenty-year celebration event for DJ Rekha's Basement Bhangra. In SAADA.

many options for "positive" representations in American film. Prior to the 1990s, Hollywood rarely depicted South Asian Americans at all, instead offering up Orientalized and exoticized portrayals of South Asians—such as the monkey-brain eaters in *Indiana Jones and the Temple of Doom* (1984). Additionally, South Asian and South Asian American characters were frequently played by white actors in brownface (brown makeup), in films such as *Gunga Din* (1939); *The Party* (1968), starring Peter Sellers; and *Short Circuit* (1986) and *Short Circuit 2* (1988). Before they were given the opportunity to make their own films, South Asian Americans generally preferred South Asian cinema—viewed first on the grainy screens of VHF television channels, and then later on VCRs, satellite television, and DVD players—

to the racism of Hollywood.

It was in the early 1990s that filmmaking gained a foothold within South Asian American communities. Mira Nair was the first South Asian American director to gain substantial access to Hollywood, and this did not happen again until the emergence of M. Night Shyamalan almost ten years later. Nair migrated from India to the United States, where she studied filmmaking at Harvard University. Her earliest foray into U.S. theaters was with *Salaam Bombay!* (1988), a fictionalized depiction of Bombay life from the perspective of those who are most disenfranchised—homeless children and sex workers. The film was controversial, and some critics felt she depicted Indians only as destitute victims.

Nair's second film, *Mississippi Masala* (1992), was the first feature film about South Asian Americans. Set in Greenwood, Mississippi, it focuses on an exiled Gujarati family who decades earlier had left Uganda when dictator Idi Amin

---

A PAKISTANI AMERICAN MUSLIM SUPERHERO

In November 2013, Marvel Comics announced that its *Ms. Marvel* series was getting a new central character: Kamala Khan, a Pakistani teenager from Jersey City, New Jersey. The new series, written by G. Willow Wilson, marked the first time a Muslim character had headlined a Marvel comic book. Sana Amanat, an editor at Marvel, was influential in the development of this Ms. Marvel and is herself a Pakistani American who was raised in New Jersey. Amanat has said that the idea for Kamala Khan was rooted in a "desire to explore the Muslim American diaspora from an authentic perspective."

In 2015, the series won a Hugo Award for Best Graphic Story, and in 2018, Kevin Feige, Marvel Studios president, confirmed that there are plans to bring Kamala Khan's *Ms. Marvel* to the big screen in the near future.

---

expelled South Asians from the country. The film's protagonist, Mina, works and lives in a motel with her parents, Kinnu and Jay. She later falls in love with an African American man named Demetrius (played by Denzel Washington). Their relationship is the target of much gossip and disapproval in the film's Indian American community—and the depiction of an interracial relationship between a South Asian American woman and an African American man also inspired heated debates within South Asian American communities. Some critics disapproved of the film's direct engagement with classism, anti-Black racism, and colorism (discrimination based on skin color) in South Asian American communities. But

---

THUSHARI JAYASEKERA

With her role on NBC's *Outsourced* (2010–11), Thushari Jayasekera became the first Sri Lankan American woman to play a principal role in a prime-time show on a major American television network.

Mississippi Masala raises important questions about how race, color, class, gender, and sexuality shape cultural belonging in these communities.

South Asian American filmmakers have sought to counter their communities' invisibility in popular culture with a two-pronged response—by representing their communities themselves and by doing so responsibly. Though Hollywood has typically offered up shallow and negative depictions, South Asian American filmmakers have been cautious not to create completely sanitized "positive" representations either. Instead, they have focused on how film, as a medium, can delve into the thorny questions of who we are and where we come from. Cinema and media are increasingly critical to how we understand and imagine ourselves, individually and collectively, in South Asian America.

Mira Nair with her family during a family road trip to the Grand Canyon in 2016, from SAADA's Road Trips Project. In SAADA, courtesy of Mira Nair.

BROWN GIRLS

Written by Fatimah Asghar and directed and produced by Sam Bailey, *Brown Girls* is a popular web series about the lives of two young women of color. According to the show's website, "Leila is a South Asian American writer just now owning her queerness. Patricia is a sex-positive Black American musician who is struggling to commit to anything: job, art, and relationships. While the two women come from completely different backgrounds, their friendship is ultimately what they lean on to get through the messiness of their mid-twenties."

In 2017, HBO announced a deal with Asghar and Bailey to develop *Brown Girls* into a series for the cable network.

Jigna Desai (she/her/hers) is a professor in the Departments of Gender, Women, and Sexuality Studies and Asian American Studies at the University of Minnesota.

SOUTH ASIAN AMERICANS IN HOLLYWOOD

Shilpa Davé

The twenty-first century has seen South Asian Americans increasingly producing, writing, directing, and acting in the American film and television industry. While network and cable television and the Hollywood film industry have included more South Asian American voices, the advent of streaming services, such as Netflix, Amazon, and Hulu, has provided opportunities for previously unheard voices to be shared on a worldwide platform. Award-winning shows like Mindy Kaling's *The Mindy Project* and Aziz Ansari and Alan Yang's *Master of None* represent the innovations and talents of South Asian Americans in the industry, but it has taken almost a hundred years to see South Asian Americans take on the role of creators and directors of their own stories in the U.S. film and television industry. The history of South Asian American representation in American popular culture is related to the relationship between the United States, South Asia, and immigrants of South Asian heritage.

Early Hollywood portrayals of Indians placed them in the context of British history, confined to British tales of adventure or spiritual discovery set in colonial India. Hollywood films focused on three thematic threads that characterized

MERLE OBERON

Merle Oberon, who was nominated for an Academy Award for her performance in 1935's *The Dark Angel*, remains the only South Asian to ever be nominated for best actress at the Oscars. She also starred in *Wuthering Heights* in 1939, opposite Laurence Olivier, and a number of other films. Oberon, though, was not known to be South Asian during the entirety of her career, and instead passed as a white woman.

In reality, Oberon was born in Mumbai to Constance Selby, who was from Ceylon (present-day Sri Lanka), and Arthur Terrence O'Brien Thompson, a white British mechanical engineer. Yet Oberon hid her origins for her entire career, claiming she was from Tasmania, Australia, until a year before her death, in 1979.

narratives of India and Indians: the spiritual guru and mystical religions, the poor rural villagers, and the treacherous or noble natives rising up against the British. Many of the distinctions between different religions in India were lost or lumped into the idea of power-hungry blood-sacrificing religious cults who threaten the rule and order of the British. Thomas Edison's *Hindoo Fakir* (1902), the first film that depicted India, emphasized these traits, and Hollywood films continued to recycle these images in depictions of India through the end of the twentieth century. One prominent example is the box-office hit *Indiana Jones and the Temple of Doom* (1984), primarily set in 1930s British India. The plot features archeologist Dr. Jones as an American hero who rescues a Hindu idol and saves the native villagers (and his friends) from the villainous Indians in power, who are members of the blood cult of Kali.

Few South Asian actors played lead roles in early Hollywood films. As with many ethnic and racial characters in Hollywood productions, Indian characters were mostly portrayed by white actors wearing makeup. During the 1930s and 1940s, one of the few Indian actors onscreen was Sabu, who starred in twenty-three films, including *The Elephant Boy* (1937), *The Thief of Baghdad* (1940), and *Song of India* (1949). His image as the wily and mischievous native youth endures and is a role model for other portrayals of native or Indian youth, such as Rudyard Kipling's Mowgli in *The Jungle Book* (1942).

After 1965, representations of Indians in television and film also provided stories of immigration and assimilation for Indians in the United States, but most of the roles were still played by white actors performing as Indians. Some of the depictions focused on Indian cultural traits and practices adopted by American youth in the counterculture movement of the 1960s and 1970s. Peter Sellers (in a brownface performance) played Indian immigrant Hrundi Bakshi in *The Party* (1968), in which he plays the sitar, has a pet monkey, and is deemed "cool" by college students. The Academy Award–winning best picture *Gandhi* (1982) was critically acclaimed, but also featured the same colonial themes of earlier times updated to show a modern India.

One of the most famous Indian Americans in American popular culture is the animated character Apu Nahasapeemapetilon, the proprietor of the Springfield Kwik-E-Mart on the longest-running television show, *The Simpsons* (1989–). White actor Hank Azaria performs an Indian accent, or a "brown voice," to simulate the voice of an Indian character. Before Apu's appearance on *The Simpsons* in 1990, there were only small parts in American television and film for South Asians, and because Apu was one of the only depictions of South Asians on popular television, it limited the types of roles and characters for South Asians. Recurring roles for South Asians only came about during the turn of the twenty-first century, as their roles in international business and the entrepreneurial arena became more prominent.

In the 1990s, satellite television, independent films, and documentaries brought other images of contemporary Indians to the United States. Indian and British Indian directors using Indian and British Indian actors made financially successful

---

APU IN THE SIMPSONS

A dominant image of South Asian Americans has been the convenience store owner Apu Nahasapeemapetilon in *The Simpsons*. With so many South Asian Americans working in convenience stores, such a character would seemingly be a fitting aspect of a television series. And yet, the representation by actor Hank Azaria, a white male who based the character in part on another white male's exaggerated representation of South Asians, played into static stereotypes. Apu's famous line, delivered in a thick accent, was "Thank you, come again." Comedian Hari Kondabolu's 2017 documentary *The Problem with Apu* challenged this portrayal, and the character has now been silenced in the show.

---

independent films in Britain, Canada, and the United States about South Asian immigrants in the United States, including *Mississippi Masala* (Mira Nair, 1991), with Denzel Washington and Sarita Choudhury; *Chutney Popcorn* (Nisha Ganatra, 1999); and *American Desi* (Piyush Pandya, 2001). Independent films, such as the critically acclaimed *Monsoon Wedding*, set in India (Nair, 2001), fostered an interest in Indian stories, and *The Namesake* (Nair, 2006) and the 2009 Academy Award–winning *Slumdog Millionaire*, set in India (Danny Boyle, 2008), were some of the first films about India in the English language to be widely recognized by an American audience. The presentations of Bollywood films in American movie theaters, and the development of ensemble multicultural and multiracial television casts that included South Asian actors playing South Asian characters, also increased the visibility of South Asians in American media.

While independent films created more complex South Asian characters, South Asians on American television and in film in the first decade of the twenty-first

---

THE PROBLEM WITH APU

In 2018, SAADA hosted a screening of Hari Kondabolu's film *The Problem with Apu* in Philadelphia. Philip Deslippe wrote about the film for *Tides* magazine:

> *The documentary film* The Problem with Apu, *written and starring comedian Hari Kondabolu, was released on truTV in November 2017.* The Problem with Apu *is not only a look at the character of Apu Nahasapeemapetilon, the owner of the Kwik-E-Mart convenience store from* The Simpsons, *but it also addresses racial stereotypes and the lack of South Asian American representation in the media. Kondabolu traces the origins of Apu and its voicing by the white actor Hank Azaria, and connects the character to the history of black-face minstrelsy in America.* The Problem with Apu *brings together a large number of South Asian American entertainers as well as former Surgeon General Vivek Murthy, who discuss the role Apu played in marginalizing South Asian Americans and the need for South Asian Americans to be visible in popular culture and to have a leading role in telling their own stories.*

Following the screening, SAADA led a community conversation about representations of South Asian Americans in popular culture. One of the audience members shared:

> *So, I grew up in a ton of different places. I was born in India, I was raised in Hong Kong, Malaysia, and Singapore. I was in an American international school, with all your typical diplomat brats, myself included. . . .*

> *So when I was in seventh grade, I was in a play called* Matilda. *This was the typical* Matilda *that we all saw—really smart girl, tremendous intellect, [etc]. And I played her father. Now, I was in seventh grade and the director said, "Hey, you know, if you put an Indian accent on it, that would be hilarious." And I thought it was hilarious. I mean, I was what? Twelve? You know? And I think about it now and it's like . . . I'm making fun of my dad.*

> *It's hurtful.*

---

century were mostly young men who played the foreign-looking, out-of-place emasculated geek who is always the sidekick and never the leader. The smart but socially awkward fresh-off-the boat Indian immigrant male character continues to appear on shows such as *The Big Bang Theory* (2007–19), whose particle astrophysicist Raj Koothrappali (Kunal Nayyar) is part of the ensemble cast. But the twenty-first century has seen alternative and expanded roles for South Asians outside this stereotype. One comedic satire of the model minority can be seen in the feature film *Harold & Kumar Go to White Castle* (2004), starring the actors Kal Penn and John Cho.

In the past twenty years, South Asians have become more visible and earned more acclaim in the U.S. film and television industry. Since M. Night Shyamalan's breakout film, the blockbuster hit *The Sixth Sense* (1999), he has been one of the most prominent South Asian American directors. South Asian American women are delivering award-winning performances on television, such as Priyanka Chopra, the lead actress in the network drama *Quantico* (2015–18). Mindy Kaling wrote for *The Office* and played the character Kelly Kapoor before starring in her own series, *The Mindy Project*. On reality television, Padma Lakshmi hosts the popular Bravo show *Top Chef* (2006–). South Asian Americans have also been prominent on the comedy scene, and many comedians have appeared on late-night talk shows, including Hari Kondabolu, Aasif Mandvi, and Aparna Nancherla.

An increasing number of South Asians are appearing in American film and television productions with more diverse storylines. While many of the colonial and immigrant images still dominate, more complex stories are being told. In addition, many South Asian characters are being played by South Asian actors and actresses, and scripts are being written by more South Asian writers and filmed by South Asian directors. The series *Outsourced* premiered on NBC in 2010, the first American television show set in India and featuring an ensemble cast with South Asian and South Asian American actors, and written by South Asian and South Asian American writers. The Asian American situation comedy *Fresh Off the Boat*, created by Nahnatchka Khan, has a diverse group of directors and writers. Following in the footsteps of the earlier groundbreakers are other South Asian Americans in all phases of the industry—writing, producing, and directing.

While network shows and Hollywood films continue to dominate in terms of publicity, streaming services like YouTube, Netflix, Amazon, and Hulu have offered more opportunities for diverse and alternative stories, and for South Asian Americans to develop a presence in different genres and multiple roles both in front of and behind the camera.

Shilpa Davé (she/her/hers) is an assistant dean in the College of Arts and Sciences and an assistant professor in the Department of Media Studies at the University of Virginia.

THEATER IN SOUTH ASIAN AMERICA

Neilesh Bose

Theater in South Asian American communities stretches back at least to the early twentieth century, in professional venues and university theater spaces. Theater has been produced both *about* South Asians, primarily through adaptations of plays from ancient India and about historic events in colonial India, as well as, recently, *by* South Asian American people and *about* South Asian American lives.

Theater produced about South Asians began in the mid-nineteenth century, just before the Civil War, in 1858, as the rebellion of Indian soldiers against the British East India Company was coming to a close. The first recorded play about South Asians to run to large audiences in the United States, *Jessie Brown; or, the Relief of Lucknow*, was written by the Irish American playwright Dion Boucicault and was focused on the rebellion. It featured a composite character, Nana Sahib (based loosely on a real person in the rebellion), as well as other Indian rebels in a spectacular drama centered on the capture and freedom of Europeans in India. This play offered exaggerated and stereotypically "savage" portrayals of the Indians in the rebellion, in contrast to the "innocent" Europeans, like the title character, Jessie Brown. Running for a year, from the summer of 1858 to the middle of

THE CONQUEST OF KAMA

working among these famine stricken people report that there is no work by which man can earn money and attribute the cause of the famine to the very low purchasing power of the people rather than to the want of foodstuff.

But famines art not unknown in India. In 145 years of British rule from 1770-1915, more than 24 famines have visited the soil. The mortality is not less appalling than the number. Five million people died in one Madras famine in 1877, and out of 500,000 population in a district, 200,000 were starved to death in another.

The cause of the present famine, and of all other famines is undoubtedly the very low purchasing power of the people which can never be removed so long India grinds under economic slavery.

Sanskrit Play.

For the benefit of the Indian Famine Relief Fund, the members of the California Chapter of Hindusthan Association of America, under the patronage of a few remarkable American friends of Hindusthan, gave a performance in the Berkeley High School Auditorium on Friday evening, October 1, 1915.

The drama was named "The Coquest of Kama." The main theme has been taken from Kalidasa while about a dogen songs,

mostly from Tagore, have been introduced to suit the time and occasion.

Mr. S. N. Guha, B. S. (Calif.), is the compiler of the drama and the director of the Abu Hossain Dramatic Club of Los Angeles. The club was started at Los Angeles only last year by Mr. Guha with a few of his friends. The chief object of this club is to represent Oriental music to the West in its true form and spirit untampered by foreigners who have a natural tendency to represent everything oriental in a light and careless manner.

Adaptation, at least a false show of it, is indispensable for Self-preservation. In this nervous age of Self-advertisement and aggression, India must go against her own tradition and advertise her Culture and Civilization systematically to save her from that psycological and consequently phy-

In SAADA.

This article, from the October 1915 issue of *The Hindusthanee Student*, details a performance of the Sanskrit play *The Conquest of Kama* at Berkeley High School on October 1, 1915. The play was performed by the Hindusthan Association of America and produced for the benefit of an Indian famine relief fund. S. N. Guha, an alumnus of the University of California, Berkeley, and the director of the Abu Hossein Dramatic Club of Los Angeles, served as the main organizer.

1859 in New York's Wallack's Theatre, the play was the first depiction of Indians on Broadway, albeit by Europeans costumed as Indians.

In the early twentieth century, universities began to stage classic Sanskrit plays using student actors and translations of American Sanskrit professors. The first such production, at the University of California, Berkeley, in 1907, was of Shudraka's *Mricchakatika*, known in English as *The Little Clay Cart* and translated by the famous Sanskrit scholar A. W. Ryder (1877–1938). Ryder's translation of Kalidasa's *Sakuntala* was also produced at the same university in 1914. Around the same time, Sanskrit classics were being produced in professional venues, such as the 1919 production of *Sakuntala* at New York's Greenwich Village Theatre and the 1924 and 1926 productions of *Mricchakatika*, the latter running for seventy-two shows. All the actors involved in these shows—from Berkeley to New York—were European Americans performing in South Asian costumes and brownface makeup.

After the 1965 Immigration and Naturalization Act, theater and the performing arts in the United States witnessed a number of changes corresponding to the increasing numbers of South Asian Americans settling in the country. By the 1990s, theater companies run by and focused on South Asian Americans themselves appeared, such as SALAAM Theatre in New York, Rasaka Theatre Company in Chicago, Rasik Arts in Toronto, Shunya Theatre in Houston, and arts organizations

---

DISGRACED

Written by Ayad Akhtar, *Disgraced* is a one-act play that won the 2013 Pulitzer Prize for Drama. It tells the story of lawyer Amir Kapoor and his artist wife, Emily, who are hosting a dinner on the Upper East Side of New York City. In a review in the *New York Times*, Charles Isherwood described *Disgraced* as a "vitally engaged play about thorny questions of identity and religion in the contemporary world. . . . In dialogue that bristles with wit and intelligence, Mr. Akhtar, a novelist and screenwriter, puts contemporary attitudes toward religion under a microscope, revealing how tenuous self-image can be for people born into one way of being who have embraced another."

From "Beware Dinner Talk on Identity and Islam" for the New York Times, *by Charles Ishwerwood.*

---

like the Indo-American Arts Council of New York City. These institutions, along with groups that have broader missions—like Silk Road Rising of Chicago, which is focused on staging plays and video essays based on stories from Asia and the Middle East—have produced plays about South Asians across the country since the turn of the twenty-first century.

Individual playwrights and theater artists, such as Aasif Mandvi, Shishir Kurup, Rehana Mirza, and Ayad Akhtar, have seen their work produced in professional theaters and recognized by the mainstream theater community. Just as the global crisis of the 1857–58 Indian Mutiny in colonial India inspired the play *Jessie Brown;*

BROKEN SEEDS

*Photo by
Amitava Sarkar.*

In 2017, Bay Area artists Rupy Tut and Nadhi Thekkek produced a mixed-media bharatanatyam performance entitled *Broken Seeds (Still Grow)*. Presented at The Flight Deck in Oakland, *Broken Seeds* featured live spoken word and music, along with projections of Tut's calligraphy and miniature paintings as a backdrop to Thekkek's choreography. The dynamic performance captured the violent and complex history of Partition—the splitting of India into the independent nations of India and Pakistan at the close of the British Empire—and connected the questions around displacement and discrimination that characterized that event with the South Asian immigrant experience in America.

As part of their research for this performance, Tut and Thekkek turned to SAADA's online repository. In particular, photographs and stories about Bhagat Singh Thind, along with archived news articles about the Bellingham riot of 1907, served as direct inspiration for sections of the show that addressed the history of anti–South Asian xenophobia in the United States.

From "From Partition to the Present: An Interview with Artists Nadhi Thekkek and Rupy Tut" for
Tides, *by Anantha Sudhakar.*

or, the Relief of Lucknow, the global crisis of the 9/11 attacks on the United States inspired a range of theatrical works by and about South Asian Americans. Shishir Kurup's *Merchant on Venice* (2007) adapts William Shakespeare's *Merchant of Venice*; the play, set in a South Asian American community in Southern California, puts an Indian Muslim named Sharuk in the Shylock role, facing a community of Indian Hindus as opposed to European Christians. Written in blank verse, Kurup's play focuses on the predicaments of South Asian Muslims in post-9/11 U.S. society and also paints a picture of South Asian American society at large. Rehana Mirza's *Barriers* (2005), about a Muslim American family with South and Southeast Asian roots, also focuses on violence and social dislocations in the wake of 9/11. Finally, Ayad Akhtar's *Disgraced* (2012), about a Pakistani American lawyer's struggles with Muslim identity and life in post-9/11 New York, won the Pulitzer Prize and has enjoyed numerous professional productions across the United States and Europe.

The twenty-first century American stage is witnessing more and more work by and about South Asian American theater artists themselves, exploring and interrogating not only the internal lives of South Asian American communities but also the broader politics of society from South Asian American vantage points.

Neilesh Bose is an associate professor of history and Canada Research Chair in global and comparative history at the University of Victoria.

"NEHRU SUITS ARE WHAT'S HAPPENING"

Meenasarani Linde Murugan

The Nehru jacket was derived from both the shalwar kameez and the British frock coat, also known as a sherwani or achkan. It is a hip-length tailored coat with a short stand-up collar. Though the sherwani is typically worn for formal occasions in India, its own history is indicative of the cultural exchange between Britain and India as a result of colonialism. Clothing was a politically fraught arena, as India's struggle for independence led Indians to turn away from Western style. While Gandhi's white dhoti was one way to assert an anti-colonial identity through sartorial display, it seemed a little too revealing for many elite, Western-educated Indian men. India's first Prime Minister Jawaharlal Nehru opted for the Muslim sherwani and pajama that were neither British nor Indian villager. Nehru's outfit solved the problem of how to look modern without appearing Western and look Indian without appearing provincial.

Prime Minister Jawaharlal Nehru (right), wearing a "Nehru jacket," during a visit with President Dwight D. Eisenhower (left). Courtesy of U.S. Embassy Archives.

Despite Nehru's visibility in the United States—he visited three times between 1949 and 1961, and appeared on CBS's *Face the Nation* in 1957—the Nehru collar and jacket, named for the prime minister, did not make an impact on U.S. fashion until the mid-1960s, when it became part of the rising trend of mod fashion. Designer Pierre Cardin is credited with "introducing" the Nehru jacket after traveling to India and Pakistan in the 1960s. The jacket was also popularly identified with the Beatles; Paul McCartney wore a Nehru-collared stage coat when the band performed at New York's Shea Stadium on August 15, 1965. Douglas Milling, who designed many of the Beatles' early stage suits, had copied Cardin's design.

In contrast to comedic adoptions of Indian clothing in U.S. popular culture of the early twentieth century, the Nehru jacket of the late 1960s became emblematic of a hip and modern masculinity. Thomas Frank emphasized the jacket's appearance on television, noting, "In February of 1968, Johnny Carson wore a Nehru jacket designed by Oleg Cassini on *The Tonight Show*, precipitating an overnight mania for the garment." Cassini was Jacqueline Kennedy's favorite designer, and on one of his visits to the White House, he claimed to have admired one of "the more conservative" jackets he had seen "Nehru himself wear." He went on to note that he "liked the clean, uncluttered simplicity of it," adding, "Then too, my mind was on India during that period." Through the borrowing of fashion design between India, Paris, London, and the United States, the Nehru jacket was seen at once as modern and exotic. Like Nehru himself, who sought to wear something that would proclaim nationalism as well as modernity, the jacket that carried his name conveyed the "exoticism" of India as well as the modernity of "Swinging London."

Besides Carson, other television performers donned the garment in 1967 and 1968. The Monkees, who had a self-titled prime-time musical television show that aired on NBC in 1966–68, capitalized on the British Invasion by often dressing

---

NEHRU JACKETS

In 2012, rapper Himanshu Suri of Das Racist released his debut mixtape as a solo artist, titled *Nehru Jackets*, in collaboration with SEVA NYC, a Richmond Hill–based immigrant rights group. The mixtape was meant to draw attention to the debate at the time around redistricting in Queens, where Suri grew up.

---

in Nehru jackets. Channeling a similar countercultural vibe, Sammy Davis Jr., playing a hip photographer named Bruce, wore a Nehru jacket and love beads when dancing with Nancy Sinatra to her pop cover of Ray Charles's "What'd I Say" on the special *Movin' with Nancy* on NBC in December 1967. On these programs, the Nehru jacket was a shorthand way to connect to youth culture and its musically hip connotations.

By 1968, the jacket had been featured in and graced the cover of many magazines, including *GQ*, *Life*, and *Ebony*. The November 25, 1968, issue of *Newsweek* featured the Nehru jacket as one of many items that exhibited "Male Plumage," as stated on its cover. *Sports Illustrated* featured the jacket on Sportsman of the Year Bill Russell on December 23, 1968, as well as on the cover of its September 2, 1968, issue with Boston Red Sox baseball player Ken Harrelson, "The Swinger." Puns abound, as he is pictured in a powder-blue Nehru suit, wearing a gold medallion and sunglasses atop his head and leaning on two bats. The hipness of the garment became so ubiquitous that in the same year, the New Good-Lookin' Talking Ken doll was released in a red Nehru jacket and red shorts.

Meenasarani Linde Murugan (she/they) is an assistant professor in the Department of Communication and Media Studies at Fordham University.

This newspaper clipping, from the March 3, 1970, issue of India News and Views, *features an illustrated guide on "How to Wear a Saree." In SAADA.*

DHAN GOPAL MUKERJI

J. Daniel Elam

One of the earliest South Asian American authors, Dhan Gopal Mukerji (1890–1936) was also among the first South Asian writers to take seriously the task of writing in English. In the United States, his books for both children and adults were best sellers. His memoir, *Caste and Outcast* (1923), introduced white Americans to life in India as well as immigrant life in California. *Gay-Neck: The Story of a Pigeon* (1927) won the Newbery Medal for distinguished contribution to literature for children. His books about Hinduism, especially *The Face of Silence* (1926), introduced white Americans to Ramakrishna Paramahamsa, an important nineteenth-century Hindu saint. His books about Indian anti-colonialism, including *My Brother's Face* (1924) and *Disillusioned India* (1930), raised awareness of and support for M. K. Gandhi, Jawaharlal Nehru, and the long struggle for Indian independence against British rule.

Mukerji's books for children combined Indian folktales, stories from the *Mahabharata* and the *Ramayana*, and his own childhood experiences. Mukerji believed his role to be the "translator" of South Asian life and culture for young American audiences, who would create the future "bridge between East and West," as he wrote in an article in 1928. He wrote often to Nehru that Americans—*Homo Americanus*, as he named the peculiar species in a letter—needed to be properly educated about India and that white American support for Indian independence was crucial for the success of the anti-colonial struggle. Nehru thought political diplomacy was key in this regard;

Photograph of Dhan Gopal Mukerji in 1916. In SAADA.

Mukerji believed that Americans needed literature instead, and he appointed himself as the cause's primary writer.

Mukerji was a friend and collaborator of Roger Nash Baldwin, the cofounder of the American Civil Liberties Union; Dr. W. E. B. Du Bois, the Black activist and intellectual; and Josephine MacLeod, a white American feminist and anti-colonialist. At the height of Mukerji's career, he was the leading spokesperson for an independent India and a widely respected public intellectual. In *A Son of Mother India Answers* (1928), he wrote one of the foremost arguments against Katherine Mayo's alleged (and misguided) public health "exposé" of Indian misogyny and "cultural impotence."

The Great Depression, however, saw a steep decrease in book sales. Mukerji wrote that Americans had ceased to care about anything other than themselves. Overworked and underpaid, he suffered a series of breakdowns. His press, E. P. Dutton & Co., began collecting the loans they had given him against future advances. He owed nearly $5,000 (equal to $95,000 in 2021). His editors grew frustrated with his inability to produce additional work. In May of 1936, Mukerji's wife, Patty, returned home to find that her husband had hanged himself. In a letter to Roger Baldwin, she consoled herself with the assertion that Mukerji had finally "completed his tasks" and given himself "to the Lord."

Mukerji was born and raised in a village outside of Calcutta. His older brother, Jadu Gopal Mukherjee, was a leader of the revolutionary Bengali anti-colonial organization Jugantar ("New Era"). In 1910, Jadu Gopal was caught by British police and urged his brother to flee to Tokyo. In 1911, Mukerji boarded a ship bound for San Francisco. Upon arriving, he likely took up farming jobs along the West Coast, along with many other undocumented Indian migrants, most of whom were arriving from Punjab (and many of whom were Sikh and Muslim). Mukerji enrolled at the University of California, Berkeley, but tended to keep his distance from his fellow South Asian students who associated with the Ghadar Party. He transferred to Stanford University, where he met his future wife, a white woman named Ethel Ray "Patty" Dugan.

E. P. Dutton & Co. was reluctant to publish *Caste and Outcast*, and the editorial staff expressed concern that most Americans had little interest in India or Indian life. The success of *Caste and Outcast* proved the editors wrong. The book paid for an extended vacation for the Mukerjis in France (where they likely went to avoid the anti-miscegenation laws prohibiting nonwhite people from marrying whites) as well as one of the only two trips Mukerji would make back to India in his short life.

Critics praised *Caste and Outcast* for its description of India, though they tended to downplay the second section, "Outcast," because of its "politics": analysis of racial inequality and white hypocrisy in the United States. Now, by contrast, critics applaud the text as offering a rare glimpse into South Asian American life before the Hart-Celler Act legalized immigration from Asia and Africa in 1965. Americans at the time often treated Mukerji's books on India as "accurate" representations of "Hindu life" in the late nineteenth and early twentieth centuries. *Caste and Outcast* is not, however, straightforward nonfiction. Instead, Mukerji's literary skill enabled him to create an idea of India that cultivated cross-cultural sympathy, rather than simply pursuing factual accuracy.

Mukerji made no secret of his alienation and depression in the United States and wrote often about "the prison of exile" that had been imposed on him by his lack of financial resources. In the early 1930s, he published a children's version of the *Ramayana* and an "American translation" of the *Bhagavad Gita* for adults; he blamed isolation and emotional fatigue for his inability to write another "original"

INITIATION INTO AMERICA

The following is an excerpt from Dhan Ghopal Mukerji's 1923 memoir, *Caste and Outcast:*

America at last! The seventeen days of Asiatic steerage seemed like the experience of another man the very moment the immigration authorities gave me permission to enter the United States. The reverence that I felt for this country was so great that nothing short of falling to my knees and kissing its soil would have sufficed to express my feelings. But Americans are strange people! No sooner did they see that I had such feelings for their country [than] they began to knock it out of me in a very unceremonious fashion.

PASHMINA

"There are family dynamics that are rarely seen from many communities—including ours. I wanted to work within a story that isn't often seen but is still relatable."

That's how Nidhi Chanani described her graphic novel *Pashmina* in a 2017 interview with *Electric Literature*. The feminist tale centers on Priyanka "Pri" Das, a teenager living with her single mother in Orange County, California. Because her mother doesn't speak much about the past, Pri searches for the truth, including the whereabouts of her father, with the help of a long-lost aunt, Shakti, and a mysterious shawl that transports her to the India of her dreams. Ultimately, Pri learns more about her mother's choices and the ways women in general are constrained by patriarchy.

---

work. In the cold winter of 1933, Dhan Gopal Mukerji wrote to his close friend Jawaharlal Nehru that he still couldn't figure out how to describe the sound of the wind off an upstate New York lake: should he borrow from the Greek poet Sappho or from the *Upanishads*? In Mukerji's writings, these literary worlds clash and coalesce. After his suicide, writers around the world—from American philosopher Will Durant to French essayist Romain Rolland—expressed gratitude for Mukerji's contribution to the West's understanding of modern South Asia. In ways that are often unacknowledged, the idea of India we have today is partly indebted to Mukerji's diasporic imagination of his home. Mukerji understood his task was to lay the groundwork for the bridge "between East and West" that he hoped future generations would build.

Adapted from "Reading a Friendship: Dhan Gopal Mukerji and Jawaharlal Nehru in the Archives" for Tides.

J. Daniel Elam is the author of World Literature for the Wretched of the Earth *and an assistant professor in the Department of Comparative Literature at the University of Hong Kong.*

THE ALI AKBAR COLLEGE OF MUSIC

Sarah Morelli

"Any music belongs to the universe. It's like the sky. No question of American. No question of Indian."

—ALI AKBAR KHAN

When Ali Akbar Khan (1922–2009) began teaching north Indian classical—or Hindustani—music in the United States in 1965, he was already a celebrated musician in India. As the only son of the legendary Ustad Allauddin Khan, primary court musician of the princely state of Maihar, he grew up during an era of courtly patronage; with the financial support of kings, musicians performed in the courts and otherwise spent much of their time practicing and training disciples. Allauddin Khan was known as a devout musician and strict teacher with the knowledge and ability to play and teach many instruments.

SAHEBJAN

Dancers Oondabai, Bhooribai, and Sahebjan posing in a photo studio a few days after their arrival in New York City shown in the New York Clipper (January 22, 1881).

In late fall 1880, a troupe of dancers from Bombay arrived in New York City, invited by the playwright Augustin Daly to perform during interludes of his latest opera. Described in the press as "nautch women," a few of the dancers—who were managed by Abdoolally Esmailjee, and joined by male jugglers and snake charmers—had already piqued the curiosity of President Ulysses Grant during his visit to Bombay in 1878. Despite the press's initial excitement about the dancers' residency in the city, the troupe faced extreme hardships and tragedy during their performances in January 1881, a story detailed in Priya Srinivasan's book *Sweating Saris.*

Most of the dancers—Sahebjan, Vagoirba, Ala Bundi, and Oondabai—were teenagers at the time, along with Bhooribai, who was twenty-six. Sahebjan, who also served as the troupe's principal dancer and singer, gave birth to her son during the trip, and he died shortly after of typhomalaria. Ala Bundi contracted the same disease and died that February in the city. As Srinivasan explains, the story of Sahebjan and her troupe reminds us that part of the story of South Asian labor in America includes women who came abroad through contract visas, and that to ignore them is to create a partial picture of early South Asian America.

Adapted from Sweating Saris: Indian Dance as Transnational Labor, *by Priya Srinivasan (Temple University Press, 2012).*

For his son, Allauddin Khan focused on teaching the twenty-five-stringed sarod, and by age twenty-one, Ali Akbar Khan was named court musician for the maharaja (king) of Jodhpur. That position lasted only seven years. With India's independence in 1947, former institutions of patronage collapsed, and musicians had to adapt to their new circumstances. Ali Akbar Khan, or Khansahib, as he is respectfully called, moved to Bombay, where he continued performing concerts, began composing film scores, and made several 78 rpm records, including the first recording of his new creation, "Rag Chandranandan," which quickly became a hit.

In Khansahib's youth, most musicians taught only their family members and a few trusted students. His own father had to go to great lengths to study music, even running away from home as a young boy. As Khansahib said, "In the past, people didn't want to teach outside their clan. My father broke that. He taught many people. [And] I'm making it even bigger." Khansahib founded a college of music, first in Calcutta (1956) and then in the United States (1967), which was open to any student, regardless of nationality, ethnicity, or family of origin.

"What my father learned, I don't want that to die. It must spread all over the world."

—Ali Akbar Khan

Khansahib first came to the United States in 1955. During that tour, he and tabla accompanist Chatur Lal performed at the Museum of Modern Art in New York and appeared on Alistair Cooke's *Omnibus*, marking the first American televised performance of Indian music. He was invited by the American Society for Eastern Arts (ASEA) to teach in the San Francisco Bay Area in the summer of 1965 and returned to teach for the following two summers. With growing American student interest, Khansahib decided to establish a college of music in the United States where he would teach year-round.

The Ali Akbar College of Music (AACM) maintains a relatively low tuition to financially enable students to engage in long-term study; as a result, the AACM operates on a tight budget relying on donations and grants. During its first ten years, "the College" moved over twenty times, renting scout camps, houses, churches, and schools until finally locating a building to purchase in 1977. As of 2016, the Ali Akbar College of Music still operates in the same building in San Rafael, California, holding concerts and classes, and now housing the Ali Akbar Khan Library, a

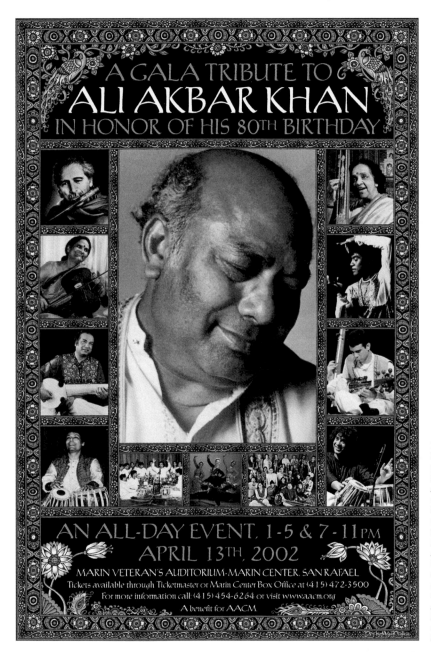

The impact of Khansahib's U.S. career can be seen in this poster for his eightieth birthday tribute concert. Artists who performed, all based in the United States, are arranged as in a mala (garland) around his neck: (L–R) G. S. Sachdev, Sisirkana Dhar Choudhury, Aashish Khan, Swapan Chaudhuri, the AACM tabla ensemble, members of the Chitresh Das Dance Company, Zakir Hussain, Alam Khan, Chitresh Das, Lakshmi Shankar. Courtesy of the Ali Akbar College of Music.

ASHA PUTHLI

Asha Puthli is a singer-songwriter, producer, and actress perhaps best known in the United States for providing vocals on Ornette Coleman's 1971 album, *Science Fiction*. Yet her long career in entertainment has been much more varied and interesting than any one moment could describe. A 2006 profile of Puthli in the *New York Times* opens with the following:

No one could blame the Indian singer Asha Puthli for a little name-dropping. The collaborators and benefactors in her career since the late 1960's include, just for starters, Ornette Coleman, Martha Graham, the Notorious B.I.G., the filmmakers Ismail Merchant and James Ivory, and the talent scout John Hammond. She has scandalized India and delighted British talk-show audiences; she has been a catalyst in German disco and an Italian B-movie actress.

With a four-octave range and a lifelong ambition to synthesize East and West, Ms. Puthli has sung jazz, disco, rock and Indian music.

From "Asha Puthli, an Indian Singer Who Embraces Countless Cultures" for the New York Times, *by Jon Pareles.*

publicly available collection of thousands of hours of performance and classroom recordings, music notation, photos, and other archival materials. Khansahib faithfully taught students each session until he passed away in 2009. His son Alam and other senior students now teach classes in vocal and instrumental music.

Khansahib's longtime musical collaborator Swapan Chaudhuri teaches tabla to students at the AACM and at the California Institute of the Arts while maintaining a rigorous international performing schedule. In celebrating Chaudhuri's twenty-five years of teaching at the AACM, Khansahib honored him with the following words: "You are the only person in my life that has continued with me for so many years, not only as a musician and artist, but as a rare kind of son. You have the same motive, like my father and I, to know and teach this wonderful art.... It is very unusual to find someone who works so hard and has dedicated their life to this art, not for themselves, but for everyone. God bless you!" Since Khansahib's passing, Swapan Chaudhuri has steadfastly continued to teach and uphold the vision of the AACM.

The college has hosted numerous renowned Indian artists over the years, serving as an important springboard for many careers. Because of the AACM, the area has become home for some of the highest-caliber artists from India, including G. S. Sachdev, Chitresh Das, Zakir Hussain, and Swapan Chaudhuri, who, like Khansahib, have had an enormous impact on the development of north Indian classical arts in the United States and internationally.

After teaching at the AACM in the early 1970s, Chitresh Das (1944–2015), a master of north Indian kathak dance, went on to found the Chitresh Das Dance Company and Chhandam School of Kathak, which trains hundreds of students each session through six locations in the Bay Area. His style is known for technical virtuosity, grace, and power. Many he has trained now perform internationally and lead schools in Boston, Toronto, Mumbai, Los Angeles, and elsewhere. Living and teaching in the United States also led to his innovative practice, Kathak Yoga, in which practitioners simultaneously sing, recite, dance, and sometimes even play an instrument, producing a form of meditation in motion.

Zakir Hussain was teaching tabla in the early years of the AACM when he began collaborating with popular musicians, ultimately leading him to expand the range and contexts for tabla performance into areas previously unknown. Groups he helped found were crucial to the development of the world-music genre, including Shakti with John McLaughlin and L. Shankar and Planet Drum with Mickey Hart of the Grateful Dead.

Because of Khansahib, the AACM, and related artists' dedication to performing and teaching, the San Francisco Bay Area is arguably the most vibrant site for north Indian classical arts in the United States. Many students have become disciples, dedicating their own lives to perpetuating the art; literally tens of thousands of people have undergone instruction as their students; and innumerable audience members have been touched by their artistry, in the Bay Area and beyond.

Sarah Morelli is an associate professor of ethnomusicology at the University of Denver and a performing kathak artist.

FAZLUR RAHMAN KHAN

Yasmin Sabina Khan

In 1960, at the age of thirty-one, Dr. Fazlur Rahman Khan took up residence in his new home in the United States, in Chicago, Illinois. A native of Bangladesh (then East Pakistan; British India at the time of his birth), he had first traveled to the United States in 1952 for advanced studies in structural engineering. Having earned two master's degrees and a doctorate in a remarkably short three years' time, he found employment with the Chicago office of Skidmore, Owings & Merrill (SOM) for a period of professional training under the terms of his Fulbright scholarship. The experience was formative. For one who was eager to participate in the shaping of the built environment, there was opportunity to do so; following a hiatus of more than twenty years, construction plans were taking form in the late 1950s as the city prepared to resume its progressive building tradition. Intent upon strengthening his talents and contributing to his profession, Khan returned to his position at SOM imbued with a spirit of possibility.

Over the course of the next decade, Khan's accomplishments in high-rise design and his keen understanding of structures earned him high regard in the engineering and architecture professions as "one of the most influential structural engineers of the century." In 1965, a time when buildings of forty stories drew attention even in the largest urban areas, he introduced a bold *trussed-tube* scheme

Fazlur Rahman Khan observes as structural steel goes up for the Sears Tower in Chicago, Engineering News-Record, *August 26, 1971. In SAADA, courtesy of Yasmin Khan.*

for a one-hundred-story tower, Chicago's John Hancock Center. Five years later, he developed another advanced building system, the *bundled tube*, for the 110-story Sears Tower, which would seize the title of "world's tallest building" in 1974 and retain it for the next twenty-two years.

Khan's first job as an engineer was with the Bureau of Roads for East Pakistan. During his six months in this government position, he worked on the design of two reinforced concrete highway bridges. Although pleased with the work, he decided to try his hand at teaching when the newly established Ahsanullah Engineering College in Dhaka offered him a lectureship in civil engineering in 1951. Khan discovered that the vocation suited him. He had a knack for presenting engineering concepts in a way that interested his students, and he felt rewarded by their eagerness to learn.

Nevertheless, he aspired to advanced studies, as did a number of his former classmates. They had grown up in communities that valued culture and education, and their families were sufficiently affluent to shelter them from famine and concern with basic necessities. Graduate work, however, implied travel overseas.

On the watch for scholarships for graduate study in engineering, Khan found two. In November 1951, he applied to the United States Education Foundation in Pakistan for a Fulbright scholarship to study prestressed concrete and develop techniques for bridge construction in East Pakistan—certainly a fitting goal for an engineer in a region traversed by rivers. He also applied for an overseas scholarship for graduate studies that had been recently introduced by Pakistan's Ministry of Commerce and Education.

Khan knew that he would face ardent competition for both scholarships. A total of fourteen hundred Pakistani students applied for the Fulbright Program, he noted in his diary. From this list, eighty candidates would be selected for further consideration; six would receive a scholarship. He carefully prepared the applications, attempted to make a favorable impression during interviews (somewhat difficult to accomplish when he could not understand the southern American English of his Fulbright interviewer), enrolled in a crash course in French to receive extra marks for a foreign language, and continued to read general knowledge books. "This time," he wrote in his diary, "I want to test the truth of the proverb, 'Where there is a will, there is a way.' I will wait to see the results."

The results, it turned out, were favorable. In May, he received notice that he had been awarded a Fulbright scholarship for study at the University of Illinois. A few weeks later, he learned that he had also been selected to receive the government scholarship for advanced studies in structures. Both scholarships were to begin that fall, and both included airfare to the United States. He realized that if he could combine the two awards, he would have the opportunity to spend a total of three years in graduate studies. With this objective, he petitioned the Ministry of Commerce and Education for postponement of his scholarship's start date by one

THE BARBOUR SCHOLARSHIP

Barbour Scholars, 1928–29. Courtesy of the University of Michigan Bentley Historical Library.

In a letter to Ruthven Hutchins, then president of the University of Michigan, Regent Levi L. Barbour explained the rationale behind a scholarship program that was to support the educational advancement of women from the Orient. Barbour wrote, "The idea of the Oriental girls' scholarships is to bring girls from the Orient, give them an Occidental education and let them take back whatever they find good and assimilate the blessings among the peoples from which they come." During his travels to Japan and China, Barbour had the opportunity to meet with three East Asian women who had been trained in medicine at the University of Michigan in the 1890s. Impressed by the kinds of work these women were doing, Barbour was inspired to create a scholarship that would allow other women from that part of the world to do the same. For its time, it should be no surprise that the discourse surrounding the scholarship was inflected by a rhetoric of uplift. As illustrated below, a Western education was seen to be key to emancipating these women:

> *Only one scholar came directly from the Indian purdah. She was accompanied from her seclusion to the secretary's office by an uncle; during the first interview, in spite of many attempts to hear her voice, the secretary could distinguish only a faint response, and she looked up but once. Not long afterward, she was a free individual able to say that her soul was her own.*

While the perception that a Western education would liberate such women was not unusual, what was striking was Barbour's hope that they would prevent future international conflicts. In a letter to Helen Hatch in 1917, he wrote, "If a thousand Japanese girls could be educated in the United States to be physicians and teachers and returned to Japan to ply their work, we certainly never would have any war with Japan . . . and I think the same is true of other Oriental countries." The scholars were imagined to be emissaries of peace.

From "The Barbour Scholarship: Early International Presence at the University of Michigan" for Tides, by Dashini Jeyathurai.

year, and the ministry accepted his proposal. The next couple of weeks rushed by as Khan prepared to leave home, an eager man of twenty-three.

In 1946, following the conclusion of World War II, Senator J. William Fulbright had sponsored a bill in the United States Congress for the establishment of an educational exchange program. The Fulbright Act aimed to broaden young people's capacity for imagination, empathy, and understanding of different ways of life, and to promote a sense of responsibility to an international community through educational exchange. Future leaders would have the opportunity to acquire a "feeling and understanding of other people's cultures—why they operate as they do, why they think as they do, why they react as they do—and of the differences among these cultures." People might "find in themselves, through intercultural education, the ways and means of living together in peace." Receptive to this view of people and life, Khan was well prepared for the program.

On July 18, 1952, he departed. The Fulbright Program flew him from Dhaka, via Calcutta and Delhi, to Karachi, then on to Basra, Beirut, Rome, Frankfurt, and London, where he boarded a Boeing Stratocruiser—"definitely an improvement over the other types we had so far journeyed in"—for New York. There he boarded a train for Ann Arbor, Michigan, where he would attend a six-week orientation program at the University of Michigan before commencing studies at the University of Illinois.

This period of travel was full of excitement, as he met many people and saw whatever he could of the places through which he passed. Once in Ann Arbor, he delighted in the intermingling of the forty-eight students from eighteen countries who had been brought together for the orientation period. He struck up a friendship with a young man from Germany, Adrian Schickler, and the two of them became the table-tennis champions of the group. With a student from Japan, they drifted into a regular threesome that would last until the completion of the orientation program. Although relatively short, the six-week program made a lasting impression. Several years later, Schickler asked Khan to be his son's godfather, though they now lived thousands of miles apart and Khan had not met his wife, nor was Khan a Christian.

Khan's experience that summer powerfully confirmed the lesson learned from his father: that all people are interconnected by their shared humanity. From then on, he greatly valued travel and contact with different peoples and cultural traditions. He came to call himself a citizen of the world; after all, he said, he had been a native first of British India, then of Pakistan, and finally of Bangladesh, and in 1967 he became an American citizen.

Excerpted from Engineering Architecture: The Vision of Fazlur R. Khan *(2004). Reprinted with permission.*

Yasmin Sabina Khan is an author and a structural engineer.

CHAPTER 9

Work, Labor, and Entrepreneurship

Protest by Andolan members during the Bangladesh Independence Day parade. Founded in 1998 by low-wage South Asians, Andolan's goal is to support and empower working-class communities to realize their rights and overcome obstacles such as language barriers, discrimination, immigration status, and gaps in social services for legal assistance and other types of support. In SAADA, courtesy of Andolan.

INTRODUCTION

Pawan Dhingra

T he first days at a first job are often quite memorable—the anxiety of getting there on time, learning what is expected of you, meeting coworkers. Now imagine that this job is the key reason you were able to immigrate to the United States. For many South Asians, work is much more than a source of income. It can be our only legal means of being in the country. It can feel as if it is a ticket to financial security. It can be a source of remittance for our family back in South Asia. It can mean working in back-breaking labor in a small business hidden from view of customers. Even if South Asians do not migrate for the sake of work, it typically becomes a defining element of our lives, a way in which we experience our new land and measure the worth of our migration.

"Work" in this case means not simply paid work but also unpaid work—often, domestic work in the home. Attending school is also a form of work. Thus, we are all shaped by a workplace, and we all experience work differently. But while there is no singular meaning of "work," what is consistent is that it often comes to define us. We have a stake in not only earning money but also in receiving dignity from work. We want to change our working conditions when treated unfairly. And in turn, we help define that workspace. We transform it in subtle or dramatic ways.

South Asian Americans' work histories are varied and fluctuate with changing economic and political environments. When South Asians first migrated to the United States, they were primarily farmers, mill workers, and merchants—occupations in which immigrants today still labor. More South Asians arrived as students in the early 1900s. By the 1940s and 1950s, South Asians began to own small businesses in the United States—one prominent example being in the hospitality industry. As immigration laws changed, so did work profiles. Physicians, nurses, and engineers arrived after the Immigration and Naturalization Act of 1965. Computer engineers arrived after the introduction of H-1B visas in the 1990s. Today, South Asian Americans are athletes, artists, actors, activists, attorneys, and much more.

And yet some current trends apply across professions. Immigration laws are constructed to bring in workers that serve the U.S. economy, and yet many U.S. residents come to resent the competition for employment. The tension between the needs of capital and the needs of residents has come to define how immigrants experience work. Racism, sexism, and xenophobia can construct South Asian Americans as the "enemy" or the "model minority" who can be paid less or given less respect. Restrictions on visas result especially under xenophobic governments, even if industries want more immigrants to enter the country to both help with the labor force and keep wages low. Employment is increasingly precarious, with fewer guarantees and protections for workers, whether professional or working class. More and more, workers are expected to take care of themselves, as benefits such as health insurance, minimum wage, and the like are no longer guarantees. A loss of a job can mean loss of one's legal status. Within these larger forces, workers put in longer hours to provide for their families at home and abroad.

In this chapter, we profile a few of these trends of South Asian American work—in medicine, domestic work, technology and entrepreneurship, small businesses, and community organizing. In looking at each of these, we pay attention not simply to successes but also to hardships, to tensions between South Asians and others and among South Asians, and how people find strength in themselves, their families, and their communities. We focus on how men and women experience work differently.

A core theme is that South Asian Americans have not simply been shaped by their workplaces but have come to define their industries—and the nation—as well. South Asian American activists have expanded the growth of human rights by reaching out to underserved populations. Motel owners have exponentially grown the hospitality business in terms of the number and geographic distribution of properties. Physicians treat patients in rural, suburban, and inner-city areas. Domestic workers connect workers' rights with women's rights, expanding the protections and dignity of many. Community organizers protect refugees and, in the process, secure work standards for everyone. And so on.

Of course, there are many relevant industries not profiled here. South Asian American farmers still toil on the West Coast. Women and men have a dominant hand in the production and canning of peaches, in growing almonds, plums, walnuts, and more. As another example, South Asians are synonymous with taxi drivers in New York City and in other major cities. The National Taxi Workers Alliance, led for many years by Bhairavi Desai, was so successful in organizing a multiethnic, multigenerational coalition of taxi drivers that it became an official member of the AFL-CIO in 2011. And as mentioned earlier, domestic labor in the home, often performed by women, is necessary for the paid labor to continue and is deeply intertwined with the issues discussed here.

What we hope becomes clear through this chapter is that there is much more that connects South Asian American workers to each other than we might imagine. Domestic workers and physicians appear to work in different worlds, and yet neither group could take for granted full rights, pay, or respect. Trailblazers and key supporters had to work together to achieve those rights. We should recognize our common bonds and see each other's struggles as our own.

Pawan Dhingra is associate provost and associate dean of the faculty at Amherst College, and professor of American studies.

NAHAR ALAM

Chitra Aiyar

When she was thirteen years old, Nahar Alam's life changed completely. She arrived home from school to discover that she was going to be forced into marriage. Her elder brother had been arrested, and in exchange for his freedom, the thirty-five-year-old arresting officer demanded Nahar as his second wife. Until that day, Nahar's life had been uneventful, spent in the Narayanganj district in Bangladesh, near the capital city of Dhaka, with a family who encouraged her education.

Unfortunately, Nahar's family did not have the power to challenge a corrupt police officer. And so, Nahar was married—her first experience of what it was to be powerless. The life that followed was torturous: She was a second wife and a second mother to four children. She cooked, cleaned, and was permitted to eat only after everyone else in the household had finished. She tried to run away, but her husband

Nahar Alam, with Andolan brochures and protest photographs behind her. In SAADA, courtesy of Andolan.

found her and dragged her back home, threatening those who helped her with jail time.

She did finally escape, thanks to a family friend whose uncle ran a travel agency. The friend told Nahar that her only chance of survival was to flee Bangladesh altogether. Slowly Nahar began to raise the money for a ticket, and through the support of family friends and neighbors and luck, Nahar secured a visa and ticket for the United States.

Nahar arrived in New York City in 1993 speaking no English and knowing one person. Her first job was in a garment factory, sewing sleeves and borders onto dresses. It was grueling work, but Nahar was committed. To her surprise, her paycheck was only for thirty-five dollars after two weeks; she was being paid per piece completed, not for the hours worked. She met an Indian woman on the train who was looking for help with cooking and taking care of her kids, and Nahar's life as a domestic worker in New York City began. She always had South Asian employers—in Brooklyn, Queens, and Long Island. Some employers yelled and threatened her, others made her work even when she was sick, and some made her shovel snow without a coat. All paid her below the minimum wage. While she did domestic work, Nahar continued ESL classes and supplemented her income by cooking in people's homes. And through these relationships, Nahar came to know about community organizations.

She attended a meeting at Sakhi for South Asian Women, an organization working to end domestic violence in the South Asian community. Nahar was a domestic worker facing abuse—technically not an area supported by Sakhi, but Nahar convinced them of the common thread of empowering immigrant women. While Nahar continued as a domestic worker, she found that her true strength was in organizing, and she was hired at Sakhi.

Organizing domestic workers is no easy task. They work in the home, out of sight of others. Nahar persisted—she followed South Asian women pushing strollers and in the park. She won their confidence and heard their stories: one had experienced boiling water being thrown on her; another was forced to eat hot chili peppers as punishment; another was never paid, but her diplomat employers had immunity.

An Andolan protest in front of a Bangladeshi diplomat's home in 2001 in response to exploitation of a worker. The worker acquired political asylum with Andolan's support, and the diplomat was transferred to another country. In SAADA, courtesy of Andolan.

ANDOLAN AND DOMESTIC WORKERS UNITED

The following excerpt is from "A Twenty-First Century Organizing Model: Lessons from the New York Domestic Workers Bill of Rights Campaign":

Domestic Workers United was born out of a joint organizing effort between two community-based organizations—CAAAV: Organizing Asian Communities and Andolan: Organizing South Asian Workers—in 1999. The two organizations had been organizing and fighting cases of injustice on behalf of workers in Asian communities for several years. However, Asian women were only a small percentage of the domestic workforce. The majority of domestic workers are Caribbean and Latina women, and no organizations were engaging them. With the intention of including all domestic workers, CAAAV and Andolan reached out to these unrepresented groups to survey them about their working conditions and gauge their interest in organizing.

Beverly Alleyne, a nanny from Barbados who worked for a young family on the Upper West Side, had waited a long time for an organization to form. "There is no place for us to go when our employers try to take advantage of us," she said, "so most of us stay silent." Beverly came to the first meeting of Caribbean workers that emerged from CAAAV and Andolan's outreach efforts. The women at these early meetings decided to form themselves into a steering committee, and Domestic Workers United (DWU) was born in 2000.

DWU helped organize individual support campaigns for workers who had been mistreated by their employers, survived trafficking, or were owed wages. DWU organized demonstrations at employers' homes and businesses, and worked with legal partner organizations—like the Urban Justice Center—to file lawsuits. Using a combination of legal pressure and direct action, DWU has helped to recover over $450,000 in workers' stolen wages.

From "A Twenty-First Century Organizing Model" for New Labor Forum, *by Ai-jen Poo.*

As the number of domestic workers grew in the United States, Nahar started her own organization focused on South Asian immigrant workers. She called it Andolan ("Movement") and began organizing against exploitative employers and educating and empowering workers. Initially, she operated Andolan from her kitchen table in her Queens apartment; over time, her efforts were recognized by local funders who supported her work, and Andolan was able to secure office space and pay its organizers.

Andolan took on a key role in organizing domestic workers of all ethnicities in New York City, helping to form an umbrella organization, Domestic Workers United (DWU), to fight for the rights of domestic workers, who were not recognized under the law. In 2005, the New York City Council required that all agencies use a standard contract for domestic workers. While this was a step forward,

Nahar recognized that the majority of Andolan's members did not enter domestic work through an agency; they operated in informal private relationships that left them vulnerable to their employers. Nahar and Andolan joined a statewide push to ensure that all domestic workers would be protected, and in 2010, New York State passed the first-ever Domestic Workers' Bill of Rights, providing sick leave and overtime.

At its peak, Andolan had close to seventy-five active members, primarily Bangladeshi immigrant women like Nahar, but also Indians, Pakistanis, Nepalis, Sri Lankans, and a number of Indonesians. Meetings were held in multiple languages and mostly on Sundays, the only day off for many domestic workers. But Andolan, like many other grassroots organizations, was hit hard by the recession in 2007 and 2008, and funding dried up.

However, Nahar continues to do the work—once again, from her kitchen table. She takes great pride in the passage of the Domestic Workers' Bill of Rights and knows that the law is not enough. There is much work to be done in raising awareness of the bill among domestic workers and ensuring that there is actual enforcement. This means that Nahar continues to stay busy looking out for her fellow domestic workers, with whom she can collectively organize and build better conditions for everyone.

Chitra Aiyar is the executive director of the Sadie Nash Leadership Project, a feminist social justice youth-leadership program.

RIGHTS, RESPECT, AND RECOGNITION

Adhikaar

Reeta K. C. was in Albany along with many other Adhikaar members on the day New York passed the Domestic Workers' Bill of Rights in 2010. Amid the cheers, joys, and hugs of the many who had fought for years for this moment, she remembered her fellow nail salon workers. Many earned no more than thirty dollars for a twelve-hour shift. Soon she was talking to the team at Adhikaar to help organize nail salon workers, envisioning a similar victory. Five years later, her dream and vision to bring about a similar change in the nail salon industry bore fruit. In July 2015, she stood in a room full of labor activists as Governor Andrew Cuomo signed a bill to reform the nail salon industry.

Adhikaar, based in Jackson Heights, Queens, is the only women-led worker and community center that serves and organizes Nepali-speaking immigrants and refugees. It seeks to raise awareness and empower low-income immigrant workers

Adhikaar's domestic worker, nail salon worker, and TPS (temporary protected status) member leaders mobilize at a #TPSjustice rally in front of New York City Hall. Courtesy of Adhikaar.

like Reeta to lead healthy, economically secure lives and develop their leadership skills to advocate for themselves and other low-income workers. Adhikaar is guided by a vision of economic justice for everyone. Through its Workers' Rights Program, it organizes low-wage workers in many informal employment sectors, including restaurants, grocery stores, gas stations, and the taxi industry. However, the organizing and campaign focus is primarily on workers in the domestic-work and nail salon industries, both of which have high concentrations of immigrant women of color.

Reeta began her career as a nail salon technician in April of 2000. The places where she worked at the beginning of her career were difficult: "The salon owners behaved as if they have bought an employee—not like staff." Employees were deprived of basic rights and were asked to work long hours without any compensation. "If [the owners] keep the doors open, the customers will keep on coming. There was no time to eat. We did manicures and pedicures nonstop, without a break," she said, shaking her head. With the new nail salon rules in effect, Reeta's

---

#METOO, #TIMESUP, AND SARU JAYARAMAN

In 2017, the Me Too movement—begun over a decade earlier when activist Tarana Burke used the phrase "Me Too" on Myspace social networks to ensure that survivors of sexual violence know they're not alone—exploded into a national conversation. After dozens of women in Hollywood came forward with stories of sexual violence at the hands of Harvey Weinstein and other powerful men in Hollywood, the #MeToo hashtag began trending globally on Twitter as thousands more women, across industries and communities, began to share their own stories of harassment and assault. *Time* magazine named the "Silence Breakers" of #MeToo the Person of the Year for 2017.

Amid this movement, a group of powerful women in entertainment banded together to create the TIME'S UP Legal Defense Fund, to provide subsidized legal support to those who have experienced sexual harassment, assault, or abuse in the workplace. This was partially in response to calls from groups like Alianza Nacional de Campesinas to include the voices of women and others with less access to media platforms in the conversation. A group of leading Hollywood actresses behind #TimesUp also brought leaders from other industries as their dates to the 2018 Golden Globes, to highlight their specific work to fight harassment and abuse in front of the millions who watched the awards ceremony.

Saru Jayaraman, director of UC Berkeley's Food Labor Research Center and president of Restaurant Opportunities Centers United, was actress Amy Poehler's date at the Golden Globes. Poehler sought to draw attention to Jayaraman's research, which shows that in restaurants, female servers making low wages and fighting for tips are often subjects of harassment from employers and customers. (Minimum wage for servers who make tips in the United States can be as low as $2.13 an hour). Nor are sick days often provided to workers.

Jayaraman explained her work to *Berkeley News*: "You live on your tips so you have to tolerate whatever a customer does to you because they are always right. When you actually give workers a living wage, then the woman is not as dependent on tips to feed her family. She doesn't have to deal with anything and everything. She can say no, and she can refuse to serve a customer."

Restaurant workers from Bangladesh, India, and elsewhere have been denied owed wages, made to work in unsafe conditions, and forced to confront other labor abuses. Workers' rights organizations such as Restaurant Opportunities Centers United are therefore working to safeguard the rights and dignity of restaurant workers.

---

salon began providing gloves and masks and instituting better work schedules. However, the biggest reward she claimed through this process was the new and improved attitude from her employer, customers, and colleagues. The milestone of this achievement is validated as more and more nail salon workers turn to Adhikaar. There is an urgency to understand the new regulations, but more important, there is a willingness to talk about shared experiences and organize together.

In the future, Adhikaar hopes to increase the leadership of Nepali-speaking immigrant workers in all communities and in the broader fight for rights, respect, and recognition of all workers. Its core strategies in this effort are threefold:

WOMEN AT WORK (LETTER TO MYSELF AT TWENTY-SIX)

I remember a professor telling me what happened was a secret. He blocked the door when I came in for our conference. Where's my hug? *he said.* Where's my kiss?

Last week something in me broke; I scrolled through the stories and comments for hours— wrecked and reeling. Across several articles, the New York Times *detailed Harvey Weinstein's predatory behavior toward women in the film industry. I couldn't work. I couldn't eat. I texted my therapist. She said,* It's like after Trump was elected. PTSD for women from things long ago.

I was twenty-six, already struggling with depression. He was attractive and had presence. If he had been a different sort of professor, I might have harbored a harmless crush. He was a Famous Male Novelist. My university paid him a full salary to teach one class a year. When I said something to him later about reporting him, he said that it was, in his era, understood to be a perk of the job. Relationships with students. He was right. They weren't going to fire him to keep me.

The New York Times *reports brought it all back to me. I hadn't known how to talk about or to give these experiences voice.*

From "Enough: America's Wholly Visible Underbelly" for the Rumpus, *by Sejal Shah.*

---

(1) to empower Nepali immigrants through increasing awareness about their rights, strengthening their employment skills, and training new leaders; (2) to amplify domestic workers' voices and power by raising awareness among domestic workers of the New York State Domestic Workers' Bill of Rights and strengthening their involvement in the national domestic workers' movement; and (3) to build a worker-led movement to create a healthy nail salon industry in New York and across the nation.

Adhikaar, meaning "rights," is a New York–based nonprofit organizing the Nepali-speaking community to promote human rights and social justice for all. Learn more about the organization at adhikaar.org.

SILICON VALLEY

Sindya Bhanoo

In 1981, when Meera Balakumar was five years old, her family left Sri Lanka. The move was supposed to be a temporary one so her father could study at the MIT Sloan School of Management, but the Balakumars never moved back to Sri Lanka. Riots in Sri Lanka against Tamils, an ethnic minority group in the island country, forced them to stay in America.

"My parents didn't feel safe after having lived through looting mobs and riots in previous years," said Balakumar, whose family is Sri Lankan Tamil.

Instead, the Balakumars raised their daughters in Orange County, California. Meera Balakumar, now forty and the founder and CEO of the startup Sterlinks, says her willingness to take risks as an entrepreneur is partially fueled by the experience of being an alien in America.

Balakumar studied economics and international development at UC Berkeley and graduated in 1997 intending to work in emerging markets. She spent time in investment banking as well as in private-equity real estate, and in between, she developed a ratings system for microlending organizations while on a Fulbright fellowship in Dhaka, Bangladesh. She also contributed to research promoting African financial markets while at the University of Cape Town in South Africa.

In 2009, Balakumar started Sterling Analytics, a company that does analytics for private-equity funds, and outsourced work to a team she put in place in Sri Lanka.

In 2012, wanting to be in the same time zone as her friends and family, she created a team in the Bay Area and built software that enables institutional investors to do their own portfolio analytics. She still runs the company, Sterlinks, today.

Immigrants from India and other South Asian countries make up a large portion of Silicon Valley's workforce. Over the years, many South Asian Americans

THE SAN FRANCISCO BAY AREA

California's Bay Area has been a hub of South Asian immigration for over 140 years. Many early immigrants from South Asia first landed on American soil at the Angel Island Immigration Station, located within the San Francisco Bay, just north of the city. The Bay Area has continued to serve as a center for South Asian immigration, including for many now arriving to work in the tech industry.

The photograph to the right, of the Sharma family overlooking San Francisco's Golden Gate Bridge in 1983, was part of an exhibition at the Smithsonian Institution from February 27, 2014, to August 16, 2015, titled "Beyond Bollywood: Indian Americans Shape the Nation." The exhibit "explore[d] the heritage, daily experience and numerous, diverse contributions that Indian immigrants and Indian Americans have made to shaping the United States."

Photo by Prithvi Sharma.

have ventured into entrepreneurship—by one estimate, between 1992 and 1998, Indian Americans ran 9 percent of all Silicon Valley startups. The story of each immigrant entrepreneur, however, is varied, and no two have taken the same path.

The same year that Balakumar's family moved to the United States from

Bangladesh, Ish Harshawat—the cofounder of Haystack TV—and his family moved from Kenya to Indiana.

"Kenya was not a safe place. [My parents] got robbed, they got hijacked, they got robbed again, and the robbers tied them up and were basically about to shoot

---

CASTE DISCRIMINATION IN SILICON VALLEY

In 2020, California's Department of Fair Employment and Housing filed a federal lawsuit against the technology corporation Cisco Systems Inc. for discrimination, harassment, and retaliation on the basis of caste. The case represents a watershed moment, as it marks the first time where a discrimination lawsuit alleged that caste is an identity category protected under United States civil rights laws. In an op-ed for the *New York Times*, Dalit author and journalist Yashica Dutt wrote:

> . . . after decades of being silenced, Dalit Americans are finally finding a voice that cannot be ignored. I was able to come out as Dalit because after moving to New York and avoiding Indian-only communities, for the first time, I was not scared of someone finding out my caste. Finding comfort and inspiration in movements like Black Lives Matter and Say Her Name and the tragic institutional murder of a Dalit student activist in India, I was able to understand and acknowledge that my history was a tapestry of pride, not shame.

---

them," Harshawat said. "So my parents decided it was time to leave, but they had me before they left."

They arrived in the Chicago area, where Harshawat's father, a physician, trained as a child psychiatrist.

The family eventually settled in Terre Haute, a small town in Indiana. Harshawat went on to attend Carnegie Mellon University, and there, in the company of other techies, he dreamed up ideas for startups.

After graduating in 2002, he took a job with the corporate giant Siebel Systems in the Bay Area, and after three years there, he joined a small startup.

"The guys running it were only a couple years older than me and I started to think, 'If they can do it, I can do it.'"

He and a friend quit their jobs and started developing mobile applications in 2007. Their first product was an app called Quip that allowed iPhone users to quickly send photo messages to other phones. Shortly after that, he and his cofounder had an idea for an Uber-like company. They released an initial app called Taxi.

NEHA RASTOGI

"I pray whenever a victim of [domestic violence] decides to rise up against their abuser, that they find the strength to follow it through and that they receive the support they need from their family, friends, community, AND the judicial system of our country."

—Neha Rastogi, addressing Judge Allison Danner of the Superior Court of Santa Clara County on June 15, 2017

In 2017, Neha Rastogi, a successful Silicon Valley professional formerly of Apple, charged Abhishek Gattani, her husband of more than a decade and former CEO of Cuberon (a customer-behavior analytics company), with abuse. Anahita Mukherji, writing about Rastogi for *Scroll.in*, described just how common such cases are in the community:

> [Rastogi's] is one of countless stories of abuse involving Indians working in Silicon Valley—a strata of society known for high educational levels and financial wealth. Non-profits that support South Asian families facing domestic violence in the Bay Area, like Maitri and Narika, are quick to point out that education levels have virtually no bearing on the prevalence of domestic violence in a community. "Domestic violence is prevalent across all backgrounds, financial, social and educational," said Maitri's outreach coordinator. . . . "It is not restricted to any particular segment of the community." Maitri received 4,330 calls for help in 2016, nearly double the number it received in 2013. Around 65%–70% of calls that Narika receives each year involve technology experts in the Valley. In many cases, both spouses, the victim and the abuser, work in the technology industry.

Tech entrepreneur Anil Dash offered some thoughts on the case via a series of tweets in April of 2017:

> This is part of the awful epidemic of domestic violence perpetrated by South Asian men. Our community has one of the highest rates of DV. We don't talk enough about it, and we Indian American men don't call each other out enough for our complicity in our toxic masculinity.

A still image from a Narika PSA video during the COVID-19 pandemic. Courtesy of Narika.

"The idea was to do pretty much what Uber does now," Harshawat said. "I guess I have some regrets, but we were inexperienced, I think our team dynamics were off, and we didn't know how to raise money."

Nearly a decade later, Harshawat's persistence has paid off with Haystack TV, a personalized news channel.

"It started with the two of us, in a dumpy office space," Harshawat said.

Soon after, they were admitted into a startup incubator, and after that, they

---

ANJALI SUD AND TECH CEOS

In 2017, Anjali Sud became the CEO of the video-sharing platform Vimeo, making her one of the few women—and one of the very few South Asian American women, at that—to head a technology company.

Sud joined a cohort of other South Asian Americans who have led tech companies in the U.S. These include Satya Nadella, the CEO of Microsoft; Shantanu Narayen, the president and CEO of Adobe Systems; and Sundar Pichai, the CEO of Google.

---

raised several rounds of funding. Today, Haystack TV has a team of ten that is growing.

"I've met a lot of really interesting people through my entrepreneurship endeavors," Harshawat said. "I hope that the journey ends well. Even if it doesn't, it's still been worthwhile."

Harshawat and Balakumar are American citizens who had the privilege of being able to leave full-time jobs to pursue their own interests. But for immigrant entrepreneurs, visa issues can be complicated.

Mitali Pattnaik came to the United States in 1996 to study computer science at Mount Holyoke College and had a successful career working at companies like Microsoft, Yahoo, Electronic Arts, Google, and Twitter. Later, she went on to found and lead Intro, a private social network for companies, and become a director of product management at LinkedIn.

Because she was on an H-1B visa, she was not able to start her own company for years. That feeling of being handcuffed to a corporation because of visa status is one that she's never forgotten.

"You seriously feel shackled," Pattnaik said. "That's literally how you feel as an immigrant—as indentured labor at a company. I was lucky to work at great companies, but some people are stuck and they just can't leave their jobs; they might have terrible managers or face horrible sexism."

The Trump administration, in the wake of the economic downturn due to coronavirus, took the opportunity to propose further restrictions on H1-B visa workers, tightening rules that determine which companies are eligible to hire such workers and shortening the length of the visa for certain contract workers.

Pattnaik's experiences led her to invest in Unshackled Ventures, one of Silicon Valley's newest startups. Unshackled is a venture-capital firm that sponsors the visas of immigrant startup founders and provides them with wages of $150,000 annually.

For Pattnaik, it's a chance to give other entrepreneurs an opportunity that she did not have.

"After all, you can't play the game unless you're in the ballpark," Pattnaik said.

Sindya Bhanoo (she/her) is a writer and journalist based in Austin, Texas.

AAPI: A BRIEF HISTORY

Vibha Bhalla

The American Association of Physicians of Indian Origin, commonly known as AAPI, originated in 1982 in a suburb of Detroit. AAPI grew out of Indian immigrant physicians' anger at questions being raised in the American press and the larger society about their competency to practice medicine in the country. These physicians believed that the assumption that they had received substandard medical training in India, their nation of origin, was a direct result of the two-tier system established by the American Medical Association (AMA), which categorized foreign physicians as foreign medical graduates (FMGs) and physicians who graduated from U.S. medical schools as USMGs and enforced different requirements for the two groups.

Mass migration of physicians to the United States increased substantially with the passage of the Hart-Celler Act of 1965. This act overturned the Johnson-Reed

Act of 1924, which based immigration to the United States on a national-origins quota system; under this act, Indians had an annual quota of one hundred. The Hart-Celler Act removed the quota system and allowed migrants with specialized skills to migrate if their skills were needed in the United States. The high demand for physicians in the country resulted in a dramatic increase in physicians migrating to the United States. In 1970, 27 percent of U.S. physicians were graduates of foreign medical schools; this percentage increased to 46 percent by 1972. The largest number of physicians were from India and the Philippines.

To work as a physician in the United States, a foreign physician was required to have completed a medical degree from his or her country of origin and pass exams, such as the Educational Commission for Foreign Medical Graduates (ECFMG) exam and an English-language exam, at which point the physician was allowed to work in a U.S. hospital as a resident or a medical trainee. On completion of this residency, the foreign physician was required to pass the board exams. The residency requirements for foreign physicians differed from those of American residents: foreign physicians' residencies were usually longer than the American physicians' residencies. AMA categorized all foreign physicians as FMGs despite their having received training in U.S. hospitals and passing exams required by the AMA.

Foreign physicians were stigmatized as inferior and less qualified since their medical training in their country of origin was not considered on par with a U.S. medical education. And even though they continued their training in the United States, these immigrants were perceived as unable to benefit from their American training. Moreover, their lack of proficiency in English and their accented English were perceived as affecting patient care. These stereotypes were especially applicable to physicians from Asia, including Indian physicians.

As a result of this discrimination, foreign-born physicians wanted the AMA to defend them and look into the problems they were facing. By forming AAPI, Indian physicians hoped to organize and collectively resolve their problems. By 1992, a decade after its formation, AAPI's dues-paying membership consisted of over eight thousand members.

AAPI's initial goals were two-pronged. First, it organized members and collected

VIVEK MURTHY, SURGEON GENERAL

Vice Admiral Vivek H. Murthy, U.S. Public Health Service, nineteenth and twenty-first surgeon general of the United States, 2015.

In a 2017 interview with the *Harvard Political Review*, Dr. Vivek Murthy, the nineteenth and, now, twenty-first surgeon general of the United States and the first of South Asian descent, was asked what specific message he hoped to bring to his community, as well as to the larger Asian American community and other minority communities. This is an excerpt of his answer:

I take my job seriously in all respects, but I also recognize that as the first Asian American Surgeon General, I have a lot to be grateful for in terms of what this country has afforded me. There are not that many countries in the world where your parents could come from very humble roots—my dad, for example, was from a small farming village in south India—and where you could be given the privilege to serve in this manner, where you're responsible for looking out for the health of the entire nation. . . .

To me, part of that gratitude needs to be expressed in making opportunities like this available for more people. As I think about the conversations that I have, particularly with immigrant communities, kids who are from minority communities, and kids who are growing up in disadvantaged situations—poverty in particular—I try to focus on making sure that I am doing everything I can to connect them to opportunities to serve and that they don't forget that even though they may be growing up in tough circumstances, this is a country where they can succeed. Clearly, we have to do more to make sure that we have more ladders of opportunity for everybody in this country. It's certainly harder for some people than it is for others to access good education and good healthcare. I see it as the responsibility of those of us who have been given opportunities to serve to ensure that others have the chance to do so as well, that they have ladders of opportunity that we are building for them, and that they can ascend and thereby serve our entire country.

From "Ladders of Opportunity: Interview with Vice Admiral Vivek Murthy, Surgeon General of the United States" for the Harvard Political Review, *by Anirudh Suresh.*

BHAIRAVI DESAI AND THE NEW YORK TAXI WORKERS ALLIANCE

After a New York City taxi driver committed suicide in early 2018, Bhairavi Desai, the executive director for the New York Taxi Workers Alliance (NYTWA), spoke with NPR's Scott Simon about how the industry has changed over the years. Desai said,

I've been organizing taxi drivers since 1996, and I've never seen the level of desperation. I've started to receive so many calls from drivers seeking resources for suicide prevention and talking about homelessness and eviction notices, and so, something has to be done here. This is not accidental, working people have a right to be protected. We have a right to work with dignity and justice.

Bhairavi Desai being interviewed by Juan Gonzalez of the Daily News on strike day, May 13, 1998. Courtesy of New York Taxi Workers Alliance (NYTWA).

In August 2018, NYTWA members celebrated a major victory as the New York City Council voted to begin regulating ride-sharing apps like Lyft and Uber by limiting the number of new for-hire vehicles on the streets and regulating minimum rates across the industry.

From "Driver's Suicide Highlights 'Race to the Bottom' in Cab Industry, Union Director Says" for NPR.

stories of discrimination from Indian physicians across the United States. Second, it tried to pressure the AMA to focus on the problems facing FMGs: it wanted the AMA to institute a single licensing exam for USMGs and FMGs; it wanted the state medical boards to accord similar treatment to USMGs and FMGs, especially in endorsing their licenses and by offering reciprocity; and it wanted the AMA to establish an FMG wing to understand their problems. AMA did not accept any of these demands, and its refusal led the AAPI to develop a new strategy of seeking a political solution.

Other FMGs were also encountering similar problems, and they also formed national professional associations. These various associations, including the AAPI, formed an umbrella organization called the International Association of American Physicians. They hired a lobbying group, and with its help succeeded in getting many bills on the agenda in Congress that promised equality between FMGs and USMGs. AAPI members wrote letters to their congressional representatives to support these bills. Along with seeking political solutions, AAPI also encouraged its members to become active in hospital and state medical boards to highlight and resolve their problems. To spread information to physicians about these issues, AAPI established the *AAPI Journal*.

These political tactics resulted in the AMA changing its earlier stance and policies to heed two of the FMGs' main demands. It established an international medical wing within the AMA to look into the problems faced by foreign physicians, and in 1992, it began administering a single exam to FMGs and USMGs. Although all problems were not resolved, AAPI succeeded in transforming the AMA. Its success demonstrated the benefit of collective action.

Vibha Bhalla is an associate professor of ethnic studies at Bowling Green State University.

SOUTH ASIAN AMERICAN MOTEL OWNERS

Pawan Dhingra

Kanjibhai Desai made his way to the United States without documents from the West Indies through Mexico. It was San Francisco, 1922. Looking for a place to stay, Desai eventually came to the Goldfield Hotel, a residential hotel where people lived for months or even longer and shared bathrooms. Years later, when Japanese Americans were being interned during World War II, Desai took over the hotel. Immigrants from Gujarat arrived in the 1940s and 1950s and pooled their resources to run similar residential hotels in San Francisco. In the following decades, more immigrants joined from India, East Africa, Britain, and elsewhere. The motel industry was in a state of transition, with ample opportunities for buyers willing to take over small properties.

Currently, about half of the motels in the United States are run by South Asian Americans, most notably Patels from Gujarat and their descendants. Gujaratis are comprised of numerous castes and subcastes. Among these, Leva Kanbis, also referred to as Leva Patels, became particularly represented in the U.S. motel business. Many of the Patels who own motels are of Kanbi and Patidar backgrounds. Their social connections to one another facilitated their rise.

The "Patel Motel" today defies easy categorization. It can range from a mom-and-pop operation with hardly any staff to an economy franchise such as Super 8

An image from artist Chiraag Bhakta's "The Arch Motel Project." The project gets its name from the New Jersey motel where Bhakta lived with his family until the age of seven.

or Days Inn to a newly constructed motel such as Holiday Inn Express to a boutique hotel. It is no surprise that motel owners have received praise from business and political leaders. The time, energy, and money that owners spend in refurbishing their establishments help rebuild not only the industry but also the cities in which they pay taxes. The Asian American Hotel Owners Association (AAHOA), which represents owners and operators, is one of the largest and most politically connected South Asian American organizations in the nation.

Behind this rise to prominence lies a more human drama. Many immigrants refer to their entrance in the hospitality industry as a forced choice. An elderly immigrant explained why she came to the United States to work in her relative's motel: "I didn't pick this country, but my sister-in-law applied . . . for us. And we came here. She is a motel owner too. . . . It's a hard life [in India]. And this is an advanced country." The only way for many owners to eke out a profit is to have the entire family living in the motel and pitching in. Another owner said, "[The motel] served multiple purposes. You can live in your own motel. Because you have an apartment in your own motel, you don't have to pay rent. The other thing is that the whole family can work in the hotel. From making beds to laundry to maintenance . . . everything." Work duties often fall along gendered lines. Men oversee the finances, decisions about large purchases, and the entrepreneurial side, while women typically handle the housekeeping and the books. Being the owner/operator of a budget motel is often referred to as the "twenty-four-hour headache."

Because the hospitality industry depends on travel and tourism, economic downturns have significant impact and can ruin businesses. The Great Recession, which began in 2007, and the devastation to the economy due to the COVID-19 pandemic have led to layoffs, the selling of motels, and cash drying up, not to mention stress and sleepless nights.

Motel owners face more than difficult working conditions and financial strain. Instances of racial discrimination against owners continue, even as customers realize they have no choice but to stay at South Asian–owned motels. It is common for owners to hire white desk clerks, preferably women, to work during check-in hours so that customers don't immediately assume the motel is owned by South Asians. Even if customers do not mind staying at these motels, owners realize that they may judge a motel more harshly or be more difficult to please if they think the owner is a "foreigner."

Making the customer feel welcome also means circumscribing one's domestic life. To live in one's motels, which is common in lower-budget establishments, requires cooking meals at times of day when fewer customers are arriving, so as to avoid the scent of South Asian food in the lobbies or hallways. Women's contributions at work are often under-recognized when they work within the home. And growing up in a motel presents its own challenges. As one youth said, living in the motel deprived him of a "normal childhood. The opportunity to play with other kids and to have friends that live next door or across the street, . . . or trick-or-treating, for that matter." Simultaneously, living in one's workplace gave children direct insights into what their parents had to go through in order to be successful.

Having grown up in a motel, many children swear off following in their parents' footsteps. An owner who grew up in motels said, "Well, I promised myself after high school, I'm going to go get a good education, and I'm gonna go work for a national company and never get into the hotel business. . . . I worked for a few years and what I noticed was, I'm working thirteen, fourteen hours a day just like my dad was [in his motel]. However, in my case, somebody else is getting fat. . . . And then I saw my dad and his cousins who were not working as many hours any more, but they're making three, four times my pay." He ended up back in the motel business. The impressive growth of South Asian Americans in the hospitality industry has relied on the children of owners staying in it, whether as owners or in related roles, such as real estate and hospitality law.

While some who grew up in the United States return to the motel industry after hitting a glass ceiling at their jobs and seeing others getting rich and making money off their work, others could not wait to take over the reins of a small business. An owner who grew up in the United States turned down a job offer at the Waldorf Astoria hotel in New York City to run an economy motel in Ohio. "[The Waldorf Astoria] offered me a position. But the bottom line is, what am I going to do there? I can work there fifteen years if I really wanted, but I'm never going to own that. So the bottom line is ownership, that was the only persuading thing. As an owner you have more freedom. Freedom is a big thing. I can do whatever I want to [this motel]. If I run it down to the ground, then I run it down to the ground. If I make it successful, then I make it successful."

Pawan Dhingra is associate provost and associate dean of the faculty at Amherst College, and professor of American studies.

CHAPTER 10

Family

Congressman Dalip Singh Saund with his wife, Marian, and their children and grandchildren. This photograph was donated to SAADA by the congressman's grandson, Eric, who is seated on his lap in this photograph. In SAADA, courtesy of Eric Saund.

INTRODUCTION

Amy Bhatt and Amber Abbas

What comes to mind when you think of South Asian American families? Perhaps you start by picturing a husband and wife, most likely from India, Sri Lanka, Pakistan, Nepal, or Bangladesh, and a few kids born or raised in the United States, maybe all living with grandparents or other extended family members. You might also think about the colorful, festive spectacle of the South Asian wedding that would have brought the couple together: brightly attired guests awaiting the arrival of the groom's party (perhaps on horseback or in a convertible sports car), a band of drummers or a DJ spinning the latest mix of Bollywood hits and hip-hop, the hours-long (or days-long!) poojas or nikah ceremonies, buffets overflowing with delicacies and sweets, exuberant dancing that goes late into the night. Even before the wedding party, you might imagine two families sitting down together over tea and snacks to discuss whether or not their children would be suited to marry.

While many fit into the "typical" mold, South Asian American families define and understand family in a variety of ways, and there is much more nuance to the lived experience. From the earliest days, South Asians have creatively constructed their families in the diaspora. Because of immigration laws that first prohibited Asian family migration (such as the Chinese Exclusion Act, which limited Asian women from coming to the United States) and later encouraged family reunification, the family has been an important, but also contested, site of community development.

In this chapter, we explore stories that demonstrate the wide range of experiences that make up South Asian American family life. First, an excerpt from Karen Leonard's book *Making Ethnic Choices* looks at the dynamics in "Mexican-Hindu" families that grew out of marriages between early South Asian migrant men and Mexican migrant women in California. Although the Catholic mothers in these families handled faith and other domestic matters, Leonard's excerpt shows how fathers conveyed their pride in their South Asian heritage to their children. This creative adaptation to life in the United States emerges as a persistent theme in the stories collected here.

Similarly, but in a more contemporary example, Shiwani Srivastava has had to navigate her children's complex identities as half Indian American, half Taiwanese American identical twins. As she says, this means "double identity trouble!" She explores how her own identity, and her relationship to her South Asian heritage, have changed throughout her life. Since her children were born, she has often been asked, "What are they?" The question makes her "bristle," as people seek to place her children into familiar and binary identity boxes. To her, the question betrays an unwillingness to embrace the creative identity that her family represents. The common denominator in their household, as it turns out, is "American." Like many immigrant families before them, Srivastava's mixed family continues to create their own traditions and to celebrate their unique identities through them.

Mixed families often find harbor abroad, ostensibly freer from the restrictions of caste and status so deeply embedded in South Asian life. Kavita Pillay, a documentary filmmaker and reporter, shares an excerpt from a radio story she originally produced for WGBH in Boston about her South Indian parents' intercaste marriage. Because both were doctors, they met professionally, fell in love, and had the means to move abroad. Intercaste marriage was rare and "scandalous" in 1960s India, but migration to the United States transformed her parents into "economic Brahmins." Pillay acknowledges the privilege that her father's higher-caste name has provided her among Indian and diasporic communities, as well as how racial difference exposed her to discrimination in the Midwest. The United States offers refuge to families like Pillay's, yet people of color still face racist marginalization. As Pillay's longer story and reports such as Equality Labs' "Caste in the United States: A Survey of Caste Among South Asian Americans" (2018) reveal, casteism persists in South Asian American communities, a reminder that inequality has a constant presence even in the "land of the free."

Nalini and Ganesh Iyer, South Asian parents in Seattle, share the challenges they have faced in raising their daughters in America. While they are both immigrants from India, Nalini and Ganesh's story reveals how difficult it can be for South Asian migrants to become South Asian Americans. On one hand, they are highly educated, upwardly mobile professionals who have assimilated many aspects of American culture; on the other hand, they have realized that assimilation is not neutral, and through their daughters especially, they have had to confront questions about their ability and right to "belong" in America. The most helpful strategy for them has been to embrace multiplicity, to encourage their children to find the joy of "navigating multiple cultures," and to take what serves them best from each. As a family, they have created a transnational model that both preserves and adapts.

Mallika Iyer, Nalini and Ganesh Iyer's daughter, weighs in on the question of identity herself as she reflects on coming of age, leaving home, and crafting the contours of her own identity as a South Asian American and as a woman. She describes her struggles fitting into post-9/11 America, especially when other students ignorantly asked if she was a "terrorist." In high school, she felt objectified as a representative of Indian "tradition," and by the time she headed off to college, it became more and more important for her to find her own path. It is in the mixed identity of a Hindu woman of color that Mallika has found her place, inspired by her South Asian family heritage but also by the challenges and opportunities of being a nonwhite American woman. Embracing these identities has brought clarity to her experience and emboldened her as she has set out on her own.

In another story about finding one's path, Vegavahini Subramaniam (Vega) and Vaijayanthimala Rettakudi Savithree Nagarajan (Mala) share the sensitive experiences of coming out as lesbians to their South Indian families and reflect on how their families have continued to cherish them and embrace them in their life together. Both struggled with their identities growing up and feared being isolated in either one identity or another: "asexual in Indian contexts, lesbian and non-Indian in Western contexts." Ultimately, Vega and Mala have resisted the "path of obligation" and found liberation in living as fully realized South Asian lesbian women in a loving relationship. They describe the strength they draw from their chosen families in addition to their birth families. It is through building community that they have truly found their home.

South Asian American lives are animated by family, both local and transnational, at all stages of life. In the stories that conclude the chapter, drawn from oral history interviews, Amber Abbas and Amy Bhatt reflect on the deaths of their fathers. Both men had lived most of their adult lives outside of South Asia: Abbas's in Saudi Arabia and the United States, Bhatt's in Philadelphia. Because of these men's distance from the lands of their birth, their children had to navigate multiple familial, medical, and religious environments in supporting their fathers through illness and the last stages of life. As the post-1965 generation of South Asian migrants ages, the challenges of death and dying are becoming more immediate. Ultimately, in the face of tremendous loss, both Abbas and Bhatt recognize the importance of maintaining connections to their South Asian families, not just for their fathers' sakes, but for their own.

While there are strong links between family life in South Asia and South Asian families in the diaspora, there are also significant adaptations. From navigating new identities and relationships to finding love on one's own terms to dealing with the end of life and what that means for future generations, family life for South Asian Americans is a complicated, joyful, and messy space that undeniably shapes the immigrant experience.

Amy Bhatt is a writer, museum curator, and former professor.

Amber Abbas (she/her) is an associate professor of history at Saint Joseph's University.

PUNJABI MEXICAN FAMILIES

Karen Isaksen Leonard, with introductory text by Amy Bhatt and Amber Abbas

Karen Leonard's research on early South Asian migrants to the United States has illuminated the variety of experiences and challenges they faced in California and along the West Coast since the early twentieth century. Many of these early migrants were agricultural workers hailing from British India's Punjab province, and even as they faced discrimination, exclusion, and restrictions on property ownership, they also built communities and the nation's first gurdwara, in Stockton, California, in 1912.

Most of the men from Punjab who migrated to the Imperial Valley in Southern California in the early twentieth century married Mexican or Mexican American women. Their children were called "Mexican-Hindus" (Hindu at the time meant anyone from Hindustan or India) and had names like Maria Jesusita Singh and Jose Khan. Hardworking farmers, the fathers left the childrearing to their wives, so

A photograph from Amelia Singh Netervala's personal collection, taken in 1951. She describes the scene as follows: "Dinner held at our home in Phoenix for Tiger Joginder Singh, a wrestler from India who performed in Phoenix and other cities." In SAADA, courtesy of Amelia Singh Netervala.

their children spoke Spanish and English more readily than Punjabi and were primarily raised Catholic (but they had great respect for the religions of their fathers, who were Sikh, Muslim, or Hindu).

The story below offers a picture of family life and particularly of father-son relations. The storyteller is Mehnga "Mike" Singh, remembering his footrace against the son of another Punjabi farmworker; he and the other boy were state-champion runners, Singh in California and the other in Arizona. The setting is a picnic ground near the California-Arizona border, where the Punjabi Mexican families were relaxing.

The old men were sitting around, drinking whiskey and boasting about their sons. . . . An Arizona man put $1,000 on a blanket, said I couldn't

AN ORAL HISTORY INTERVIEW WITH AMELIA SINGH NETERVALA

Interviewer: And where were you born?

Netervala: In Texas in a small farming town.

Interviewer: Where in India did your father come from?

Netervala: He came from Patiala . . . Jalandhar in the northern part of India. Punjab.

Interviewer: And what were his family circumstances in India before he came?

Netervala: He didn't talk much about it. . . . I think they were farmers, because that's what he and his brother did and why they came to this country too . . . to work here. And they heard about America being a very rich country where you could make money. . . .

Interviewer: When did he arrive in the United States and how did he get here?

Netervala: He arrived in 1907 in San Francisco, both he and his brother. My father's name was Jiwan Singh and his brother Jagat Singh, and they . . . I believe it was twenty dollars that they had to have, at least twenty. . . .

Interviewer: When they arrived there?

Netervala: When they arrived there in San Francisco. And those that didn't have [money] were rejected, but what some of them did was pass their money to the fellow behind him. And then I have heard also from researchers that some of them would, if they didn't look tall enough, strong enough to be labor, they would put a little stool. . . . [And] I guess they would step up, you know, and be a little taller. But . . . those [who] were rejected, I understand that they . . . some of them jumped off the ship. They didn't want to go back. . . .

Interviewer: How much did your dad talk about his immigrant experience when you were growing up?

Jiwan Singh with his grandchildren in 1956. In SAADA, courtesy of Amelia Singh Netervala.

Netervala: I would ask him, but he didn't talk much, you know. He would say, "Why do you want to know?" And as I heard from other researchers or interviewers, this is the same answer they got from their fathers, most of the fathers. They just didn't want to talk about it. I guess it was such a bad experience. I asked him after he came to this country what it was like, where he was, and he wouldn't talk about it. . . .

Interviewer: What about your mother? Where was she born and what were the circumstances of her family before she met your father?

Netervala: Well, she was born in Mexico—

Interviewer: Where in Mexico?

Netervala: Um, what was the name of the town . . . it was a small town across Texas. Oh, San Ygnacio! That's what it was. It's just a border town. And she had cousins in Texas, which was all, you know—Texas and Mexico was the same. There was no border there, and my grandmother was a Native American, so she had relatives or cousins in that small town in Texas. And so when [my mother] was visiting those relatives there, she saw these Indians. . . . There were about four of them that were working . . . that had farmed or [were] working on the farms. And somehow she and my father got to talking, and that's how they met, but they never really went into detail. They always [said,] "Why do you want to know?" They never discussed any of those things . . . with us.

Amelia Singh and Helen Ram at Westwood Village Hall, 1953. In SAADA, courtesy of Amelia Singh Netervala.

beat the Arizona boy. Dad threw in $5,000, then others put down money. . . . We kids were off shooting .22 rifles at tin cans.

Dad came, took me aside, and asked me, "Who are you?"

I could tell something was up. I replied, "Mehnga Singh [his Punjabi name, seldom used]."

"Yes," he replied, "a lionhearted Sikh warrior. Nobody can beat you, run and *win*, you're going to race this boy."

"Okay," I said, "I'll run. Where is it?"

"No," he said, "run and *win*, that's what you're going to do." He pointed to a course along the canal. "You are my blood," he said. . . . The women ran out, Mother among them, to see what was happening, and she remonstrated with him; Dad hushed her, she shut up. There was one drunken old man, he shot off a .22 to start the race, he called out, "You *chobdars*, run!" in Punjabi. Dad stood there with a deadpan look. . . . I ran but the other boy was ahead of me most of the way. . . . Then I hit it and ran, a Sikh warrior, ran for my heart, and beat him by two yards. Father just stood there looking impassive, elders all around him. Then he spoke, "As I said, no one can beat my son, he's of my blood and he's a

JOTI SINGH'S HALF AND HALVES

Photo by Vijay Rakhra.

Joti Singh is a dance creator and innovator who serves as the artistic director of the Duniya Dance and Drum Company. She explores issues of race, ethnic identity, and belonging through her choreography, and in 2010 she used her Bhangra expertise in collaboration with Ensambles Ballet Folklórico de San Francisco, a company dedicated to traditional Mexican folk dance, to create *Half and Halves*—a series of dances that celebrates the history of Punjabi Mexican marriages and the overlapping histories of these American communities.

Sikh warrior." The other boy's father didn't say a word to him and they left within thirty minutes.

Excerpted from Making Ethnic Choices: California's Punjabi Mexican Americans *by Karen Leonard (Temple University Press).*

Karen Isaksen Leonard (she/her) is a historian and anthropologist who is retired from the Department of Anthropology at the University of California, Irvine.

DOUBLE IDENTITY TROUBLE

Shiwani Srivastava

"What are they?"

As the parent of half Indian American, half Taiwanese American identical twin boys, I've gotten used to hearing this question fairly regularly. I sometimes wonder if for the past two years, I've unknowingly been walking down the streets of San Francisco with a sign on my back that says, "Will stop to discuss identity."

I've learned that "What are they?" typically means one of the following: Are they twins? Identical or fraternal? Boys or girls? What race/ethnicity? For identical twins, there's usually another layer of identity questioning that happens as well—who's who, and how do you tell them apart?

"They're innocent questions," my friends remind me. I often ask myself why seemingly innocuous questions make me bristle. Perhaps it's the realization that

PEANUT BUTTER DOSAS

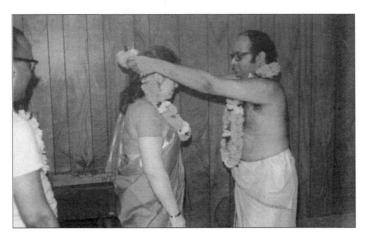

Jessica Namakkal's parents during their Hindu marriage ceremony in 1975. In SAADA, courtesy of Jessica Namakkal.

In this excerpt from an article in *Tides*, historian and writer Jessica Namakkal reflects on the impact of the choice that her parents—one white and born in Nebraska, the other Brown and born in India—made in marrying in 1975, less than a decade after the Supreme Court decision in *Loving v. Virginia* (1967) lifted the ban on interracial marriages in the United States.

Outside of social expectations, many negotiations had to be made on a personal and cultural level, especially around food. The first time my dad, a lifelong vegetarian, went to my mom's house for dinner, she made him a steak. Whenever they told this story, my mom would laugh deviously as my dad detailed how he carefully picked the red peppers off the top and ate those along with some Spanish rice. My mom may not have been fazed by dating an Indian, but she had no idea how to feed a vegetarian. She was from Nebraska: a good steak was the ultimate meal. By the time I was born, my dad had given up his vegetarianism in favor of my mom's meatloaf and those Jell-O salads so popular in the Midwest in the 1980s (lime Jell-O, canned pineapple, carrot shavings). Despite my father's adaptations to Midwestern eating habits, he was (and is still) known at the local diner for asking for a side of salsa with his pancakes, and he regularly made my sister and me peanut butter or (processed) cheese dosas on the weekends.

Mixed marriages have become much more popular in the South Asian diaspora since the 1970s, although there is not much discussion about what this means or of the great amount of diversity these "new" family formations have brought to the community, both in South Asia and globally. By the mid-1980s, most of my Indian family, including my grandfather, my five aunts and their families, and my cousins, had left India and lived in Canada, the United States, and areas of the Gulf States. This meant that growing up, instead of learning about India by going there, I developed ideas of India that were largely shaped by people and places in the diaspora. Most of the Indian family I saw were in Toronto or came to stay with us in Minnesota—our house became a sort of way station for Indian family on the way to bigger cities. When I was in Toronto, I interacted primarily with Indian people, ate Indian food, heard people speaking Tamil and Hindi, went to Hindu temples, and watched Indian films.

> *Despite the white landscape (including both the snow and the people), when I was young, I practically thought Canada was India.*
>
> *For many years, I thought my knowledge, of India and of myself, was inauthentic because I learned it in North America, not in India. I expected that, had I been in India, I would somehow have a deeper understanding of "my" culture. This is an idea that many immigrants and diasporic peoples seem to carry with them and pass on to their children, perhaps because of the sadness that comes with the loss of homeland, or with the realization that you have produced children who are culturally different than you. For my father, what must it feel like to be an Indian but have children who are Americans, who do not desire the foods of his youth and do not understand his mother's native tongue? And for my mother, what must it feel like to have children who have a different last name from her and are often assumed to not be her children because of their brown skin and dark hair?*
>
> From *"Peanut Butter Dosas: Becoming Desi in the Midwest"* for Tides, by Jessica Namakkal.

even in a diverse city like San Francisco, we act like overeager census takers, feeling the immediate need to categorize anyone who seems different.

Or maybe it's because throughout my life, like many children of immigrants, I've had a complicated history with being asked "What are you?" or "Where are you from?" I've often struggled to come up with the "right" answer out of a host of options: (a) American, (b) Indian American, (c) from New Jersey, and (d) the child of Indian parents.

My automatic answer has become Indian American, although even that categorization carries its own baggage. As a child, it felt arbitrary. As a teenager, it felt constraining. And as a young adult, it felt like something to cling to as a way to proclaim who I am. These days, I believe each of these categories contains vast multitudes of identities, which is why they actually tell you very little about an individual.

But as much as I shirk categorization, there's no doubt that being part of a multiracial marriage and family has forced me to grapple with self-identification. This is especially true as my husband and I attempt to establish new multiethnic traditions, and being American ends up being the common thread in our hyphenated Indian American and Taiwanese American families.

This has become most evident with holidays. We always celebrated Halloween, Thanksgiving, and Christmas as children. But because I grew up with Hindu

LOVING V. VIRGINIA

On June 12, 1967, the Supreme Court of the United States decided the case of *Loving v. Virginia*, unanimously striking down state laws prohibiting interracial marriages. Mildred and Richard Loving were married in Washington, D.C., in 1958, but when they returned to Virginia, they were arrested for violating the state's anti-miscegenation statute. Mildred was Black (and part Native American), while Richard was white. For nearly three hundred years, interracial marriage in the state, as well as in the country, had been carefully regulated—and had even led to the denaturalization of American citizens who married Indian men (under the Expatriation Act of 1907, American women automatically assumed the nationality of their husbands upon marriage).

The American Civil Liberties Union began representing the Lovings in 1963, and after failed appeals in Virginia, the case eventually went to the U.S. Supreme Court. The decision in favor of the Lovings in 1967 redefined marriage in the country and opened the door for interracial couples everywhere. In 2015, *Loving v. Virginia* was also used as precedent in the case of *Obergefell v. Hodges*, which legalized same-sex marriage in the United States.

parents from India in New Jersey, Diwali was my time to shine—literally. We'd put up bright decorations, light candles, and go to vibrant parties. Similarly, my husband's Taiwanese parents celebrated the Mid-Autumn Festival and Chinese New Year every year with equal exuberance.

We each have a strong desire to preserve these traditions that were a big part of our childhoods and pass them on to our children—yet what's familiar to one side of the family is foreign to the other. The reality is that Christmas and Thanksgiving have become our shared traditions—our common ground across families that speak different languages and celebrate different holidays.

This has sparked the realization that when you erase the hyphens altogether, what's left is that we are American.

Our Americanness is accentuated by the reality of our children acquiring language. When the twins were infants, people told us how lucky we were that our children could be trilingual in Mandarin, Hindi, and English. I hoped this might come true. But my husband and I can only communicate with each other in English, and our parents live in different states—without immersion, our trilingual dream is fading. The twins' coos and babbles are giving way to very English words, like "applesauce" and "uh-oh."

While there is some sadness in this erasure, I also see it strengthening my own hold on some amorphous definition of Indian culture. I cannot rely on my

---

TONGUE TIED: KUTCHI ACROSS BORDERS

In her essay on the complexity of claiming and losing language, 2020–21 Archival Creators Fellow Omme-Salma Rahemtullah discusses the historical origins of her family language, Kutchi, and its enduring legacy through years of migration and settlement across continents:

> I grew up speaking Kutchi at home and, as I grew older, spoke a mix of Kutchi and English. As long as I can remember, Swahili was the language my parents spoke to each other when they did not want us kids to understand. And in turn my sister and I spoke to each other in French, which, being Canadian, we learned in school, when we didn't want our parents to understand. My nephews, currently ranging in age from three to ten, do not speak Kutchi at all, but understand a few Gujarati words as well as a few Tamil words, as their father is Tamil. The Kutchi language, it seems, is dying with subsequent generations, but growing in its place is a unique mixture of all the languages that have defined our migrations. Like my family in Toronto, the families in South Carolina that I interviewed can fall in and out of several languages in one sentence, taking words from one, syntax from another, and conjugation from yet another.
>
> There is, though, something incredibly distinctive about Kutchi for me: the way it tells the history of the migration of my family, and the way it conjures a strong sense of African Asian identity. This identity is one of mixed migrations and imperial dislocations: from West India to East Africa to North America, from Kutchi to Swahili to English, each piece adding to the road maps of our lives, never fully leaving any one place or language behind.

From "Tongue Tied" for Tides, by Omme-Salma Rahemtullah.

---

husband to "do the Indian stuff." This has to come from me. I must be the one to keep track of the holidays, cook the traditional dishes, and tell the stories. And my husband finds himself in the same boat with Taiwanese culture. But we try to learn and buoy each other along the way, until we form a new family identity and new traditions that stand on their own.

Maybe this is why the question of "What are they?" or "What are you?" is so fraught. It reminds us that we are still wrestling with who we are. In the case of our twins, they'll spend a lifetime figuring out who they are not only in relation to their parents, their multiracial identity, and the world around them, but also and especially in relation to each other.

So next time I hear the question "What are they?" I will give what is actually the most accurate answer: "They're still figuring that out."

Shiwani Srivastava (she/her) is a screenwriter and freelance editorial consultant based in Seattle.

LOVE ACROSS CASTE LINES

Kavita Pillay

For years, my mom, Indira Pillay, told her American friends and colleagues that she and my dad had had a shotgun wedding. Then one day, someone informed her that a shotgun wedding takes place when the bride is pregnant.

"We hardly touched each other before we got married," she explains. "I thought it meant any no-frills wedding ceremony."

Though my mom was not a pregnant bride, my parents' simple and hurried wedding was cause for gossip and some scandal for one reason: they had fallen in love across caste lines.

"It was not scandalous," says my dad, Bala Pillay. "It was not common. It was rare."

My dad's parents accused my mom of having performed black magic on their son to make him fall for her.

"That is why it was scandalous," says my mom. "Anything which was rare was

Studio photo of Indira and Bala Pillay. Courtesy of Kavita Pillay.

scandalous."

My dad is a Nair, which is a dominant, upper caste. Nairs consider themselves to be the descendants of warriors, landowners, and, in some cases, royalty. My mom, on the other hand, is from a lower caste called the Ezhavas. They were traditionally low-level agricultural workers who did jobs that were considered "unclean" by upper-caste Hindus, such as tapping sap from palm trees to make wine.

As one of my parents' friends put it: "Bala is from the lowest of the high castes, and Indira is from the highest of the low." Yet, once upon a time, the social chasm between these two groups was so vast that it was unthinkable for even the shadow of someone from my mom's caste to fall on someone of my dad's caste.

In addition to accusing my mom of black magic, my dad's parents said that nobody would marry the children of an intercaste marriage.

"I told [my parents], 'Listen, I don't care about what all these relatives are talking about,'" my dad recalls. "'I love her, I want to marry her. If you don't like it, you can go to hell.'"

To my American ears, it sounds brave and romantic. To my grandparents, it was unimaginable.

My favorite aunt even claims that there were relatives who threatened to kill themselves and kill my parents for this "love marriage," for transgressing the Indian tradition of unions arranged by parents. My mom maintains that my aunt is exaggerating, though from what I can surmise, it probably is not much of a stretch. The more I learn about the obstacles my parents and other intercaste couples have faced, the more I think that it's comparable to what a Black woman and a white man might have encountered had they planned to get married in the American South just after Jim Crow.

My parents' marriage was possible because they met in medical school. They were both doctors, they saw each other as equals, and they had the wherewithal to leave India. In 1970—five years after the Immigration and Nationality Act loosened restrictions on immigrants from non-European countries—my mom and dad arrived in Cleveland to escape their feuding families and begin their medical residencies.

In doing so, they entered the complicated caste system of America. We became what I would call "economic Brahmins," but we inhabited murky racial terrain. Growing up in the hypersegregated suburbs of Cleveland, I was asked "What are you?" more times than I can count. We were called the n-word more often than I care to remember.

Today, my parents live in Hingham, Massachusetts, where they are busy enjoying the spoils of retirement. This includes spending winters in the South Indian state of Kerala, which is where our family is originally from. Kerala has become a tourist hot spot in recent years and has India's highest literacy and life-expectancy rates. Compared with the rest of India, the state is known for being highly progressive.

Yet while intercaste marriages have become more common than they were in 1969, they are still far from the norm in Kerala, let alone in the rest of India. More people migrated out of India than any other country in 2017, according to a United Nations report. For this growing diaspora, the option to marry someone of the same caste has been made easier by an array of matrimonial websites that list potential brides and grooms, specifying their caste and desire for a spouse from the same one.

I was born and brought up in America, and my Indian American friends and I never discuss caste, probably because the vast majority of Indian Americans are like my dad, and come from India's upper and dominant castes, as research by the University of Pennsylvania has found. Though we are all well versed in the stories of how our mothers and fathers came here with one suitcase and a handful of dollars in their pocket, we have little understanding of how generations of caste privilege in India helped pave the way for our parents, for us, and for our children to do well in this country.

This excerpted story is part of the "Caste in America" series, produced with funding from the Pulitzer Center and in partnership with WGBH Boston. It is reprinted with permission by the author.

Kavita Pillay (she/her(s)/hän) is a documentary filmmaker and journalist.

RACE, GENDER, AND TRANSNATIONAL PARENTING

Nalini and Ganesh Iyer

When our daughter Mallika was three years old, she came home from day care and asked, "Daddy, can you make my eyes blue?" We were surprised by the question, because we didn't expect our child to be conscious of racial difference so early. We explained genetics to her by saying, "Parents with brown eyes have children who have brown eyes; brown-eyed parents cannot have blue-eyed children." Some six months later, we had our second daughter, Geetanjali. Much to our surprise, she was born with blue eyes! While we understood recessive genes and the mixing of races in the history of the Indian subcontinent, we had no clue how to explain this difference to our preschooler. A few days after we brought baby Geetanjali home, we gently checked in with Mallika and asked her what she thought of her sister's eye color. Mallika casually replied, "God made a mistake; he forgot that brown-eyed parents cannot have blue-eyed children!" The issue of

Geetanjali's eye color came up often—from random strangers commenting on it in public places to Indian friends and family admiring her eye color as something special and superior and not just a quirk of genetics.

We share this anecdote because race is a vexed question for South Asian Americans like us. We grew up in urban India and came from positions of economic and cultural privilege. But when we arrived in the United States as graduate students (California and Indiana, respectively), we suddenly became racial minorities. Although we had studied American history in school in India and knew a bit about racial politics, nothing prepared us for how people would treat us as nonwhite foreigners. Some people were curious about our exotic and foreign culture, others wondered why we spoke such good English, and many assumed a color-blind attitude and refused to recognize that we didn't experience the world as they did. South Asians we encountered also took a variety of positions, from assuming cultural superiority about coming from an ancient culture, to sticking to insular ethnic groups, to eagerly assimilating into the melting pot of America. As adult

---

ROOTS AND REFLECTIONS: SOUTH ASIANS IN THE PACIFIC NORTHWEST

Sometimes I would write home, write a letter. You know, in those days telephone was impossible. As a matter of fact, when I came to Seattle and I moved into the house, if you wanted to call India, we would place the call in the evening about six o'clock. And we'll get the connection about four or five in the morning. You called the operator—"I want to call India, such and such number," and then she called you back. . . . That was a big deal, getting a call through to India [and you had to shout at the top of your voice to be heard on the other end]. . . . Now you just pick up the phone and dial and there it is. And the connection is very, very clear—like you're talking to anybody here in Redmond or Seattle.

—Sat Kapahi

The India that Sat Kapahi left in the 1950s had no private telephone companies and few phone lines in most family homes, and mailing a letter from Seattle to Delhi took almost three weeks. Today, India is but a Skype call or email away. Over the past six decades, South Asian migration to the Pacific Northwest has changed dramatically, and the world in which immigrants live has also expanded to include new diversities and experiences. *Roots and Reflections: South Asians in the Pacific Northwest* is a cultural history of South Asian immigration that explores these changes through the life stories of settlers who came to the Pacific Northwest between the 1940s and the 1990s.

Adapted from the description for Roots and Reflections: South Asians in the Pacific Northwest, *by Amy Bhatt and Nalini Iyer (University of Washington Press, 2014).*

immigrants, we were able to make choices about how much of our culture we pre-served, how much we assimilated, and how to be both critical and appreciative of the United States and India. However, raising bicultural children, particularly daughters, has been quite a different journey.

We live in the Seattle area, which has a large South Asian community because of the presence of high-tech companies like Microsoft and Amazon. This commu-nity has a long presence in the region (since the early twentieth century) and has grown rapidly since the passage of the Hart-Celler Immigration and Nationality Act of 1965. We live in a middle-class suburb, and it is common for us to encounter South Asians in our everyday life. Yet our daughters struggle with their identities because they are constantly navigating where they belong. They must explain that they are Americans, in contrast to the children of first-generation white immi-grants from Europe or Canada whose nationality is rarely called into question. This racialization has become particularly acute post-9/11. As recently as February 2015, our family encountered racial slurs painted across the local Hindu temple walls, shaking us to the core and emphasizing our status as outsiders. When Geetanjali was nine years old, she was stopped and searched at the Minneapolis airport. At the time, the terror alert was high, and the cast on her broken arm tested falsely positive for explosive residue because of a lotion she had used. She was terrified by the search and wept while we wondered if the same thing would have happened to a little girl who did not have brown skin. Neither of us challenged the TSA agents although we were very angry.

Now when we travel, we carry our passports (even within the United States), be-cause we might be called upon to prove that we are citizens and belong here. This outsider status is not resolved when we travel to India, either. Many loving family and friends wonder about our choice to raise daughters in the United States. Will they become too American? Will they date or marry non-Indians? In India, they seem very American, because they do not speak an Indian language fluently, they are unfamiliar with Indian traditions and popular culture, and they speak and act like Americans! We explain to our Indian family and friends that our daughters have the freedom to choose their life partners and that we are raising them with

ECHOES OF THE DOTBUSTERS

In an op-ed for the *Washington Post* titled "Indian Americans Won't Be Safe As Long As the White House Is Inciting Fear," Philadelphia-based rapper and producer Raj Haldar (aka Lushlife) reflects on the hate-crime killing of Srinivas Kuchibhotla on February 22, 2017:

Photo by Corky Lee.

The recent rash of attacks on people of Indian origin has incited an all-too-familiar mix of anger, sadness and fear in our community. In 1988, when I was 7 years old, a hate group called the Dotbusters began threatening and attacking South Asians in Jersey City, near where I grew up. Their name comes from the traditional bindi that Indian women sometimes wear on their forehead. Over the course of several years, this loosely organized group terrorized the Indian community in New Jersey and New York with an escalating campaign of vandalism, burglary and murder. At the height of their attacks, I can remember sitting in the back of our family car, panic-stricken as my dad drove us to a Hindu puja celebration in downtown Jersey City. I was one of the only brown kids at my school, and the climate of otherization created by the Dotbusters made me feel even more alone. Today, the senseless murder of Kuchibhotla is undoubtedly creating a new generation of South Asian children who, despite their best efforts, don't feel like they belong.

During an October 2016 campaign fundraising stop in Edison, N.J.—a suburb not far from the epicenter of Dotbuster activity two decades earlier—then-candidate Donald Trump held court with a glitzy audience of Indian business executives and Bollywood actresses. South Asians voted overwhelmingly for Hillary Clinton in last year's election, but Trump's anti-Muslim, hyper-nationalistic message resonated with some who found it complementary to their views on politics in India. . . .

Back in the early '90s, the Dotbusters were eventually quelled only by grass-roots organizing among the South Asian Hindu, Sikh and Muslim communities—setting aside their differences as they were collectively jarred into political action by more than 58 attacks in 1990 alone. Today, Indian Americans need to follow suit. Instead of agonizing over Facebook posts that beg for acknowledgment, we need to organize and insist on outreach and cooperation when it comes to bias-motivated crimes, immigration policy and other issues that affect the South Asian community at large. . . . This doesn't end with our own community, either. The tone from the top has set a collision course for otherization, and hate crimes are on the rise against Muslims, Arabs, South Asians and Jewish Americans alike.

If we learn anything from Srinivas Kuchibhotla's tragic death, it should be that we're all in danger as long as anti-immigrant prejudice exists. And as I prepare for another turn of performances in the Midwest later this year, it's hard not to be more than a little on edge.

an awareness of global cultures and histories. In America, raising daughters of South Asian origin means we also have to navigate the inherent gender norms and biases in American culture—from clothing and career choices to passions and interests.

Despite these challenges, as parents we seek to inculcate in our daughters the joy of navigating multiple cultures and to allow them to choose the pieces that resonate. We recognize that each of them has her own road to travel, and we see ourselves as their companions on this journey.

Nalini Iyer (she/her) is a professor of English with an associate appointment in the Asian Studies Program and the Women and Gender Studies Program at Seattle University.

Ganesh Iyer is a business-development executive in the life sciences industry. He lives in Kirkland, Washington, with his wife, Nalini.

LAKSHMAN KALASPUDI'S ROAD TRIP STORY

In SAADA, courtesy of Lakshman Kalaspudi.

I am the deputy director of the only professionally managed senior center for South Asian older adults in the Northeast, called India Home. These pictures are from a road trip we took our seniors on to Amish country in Pennsylvania. They had never seen anything like the culture they encountered there because it was not a standard destination for South Asians. They played Anthakshari on the bus, teams competing fiercely on who could sing the most songs from Bollywood's golden oldies. They ate Bombay mix and samosas and drank chai all the way there. The sight of fifty seniors eating puri bhaji *and pickle on the grounds of an Amish farm didn't seem to faze the Amish, by the way. The guide at the Amish center was a refugee from Afghanistan, and he was great about making our South Asian seniors feel right at home. The trip showed our seniors a side of America they hadn't seen and provided an encounter with another marginal culture in America, one that they recognized had its own peculiarities and deeply held beliefs, just like their own.*

SAADA's Road Trips Project aims to reframe a major American tradition by sharing stories of South Asian Americans traveling across the country.

VIJAYA SUBRAMANIAM'S FIRST DAYS

Interviewed by Sindya N. Bhanoo

Vijaya Subramaniam departed from Chennai, India, and arrived in Akron, Ohio, in 1986 at the age of 55.

My name is Vijaya Subramaniam. I came here in 1986. . . . [In] November, I'll be eighty-four.

I came with my youngest daughter. She got admission in Akron, Ohio. So I came with her on a tourist visa. My son was here in Ohio, so I came and stayed with him for six months. And then he extended my trip another six months, and . . . [then] I went to India to see my older daughter, and then I came back after one year or something. By that time, he got me the green card, and I stayed here forever [laughs].

I was surprised because I am used to living in India for fifty-five years. The first day seeing America, it was a thrill. Everything is new and so exciting. And when I visit India I feel like staying there also, but now I am getting to the age where . . . I am in a bit of confusion. . . . My son and my youngest daughter are here. So they say, "We are here, so you stay here. . . ." My oldest daughter is in India, Bangalore. She says, "Come and stay with me." I'm a bit confused, but better to be here, I think, for all the medical benefits and everything. . . . Every once in a year I go to India . . . to visit my daughter, my brothers, sisters. I feel happy there also.

MAGANBHAI PATEL'S FIRST DAYS

Interviewed by Renuka Sharma

Maganbhai Patel departed from Chikhli, India, and arrived in Chicago, Illinois, in 2010 at the age of 76.

My name is Maganbhai Patel. I came from Gujarat, India. . . .

I arrived on April 20, 2010, at O'Hare Airport. On that day, my wife and I were only welcomed by my daughter, grandkids, and son-in-law. We arrived at the airport at 3 p.m. The weather was clear. I saw the third-largest international airport. . . . It covered a wide area. More than a thousand airplanes land and take off every day. The airport looked so busy.

After that we sat in the car and took the road home. Chicago's roads were good. The roads were three and four lanes up and down. All the cars were going fast. We saw big bridges. It was spring. There was green scenery on both [sides of the road]. . . . There were red, white, yellow, brown, and sky-colored flowers. We saw them like they were welcoming us heartily. That time I was feeling so happy. I saw in our car a new thing, a GPS. The GPS was announcing where and when to turn right or left and how far away our home was. It wasn't necessary to ask any person. The car would reach the address. I thought that was wonderful.

GROWING UP DESI

Mallika Iyer

I t was seventh grade, and I was trying to do some problem about pigs and chick-
ens in algebra class when the boy sitting in front of me turned around and asked
me if I was a terrorist. Until then, as a child of Indian immigrants, I had always
thought of myself as American. Once I entered junior high, things changed. To
some, my perpetually tan skin despite the gray Seattle weather was an asset. To
others, it was something to be feared.

It didn't matter that we had barely been in kindergarten for a week when 9/11
happened, or that the 9/11 perpetrators were not Indian, or that I was an American
citizen. People would ask, "Oh you're Indian, so you're a Muslim, right?" This was a
complex question that I always answered defensively, insisting that I was a Hindu.
But then I would think to myself, "Why would I be ashamed to be a Muslim?" I felt
guilty for feeling offended, but I knew it was because of all the negative associations

with Islam in post-9/11 America. And there was another question: by asserting my Hinduism, did that make me a fundamentalist, despite my upbringing in a secular household?

In my freshman year of high school, my English teacher, too, made me a spectacle. I became an object to be studied during our India unit (which felt like an eternity but really only lasted about three months). I was constantly being asked questions

---

ALI KHATAW'S FIRST DAYS

Ali Khataw departed from Karachi, Pakistan, and arrived in Fayetteville, Arkansas, in 1980 at the age of 21 to attend the University of Arkansas.

I've lived only in Pakistan approximately eight to nine years of my life. I have lived in Hong Kong and I have lived in England, so it's not a culture shock for me at all to come here. But when I did come here the one thing was that I was . . . throughout my life when I was living with my parents when I was young and lived in Hong Kong and England, I was very close to them. So the biggest thing was the home-sickness. That was just out of this world. . . .

But the first day when I arrived it was . . . I don't know what to say . . . it was . . . very lonely. You don't have the people that you have been growing up with. Your friends, your parents, your sister, brother. And then you come over and then suddenly it's a different environment and you don't have a single friend. I mean zero. Zilch. You're starting with a blank slate. And I create friends very easily and all that, but loneliness was the number one . . . if you want me to put it in one word . . . initially the first day was "loneliness," because you don't have anybody to count on, you don't know who to ask for advice, and you don't know if they're going to give you the right advice. It was very interesting. It was different. I think "helpless" and "loneliness" were the two words that I would put the experience into the first day. Now . . . ask me about after a month? Oh my god, I was a party animal!

---

about Hinduism and India, not all of which I could answer. To top it off, my teacher asked me personal questions like "Are you having an arranged marriage when you grow up?" and "Would your parents be upset if you married outside your caste?" For a fifteen-year-old, these questions made me feel alien and weird. Looking back now, I am able to see how much prejudice and discrimination was passed off as being "curious" about my "exotic" culture and was perfectly acceptable in a class focused on "world cultures." In my predominantly white high school, I couldn't help but constantly feel different from my classmates regardless of how hard I tried to blend in with them.

When it came time to apply for college, I knew I wanted to get the heck out of the Seattle suburbs. I was ready to live in a big city in a different part of the country and to truly be independent. So I chose a school in Chicago. One thing that struck

COLLEGE LIFE: A SCENE

A SCENE OF THE HINDU MARRIAGE CEREMONIAL IN THE HINDUSTHANI NIGHT:

A Chinese student played the part of the Hindu bride, an Argentine student that of the bridegroom, a Brazilian student that of the bride's mother, and a Filipino student that of the bridegroom's mother. Prince Victor N. Narayan (third figure from the left) played the part of the bride's father, and B. M. Chatterjee, who is shown in the picture as blessing the couple, played the part of the Brahmin priest.

[To face p. 155.

In SAADA.

Taken sometime prior to 1918, and appearing in Indu Bhushan De Majumdar's *America through Hindu Eyes*, this photograph depicts a "scene" of a Hindu marriage ceremony during "Hindusthani Night" at Cornell University. It shows several students of various nationalities enacting the parts of bride, groom, Brahmin priest, and family. The caption explains, "A Chinese student played the part of the Hindu bride, an Argentine student that of the bridegroom, a Brazilian student that of the bride's mother, and a Filipino student that of the bridegroom's mother. Prince Victor N. Narayan (third figure from the left) played the part of the bride's father, and B. M. Chatterjee, who is shown in the picture as blessing the couple, played the part of the Brahmin priest."

Today, South Asian student groups on college campuses across the country continue to play a large and active role in campus life—for South Asian and non–South Asian students alike. For instance, at the University of Virginia and the University of Illinois at Urbana-Champaign, the Indian Student Association is often the largest student group on campus, with annual events, like "India Night," that are attended by thousands. These events, which are not without their controversies or issues of inclusion, include religious and cultural celebrations that serve both an educational and a bonding purpose—just as they did at Cornell in the early twentieth century.

me right away was that there are regional differences in the Indian immigrant community. In the Pacific Northwest, particularly in western Washington, the Indian community is relatively small, made up mostly of people working in Microsoft or other similarly "techie" jobs. This was a stark contrast to the large, vibrant, and tight-knit South Asian community I encountered in the Chicago area. My university is just five minutes from Devon Avenue, a street lined with Indian and Pakistani shops and restaurants that can make you forget you are even in the United States! I loved being in a place where there were plenty of kids just like me, who had grown up with Indian immigrant parents and had also struggled to navigate two worlds. My freshman-year roommate was also South Asian, and living with another Indian girl helped me start to understand more of my Indian American identity. She introduced me to Bollywood movies and songs, beyond

NICOLETTE KHAN'S ROAD TRIP SOUNDTRACKS

The thing I remember most about road trips with my father were the soundtracks. We had dozens of mixtapes that he would buy from markets during his trips back home to Kara-chi. They featured songs from playback singers like Suraiya, Noor Jehan, and Geeta Dutt, and ghazals from poets like Jagjit Singh. We would play these tapes alongside American greatest-hits albums from Journey, Air Supply, Pat Benatar, and Fleetwood Mac. Music was always something that brought our family closer together.

From SAADA's Road Trips Project, which aims to reframe a major American tradition by sharing stories of South Asian Americans traveling across the country.

just those of *Kabhi Khushi Kabhie Gham*. We formed a special bond—she made me feel like I was at home with family, something I may not have had if we had not shared a similar cultural background and history.

It was during my freshman year of college that I began to finally embrace two identities that I had been struggling with: being a Hindu and being a woman of color in America. I began to take more ownership of my Indian American identity by exploring more of my Hindu heritage. I attended many events put on by my school's Hindu Students Organization, including Garba, Diwali, and Holi celebrations, *aarti*, and a retreat. These experiences allowed me to delve deeper into what it meant to identify as Hindu personally, instead of just being labeled as different, as I was in high school. I found a community of people with shared beliefs and grew more confident about my cultural knowledge and involvement.

Also in my first year at college, I joined an intergenerational group for women of color, LUCES (Loyola University Chicago Empowering Sisterhood), which allowed me to explore what being a woman of color means in today's world. I was paired with a faculty mentor who helped me understand how being a woman of color can impact one's career paths and who empathized with my experience. This relationship helped me to establish an identity that incorporated being South Asian with being a woman of color, without the two being mutually exclusive.

I used to tone down my identity in order to fit into my high school's homogenous landscape. Now, I am a proud Indian American woman who fully embraces her desi side and loves to participate in Hindu cultural celebrations and religious events. I have also become much prouder of my identity as a woman of color. By embracing these identities and making them my own, I've found my own niche as an Indian American growing up today.

Mallika Iyer (she/her/hers) is a medical student at the University of Washington.

FINDING LOVE, FORMING FAMILY

Vega Subramaniam and Mala Nagarajan

Vegavahini Subramaniam (Vega) and Vaijayanthimala Rettakudi Savithree Nagarajan (Mala) were raised in Hindu families who emigrated from South India to the United States in the 1960s. In June 2002, they got married in a lesbian Hindu wedding. Despite the fact that Vega is atheist and Mala agnostic, they chose a Hindu ceremony in order to reclaim their cultural heritage. In March 2004, Vega and Mala joined the Washington State marriage-equality lawsuit to have their relationship recognized legally. Here, they reflect on their journey with relationships, marriage, and given and chosen families.

Vega, on coming out: Like many desis, I was raised to assume that I would get married to the man my parents helped me choose, and that I would have two kids. But something happened during my teens that my parents didn't expect: I became a feminist. And when I was eighteen, I started coming to terms with being

---

GOOD GIRLS MARRY DOCTORS

Good Girls Marry Doctors: South Asian American Daughters on Obedience and Rebellion is a 2016 anthology of stories written by South Asian Americans, edited by Piyali Bhattacharya. Below is an excerpt from Preeti Aroon's review of the book for the *Aerogram*.

Many readers of South Asian heritage will likely see in this book echoes of their own experiences, when the values and norms stressed at home are incongruent with the values and norms stressed outside the home. One woman reflects on her life at age 17: "In my school life, I am in my senior year and being asked to cast votes for 'cutest couple.'" Meanwhile, she's having this exchange with her father:

"You are too young for dating."

"My friends have been dating since they were 12."

"Your friends are Canadian."

"I am Canadian," I laugh through my tears.

Not everyone has complete discord with their parents, though, and there are heartwarming stories of parental acceptance when daughters don't follow the expected path. Jyothi Natarajan and her partner, Anand, had a "non-wedding" party because they didn't believe politically in the institution of marriage. Her queer sister, Vani, met a white trans man in 2012. While the two sisters and their partners were visiting their parents, Jyothi's mother says, "So, now that both you and Vani are not getting married but are living with partners . . . I want to get you something." Jyothi wonders what's going on. Mom explains: "You won't get any wedding gifts. . . . So I want to get each of you a Vitamix." Yes, the $450 Vitamix 5200 blender—apparently the maternal stamp of approval on your relationship.

What surprised me most—but probably shouldn't have—was the diversity of experiences. The daughters whose families have struggled with money, breaking the stereotype of the financially secure South Asian American family. The daughter whose parents separated after 30 years of marriage and eventually divorced. The daughter whose parents didn't flinch at all when she decided not to go to college straight out of high school and chose instead to pursue an opportunity to work as a singer.

These moving essays on sensitive topics provide hope and inspiration for those South Asian American daughters on the precipice of Good Girldom. Jumping is not easy. But other daughters have gone before you—and they have not just survived but have come out stronger. These are their stories.

From "Good Girls Marry Doctors—Brave Voices on Daughterhood in South Asian American Families" for the Aerogram, *by Preeti Aroon.*

---

a lesbian. It was painful and confusing. I had no idea how I was going to make it, or *if* I was going to make it. In my mind, you could be Indian or queer, but not both. And that's how I lived my life: asexual in Indian contexts, lesbian and non-Indian in Western contexts. It was completely natural while I was doing it, but it was destroying me inside.

I came out to my parents around 1997. To this day, it remains probably the most courageous thing I've ever done. That conversation was extraordinarily painful, and it stayed painful for many years—tears, hysteria, shouting, and grief, huge, huge loads of grief.

But we never stopped talking. We never closed our doors to each other. We never stopped doing the things that we'd always done as a family. I also never compromised my core values or my relationship with Mala to ease the discomfort of family members. Over time, our relationships became closer than they'd ever been.

Mala, on family: Growing up was painful. I was depressed. I resented my parents for bringing me into the world. And I had no desire to fill societal expectations

---

STRANGER INTIMACY

Using archival records dug up in county courthouses as well as the U.S. National Archives, Nayan Shah uncovers the stories of the lives of South Asian migrants on the West Coast of the United States and Canada in the early twentieth century in Stranger Intimacy: Contesting Race, Sexuality, and the Law in the North American West. The book, however, is not so much about the history of South Asian migrants as it is about what the intimate lives and relationships of this particular transient group can tell us about migrant mobility and how it leads to nonnormative kinship, social, and sexual associations among migrants.

As Shah notes, South Asian migrants to the United States and Canada in the early twentieth century were a predominantly male, transient group. Their communities remained in constant flux as they moved from place to place in search of a livelihood and to escape racial persecution. Their movements were often under surveillance, both by the state and the local white populace, who viewed them as racial and economic threats. Canadian and U.S. laws that regulated their migration, restricted family reunification, and prohibited property ownership rendered South Asian migrants as "marginal and replaceable labor" whose very presence threatened the settled, white republic.

Building on some of the emergent themes from his previous book, Contagious Divides: Epidemics and Race in San Francisco's Chinatown (2001), Shah illuminates how transient migrants often developed "intimate ties that [were] expressed in transnational kin networks, interracial marriages, and various temporary intimate encounters," including prostitution and same-sex relations. These experiences, Shah argues, are often marginalized in historical scholarship, which tends to focus on settled, heterosexual households in favor of the idea that the "nuclear family is the necessary model for social vitality and political participation." Thus, Shah places special emphasis on spaces such as streets, saloons, ranches, dormitories, and boardinghouses and the possibilities they offered to migrants to forge intimate, yet often transitory, social, sexual, and economic relationships.

Adapted from "Forbidden Desires and the Racialization of Citizenship" for Tides, *by Kritika Agarwal.*

Courtesy of Vega Subramaniam and Mala Nagarajan. Photo by Jannine Young.

for family's sake. I didn't follow the path of obligation, so I've approached both chosen and given families on my own terms.

As an adult, I finally appreciate the sacrifices my parents made. Talking with my parents about my sexuality was a painful journey. Still, staying in dialogue brought us closer. All around me, parents were rejecting their queer children. My parents were trying to understand, and they became my role models. My mom is deaf and speaks very little English. Still, she came to PFLAG [Parents, Families, and Friends of Lesbians and Gays] meetings with me in the mid-1990s. She was the only parent speaker at DesiQ2000, a conference for queer South Asians. She marched with me in the 2005 Seattle Pride Parade. My dad struggled with acceptance. Still, he supported us in the only ways he knew how. He did our taxes; twenty years after I came out, he voted in support of marriage equality; on his deathbed, he asked Vega to stand for a family photo with him.

Vega and Mala, on their wedding: With some effort, we found a Hindu priest to perform our marriage ceremony. As we requested, he performed the poojas without patriarchal messages about marriage and recited Vedic *shlokas* referring to two (genderless) souls. Our friends, community, and accepting family members participated in poetry readings, songs, dances, and the *aarti*. With 155 friends and

---

QUEER BROWN FEELINGS

In 2020, SAADA Archival Creators Fellow Mustafa Saifuddin built an ongoing archive of South Asian American queer and trans stories titled Queer Brown Feelings. Included in that archive is a series of oral histories of queer and trans South Asian Americans that highlight personal stories of inspiration, resistance, and resilience. An excerpt from one of those oral histories, narrated by Aveena, is included below. Please visit Queer Brown Feelings at saada.org/qbf to read others.

My coming out to my family & community was difficult, to say the least. Unfortunately, that is a resounding statement amongst the LGBTQIA+ community. When I came out to my family & community everything changed from their perspective. I was no longer the woman they knew me as. My faith, my accolades, my character, everything was impacted because (in their minds), I was "now" gay. Instead of me defending my faith to them or my relationship with my wife, I wish I can tell them that I have not changed. I am the same person. Yes, I am gay, but that does not impact who I am and who my character is. Despite not agreeing with my sexuality and [believing] that my sexuality and my faith cannot coexist, I am still the daughter you raised. I am still the cousin that you joked around with. I am still a woman. Lastly, I still love you. I understand that we might never see eye-to-eye, but I love you. Period.

---

family as witnesses, we experienced something very unexpected: a heightened level of trust and commitment.

Vega and Mala, on intentional relationships: In Hollywood and Bollywood, relationships are dramatic and "meant to be." In reality, relationships are hard work. We have tried to build an intentional relationship and family structure. We talk constantly about our views on family, money, and children. On desire, sex, and polyamory. On activism, our role in social change, and homeownership. On household roles and responsibilities. We are changing all the time, and we build our discovery process into our relationship.

Vega and Mala, on chosen families: One of the biggest challenges for many lesbian, gay, bisexual, transgender, and queer South Asians is the isolation we experience because we are at the intersection of more than one marginalized community. Some of us, including the two of us, have been suicidal because we couldn't imagine a positive future. We found few, if any, role models willing to speak in support of lesbian, gay, bisexual, transgender, and queer communities. Queer South Asians, even those of us who appear successful, continue to suffer. We're still fighting for our lives.

But it is possible to survive! Our chosen families—our community of friends, lovers, and significant others—are our lifelines. Queer South Asian spaces—

Courtesy of Vega Subramaniam and Mala Nagarajan.

magazines like *Trikone,* the book *A Lotus of Another Color,* the internet community, and newsletters—gave us room to come up for air, breathe, and build our fortitude and community. In other words: to fight and live and love like family.

Vega Subramaniam (she/her) is a lifelong social justice activist currently working as a leadership coach for nonprofit leaders.

Mala Nagarajan (she/he), cofounder of the Seattle-based Trikone-Northwest, is a caregiver and nonprofit consultant.

"HIS CYCLE AS PRADIP WAS DONE": LOSING A FATHER IN PHILADELPHIA

Amber Abbas, based on an interview with Amy Bhatt

"It was a testament to who he was and [to] the community. . . . People were coming to say goodbye, and it was important for them to be able to come and say that. . . . It was really amazing to witness."

Amy Bhatt remembered that 250 people attended her father's funeral rites. The experience of losing her father was deeply and intensely personal, but it was also a blow for the working-class Gujarati Hindu community in which she grew up.

After thirty years as a small-business owner in North Philadelphia, her father, Pradip Bhatt, suffered a heart attack. He spent two weeks on life support, and during that time, her family—immediate and extended—set up camp in the hospital waiting room. The many relationships her family had built were so important in this period: her aunt and uncle took turns bringing food and sleeping at the hospital; her husband, Kevin, and her sister's then-boyfriend (now husband),

Mike, were there too; a family friend, another Indian small-business owner, gave them discounted rooms at his hotel nearby; and dozens of relatives and friends came from across the country to pay their respects. The vigil ultimately concluded with a family meeting. It was then that the whole family decided together to stop the life support. With the help of an astrologer, who determined the auspicious time, the family turned off the machines keeping Amy's father alive at midnight on March 28, 2012.

"It happened really fast. We were able to—I don't even know where it came from—but there was Ganga jal, which is the water which is supposed to be blessed, representative of the Ganga; we were able to put drops in his mouth. I think my mom did that part. The immediate family were touching him."

ANANDIBAI JOSHEE'S GRAVE

In SAADA, courtesy of Legacy Center Archives at Drexel University.

In 1886, Anandibai Joshee graduated from the Woman's Medical College of Pennsylvania to become the first Indian woman to earn her MD. She died shortly after returning to India, at the age of twenty-one.

She initially made her way to the United States partially because New Jersey resident Theodicia Carpenter had read a request for help from Joshee and her husband that was published in the *Missionary Review*. Carpenter eventually housed Joshee when she arrived from India, and the two became close, so much so that, upon her death, Joshee's ashes were sent to Carpenter—who placed them in her family cemetery at the Poughkeepsie Rural Cemetery in New York, which is where the headstone pictured here still stands.

To Amy, it felt important that her father be led into the next stage, and she suddenly realized that she didn't possess the tools to do it. She could make the decisions about how to manage his care—and as the oldest child, that task was hers—but the spiritual part? She needed the community for that.

"Another aunt came up from South Carolina, and she is well versed in the *Bhagavad Gita*. She was saying the prayers that you say at the end. We had had music going the whole time, all the chants and prayers and stuff. And she was able to kind of lead him out, in that way."

In the days that followed, as they hastily prepared a cremation and memorial—after twenty-four hours of death, as is the Hindu tradition—her dynamic family came together to ensure the correct rituals were observed while creating new ones. The men who carried her father's body to his cremation were mostly non-Indian: her husband, her sister's boyfriend, and her cousin's husband (along with her brother and a cousin who had come from India). "We didn't really plan on a formal funeral, but so many people came—Indian and American—that my sister and I gave a short speech." Afterward, the mourners came up to pay their respects and drop rose petals on Pradip's body. Roses were his favorite flower, and he was known in the neighborhood for growing several fragrant varieties.

Once the ceremony was complete, there were some complications. What to do with the ashes? Her Indian cousin said the ashes could not be stored in the home. Amy put them in the shed behind the house. The cousin offered to carry them to India and to dispose of them appropriately. But Amy and her family weren't ready for this. After all, though Pradip loved India, he had made his home here. He loved Philadelphia, too; he even hosted the annual neighborhood Super Bowl party! In the end, they spread half of the ashes at their home in Pennsylvania and "returned" the rest to India the following year. Amy recalls sadly that this was the only time she traveled to India with her father. But she remembered "the images he would conjure up and the happiness that he experienced while being a young person [in Bombay]. That was so special and was part of how I always understood and saw him."

In the grief of losing a parent, one's transformation is immediate, but Pradip's death also permanently altered the shape of Amy's family. She began to see her mother, Ranjana, differently, as she too entered "into the next stage of life" as a widow and grandmother. Amy grew up with her grandparents at home and remembers a childhood filled with Indian relatives. She longed for privacy, for the intimacy of a small nuclear family. She never planned to recreate a joint family home. Yet now, as her daughter begins to toddle, and her mother considers retirement, Amy is equally sure that she and her husband will remain really close to her

RANJANA BHATT'S FIRST DAYS

Interviewed by Isabella Nugent

Ranjana Bhatt departed from Bombay, India, and arrived in New York City in 1976 at the age of 22.

In SAADA, courtesy of Ranjana Bhatt.

Reflecting on her first days in the United States, Ranjana Bhatt (Pradip Bhatt's wife and Amy Bhatt's mother), shared:

I landed at JFK, New York. It was in the late evening and I came from Bombay. It was a very busy, crowded airport [in Bombay], and here I didn't see that many people, and my first impression was "Where did everybody go?"

And of course my husband and my sister-in-law came to pick me up, and we took the turnpike and I-95 and came home to Pennsylvania, and there was nobody, but . . . cars everywhere. That's all I saw. And I was wondering, "Do people ever walk here?" or "Am I going to see anybody or not?"

It's bittersweet feeling because I was leaving my parents and my family. . . . I was nervous and excited too, because I was going to see my husband after six months and start a new life.

family. This was a surprise. "I thought that as a second-generation Indian American, I would not be making those choices . . . but seeing the work my mom did to care for her parents at their end of life, I wouldn't want anything *but* that." Now she says the caring work of her family and community "changed it for me."

Amber Abbas (she/her) is an associate professor of history at Saint Joseph's University.

"A SERIES OF MIGRATIONS": LOSING A FATHER IN TEXAS

Amy Bhatt, based on an interview with Amber Abbas

"When I think about my dad's life, it was a series of migrations. That turns out to be a really big part of the story of his death because of the way it affected and changed his relationship with his family and, in turn, our relationship with his family."

Amber's father, Tariq Azhar Abbas, came from Pakistan as a teenager to study in the United States in 1959. This was a time when few South Asians came to the country, and even fewer came as young adults. His journey from Lahore to Dallas kicked off a chain of events that would forever separate him from his ancestral home. However, for Tariq Abbas, home was where his family was, and that was the case until the very end of his life, in 2013.

Tariq met and married Amber's mother, Cynthia, who was not Pakistani but a white American woman, while living in the United States. After a few years, they

TARIQ ABBAS'S FIRST DAYS

Interviewed by Amber Abbas

Tariq Abbas departed from Lahore, Pakistan, and arrived in New York City in 1959 at the age of 18.

I had no idea where Dallas was! In fact, after I was selected [for the American Field Service foreign-exchange program], I went back and asked them, "What is this Dallas place?" . . . That lady, she was very nice, she showed me on the map where Dallas was. . . . I only knew of New York. I only wanted to go to New York. I was kind of disappointed when they said I was going to Dallas. I didn't really know what to expect. . . .

[The Weeks family, my hosts] picked me up at the airport and we went home. I went to bed and woke up the next morning, and the dog was licking my face! . . . I was just disgusted. This dog! Anyway, so that was my [laughs] . . . my first experience.

But then, after that, I did have trouble with the food, adjusting to the food. I could not take mashed potatoes! Mashed potatoes! If you've never had any mashed potatoes in your life, let me tell you they are the worst-tasting thing in the world! They are just like glue, for eating. It is something you have to get used to. . . . I loved hamburgers, and we went out for picnics and such and Mr. Weeks would fix hamburgers. That was my favorite food. And grilled cheese sandwiches. I ate grilled cheese sandwiches for a long time.

Tariq Abbas ice skating in Dallas, Texas. Circa 1960–1. Courtesy of Amber Abbas.

moved abroad to Saudi Arabia, where they lived for more than twenty years. While living in the Middle East, the Abbas family would frequently visit Pakistan and remained close with their relatives. For Amber, those relationships continued even after she moved back to the United States and were important as she trained to become a South Asian historian.

This connection to Pakistan was an ingrained part of her father, who maintained close ties to his family even though he settled abroad permanently. His family would await his visits, and as one of Amber's cousins remembered, "When he used to come to Pakistan to visit, we would all go and greet him. We would take five or six cars and stuff ourselves in there. There was never enough room for luggage coming home, but we would still all go. And we only did that for him." When in the United States, he shuttled information about illnesses, births, deaths, and new jobs and other bits of news across borders, creating a web of connection between Amber and her sisters and the vast network of relatives living away from them.

When he was diagnosed with colorectal cancer, his family came to his bedside to care for him in his last days. Amber and her sisters, along with their mother, took care of the majority of his day-to-day needs, but they were helped by Tariq's sisters, brother, nieces, and nephews, who flew to Texas from Pakistan, New York, and South Africa to spend his final days with him.

At the end of that excruciating period, he passed away peacefully, surrounded by his daughters, former wife, and extended family. After his death, Amber faced a new challenge: how to deal with her father's wishes regarding his funeral. In Muslim tradition, bodies are interred after family members and religious leaders have completed the appropriate rituals and prayers. The burial is important in Islam because of the belief that family members will be reunited in heaven, after the correct funeral rituals are observed. However, Tariq wished instead to be cremated. Amber recalls: "He had spent his whole life making up his own rules. He broke all the rules that people said he should follow and he did his own thing. I think the cremation thing was just another part of that." His Pakistani family was heartbroken by his decision, because it was antithetical to their Muslim beliefs. In the end, they accepted the decision and came together to celebrate the life of a man loved by so many.

Since his death, Amber has struggled to pick up the connections that her father had so diligently maintained. Without him as the link, new relationships must be forged. Amber notes: "He was so important. And I think what's hard is that everyone feels that loss. Everyone is suffering and grieving from it. It's hard to figure out . . . It's not even putting pieces together. It's trying to make a new puzzle."

As the extended family works on that puzzle together, Amber knows that the road ahead isn't going to be easy, but it's worth the effort: "It's a challenge. But we keep trying, because it's important. We need to be there to support them, and we need them to support us. Not just in our grief, but in our lives and our happiness. Because we are a family. But we are a family that is separated by many years and many miles. And that's a challenge."

Amy Bhatt is a writer, museum curator, and former professor.

Courtesy of Amber Abbas.

AUTHOR BIOS

Dr. Amber Abbas is an associate professor of history at Saint Joseph's University in Philadelphia. Her book, *Partition's First Generation: Space, Place, and Identity in Muslim South Asia* (I.B. Tauris, 2021), focuses on the period of transition associated with the 1947 Independence and Partition of India and its particular impact on South Asian Muslims. As an oral historian, she focuses on storytelling, the voice, and memory. This research also extends into the South Asian diaspora, where she is researching death, dying, and distance. In addition to dozens of oral interviews with men and women in South Asia, Abbas has consulted archives in England, Pakistan, India, and Bangladesh. Her publications include "A Living Legacy: Sir Sayyid Today," in the *Cambridge Companion to Sayyid Ahmad Khan* (Cambridge University Press, 2018); "Disruption and Belonging: Aligarh University and the Changing Meaning of Place Since Partition" (*The Oral History Review*, September 2017); and "The Solidarity Agenda: Aligarh Students and the Demand for Pakistan" (*South Asian History and Culture Special Issue: Defying the Perpetual Exception: Culture and Power in South Asian Islam*, 2014). She served as the president of SAADA's Board of Directors from 2019 to 2021.

Dr. Retika Adhikari is the Chancellor's Postdoctoral Research Fellow in the Department of Asian American Studies at the University of Illinois at Urbana-Champaign. She earned her PhD in cultural anthropology from Syracuse University in 2018. Retika's research interests include contemporary experiences of forced migration and humanitarian interventions, and her writing has appeared in *American Anthropologist*.

Dr. Shweta Majumdar Adur is an assistant professor of sociology at California State University, Los Angeles. She completed her PhD in sociology from the University of Connecticut and has received a master's in international development from the University of Pittsburgh. She also has a master's in sociology from Jawaharlal Nehru University, New Delhi, and an undergraduate degree from Lady Shri Ram

College, New Delhi. Her research interests include sexuality, gender, gender-based violence, human rights, and immigration. She was the chair of the Discrimination Committee for Sociologists for Women in Society and is the newsletter editor for RC32 of the International Sociological Association. She is also the coauthor of the book *As the Leaves Turn Gold: Asian Americans and Experiences of Aging*, which engages with issues surrounding aging and social inequality from a transnational perspective. She has authored publications in peer-reviewed journals as well as edited collections, and some of her most recent works have appeared in *Current Sociology* and *Journal of Gender Studies*.

Dr. Kritika Agarwal is website editorial manager at the American Immigration Lawyers Association. She previously served as managing editor for *Perspectives on History*, the newsmagazine of the American Historical Association. She holds a PhD in American studies from the University at Buffalo (SUNY).

Chitra Aiyar is the executive director of the Sadie Nash Leadership Project, a feminist social justice youth-leadership program that strengthens, empowers, and equips low-income young women of color to be agents of change in their lives and communities. Prior to joining Sadie Nash, Aiyar was a senior staff attorney at African Services Committee, representing African and Caribbean immigrants at the intersection of poverty, HIV, and migration. She has also worked in international development at Grameen Foundation USA, supporting microcredit replication programs in East Africa and India, and was a Fulbright Scholar in Bangladesh researching BRAC's expansion of accessible schooling for poor rural girls, the world's largest and most successful nonformal primary education program. She has taught at various women's prisons and at high schools, and she founded the Berkeley-based People's Test Preparation Service (a nonprofit that was awarded the Presidential Service Award by Bill Clinton in 1995). Aiyar has worked in radio as one of the hosts of Asia Pacific Forum, a show that covers progressive issues in Asia and Asian America, and in film as coproducer of *Claiming Our Voice*, a short documentary on Queens-based migrant domestic workers engaging in art and activism. She has been an adjunct professor at Hunter College, Teachers College/ Columbia University, and New York Law School, teaching courses on gender and migration, human rights, and negotiation skills for attorneys.

Dr. Anupama Arora is a professor of English and women's and gender studies at University of Massachusetts Dartmouth. She received her PhD in English from Tufts University. She teaches courses on postcolonial and global literatures, among others. She was the recipient of the Scholar of the Year Award in 2020, and the Provost's Best Practices Award for the Recognition of Excellence in Teaching and Learning with Technology in 2011 and 2014. She is coeditor of the *Journal of Feminist Scholarship*, an open-access journal. In addition to publications in edited volumes, her work has appeared in the *Journal of Commonwealth Literature*, *Women's Studies*, *Journeys: The International Journal of Travel and Travel Writing*, *TOPIA: Canadian Journal of Cultural Studies*, and *LIT: Literature Interpretation Theory*. Her current research projects focus on India in the U.S. in the late nineteenth century and Bollywood.

Dr. Vivek Bald is a scholar, writer, and documentary filmmaker whose work focuses on histories of migration and diaspora, particularly from the South Asian subcontinent. He is the author of *Bengali Harlem and the Lost Histories of South Asian America* (Harvard University Press, 2013) and coeditor, with Miabi Chatterji, Sujani Reddy, and Manu Vimalassery, of *The Sun Never Sets: South Asian Migrants in an Age of U.S. Power* (NYU Press, 2013). His films include *Taxi-vala/Auto-biography* (1994), which explores the lives, struggles, and activism of New York City taxi drivers from India, Pakistan, and Bangladesh, and *Mutiny: Asians Storm British Music* (2003), a hybrid music documentary/social documentary about South Asian youth, music, and anti-racist politics in 1970s–90s Britain. Bald is currently working on a transmedia project aimed at recovering the histories of peddlers and steamship workers from British colonial India who came to the United States under the shadows of anti-Asian immigration laws and settled within U.S. communities of color in the early twentieth century. The project consists of the Bengali Harlem book as well as a documentary film, *In Search of Bengali Harlem* (currently in production), and a digital oral history website in development at bengaliharlem.com.

Neelanjana Banerjee is a writer, editor, and teacher whose poetry, fiction, essays, and journalism have appeared widely in places like *Prairie Schooner*, *PANK Magazine*, the *Rumpus*, *World Literature Today*, *Harper's Bazaar*, and many others. She is coeditor of *Indivisible: An Anthology of Contemporary South Asian American Poetry* (University of Arkansas Press, 2010) and *The Coiled Serpent: Poets Arising from the Cultural Quakes and Shifts of Los Angeles* (Tia Chucha Press, 2016). She is the managing editor of Kaya Press, an independent publishing house dedicated to Asian Pacific American and Asian diasporic literature, and teaches writing in the Asian American Studies Departments at UCLA and Loyola Marymount University.

Dr. Vibha Bhalla is an associate professor of ethnic studies at Bowling Green State University. Her research interests focus on gender, migration, and urban studies. She is currently working on her book manuscript tracing the migration and settlement of Indian immigrants in metropolitan Detroit.

Sindya Bhanoo is a writer and journalist based in Austin, Texas. Her first collection of fiction, *Seeking Fortune Elsewhere*, is forthcoming from Catapult in 2022. She has worked as a reporter for the *New York Times* and the *Washington Post* and is currently a Knight-Wallace Reporting Fellow at the University of Michigan. Bhanoo is a graduate of UC Berkeley's Graduate School of Journalism and the Michener Center for Writers.

Dr. Amy Bhatt is a guest curator at Seattle's Museum of History and Industry (MOHAI). She cocurated the traveling Smithsonian exhibit *Beyond Bollywood: Indian Americans Shape the Nation*, and *Stand Up Seattle: The Democracy Project*. She received her PhD in feminist studies from the University of Washington in Seattle and was an associate professor of gender and women's studies at the University of Maryland, Baltimore County (UMBC). She is the author of *High-Tech Housewives: Indian IT Workers, Gendered Labor, and Transmigration* (University of Washington

Press, 2018) and coauthor, with Nalini Iyer, of *Roots and Reflections: South Asians in the Pacific Northwest* (University of Washington Press, 2013). She was the oral historian for the South Asian Oral History Project and has written for and appeared in news outlets such as NPR, the *Conversation*, the *Society Pages*, *AsiaGlobal Online*, the *Indian Express*, *Quartz*, and the *Seattle Times*. She also serves on SAADA's Board of Directors.

Dr. Nilanjana Bhattacharjya is a principal lecturer and Honors Faculty Fellow at Barrett, the Honors College at Arizona State University, where she teaches interdisciplinary courses on the humanities, Asian studies, music, and film. Her research focuses on popular music, film, and visual culture from South Asia and its diasporic communities. Her articles and essays appear in the journals *Asian Music*, *Framework*, *South Asian History and Culture*, and *South Asian Popular Culture*, as well as in the edited collections *Global Bollywood: Travels of Hindi Song and Dance*, *South Asian Transnationalisms: Cultural Exchange in the Twentieth Century*, *Writing about Screen Media*, *Industrial Networks and Cinemas of India*, and *Scattered Musics*.

Dr. Neilesh Bose is an associate professor of history and Canada Research Chair in global and comparative history at the University of Victoria. His research and teaching interests include the history of modern South Asia (the Indian subcontinent), the British Empire, decolonization, and the history of diasporas and migrations, as well as theater, performance studies, and popular culture. He is the editor of *South Asian Migrations in Global History: Labour, Law, and Wayward Lives* (Bloomsbury, 2020), author of *Recasting the Region: Language, Culture, and Islam in Colonial Bengal* (Oxford University Press, 2014), editor of *Culture and Power in South Asian Islam: Defying the Perpetual Exception* (Routledge, 2015), and author of numerous articles and book chapters. His book *Beyond Bollywood and Broadway: Plays from the South Asian Diaspora* (Indiana, 2009), is the first-ever collection of plays from South Asian diasporic playwrights from the U.S., the U.K., South Africa, and Canada. He is a senior editor in the collective *SAAG: South Asian Avant-Garde: A Dissident Literary Anthology* (saaganthology.com/info).

Marina Budhos is an author of several books of fiction and nonfiction and a professor of English at William Paterson University. Her most recent novel is *The Long Ride* (Wendy Lamb Books/Random House, 2019), about three mixed-race girls during a 1970s integration struggle. She is also the author of *Watched* (Wendy Lamb Books/Random House, 2016), which received an Asian/Pacific American Award for Literature YA Honor (APALA) and is an Honor Book for The Walter Award (We Need Diverse Books); *Tell Us We're Home* (Atheneum Books for Young Readers, 2010), a 2017 Essex County Big Read YA pick; and *Ask Me No Questions* (Simon Pulse, 2006), recipient of the first James Cook Teen Book Award, an ALA Best Book, and Chicago Library's Best of the Best, among other awards. She has published the adult novels *The Professor of Light* (Putnam, 1999) and *House of Waiting* (Global City Press, 1995) and a nonfiction book, *Remix: Conversations with Immigrant Teenagers* (Resource, 2007). She is coauthor, with her husband, Marc Aronson, of *Eyes of the World: Robert Capa & Gerda Taro & The Invention of Modern Photojournalism* (Henry Holt & Co., 2017) and *Sugar Changed the World: A Story of Magic, Spice, Slavery, Freedom & Science* (Clarion Books, 2010), an *L.A. Times* Book Prize finalist. Her books have been published in several countries, and her short stories, articles, essays, and book reviews have appeared in publications such as the *Daily Beast*, the *Awl*, the *Huffington Post*, LitHub, the *Kenyon Review*, *Ploughshares*, the *Nation*, *Dissent*, *Marie Claire*, *Redbook*, the *L.A. Times*, and in anthologies. Budhos has been a Fulbright Scholar to India, and has received an NEA Literature Fellowship in Fiction, an EMMA (Exceptional Merit Media Award), a Rona Jaffe Award for Women Writers, and two fellowships from the New Jersey Council on the Arts.

Dr. Monisha Das Gupta participates in and researches migrant-led social justice movements. She has published extensively in this area. She and Lynn Fijiwara recently coedited a special issue of the *Amerasia Journal, Law and Life: Immigrant and Refugee Acts amid White Nationalism* (2020). She is finishing a book on anti-deportation organizing. During the pandemic, she has been working with the local hotel workers' union and the Hawaii Workers Center to advocate safe working conditions and worker recall. She is the author of *Unruly Immigrants: Rights, Activism, and*

Transnational South Asian Politics in the United States (Duke University Press, 2006), which has won awards from the Association of Asian American Studies and the Asia and Asian America section of the American Sociological Association.

Dr. Shilpa Davé is an assistant dean in the College of Arts and Sciences and an assistant professor in the Department of Media Studies at the University of Virginia. She is the author of *Indian Accents: Brown Voice and Racial Performance in American Television and Film* (2013) and is coeditor of *Global Asian American Popular Cultures* (2016) and *East Main Street: Asian American Popular Culture* (2005). Dr. Davé researches and teaches about representations of race and gender in media and popular culture; American cultural narratives of immigration and border crossings; Asian American and South Asian American studies; and film, television, and literary studies. She has published on topics ranging from teaching Asian American studies and "No Life without Wife: Masculinity and Modern Arranged Meetings for Indian Americans" to "Apu's Brown Voice: Cultural Inflection and South Asian Accents," comics narratives on Ms. Marvel and Spider-Man: India, and South Asians and the spelling bee.

Mashuq Mushtaq Deen is a 2018 Lambda Literary Award winner, a 2020 silver medalist for India's international Sulthan Padamsee Playwriting Prize, and the first runner-up for the Woodward International Playwriting Prize. His publications include two plays, *Draw the Circle* (Dramatists Play Service) and *The Betterment Society* (Methuen Books), as well as short stories and essays, which have been published in *JAAS*, *In the Margins* (an online publication of the Asian American Writers Workshop), and elsewhere. His plays have been produced in N.Y.C., D.C., and Chapel Hill, NC. He is a resident playwright at New Dramatists and a core writer at the Playwrights Center in Minneapolis, and his work has been supported by the Sundance Institute, Blue Mountain Center, MacDowell, Bogliasco Foundation, and Helene Wurlitzer Foundation, among others. He will be heading to the Sewanee Writers' Conference and Siena Art Institute in the coming year. He is currently working on a memoir. Learn more at mashuqmushtaqdeen.com.

Dr. Jigna Desai did her undergraduate education at MIT in cognitive science, earth atmospheric and planetary sciences (astrophysics), English literature, and women's studies. Deciding between being a scientist and being a feminist professor, she chose the latter. She is now a professor in the Deptartment of Gender, Women, and Sexuality Studies (GWSS, pronounced "Gee Whiz") and the Asian American Studies Program at the University of Minnesota, and her research spans media and cultural studies, transnational and postcolonial feminisms, disability studies, Asian American studies, and critical sexuality and queer studies. Her book on cinema, *Beyond Bollywood*, is the first feminist and queer book on South Asian diasporas. Desai is deeply committed to transforming K–12 education and higher education for BIPOC students. She is the codirector of the MN Youth Story Squad (youthstorysquad.org), a university–K–12 partnership that does digital media–making about racial justice in underserved public schools in Minneapolis and St. Paul, working primarily with BIPOC youth.

Dr. Manan Desai is an associate professor of Asian/Pacific Islander American studies in the American Culture Department at the University of Michigan. His book, *The United States of India: Anticolonial Literature and Transnational Refraction* (2020), was published by Temple University Press as part of the Asian American History and Culture series. From 2010 to 2016, Manan served as a member of the board of directors for SAADA, where he contributed original archival research, assisted in building digital collections, and served as an editor and contributor to *Tides*, the online publication of SAADA.

Philip Deslippe is a doctoral candidate in the Department of Religious Studies at the University of California, Santa Barbara. He has written articles for academic journals such as *Sikh Formations*, *Amerasia*, and *Japanese Religions*, and for popular magazines including *Tricycle: The Buddhist Review*, *Yoga Journal*, *Air & Space Smithsonian*, the Indian news site *Scroll.in*, and *Tides*, the magazine of the South Asian American Digital Archive.

412

Kartar Dhillon (or Kar, as she was known) was born on April 30, 1915, in California's Simi Valley. Her father, Bakhshish Singh, immigrated to the U.S. in 1897, and her mother, Rattan Kaur, arrived in 1910. One of the first South Asian families in the U.S., the Dhillon family was involved in the Ghadar Party, agitating for India's independence from British rule, and with labor organizing through the Industrial Workers of the World. When her brother Bud Dillon was just twelve years old, he volunteered to join a mission for India's freedom, which took him around the world. Kar was herself an activist and writer involved with India's freedom struggle, and later supported organizations like the Black Panthers and helped organize farm workers in California. She passed away on June 15, 2008.

Dr. Pawan Dhingra is associate provost and associate dean of the faculty, and professor of American Studies, at Amherst College. He is a former curator at the Smithsonian Institution's *Beyond Bollywood: Asian Indian Americans Shape the Nation*. He has been published in the *New York Times*, CNN, *Salon*, and elsewhere, and his work has been profiled in the *Washington Post*, the *Wall Street Journal*, National Public Radio, and other venues. He is an award-winning author whose latest book is *Hyper Education: Why Good Schools, Good Grades, and Good Behavior Are Not Enough* (New York University Press, 2020). His other books include *Life Behind the Lobby: Indian American Motel Owners and the American Dream* (Stanford University Press, 2012), chosen by the *Los Angeles Times* as a key book on Asian America; *Managing Multicultural Lives: Asian American Professionals and the Challenge of Multiple Identities* (Stanford University Press, 2007); and, the coauthored *Asian America: Sociological and Interdisciplinary Perspectives*, Second Edition (Polity Press, 2021). He also appears in the Netflix documentary *Spelling the Dream*. He has been president of the board of SAADA and is currently president-elect of the Association for Asian American Studies. An award-winning teacher, he has held tenured positions at Tufts University and Oberlin College.

Dr. J. Daniel Elam is an assistant professor in the Department of Comparative Literature at the University of Hong Kong. He writes about activism: anti-colonial revolutionaries in the 1910s–20s; anti-racist thinkers in the 1930s–40s; Third World solidarity in the 1950s–60s; anti-apartheid movements in the 1970s; and AIDS activism in the 1980s–90s. He is the author of *World Literature for the Wretched of the Earth: Anticolonial Aesthetics, Postcolonial Politics* (2020). His essays have been published in journals such as *Postcolonial Studies*, *Interventions*, and the *PMLA*. He is currently working on an anthology of political theory from the Global South, a series of essays on Hong Kong, and a biography of his great-uncle.

Dr. Paul Englesberg is a retired faculty member at the School of Education at Walden University. From 2008 to 2018, he taught courses in research methodology, adult education, and higher education. He served as editor of the *Journal of Educational Research and Practice*, an online journal sponsored by Walden University. For thirteen years, he taught undergraduate and graduate courses at Western Washington University, in Bellingham, Washington, and directed the Asian American Curriculum and Research Project. He is currently writing a book about immigrants, racism, and conflict in the Pacific Northwest, focusing on the arrival of several hundred workers from Punjab, India, and their forced expulsion from Bellingham and Everett, Washington, in 1907.

Hasan Ferdous is a writer and journalist who worked for the United Nations until 2015. He studied English language and literature at Dhaka University and later obtained an MA from Kiev State University, Ukraine. He has published numerous books, including four monographs on Bangladesh's Liberation War and six volumes of essays on literature and aesthetics. He currently writes for Dhaka's *Daily Prothom Alo* and the *Dhaka Courier*.

V. V. Ganeshananthan teaches fiction and nonfiction writing in the MFA program at the University of Minnesota and is the author of a novel, *Love Marriage*. The book was longlisted for the Orange Prize and named one of *Washington Post Book World's* Best of 2008, as well as a Barnes & Noble Discover Great New Writers pick. A former vice president of the South Asian Journalists Association, she has also served on the board of the Asian American Writers' Workshop. She is a founding member of Lanka Solidarity and a member of the board of directors of the American Institute for Sri Lankan Studies. She has received fellowships from Radcliffe, the National Endowment for the Arts, the American Academy in Berlin, Yaddo, and MacDowell. Her work has appeared in the *New York Times*, the *Washington Post*, *Columbia Journalism Review*, *Himal Southasian*, and the *American Prospect*, among others. *Granta, Ploughshares,* and *Best American Nonrequired Reading* have published excerpts of her second novel, which is forthcoming from Random House in 2022. She is the cohost of the *Fiction/Non/Fiction* podcast on Literary Hub.

Deepa Iyer is a South Asian American writer, strategist, lawyer, and racial justice advocate. Currently, she is director of strategic initiatives at Building Movement Project, where she develops tools and conducts workshops on solidarity and social change. Iyer serves on the advisory council of the Emergent Fund, which resources grassroots organizing and power building in communities of color who are facing injustice based on racial, ethnic, religious, and other forms of discrimination, and is the former executive director of South Asian Americans Leading Together (SAALT). Her book, *We Too Sing America: South Asian, Arab, Muslim, and Sikh Immigrants Shape Our Multiracial Future* (The New Press, 2015), received a 2016 American Book Award and was selected as a top-ten multicultural nonfiction book of 2015 by Booklist. Iyer has been recognized for her work with the 2017 Justice in Action Award from the Asian American Legal Defense and Education Fund (AALDEF), the 2014 Pioneer Award from the South Asian Bar Association of North America, and the 2013 Dorothy Height Coalition Building Award from the Sikh American Legal Defense and Education Fund (SALDEF). She has also served as an adjunct professor at the University of Maryland (where she was an activist-in-residence in 2015), Hunter College, and Columbia University. Her areas of expertise include the post-9/11 America experiences of South Asian, Muslim, Arab, and Sikh immigrants; immigration and civil rights policies; and racial equity and solidarity practices.

Ganesh Iyer was born and raised in India. An alumnus of IIT-Bombay, he received his PhD in chemical engineering from Purdue University and an MBA from Seattle University. He is a business-development executive in the life sciences industry. He lives in Kirkland, Washington, with his wife, Nalini.

Mallika Iyer is a medical student at the University of Washington. She graduated in 2018 from Loyola University Chicago with a degree in biology. She aspires to practice medicine with the values of inclusivity, intersectionality, and centering those who are marginalized.

Dr. Nalini Iyer is a professor of English with an associate appointment in the Asian Studies Program and the Women and Gender Studies Program at Seattle University. Her research interests include postcolonial literatures and theory, nineteenth- and twentieth-century British literatures, South Asian and South Asian diasporic literatures, African and African diasporic literatures, and non-Western women's writing. In addition to writing essays, book chapters, and book reviews, she is the coeditor of *Other Tongues: Rethinking the Language Debates in Indian Literature* (with Bonnie Zare; Rodopi, 2009) and *Revisiting India's Partition: New Essays on Memory, Culture, and Politics* (with Amritjit Singh and Rahul K. Gairola; Lexington, 2016), and the coauthor of *Roots and Reflections: South Asians in the Pacific Northwest* (with Amy Bhatt; University of Washington Press, 2013). She is editor-in-chief of *South Asian Review* and is the Theiline Pigott McCone Endowed Chair in the Humanities at Seattle University (2020–22).

Dr. Khyati Y. Joshi is a professor of education at Fairleigh Dickinson University and a social-science researcher whose work focuses on the intersections of race and religion in the United States. Her most recent book is *White Christian Privilege: The Illusion of Religious Equality in America* (NYU Press, 2020). She is the author and coeditor of *Teaching for Diversity and Social Justice*, Third Edition (Routledge, 2016); *New Roots in America's Sacred Ground: Religion, Race, and Ethnicity in Indian America* (Rutgers U. Press, 2006); *Asian Americans in Dixie: Race and Migration in the South* (U. of Illinois Press, 2013); and numerous book chapters and articles. She has lectured around the world, including at the White House; to policy makers at the Organization for Security and Cooperation in Europe (OSCE); and for university and popular audiences in Denmark, India, and Lebanon and across the United States. She consults on equity and inclusion for schools, colleges and universities, nonprofit organizations, and businesses. Dr. Joshi was a consultant for the Pew Research Forum's groundbreaking 2015 survey on Asian Americans and religion. Often contacted by journalists, Dr. Joshi has appeared on television and radio programs such as MSNBC, C-Span, Voice of America, PRI's *The World*, and NPR's *Morning Edition* and has been quoted in numerous publications in the U.S. and abroad, including the *New York Times*, the *Wall Street Journal*, the *Washington Post*, the *Boston Globe*, the *Times of India*, the *Atlanta Journal-Constitution*, and the *Record*.

Nivetha Karthikeyan is the special projects coordinator at SAADA and the 2020 Caltech Milton and Rosalind Chang Prize Fellow. Through the Chang Prize, she is working on a project titled "Intersections: Building Solidarity through Community Archives," which explores the ways in which community memory work may inform, ground, and inspire new means of solidarity building. An aspiring historian of science, her research interests revolve around how histories of "tech" as industry and cultural phenomenon can be intertwined with histories of migration, transnational labor, and the construction of minoritized identity—particularly South Asian American identity—in the United States.

Dr. Rajender Kaur is a professor of English and director of the Asian Studies Program at William Paterson University. She is coeditor most recently of *India in the American Imaginary, 1780–1880* (2017). Her research work and pedagogy ranges across the fields of Anglophone South Asian literatures, postcolonial studies, contemporary and world literatures, and Asian American literature, where she has published articles and edited journals on issues of social justice, gender, class, and culture in South Asia. Her articles and book reviews have appeared in a host of scholarly journals, including the *Journal of Postcolonial Writing*, *South Asian Popular Culture*, *Postcolonial Text*, the *South Asian Review*, *Journal of Contemporary Thought*,

Early American Literature, the *Journal of Transnational American Studies*, *Transnational Literature*, and *ISLE: Interdisciplinary Studies in Literature and Environment*, among others. She is currently working on a monograph on India in the early republic, where she explores the pervasiveness of Indo-American interactions in print and popular culture.

Valarie Kaur is a renowned civil rights leader and celebrated prophetic voice "at the forefront of progressive change" (Center for American Progress). Valarie burst into American consciousness in the wake of the 2016 election when her Watch Night Service address went viral, with forty million views worldwide. Her question "Is this the darkness of the tomb—or the darkness of the womb?" reframed the political moment and became a mantra for people fighting for change. Valarie now leads the Revolutionary Love Project to reclaim love as a force for justice in America. In the last twenty years, as a lawyer, innovator, and award-winning filmmaker, Valarie has helped win policy change on multiple fronts—hate crimes, racial profiling, immigration detention, solitary confinement, internet freedom, and more. She founded Groundswell Movement, Faithful Internet, and the Yale Visual Law Project to equip new generations of advocates. Valarie has been a regular TV commentator on MSNBC and contributor to CNN, NPR, PBS, the *Hill*, *Huffington Post*, and the *Washington Post*. A daughter of Sikh farmers in California's heartland, Valarie earned degrees at Stanford University, Harvard Divinity School, and Yale Law School. Valarie's debut book, *See No Stranger: A Memoir and Manifesto of Revolutionary Love*, expands on her "blockbuster" TED Talk and is available wherever books are sold.

Dr. Fariha Khan is the associate director of the Asian American Studies Program at the University of Pennsylvania, where she also teaches courses on South Asians in the U.S., Asian American community, Asian American food, and Muslim identity in America. She received a master's degree in Arabic and Islamic studies from Yale University and a PhD in folklore and folklife from the University of Pennsylvania. Her current research focuses on South Asian American Muslims and the

Asian American community. Actively involved in the Philadelphia community, Dr. Khan is a member of the board of the Philadelphia Folklore Project, the Philadelphia Asian American Film Festival, and the Samuel S. Fels Fund. She also serves on the board of the American Folklore Society and is a member of the James Brister Alumni Society at the University of Pennsylvania. Dr. Khan was appointed in 2015 to the Pennsylvania Governor's Advisory Commission on Asian Pacific American Affairs and served until 2019.

Hamid Khan is an organizer and coordinator with the Stop LAPD Spying Coalition. The mission of the coalition is to build community-based power to dismantle police surveillance, spying, and infiltration programs. The coalition utilizes multiple campaigns to advance an innovative organizing model that is Los Angeles–based but has implications regionally, nationally, and internationally. An immigrant from Pakistan, Hamid came to the United States in 1979. As founder and former executive director of South Asian Network (1990–2010), Hamid helped create the first grassroots community-based organization in Los Angeles committed to informing and empowering thousands of South Asians in Southern California to act as agents of change in eliminating biases, discrimination, and injustices. Hamid also serves on the board of May First Technology, a membership organization that engages in building movements by advancing the strategic use and collective control of technology for local struggles, global transformation, and emancipation without borders.

Yasmin Sabina Khan is an author and a structural engineer. She followed her father, Fazlur R. Khan, into the field of engineering and so was able to write about his life and accomplishments from a unique perspective. After graduating from the University of Michigan and the University of California, Berkeley, she worked as a structural engineer designing buildings for about fourteen years. She is the author of *Engineering Architecture: The Vision of Fazlur R. Khan*, which describes the development and design of her father's building projects and offers insight into the personal qualities that shaped his work; and *Enlightening the World: The*

Creation of the Statue of Liberty, in which she explores the story of the creation of the record-setting statue in its historical context.

Dr. Erika Lee is an award-winning historian and author, Regents Professor of history and Asian American studies, and director of the Immigration History Research Center at the University of Minnesota. The granddaughter of Chinese immigrants, Lee was recently elected to the American Academy of Arts and Sciences and testified before Congress during its historic hearings on anti-Asian discrimination and violence. She is the author of four award-winning books, including, most recently, *The Making of Asian America and America for Americans: A History of Xenophobia in America*, which won the American Book Award and the Asian/Pacific American Award for Literature, as well as other honors. Named to many best books lists and identified as an essential book illuminating the Trump era and the 2020 elections, it will be published with a new epilogue on xenophobia and racism during the COVID-19 pandemic in June 2021. A former member of SAADA's Academic Council, she is president-elect of the Organization of American Historians and directs three major digital humanities projects: Immigrant Stories, #ImmigrationSyllabus, and Immigrants in COVID America.

Dr. Karen Isaksen Leonard is a historian and anthropologist who retired from the Department of Anthropology at the University of California, Irvine, after chairing the department for three years. With a 1969 PhD from the University of Wisconsin on the history of India, she has published on the social history and anthropology of India, especially Hyderabad State, and on Punjabi Mexican Americans, South Asian Americans, and Muslim Americans. Her most recent book is on the construction of identity in the diaspora by emigrants from Hyderabad, India, settling in Pakistan, Britain, Canada, the United States, Australia, and the Gulf States of the Middle East: *Locating Home: India's Hyderabadis Abroad* (Stanford University Press, 2007; Oxford University Press in India, 2008). A third edition of her first book, *Social History of an Indian Caste: the Kayasths of Hyderabad* (University of California Press, 1978), was published in Hyderabad, India, by Orient Black Swan in

2020. Leonard's other recent book, *Muslims in the United States: The State of Research* (Russell Sage Foundation, 2003), is an extended bibliographic essay relating Muslim Americans to the changing religious, social, and political landscapes in America. Leonard's other books are *Making Ethnic Choices: California's Punjabi Mexican Americans* (Temple University Press, 1994) and *South Asian Americans* (Greenwood Press, The New Americans series, 1997).

Samip Mallick is the cofounder and executive director of the South Asian American Digital Archive, guiding the organization from its founding in 2008 to today. Working at the intersection of technology and storytelling, Mallick has degrees in library and information sciences and computer science and has done graduate training in history. He previously worked in the Southern Asia collection at the University of Chicago Library and for the International Migration and South Asia Programs at the Social Science Research Council. Mallick has served as an archival consultant for the Ford Foundation and as an advisor to the Library of Congress and University of Minnesota's Immigration History Research Center.

Dr. Sangay Mishra is an assistant professor of political science and international relations at Drew University. He specializes in immigrant political incorporation, transnationalism, and racial and ethnic politics. His work engages with political participation of South Asian immigrants in the United States as well as countries of origin, with a particular focus on immigrants from India, Pakistan, and Bangladesh. He has also been analyzing the experiences of Muslim American communities with law-enforcement agencies. His book, *Desis Divided: The Political Lives of South Asian Americans*, was published by the University of Minnesota Press in 2016 and Sage India in 2017. The book focuses on Indian, Pakistani, and Bangladeshi American communities and analyzes features such as class, religion, nation of origin, language, caste, gender, and sexuality in mobilization, showing how these internal characteristics lead to multiple paths of political inclusion, defying a unified group experience. It was awarded the best book on Asian America (2017) by the American Sociological Association's section on Asia and Asian America.

Nadia Misir is a writer from South Ozone Park, Queens. She is a former Asian American Writers' Workshop Open City fellow. She received her BA in English from SUNY Oswego and an MA in American studies from Columbia University. She is pursuing an MFA in fiction writing at Queens College, CUNY, and was a writer-in-residence at the Louis Armstrong House Museum. Her writing has been published in AAWW's *Open City* magazine, *No, Dear Mag,* and *Kweli Journal.* She is working on a collection of lyric essays and watercolor-marker doodles that explore grief and intimacy.

Dr. Diditi Mitra is an associate professor of sociology at Brookdale Community College. Her research focuses on race and immigration. In addition to publishing in peer-reviewed articles, she has authored *Punjabi Immigrant Mobility in the United States: Adaptation through Race and Class* and coedited *Race and the Lifecourse: Readings from the Intersection of Race, Ethnicity and Age* with colleague Dr. Joyce Weil. As well, Diditi currently serves on the editorial board of *Sikh Research Journal* (sikhresearchjournal.org). Diditi is also a kathak dancer and dabbles in poetry. Learn more at diditimitra.com.

Dr. Radha Modi is an assistant teaching professor at Florida State University. She specializes in research on race relations, immigrant incorporation, and economic inequality. Her research investigates the role of skin color in the racialization of second-generation South Asians in the U.S. She has a chapter in the *Oxford Handbook on Caste* detailing caste presentation in the South Asian diaspora. In collaboration with South Asian Americans Leading Together (SAALT), a national nonpartisan organization working on civil rights, she authored a report entitled "Communities on Fire: Confronting Hate Violence and Xenophobic Political Rhetoric," documenting the hate violence experienced by South Asian, Middle Eastern, and Arab communities following the 2016 election. In addition to research, Dr. Modi works with national organizations such as SAADA and previously SALGA-NYC in areas of organizing and fundraising.

Dr. Sarah Morelli is an associate professor and chair of the Department of Musicology and Ethnomusicology at the University of Denver's Lamont School of Music. She is active as a scholar and performer of North Indian classical music and dance; her work draws on training with Hindustani music maestro Ali Akbar Khan (voice and sarod), with kathak dance master Pandit Chitresh Das, and with noted disciples. Her monograph, *A Guru's Journey: Pandit Chitresh Das and Indian Classical Dance in Diaspora* (University of Illinois Press, 2019), is an ethnographic examination of Pandit Das's artistic contributions and the development of kathak's "California gharana." She performs kathak nationally and internationally as a solo artist and founding member of the Leela Dance Collective, most recently playing the role of Sri Ramachandra in the production *Son of the Wind*. She is also the founder and artistic director of Sureela, a kathak academy in Denver that recently joined sister schools in Los Angeles, San Francisco, and New York to create the national institution the Leela Institute of Kathak. Her kathak research has also led to various other publications, such as a chapter in *The Music of Multicultural America* (University Press of Mississippi, 2016). She is the author of the instructor's manual for the college-level world music textbook *Soundscapes*, Third Edition (W. W. Norton, 2015) and is currently coediting the volume *Music and Dance as Everyday South Asia* (Oxford University Press, forthcoming). She currently serves on the board of directors for the Chhandam Chitresh Das Dance Company in San Francisco and the Society for Asian Music.

Dr. Soniya Munshi is an associate professor in the Department of Ethnic and Race Studies at the Borough of Manhattan Community College/CUNY, where she also teaches gender and women's studies. Her research looks at relationships between the carceral state, public health, gendered violence in migrant communities, and women of color feminisms. Her research interests are grounded in over twenty years of organizing for gender justice, primarily in South Asian, immigrant, people of color, and/or LGBTQ communities in New York City and beyond.

Dr. Meenasarani Linde Murugan is an assistant professor in the Department of Communication and Media Studies at Fordham University. Her research focuses on television and theories of race and diaspora. She has written on contemporary Asian diasporic pop culture for the *Los Angeles Review of Books* and the *Platform*. She recently published an essay on the late-1960s U.S. teen idol stardom of Sajid Khan for the edited collection *Indian Film Stars: New Critical Perspectives* (ed. Michael Lawrence, BFI, 2020). Her book, *Gender and Race in Postwar Variety Television: Colorful Performance*, is forthcoming from Routledge.

Mala Nagarajan is a middle-class, queer/bigender/lesbian, East Indian American. Raised Hindu, her deep agnostic spirituality arose from her parents having been deeply religious and founding members of the Sri Siva Vishnu Temple in Lanham, Maryland. That informs and ignites her hopes and beliefs that people and communities can change to embrace social justice. Since 2013, she has held the primary caregiver responsibility for her now late father and her surviving mother. Mala recalls the isolation in high school with very few like-minded brown-skinned desis. Despite being in the honors program, in band, and an avid high school athlete, Mala dropped out after tenth grade, lost, in crisis, and without role models—queer or Indian. She went on to receive her GED and enrolled in a local community college, before the days of early- or dual-enrollment programs. Moving to Seattle to study Tamil and linguistics, she made home in the Pacific Northwest and cofounded Trikone-Northwest, an organization serving the local South Asian lesbian, gay, bisexual, transgender, and queer community. Mala served as a steering committee member for the Queer South Asian National Network (QSANN). Now, Mala is a principal with Vega Mala Consulting, with her wife and business partner, Vega Subramaniam. As a nonprofit consultant, she focuses on supporting organizations with values-based, people-centered, and movement-aligned human resources management practices. With experience across government, nonprofit, and for-profit sectors, Mala has a personal and professional mission to break down barriers, nurture learning spaces, and inspire transformations that advance justice. For fun, she loves playing basketball, writing songs on guitar, digging into

Excel worksheets, and bird-watching.

Dr. Samina Najmi teaches multiethnic U.S. literature at California State University, Fresno. Her scholarly work focuses on race, gender, and war and spotlights post-9/11 Muslim American literature. Her books include *Form and Transformation in Asian American Literature* (University of Washington Press, 2005), coedited with Zhou Xiaojing; *White Women in Racialized Spaces* (SUNY, 2002), coedited with Rajini Srikanth; and the reissue of *The Heart of Hyacinth* (University of Washington Press, 2000), by Onoto Watanna, Asian America's first-known novelist. A collection of essays on Chitra Divakaruni, coedited with Amrijit Singh and Robin Field, is forthcoming from Lexington Books. Samina's literary address on the state and future of Asian American literature may be found on the website of the Smithsonian Asian Pacific American Center. She has also published some thirty essays in creative nonfiction, including in *World Literature Today*. An early memoir piece, "Abdul," won *Map Literary*'s 2012 nonfiction prize. Penguin Random House's online magazine Signature refers to her essay "Triptych" as an example of the possibilities of the genre. Samina's creative energies are currently focused on a book manuscript of personal essays, and her scholarly energies on the work of Sherley Anne Williams, a multifaceted Black writer from Fresno who won national recognition in her lifetime.

Dr. Alisa Perkins is an associate professor in the Department of Comparative Religion at Western Michigan University. Perkins earned her doctoral degree in anthropology at the University of Texas at Austin. Perkins specializes in ethnographic research about Muslim American civic engagement in the Detroit metro area. Her book, *Muslim American City: Gender and Religion in Metro Detroit*, published by NYU Press in 2020, focuses on African American, Bangladeshi American, and Yemeni American communities in Hamtramck, Michigan. Perkins's current focus is on African American Muslim and African Muslim community leadership in Detroit, both historically and today.

Suzanne C. Persard was born and raised in Bronx, New York, to parents from Kingston, Jamaica. Currently a PhD candidate at Emory University in the Department of Women's, Gender and Sexuality Studies, Suzanne has published academic scholarship and public essays engaging with queer archives, post-indenture visual art, and decolonial feminist theory. Suzanne is a founding member of Jahajee Sisters, the first Indo-Caribbean organization in the U.S. to address gender-based violence, and organized in social justice movements for over a decade. Suzanne is the recipient of a 2018 Small Axe Literary Prize in poetry and has held writing residencies from Hedgebrook in Seattle and Mumbai.

Kavita Pillay is a documentary filmmaker and journalist. From documenting the lives of South Indian men named after Stalin and Lenin to reporting on Finnish tango stars, Kavita loves sharing stories that inform, surprise, and delight audiences. In addition to reporting for WGBH Boston, The World, and NPR, she was one of five filmmakers selected to produce radio documentaries for "Neighborhood," a collaboration between the BBC World Service and the Sundance Institute. As a filmmaker and journalist, Kavita's work has received support from the LEF Foundation, the Sundance Documentary Film Program, the Massachusetts Cultural Council, the Garrett Scott Documentary Development Grant, WGBH Boston's Filmmaker in Residence Program, and the Pulitzer Center. She is a two-time Fulbright grantee to India, where she gained new insights into caste and the complex ways in which it shapes people's lives.

Dr. Bandana Purkayastha is a professor of sociology and Asian and Asian American Studies at the University of Connecticut. Her research interests focus on human rights/human security, migration and migrants, intersectionality, and violence. She is currently working on a project focused on water, inequalities, and rights, for which she spent several months in India as a fellow of the Institute for Advanced Studies at Jawaharlal Nehru University (2016) and on a senior Fulbright-Nehru Professional Excellence Fellowship (2017), gathering data. She writes about migrants, human rights, and human insecurity, reflecting on the rapidly changing structures that shape migrant experiences across the world. Her writing has appeared in *Gender & Society*, *South Asian Diaspora*, *Sociology of Race & Ethnicity*, and Frontpage Publications' Human Rights series. In 2018, she edited a special issue of *Current Sociology* on migration, migrants, and human security. Other recent publications include *Human Trafficking: Trade for Sex, Labor, and Organs* (with Farhan Navid Yousaf, Polity Press, 2019) and the *Routledge Handbook of Indian Transnationalism*, which she coedited with Ajaya Sahoo (forthcoming). Dr. Purkayastha currently serves on the International Sociological Association's executive committee (2018–22). She was awarded the American Sociological Association (ASA)/Asian American section's Contributions to the Field (career) Award in 2016, the UCONN College of Liberal Arts and Sciences Research Excellence Award in 2019, and ASA's Jessie Bernard (career) Award in 2019. She was president of Sociologists for Women in Society (SWS) from 2013 to 2014, and served as an expert advisor for many international and state entities, including WHO's expert group on female migrants and health.

Anant Raut is the global head of competition policy for Facebook. Previously, he was a presidential appointee in the Obama administration, where he served in the Department of Justice Antitrust Division, the Office of Privacy and Civil Liberties, and as a special advisor to the office of Vice President Biden and President Obama's National Economic Council. Anant is a former Democratic counsel to both the House and Senate Judiciary Committees. While in private practice, he provided pro bono representation to terrorism suspects held in Guantánamo Bay, whose stories he tells in this book. His work culminated in joining the team that successfully argued *Boumediene v. Bush* (2008). Notable awards and achievements include being a member of President Obama's Economic Leadership working group (2016), receiving the National Legal Aid & Defender Association's Beacon of Justice Award (2007), and receiving the Southern Center for Human Rights' Frederick Douglass Award (2007). Anant is a graduate of Yale University and the Harvard Law School, and loves them each in very different ways.

Vasef Sajid is a Pakistani American with extensive experience in sales and technology and with basketball. He is a former high-school and collegiate athlete who has used his knowledge of sports to excel in everyday life. He is a husband and a father of three beautiful children, and in his spare time you can catch him in the driveway shooting hoops and passing down his legacy to his kids.

Imran Siddiquee is a writer, filmmaker, and speaker challenging systems of domination. Their writing on white supremacy, patriarchy, and popular media has been published by the *Atlantic*, *Bitch* magazine, Buzzfeed, Literary Hub, Longreads, and others. They are the current communications director for BlackStar Projects, home of the BlackStar Film Festival, and a cocreator of SAADA's *Revolution Remix* Walking Tour, which they help lead in Philadelphia. Find them on Twitter @ imransiddiquee.

Dr. Nico Slate is a professor of history and head of the History Department at Carnegie Mellon University. His research and teaching focus on the history of social movements in the United States and India. He is the author of four books: *Lord Cornwallis Is Dead: The Struggle for Democracy in the United States and India* (Harvard University Press, 2019), *Gandhi's Search for the Perfect Diet: Eating with the World in Mind* (University of Washington Press, 2019), *The Prism of Race: W. E. B. Du Bois, Langston Hughes, Paul Robeson and the Colored World of Cedric Dover* (Palgrave Macmillan, 2014), and *Colored Cosmopolitanism: The Shared Struggle for Freedom in the United States and India* (Harvard University Press, 2012). He is also the editor of *Black Power Beyond Borders* (Palgrave MacMillan, 2013), a volume that tracks the global dimensions of the Black Power movement. Dr. Slate is the founder and director of the Bajaj Rural Development Lab and SocialChange101.org. Born in Los Angeles and raised in California's Mojave Desert, he earned degrees in earth systems and the interdisciplinary studies in the humanities from Stanford University and in environmental change and management from Oxford University before completing his PhD in history at Harvard University.

Dr. Seema Sohi is an associate professor of ethnic studies at the University of Colorado Boulder, where she focuses on twentieth-century U.S. history and Asian American studies. Her book, *Echoes of Mutiny: Race, Surveillance, and Indian Anticolonialism in North America* (Oxford University Press, 2014), examines the radical anti-colonial politics of South Asian intellectuals and migrant workers based in North America during the early twentieth century as well as the interimperial efforts of the U.S. and British states to repress them. A history of radicalism and anti-radicalism, this project also looks at the racial formations of South Asians through the lens of anti-radicalism during the early years of South Asian migration to the United States. She has also published essays and articles in the *Journal of American History*, *Sikh Formations*, and an anthology titled *The Sun Never Sets: South Asian Migrants in an Age of U.S. Power* (New York University Press, 2013).

Dr. Rajini Srikanth is a professor of English and dean of the Honors College at UMass Boston. She is the author of the award-winning *The World Next Door: South Asian American Literature and the Idea of America* (Temple University Press, 2004), *Constructing the Enemy: Empathy/Antipathy in U. S. Literature and Law* (Temple University Press, 2012), and *White Women in Racialized Spaces: Imaginative Transformation and Ethical Action in Literature* (SUNY Press, 2002) and the coeditor of *Interdisciplinary Approaches to Human Rights: History, Politics, Practice* (Routledge, 2018), *The Cambridge History of Asian American Literature* (Cambridge University Press, 2015), and *A Part, Yet Apart: South Asians in Asian America* (Temple University Press, 1998), among others. Her publications have appeared in *Pedagogy*, the *Comparatist*, *International Journal of Feminist Studies*, and the *Journal of Asian American Studies*. Her research and teaching interests are in human rights and literature, American literature (including Asian American literature), diaspora studies, and comparative race and ethnic studies. She is on the board of the UMass Boston Center for Gender, Security, and Human Rights.

Shiwani Srivastava is a screenwriter and freelance editorial consultant based in Seattle. As a screenwriter, Shiwani examines immigrant experiences through the

429

lens of comedy, and her first feature film was set up at Netflix. As an editorial consultant, she has worked with clients and publications including Microsoft, Entrepreneur.com, and the Nasdaq Entrepreneurial Center. Shiwani has BA degrees in English and journalism from New York University and a master's in South Asian Studies from the University of Washington.

Vega Subramaniam is a cofounder and principal, with her wife and business partner, Mala Nagarajan, of Vega Mala Consulting. As a professional certified coach, she specializes in leadership development, career transition, and intentional life planning. She works primarily with highly motivated, creative, thoughtful social-change activists and nonprofit staff. Her nonprofit and philanthropic work focuses on LGBTQ equality, racial and gender justice, and education equity. Vega has been involved in LGBTQ organizing since 1983 and active in the South Asian queer community since 1997. In 2004, she and Mala were one of the plaintiff couples in Washington State's marriage equality lawsuit. She is also a social scientist and academic, with thirteen years of experience teaching sociology and advising low-income college students and students of color. In that time, she led student service programs at universities and foundations designed to increase access to higher education for low-income and underrepresented students.

Akshat Tewary practices as an immigration attorney in the United States and works as an advocate for financial reform as president/founder of Occupy the SEC, an offshoot of the Occupy Wall Street movement. He has played basketball collegiately and at the semiprofessional levels, and has been involved in the North American Indo-Pak Basketball circuit as an organizer and participant. He is currently a PhD student with an interest in South Asian American film.

Dr. Stanley Thangaraj is an associate professor of anthropology, gender studies, and international studies at the City College of New York. He is a sociocultural anthropologist with interests in race, gender, sexuality, class, and ethnicity in Asian America in particular and in immigrant America in general. He is a former high-school and collegiate athlete and coach who considers sport a key site to understand immigrant enculturation, racialization, and cultural citizenship. He is the author of *Desi Hoop Dreams: Pick-Up Basketball and the Making of Asian American Masculinity* (New York University Press, 2015) and coeditor of *Asian American Sporting Cultures* (New York University Press, 2016) and *Sport and South Asian Diasporas: Playing through Space and Time* (Routledge, 2014). Dr. Thangaraj was awarded the Comparative Ethnic Studies Award from the American Studies Association for his newest work on Kurdish diasporas.

Dr. SaunJuhi Verma is an assistant professor in the School of Management and Labor Relations at Rutgers University. She received a 2014 Fulbright-Nehru Fellowship to Tata Institute of Social Sciences in Mumbai for her project "How Does a State Identify Citizen Need? A Case Study of Government Rationale in Social Policy Design." Her dissertation, entitled *Black Gold, Brown Labor: Selling Migrants in Global Recruitment Markets*, outlines how a dubious migrant legality is generated through the socio-legal infrastructure of labor-recruitment chains. In addition to her scholarly work, she is a writer, an artist, and a creator working on immigrant-rights issues in a transnational context. She has more than fourteen years of experience in labor organizing, policy, and research on devaluation of Brown femme labor, racialization, and settler colonialism in a global context.

Sasha Wijeyeratne is the former organizing director at the National Queer Asian Pacific Islander Alliance (NQAPIA), working to build the power of LGBTQ API communities toward a world where all queer and trans people of color can thrive. Sasha is currently the executive director of CAAAV: Organizing Asian Communities, organizing working-class Chinese, Bangladeshi, and Korean immigrants in Chinatown and Queens in New York City. Sasha has been part of a number of grassroots and national organizing campaigns and deeply believes in the power of organizing to win impossible battles. They are confident that we have what we need to transform ourselves and our world and that working-class immigrant and people of color organizing will get us free. Sasha has also been part of a variety of organizing and political-education projects, including South Asian Youth Movement, No Dane County Jail Coalition, VigilantLove, Asians for Black Lives, DC Desi Summer, hotpot!, Queer South Asian National Network, and more.

ACKNOWLEDGMENTS

What started in 2015 as a book about community has, over the course of six years, become a community of its own. And it is only because of the support from that community that this book is in your hands today.

We are deeply grateful to the 407 backers who supported *Our Stories* on Kickstarter, believing in the importance of this project before a single page was written. The generosity of these supporters, whose names you will find in the following pages, has ensured that South Asian American stories can now be shared in homes, schools, and libraries across the country.

The sixty-four authors who contributed essays to *Our Stories* did so without remuneration, and it is because of their incredible generosity that the proceeds from *Our Stories* will go directly to supporting SAADA's continued work of documenting, preserving, and sharing stories from our community. We are grateful to you for believing in the vision for this project and sharing your immense talents with us to allow for its success.

Our thanks also go to the twenty-two community members who served as early readers for *Our Stories*, and whose thoughtful feedback improved the book immeasurably.

So many have shared their time, labor, and love to bring this book to life. We extend our heartfelt gratitude to each and every one of you who has been part of this process. We hope that you are as proud of what we have accomplished together as we are.

,

The SAADA Team

With immense gratitude to the following individuals who supported Our Stories *on Kickstarter and whose generosity is making it possible to donate the book to schools and libraries across the United States.*

JAY A. BANSAL

MITHUN BARGAV

SHAILESH & AARTI
BHAT

BOBBY CHACKO

MADURAI G. GANESAN
FAMILY

ANIRVAN CHATTERJEE
& BARNALI GHOSH

SABIR A. KHAN

ANIL & CHRISTIE
LINCOLN

J. ASHWIN MADIA

PANKAJ & SUNANDA
MALLICK

RADHIKA & MAT
MATHEWS

RAMAN MUTHUSAMY

SANDHYA NANKANI

GOUTHAM NARLA

NEAL NATHANI

URMILA & PRAVIN PATEL
AND GEETA & NARENDRA
AHYA

RAJ AND LATHA PILLAI

SHUBHADA SAXENA
AND FAMILY

DANIELLE WILLIAMS
& MATT SIMON

AMRITJIT SINGH

RAJINI SRIKANTH AND
K. S. (SRI) SRIKANTH

ANONYMOUS

For Meera, Abhay, Noah, and Aadhya

Amber H. Abbas

Sara & Rukhsana Khan Afridi, in loving memory of Saeed Khan Afridi

Suchita Malik & Ankit Agarwal

Kritika Agarwal

Ashima Aggarwal

Namita Agravat

Alka R. Agrawal

Alok & Jennifer in honor of Hari N. Agrawal

Hari & Sharda Agrawal

Shameel Ahmad

Manan Ahmed

Chitra Aiyar

Gayatri & Ajit

Charlotte Karem Albrecht

Eileen Kaur Alden

AMS316

Amarinder Anand

Anonymous

Ranjit Arab

Cly Wallace Aramian

Shaheena Arshad-Trijillo

Kaavya Asoka

Liz Li & Amish Babu

Kamal Badhey

Monisha Bajaj & Bikku Kuruvila

Gino & Kishwer Barrica

Daniel Bass

Eugenia Beh

Amanda Bergson-Shilcock

Sindya & Hemant Bhanoo

Alka Bhanot

Vivek G. Bharathan

Nilanjana Bhattacharjya

Anand Subramanian & Jhumpa Bhattacharya

Mona Bhuta

Md. Farid Uddin and Mosfika Yeasmin

Kaushlesh Biyani | Biyani Photo & Cinema

Bronwen Bledsoe

Luke Bohanon

Four Windows Books

Surajit Bose

Jessica Bray

Anonymous

Brian

Michelle Caswell

Amish Chadha

Chandra Chaki

Anonymous

Rita & Ara Chakrabarti

Manisha Chakravarthy

Hirak Chanda

Sundar Chari

Anubhav Chopra

M. Choudhury

Shyamal Chuki

Alice W. Clark

Anna Mala Coats

Nithin Coca

Elizabeth Coleman

Cornell University Asian Pacific Americans for Action

Corwin-Silva Family

Clare Counihan

Anonymous

Adam Dacey

Parag Dalsania

Avik Kumar Das & Family

Kavita Das

Sakti Das

Anil Dash

Shilpa S. Davé

Anuja Deo

Arati Desai & Rajat Deo

Manan Desai

Dipti Desai

Odessa Devi Despot

Anonymous

Dev

Josh DeWind & Dee Ratterree

Sonia Patyal Dhawan

Dhingra Family

Arjun Dirghangi

Sheela Doraiswamy

Duniya Dance and Drum Company

L. Dudley

Dulam Family

Jeannette Eaton

Jan Eberhart

Mehrin ("Mir") Masud-Elias & Jamal J. Elias

Anonymous

Eric

Badrul Farooqi

Eshana Fehrenbach-Karipineni

Kalyani Fernando

Kevin W. Fogg

The Goradia Foundation

LisaRuth Elliott,
Shaping San Francisco/
Foundsf.org

Bix Gabriel

Tarun Galagali

Manisha Gangopadhyay

Tejaswini Ganti

Mukesh Garg

David Gerber

Tribhawan Gill

Vedika Gopal

R. S. Gopalan

Sneh Goyal

Vipin Goyal

Jay Goyal

Grayson

Michael Green

Varsha Grogan

Anonymous

Meagen Grundberg

Nila Gupta

Anushtup Haldar

Katherine Halliday

Aimee Hamilton

Matt Haynie

Kaitlyn S. Higa

Anonymous

Stephen Higa

Nikhil Hira

Harshitha
Ramesh Holmes

Apna Ghar, Inc.
(Our Home)

Annie Huynh

Ajit Jagdale

Jyoti Jain

Vaibhav Jain

Navin Jain

Priya Jain

Dimpal Jain

Shakti Jaising

Rupin Jayal

Chaitanya Jayaraman

Sarah Tulman Jesudason

Dashini Jeyathurai

Uday Jhunjhunwala

Sajni Jobanputra

Denise Johnson

Amee Joshi

Robert R. Daniel Jr.

Anonymous

A. Kabel

Ann Kalayil

Prithi Kanakamedala

Kandeya

Kamini Kannan

Sockalingam Sam
Kannappan

Reena Karia

Kel Karpinski

Anu Kasarabada

Nabil Kashyap

Sheeji Kathuria

Lakhpreet Kaur

Karthik Kavasseri

Matt Kawecki

Fariha Khan

In honor of
my father Aijaz M. Khan
& uncle M. Aslam Khan

Ayshea Khan

Meena Rani Khandelwal

Vivek Khanna

Ali Khataw

The Kidd-Kattakuzhy
Family

Rupa Kitchens

Alexander A. Klimenko

Amitha Jagannath
Knight

Kelsey Knox

Nidhi Kohli

Anjalee Kohli

Laura Kopen

Aaleya Koreishi

Aashiyana Koreishi

Sonia Kotecha

Aparna Kothary

Veer, Asha, Ellora, and Zara Vaidya Krishna

Mekala Krishnan

Jennifer Lange-Pomes

Brian D. Leaf

Katie Lennard

Richard Lesage

Zoe Lewycky

Anonymous

Ed Lin

Robert Liu-Trujillo

Freia Lobo

Aysha G. Long

Lisa Lowe

Philip Lutgendorf

Christine Madden

Nick Mader

Anand Madhvani

Darshan & Carlee Mahajan Family

Mohinder Mahal

Nupur Maheshwari

Anya, Diya, Sunita, and Mahesh Mahtani

Yifan Mai

Savita Malik & Ezekiel Robles

Kinnari, Samip, & Sejal

Meenal Mamdani

Renee Mancuso

Erin Mao

Anonymous

Mahnaz Maqbool

Chandrika Marla

Neil C. Maskeri

Marvin J. Mathew

Joe Mathew

Raj and Dheepa Maturi

Emily McNish

Tasveer - Rita Meher

Anjali Mehta

Devanshu Mehta

Hemal & Parikha Mehta

Samir Mehta

Sarika D. Mehta

Karl Mendonca

Nayantara Mhatre

Anjal Chande & Samir Mirza

Anna Misra

Pulin Modi

Shalin H. Mody

Vyasachar Mohan

Anonymous

Jyoti Mohan

Mukta Mohapatra

Chris Morrison

Aditya Mukerjee

Sherally Munshi

Anne Murphy & Raghavendra Rao K. V.

Sameena Mustafa

Dr. Todd Nachowitz, PhD

C . M. Naim

Chand Nair, MD

Jessica Namakkal

Murali Nandula

Sujata Narayan

R. Sekhar & Monali Narayanaswami

Elin Nelson

International News Books & Gifts | int-news.com

sine hwang jensen & linda nguyễn

Nina

Ninad

Safiya Noble

Johanna Ogden

Manish Oza

Paayal

Arunima Pande

Nitai Pandya

Kaumudi Pandya-Panigrahi

Kerishma Panigrahi

An Immigrant Parent

Ashish and Viraj Parikh

Stootee Parikh

Sunil Patel

Priti Patel & Praveen Raju

Aniruddh Patel

Archana D. Patel

Rita Patel

Anonymous

Viraj Patel

Avni Patel

Kirti Patel, PhD

Maneesh Kenia &
Reva Patwardhan

Leena Pendharkar

P. R. Perumalswami

Ian Petrie

Anonymous

Remoy Philip

Shaji Philip

Naveena Ponnusamy

Laura Popova

Gautam and Anjali
Prakash

Shubhra Prakash

Ankita Prasad

Smitha Prasadh

Aswin Punathambekar

Natasha Raheja

Govinda Rajan

Venkat R. Ramaprasad

Muthuramanan
Rameswaran

Kavita Daiya &
Sunny Rao

Aditi Rao

Shilpa Rao

Qasim Rashid

Ratnakaram Family

Ina Adele Ray

The Reddy Family

Sravana Reddy

Sumana Reddy

Gayatri Reddy

Gopal & Rina Roy

Anonymous

Russell

Dinesh Das Sabu

Suhail Salim

Niranjan Sampat

Sarah

Salas Saraiya

Anand D. Sarwate

Marthine Satris

Nitasha Sawhney

Shahana Sen

Kushkarn Singh
Senghera

Mahesh K. Seth

Anonymous

Nayan Shah

Janak and Shamita Shah

Jugna Shah

Mimosa Shah

Nilay & Marjorie Shah

Palak Shah

Seema Shah

Mona Shah

Shajuti

Shane

Sudeep Sharma

Ashish Shenoy

Zack Chatterjee
Shlachter

Fazeela Siddiqui

The Sidharaju Family

The Silvermans

Noah D. Simons

Julie and Inder Singh

Gayatri Singh

Kartikeya Singh

Tito Sinha

Siraj

Anonymous

Gene Smith

A. Springmann

Jyotsna Sreenivasan

Harini Srinivasan

Venkat Srinivasan

Ragini Tharoor
Srinivasan

Shobha Tharoor
Srinivasan

Subramanian/Chopra

Anantha Sudhakar

Bob Sundar

Lakshmi Sundaresan

Kirin Suri

Swami and Family

Robynn Takayama

Nancy Ng Tam

Sharmila Rao Thakkar &
Rakesh Thakkar

Mitali Thakor

Sujeeth Thirumalai

THANK YOU

Lesley M. Varghese &
Dr. Harry J. Thomas

Elizabeth Thompson

Creatrix Tiara

Anonymous

Ishaan Tipirneni

Christina Tom

Mukhtyar Tomar

Grant Din &
Rosalyn Tonai

Anonymous

Nicole Topich

Manan Trivedi

Lhakpa Tsering

Rajal, Radha, and Batian
Upadhyaya

Anne Vagts

Aditi Vaidya

Kersey Vakharia

Neville Vakharia

Lindsey Varghese

Linta Varghese

Hetal Vidwans

Vrushali

Arzan Sam Wadia

Natasha Warikoo

Anonymous

Nate Warren

Rai Wilson

Lia Wolock

Cynthia Wu

Nitesh Yadav

Pavani Yalamanchili

Shanna Yue

Asad Zaidi

Paayal Zaveri

ABOUT SAADA

SAADA documents, preserves, and shares stories of South Asian Americans, ensuring that today's struggles for inclusion and belonging are not the same ones we leave to the next generation. SAADA's collections represent the largest publicly accessible South Asian American archive, enabling academics, artists, filmmakers, journalists, students, and community members to write books, create new content, and shape public understanding about the South Asian American community. By writing South Asian Americans into the American story, SAADA's work poses a direct challenge to narratives that exclude immigrants and people of color, and serves as a powerful response to the question of who belongs.

Learn more at saada.org.